Henry Wood Elliott

Report on the Condition of the Fur-SealFfisheries of the Pribylov Islands in 1890

Henry Wood Elliott

Report on the Condition of the Fur-SealFfisheries of the Pribylov Islands in 1890

ISBN/EAN: 9783744725828

Printed in Europe, USA, Canada, Australia, Japan

Cover: Foto ©ninafisch / pixelio.de

More available books at **www.hansebooks.com**

BEHRING SEA ARBITRATION

REPORT

ON

THE CONDITION OF THE FUR-SEAL FISHERIES

OF THE

PRIBYLOV ISLANDS

IN 1890

BY

HENRY W. ELLIOTT

SPECIAL AGENT APPOINTED UNDER AN ACT OF CONGRESS
OF THE UNITED STATES APPROVED APRIL 5, 1890

Produced on the 4th April 1893
by the Agent of the United States to the Tribunal
of Arbitration convened at Paris

PARIS

PRINTED BY CHAMEROT & RENOUARD

19, RUE DES SAINTS-PÈRES, 19

1893

NOTE

This report by Mr. H. W. Elliott is accompained, in the original manuscript, by 48 plates, representing various « rookeries », etc. : also by 15 maps and plans chiefly intended to show the relative extent of ground occupied by seals on the Pribyloff Islands in 1890 and 1872-1874. It has been found impossible to reproduce these plates and maps in the time available.

The titles of the various maps and plans are as follows :

North Rookery, St. George Island, July 19th 1890.

Zapadnie Rookery, St. George Island, July 20th 1890.

Little East Rookery, St. George Island, July 20th 1890.

Starry Arteel Rookery, St. George Island, July 20th 1890.

Hauling-grounds at South-west Point, St. Paul Island, 1872.

Great Eastern Rookery, St. George Island, July 20th 1890.

Tolstoi Rookery, St. Paul Island, July 10th 1890.

Polavina Rookery, St. Paul Island, July 13th 1890.

Lukannon and Ketavie Rookeries, St. Paul Island, July 10th 1890.

NOTE.

Lagoon, Nah Speel and Zoltoi Rookeries and Hauling-grounds, St. Paul Island, 1890.

Reef and Garbotch Rookeries, St. Paul Island, May, June and July 1890.

Zapadnie Rookeries, St. Paul Island, July 1890.

Novastoohnah Rookeries (North-east Point), St. Paul Island. June, July 1890.

St. George Island, Pribyloff Group, 1890.

St. Paul Island, Pribyloff Group, 1890.

C. H. TUPPER.
Agent for Her Britannic Majesty.

Paris, April 1893.

LETTER

TO THE SECRETARY OF THE TREASURY

Hon. William Windom, Secretary of the Treasury.

Cleveland, Ohio, November 17th, 1890.

SIR : —

On the 7th of last 'April, I received from your hands my appointment as the Special Agent under the act of Congress, approved April 5th, 1890, which orders and provides for a thorough examination into the present status of the fur-seal industry of our Government as embodied on the Seal Islands of Alaska, so as to make known its relative condition now as compared with its prior form and well being in 1872 : and, for other kindred lines of enquiry.

I may as well frankly confess, at the outset, that I was wholly unaware of the extraordinary state of affairs which stared me in the face at the moment of my first landing, last May, on the Seal Islands of Alaska. I embarked upon this mission with only a faint apprehension of viewing anything more than a decided diminution of the Pribylov rookeries, caused by pelagic poaching during the last five or six years.

But, from the moment of my landing at St. Paul Island on the 21st of last May, until the close of the breeding season those famous " rookeries " and " hauling-grounds " of the fur-seal thereon, and of St. George Island too, began to declare and have declared to my astonished senses the fact that their utter ruin and extermination is only a question of a few short years from date, unless prompt and thorough measures of relief and protection are at once ordered on sea and on land by the Treasury Department, and enforced by it.

a

Quickly realizing after my arrival upon these islands that a remarkable change for the worse had taken place since my finished work of 1874, was given to the public in that same year, and the year also of my last survey of those rookeries, I took the field at once, carrying hourly and daily with me a series of note books opened under the following heads :

I. The " Rookeries "; their area, position and condition (1872-1874 and in 1890).
II. The " Hauling-Grounds »; their appearance (1872-1874 and in 1890).
III. The Method of " driving " and taking fur-seals (1872-1874 and in 1890).
IV. The Selection of Skins, grade and supply (1872-1874 and in 1890).
V. Character, condition and number of natives (1872-1874 and in 1890).
VI. Conduct of native labour and pay (1872-1874 and in 1890).

To these heads I add the following sections; the whole series making up my report in the order as they are here given.

VII. The Protection and Preservation of these fur bearing interests of our Government on the Pribylov Islands and that immediate action necessary, viewed in the full light of existing danger.
VIII. Appendix, in which the author's daily field notes appear, *verbatim et literatim*, in order of day and date.
IX. Revised general maps of St. Paul and St. George showing the area and position of the hauling-grounds of the fur-seal thereon in 1872-1874, and again in 1890.
X. A series of special maps showing the exact topography, area and position of the breeding rookeries of St. Paul and St. George Islands in 1872-1874 and again in 1890, together with an illustration of each rookery drawn from life by the author.

Although I was unable to detect any sign of existing danger or injury to these interests of our Government on the Islands of Pribylov in 1872-1874, yet the need of caution on the part of the Government, and their close annual scrutiny was pointed out and urged in my published work of 1874 [1], in the following language : (pp.75-77).

1. A Report upon the Condition of Affairs in the Territory of Alaska, by Henry W. Elliott, Special Agent Treasury Department, Washington. Government Printing Office, 1875. (pp. 277 ; 8 vo.).

Until my arrival on the Seal Islands, April, 1872, no steps had been taken toward ascertaining the extent or the importance of these interests of the Government by either the Treasury Agent in charge, or the Agent of the company leasing the islands. This was a matter of no especial concern to the latter, but was of the first importance to the Government. It had, however, failed to obtain definite knowledge upon the subject, on account of the inaccurate mode of ascertaining the number of seals which had been adopted by its agent, who relied upon an assumption of the area of the breeding " rookeries " but who never took the trouble to ascertain the area and position of these great seal grounds intrusted to his care.

After a careful study of the subject during two whole seasons, and a thorough review of it during this season of 1874, in company with my associate, Lieutenant Maynard, I propose to show plainly and in sequence the steps which have led me to a solution of the question as to the number of fur-seals on the Pribylov Islands, together with the determination of means by which the agent of the Government will be able to correctly report upon the condition of the seal life from year to year.

At the close of my investigation for the season of 1872, the fact became evident that the breeding seals obeyed implicitly a fine, instinctive *law of distribution*, so that the breeding ground occupied by them was always covered by seals in an exact ratio, greater or less to the area to be held : that they always covered the ground evenly, never crowding in at one place and scattering out at another; that the seals lay just as thickly together where the rookery is a small one of only a few thousand, as at Nah Speel, near the village, as they do where a million of them came together, as at North-east Point.

This fact being determined, it is at once plain, *that just as the breeding grounds of the fur-seal on these islands, expand or contract in area from their present dimensions, so the seals will have increased or diminished.*

Impressed, therefore, with the necessity and the importance of obtaining the exact area and position of these breeding grounds, I surveyed them in 1872-1873 for that purpose, and re-surveyed them this season of 1874 : the result has been carefully drawn and plotted out, as presented in the accompanying maps.

The time for taking the boundaries of the rookeries is during the week of their greatest expansion, or when they are as full as they are to be for the season, *and before the regular system of compact, even organisation breaks up,* the seals then scattering out in pods or clusters, straying far back, the same number covering then twice as much ground in places as they did before, when marshalled on the rookery ground proper : the breeding seals remain on the rookery perfectly quiet, and *en masse* for a week or ten days during the period of greatest expansion, which is between the 10th and 20th of July, giving ample time for the agent to correctly note the exact boundaries of the area covered by them : this step on the part of the Government officer puts him in possession every year of exact data upon which, to base a report as to the condition of the seal-life as compared with the year or years previous. In this way my record of the precise area and position of the fur-seal breeding grounds on St. Paul Island in the season of 1872, and that of St. George i nthe season of 1873, correctly serves as a definite basis for all the time to come upon which to found authoritative reports from year to year, as to any change, increase or diminution of the seal-life. It is therefore very important that the Government should have an agent in charge of these novel and valuable interests who is capable by virtue of education and energy, to correctly observe and report the area and position of the rookeries year by year.

Therefore, in the light of the foregoing you will observe, that although I was unable to detect myself, any danger to or diminution of the seal-life on the Pribylov Islands, after three seasons of close study in the field, ending with the season of 1874, yet I was deeply impressed with the need of an intelligent careful search, every year for the signs of or real existence of such danger : that I urged the Department to select men who were fit to make such a search, and who could be trusted to do it honestly and thoroughly. I made this request on the 16th of November, 1874, as I gave in my detailed report above cited to the Secretary of the Treasury, who ordered it published at once, and caused it to be widely circulated by the Department.

In 1872-1874 I observed that all the young male seals needed for the annual quota, of 75,000 or 90,000 as it was ordered in the latter year, were easily obtained every season, between the 1st of June and the 20th of July following, from the " hauling-grounds " of " Tolstoi, " " Lukannon " and " Zoltoi Sands " — from these hauling-grounds adjacent to the " rookeries ," or breeding-grounds of " Tolstoi, " " Lukannon, " " Reef " and " Garbotch. " All of these points of supply being not more than one and a half miles distant from the St. Paul village killing grounds — the " Zoltoi " drive being less than 600 feet away.

At North-east Point on this island, Webster got all the seals desired towards filling the above cited quota of 90,000, from that sand reach between the foot of Cross Hill and the Big Lake sand-dunes on the north shore beach.

Then, that immense spread of hauling-ground covered by swarms of young male seals, at Zapadnie, at South-west Point, at English Bay beyond Middle Hill, west, at Polavina, and over all that eight long miles of beach and upland hauling-ground between Lukannon Bay and Webster's House at Novastoshnah — all of this extensive sealing area was not visited by sealing gangs, or spoken of by them as necessary to be driven from.

Therefore, when attentively studying in 1872-1874, the subject of what was the effect of killing annually 100,000, young male seals on these islands (90,000 on St. Paul and 10,000 on St. George), in view of the foregoing statement of fact I was unable to see how any harm was being done to the regular supply of fresh blood for the breeding rookeries, since those large reservoirs of surplus male life, above named, held at least just half of the young male seal-life then belonging to the islands — these large sources of supply were never driven from — never even visited by the sealers, and out of their overwhelming abundance, I thought that surely enough fresh male seal-life must, did annually mature for service on the breeding rookeries.

Therefore, when summing up in my published work of 1872-1874, I was positive in declaring that although I was firmly convinced that no increase to the then existing number of seals on these Islands would follow any effort that we might make (giving my reasons in detail for so believing), yet I was as firmly satisfied that as matters were then conducted, nothing was being done which would injure the regular annual supply of male life necessary for the full demand of the rookeries. I then declared " that *provided* matters are conducted on the seal-islands in the future, *as they are to day* 100,000 male seals, under the age of five years, and over one, may be safely taken every year from the Pribylov Islands without the slightest injury to the regular birth rates, or natural increase thereon : *provided* also that the fur-seals are not visited by any plague, or pests, or any abnormal cause for their destruction, which might be beyond the control of men." (*Monograph of the Seal Islands of Alaska*, p. 62.)

I repeatedly called attention to this fact, in my published report, that all of the killable seals required, were easily taken in thirty working days, between June 14th and July 20th of every year from those points above specified, and that those reservoirs of surplus male life at South-west Point, Zapadnie, English Bay, Polavina, Tonkie Mees, etc., were full and overflowing : that more than enough was untouched which sufficed to meet the demands of nature on the breeding grounds. But, to make certain that my theory was a good one, and would be confirmed by time, for I qualified my statement, at that time, as a theory only, I made a careful and elaborate triangulation of the area and position of the breeding-grounds in 1872-'73 on St. Paul and St. George Islands, aided and elaborated by my associate in 1874, Lt. Washburn Maynard, U. S. N. This I did in order that any increase or diminution following our work could be authoritatively stated — that a foundation of fact and not assumption should exist for such a comparison of the past order with that of the present or the future.

Sixteen years have elapsed since that work was finished : its accuracy as to the statements of fact then published was at that time unquestioned on these islands, and it is to day freely acknowledged there : but, what has been the logic of events? Why is it that we find now only a scant tenth of the number of young male seals which I saw there in 1872? When did this work of decrease and destruction so marked on the breeding-grounds there, begin? And how? This answer follows :

1sts. *From overdriving without heeding its warning,* first begun in 1879, dropped then, until 1882, then suddenly renewed again with increased energy from year to year, until the end is abruptly reached, this season of 1890.

2nd. *From the shooting of fur-seals* (*chiefly females*) in the open waters of the North Pacific Ocean and Bering Sea, begun as a business in 1888, and continued to date.

Thus, the seal-life candle has been literally " burning at both ends " during the last five years.

That day in 1879, when it became necessary to send a sealing gang from St. Paul village over to Zapadnie to regularly drive from that hitherto untouched reserve, was the day that danger first appeared in tangible form since 1870—since 1857 for that matter.

The fact then, that that abundant source of supply which had served so well and steadily since 1870-81, should fail to yield its accustomed returns to the drivers—that fact ought to have aroused some comment— ought then to have been recorded by the officer in charge in behalf of the Government at the close of the season's work in 1882; but, it did not : possibly, the gravity of the change was not then fully appreciated by the sealers themselves either through ignorance or inattention.

But, when in 1882 it became absolutely necessary to draw from that time on until the end of the present season, heavily and repeatedly upon these hitherto untouched sources of supply for the rookeries, in order to get the customary annual quota—at that time that fact, that glaring change from the prosperous and healthy precedent and record of 1870-'81, should have been it was ample warning of danger ahead :—it seems however, to have been entirely ignored—to have fallen upon inattentive or incapable minds : for, not until the report for 1889 from the agent of the Government in charge, who went up in the spring of that year for his first season of service and experience— not until his report came down to the Treasury Department, has there been the slightest intimation in the annual declarations of the officers of the Government, of the least diminution or decrease of seal-life on these islands since my work of 1874 was finished and given to the world.

On the contrary strange as it may seem, all the Treasury Agents since 1879 have, whenever they have spoken at all, each vied with the other in their laudations of the " splendid condition of the rookeries "— "fully up to their best standard", etc., and one report in 1888, declares a vast increase over the large figures which I published in 1872-'74 which is again reiterated by the same officer in 1888.

But, how could these gentlemen reconcile their statements with that remarkable evidence of the decrease in supply of young males from the records made and before them—staring them in the face—of 1872-74? When they saw and daily recorded the fact that sealing gangs were being daily sent out from the village, miles and miles away to hitherto undisturbed fields, for killable seals—*the regular, customary hauling-grounds, then at the point of exhaustion, from which an abundant supply had been easily secured during the last thirty years,* and grass growing all over the hauling grounds of 1872,—how indeed did that fact escape their attention? it did however; it was utterly ignored.

I can see now, in the light of the record of the work of sixteen consecutive years of sealing, very clearly one or two points which were wholly invisible to my sight in 1872-'74. I can now see what that effect of driving overland is upon the physical well being of a normal fur-seal, and from that sight, feel warranted in taking the following ground.

The least reflection will declare to an observer that while a fur-seal moves easier on land and freer than any or all other seals, yet, at the same time it is an unsual and laborious effort, even when it is voluntary; therefore, when thousands of young male seals are suddenly aroused to their utmost power of land locomotion, over rough, sharp rocks, rolling clinker stones, deep, loose sand, mossy tussocks and other equally severe impediments, they in their fright exert themselves violently, crowd in confused sweltering heaps one upon the other so that many are often " smothered " to death; and, in this manner of most extraordinary effort to be urged along over stretches of unbroken miles, they are obliged to use muscles and nerves that nature never intended them to use, and which are not fitted for the action.

This prolonged, sudden and unusual effort, unnatural and violent strain must leave a lasting mark upon the physical condition of every seal thus driven, and then suffered to escape from the clubbed pods or the killing grounds; they are alternately heated to the point of suffocation, gasping, panting, allowed to cool down at intervals, then abruptly started up on the road for a fresh renewal of this heating as they lunge, shamble and creep along; when they arrive on the killing grounds after four or five hours of this distressing effort on their part, they are then suddenly cooled off for the last time prior to the final ordeal of clubbing; then when driven up into the last surround or " pod, " as the seals are spared from cause of being unfit to take, too big or too little, bitten, etc., they are permitted to go off from the killing ground back to the sea, outwardly unhurt, most of them; but I am now satisfied that they sustain in a vast majority of cases, internal injuries of greater or less degree[1], that remain to work physical disability or death thereafter to nearly every seal thus released, and certain destruction of its virility and courage necessary for a station on the rookery even if it can possibly run this gauntlet of driving throughout every sealing season for five or six consecutive years; driven over and over again as it is during each one of these sealing seasons.

Therefore it now appears plain to me that those young male fur seals which may happen to survive this terrible strain of seven years of driving overland, are rendered by this act of driving wholly worthless for breeding purposes — that they never go to the breeding grounds and take up stations there, being utterly demoralized in spirit and in body.

With this knowledge, then, the full effect of " driving " becomes apparent, and that result of slowly but surely robbing the rookeries of a full and sustained supply of fresh young male blood, demanded by nature imperatively, for their support up to the standard of full expan-

1. I have been repeatedly astonished at the amazing power possessed by the fur-seal, of resistance to shocks which would certainly kill any other animal. To explain clearly, you will observe, by reference to my maps, that there are a great many cliffy places between the rookeries on the shore-lines of the islands. Some of these cliffs, are more than 100 feet in abrupt elevation above the surf and rocks awash below, Frequently " hollusckickie, " in ones, or twos, or threes will stray far away back from the great masses of their kind, and fall asleep in the thick grass and herbage which covers these mural reaches. Sometimes they will lie down and rest very close to the edge, and then as you come tramping along you discover and startle them and yourself, alike. They, blinded by their first transports of alarm, leap promptly over the brink, snorting, coughing, and spitting as they go. Curiously peering after them and looking down upon the rocks, 50 to 100 feet below, instead of seeing their stunned and motionless bodies, you will invariably catch sight of them rapidly scrambling into the water; and, when in it, swimming off like arrows from the bow. Three " holluschickie " were thus inadvertantly surprised by me on the edge of the west face of Otter island. They plunged over from an elevation, there, not less then 200 feet in sheer elevation, and I distinctly saw them fall in scrambling, whirling evolutions, down, thumping upon the rocky shingle beneath, from which they bounded, as they struck, like so many rubber balls. Two of them never moved after the rebound ceased, but the third one reached the water and swam away like a bird on the wing.

While they seem to escape without bodily injury incident to such hard falls as ensue from dropping 50 or 60 feet upon pebbly beaches and rough bowlders below, and even greater elevations, yet I am inclined to think that some internal injuries are necessarily sustained in most every case, which soon develop and cause death; the excitement and the vitality of the seal, at the moment of the terrific shock, is able to sustain and conceal the real injury for the time being.

sion (such as I recorded in 1872-1874) — that result began, it now seems clear, to set in from the very beginning, 20 years ago under the present system.

Had, however, a check been as slowly and steadily applied to that " driving " as it progressed in 1879-1882 upon those great reserves of Zapadnie, South-west Point and Polavina, then the present condition of exhaustion, complete exhaustion of the surplus supply of young male seals would not be observed — it would not have happened.

But, however, no attention was given whatever to the fact that in 1882 the reserves were suddenly, very suddenly drawn upon, steadily and heavily for the first time, in order that a prompt filling of the regular annual quota should be made before or by the usual time of closing the sealing season for the year, viz :, July 20th; — and until the report for 1889, above cited, of the Treasury Agent in charge came into the Treasury Department, not a suggestion ever had been made in official writing, from 1872-1874 to that time, of the slightest prospect even of the amazing diminution of seal-life which is now so painfully apparent.

. Naturally enough, being so long away from the field, on reading Mr Charles J. Goff's report for the season's work of 1889, I at once jumped to the conclusion that the pelagic sealing, the poaching of 1886-1889 was the sole cause for that shrinkage which he declared manifest, on those rookeries and hauling grounds of the Pribylov Islands, — such a great shrinkage as to warrant him in the declaration which he makes in that report, that he believes that not over 60,000 young male seals can be secured here in 1890 — and if more can be, that they should not be taken.

Still, even then, charging it in this manner all to the poachers was not quite satisfactory to my mind; I could figure out from the known number of skins which these hunters had placed on the market, a statement of the loss and damage to the rookeries — to the females and young born and unborn, for that is the class from which the poacher secures at least 85 %, of his catch from; and, I was prepared to find, by these figures that the breeding grounds had lost heavily, but that did not even satisfy me as to his statement which came so suddenly in 1889, that little more than half of the established annual quota of 100,000 holluschickie suitable for killing could or should be secured here in 1890; for great as my estimated shrinkage on the breeding grounds was, due to the work of the poacher, yet that would not, could not explain to my mind the ninefold greater shrinkage of that supply from the hauling grounds which must exist, or else 60,000 young males might be easily taken, judging from my notes of such work in 1872.

Therefore I landed here very much confused in thought as to what I should observe.

I began at once and finished by the 9th of June, an entire new topographical survey and triangulation of the landed area of the seven rookeries of St. Paul Island, and those of St. George Island on the 19th and 20th of July, so as to have these charts ready for instant use when the time came in which to observe the full form and number of the breeding seals as they laid upon this ground, viz., July 10th-20th inclusive:— Thereafter until the closing of the season on St. Paul, July 19th, and on St. George up to August 4th, I have daily recorded the full details of the hauling, the driving and killing of seals there, the condition of the breeding animals, their arrival and behavior, etc., — a thousand varied incidents have been faithfully observed as my field notes will testify and which appear in all their detail in the following appendix to this report.

The present condition of these fur-seal preserves, is nothing new to the history of their case while in the hands of the Russians. Twice before in the comparatively short period of a century since they were first opened to the cupidity of man, have they been threatened with the same ruin that threatens them to day : in 1806 and 1807 all killing was stopped to save them, but resumed again in 1808 — too soon, for after seventeen years of halfway measures, the full and necessary term of rest was given to them in 1834; the story of this "Zapooska" of the Russians in 1834, and the causes which led then to threatened extermination of those fur-seal interests on the Pribylov Islands, is one that is now timely in its repetition and should be heeded.

When these islands were first discovered in 1786-'87 an indiscriminate rush was made to them by the representative of every Russian trading organization then in Alaska — by every one then able to fit out a vessel and hire a number of men. These eager, greedy parties located on and near all of the large rookeries and hauling grounds, and killed as many as they could handle; in those days all the skins were air dried, and not salted, and that made the work of scaling then far slower and much more difficult than it is now, since the present system of salting skins practically offers no delay whatever to the work of killing and skinning. In my mind there is no doubt but what this inability to cure rapidly the skins for shipment in 1786-1803, as fast as they could then be killed and skinned — not one tenth as fast as they can be to day — that this delay alone saved the Pribylov rookeries from utter extermination in those early days. Certainly it was and must have been the cause, for, at least thirteen different trading organizations had their vessels and their men around and on these two islands of St. Paul and St. George engaged to their utmost ability throughout full seventeen years in unbroken succession, in taking fur-seal skins.

Had these early Russian fur hunters then possessed the knowledge and means of curing skins in salt, that we now have, together with those appliances in use to day on the Seal Islands of Alaska, I am well satisfied in my own mind, that they would have killed every fur-seal that remained to show itself in less than three years after they began operations — that they would have swept every animal from these ground long before the old Russian American Company assumed autocratic control of those interests in 1799, and extended it, in 1805, and to all Alaska as well.

But fortunately for us and the world as well, they did not know anything about curing skins in salt — they had but one method, and that was to stretch out the green skins and air dry them upon frames in long, low drying houses, or in bright weather during August, September, and October to peg them out upon the ground.

Thus, this tedious process in a climate as damp foggy and stormy as is that peculiar to the Seal Islands of Alaska, made these Slavonian sealers spend ten times as much time in the act of curing their fur-seal pelts as it took them to drive out and kill; then too, in those early days they were remote from a market, had no prompt, economical means of transportation to London, and depended wholly upon the idiosyncrasies of the Chinese trade, via Kiachta; but even with this extraordinary hindrance, it seems that they took in that laborious and risky manner, at least one hundred thousand fur-seal skins every year[1].

They took so many that by 1803, several hundred thousand of these air dried pelts had accumulated over the ability of the Old Russian Company to profitably dispose of them in time to prevent their decay, — moulding and damp, then abruptly decaying — rotting in large piles, as they were stacked up in the warehouses at Kodiak — so it became necessary to cut or throw into the sea, 700,000 pelts " during that year. Naturally this loss of labor, time and money cooled the ardor of the sealing gangs which were working the Pribylov Islands, they worked slower, when they did work, and most likely never worked at all in wet weather; obliged to bow to the caprices of the climate, or

---

1. " In the first years on St. Paul Island from 50,000 to 60,000 were taken annually, and on S. George from 40,000 to 50,000 every year. Such horrible killing was neither necessary nor demanded. The skins were frequently taken without any list or count. In 1803, 800,000 seals skins had accumulated, and it was impossible to make advantageous sale of so many skins; for in this great number so many were spoiled, that it became necessary to cut or throw into the sea, 700,000 pelts!" (Bishop Veniaminov, " Zapieskie " etc. 1848, Vol. I, chap. XII.)

lose their labor, they were thus obliged to spare the seals and this enforced delay in 1788-1806 has saved the Pribylov Rookeries from that swift destruction which the keen quick witted American and English sealers visited in 1806-26 upon the great breeding grounds of the fur-seal in the Antarctic : — they, our countrymen, then used the kench and salt, they were never bothered with the question of how to dispose of their skins after killing and skinning so as to save them; and, they brought their methods of 1806-'26 — the same methods of to-day, up to these Seal Islands of Alaska for the first time in 1868[1].

No one can state with more than mere estimation on his part, the full number of seals slaughtered by the Russians on the Pribylov islands from 1786 to 1817 : no lists — no check whatever on it appears to have been made, and the record certainly never was made, since Bishop Venianimov who from 1825 up to 1838 was at the head of all matters connected with the church in this Onalaska district where the seal islands belonged, and who had the respect and confidence of the old Russian American Company, made a zealous search for such a record in 1834-35 among the archives of the Company at Sitka, where he had full access: by the result of his painstaking search he sums up in the following terse statement, " Of the number of skins taken up to 1815, I have no knowledge to rely upon; but, from that time up to the present writing, I have true and reliable accounts, " which he puts into the appendix of his published work[2].

The Bishop (who is the only Russian who has given us the faintest idea of how matters were conducted in his time upon these islands), seems to have witnessed them in a uniform condition of decline as to yield, for in the time of his writing and up to its closing in 1837, the record was one of steady diminution; until 1834, the killing seems to have been permitted with all sorts of half measures, since 1817 adopted one after the other, to no good result whatever; finally

---

1. They began at once that system of disciplined exhaustive slaughter which had proved so effective in their hands throughout the Antarctic — took nearly 250,000 seal skins on these islands in the short space of four months; ceased then only for the want of salt; but happily the Government intervened early in 1869 before they could resume their work of swift destruction.

In 1857 the first salting of fur seal skins was attempted on the Pribylov Islands : but the rudeness of the method caused trouble when the shipment reached London. In 1862 it was tried again by the Russians, but it was still rudely done until our people went to work in 1868 with their thorough methods. The Russians never bundled their skins when salted: they allowed them to dry without kenching in salt, and shipped them just as they did their air dried skins, or " parcment " peots.

2. " Zapieskie ob Onalashkenskaho Otdayla : St. Petersburg, 1842; 2 vols 8vo. A full translation of that chapter which treats of that question will follow this introduction.

however, the supply abruptly fell from an expected 20,000 to 12,000 only from both islands in 1834 — " all that could be got with all possible exertion. "

Then the Russians awoke to the fact that if they wished to preserve these fur bearing interests on the Pribylov Islands from ruin that they must stop killing, *wholly* stop for a number of years — stop until the renewal of the exhausted rookeries was manifest, and easily recognized : this Zapooska of 1835 which they then ordered is the date of the renewed lease of life which these rookeries took and which by 1857 had restored them to the splendid condition in which they were when they passed in the hands of the United States, and which now, after 22 years of killing since 1868 and under the recent regulations of 1870 together with the pelagic sealing since 1886, we find again threatened with speedy extinction unless *full* measures are at once adopted for their preservation and restoration on land, and in the sea, — *half measures will not do* — they failed in the Russian period signally, and they will as signally fail with us if we yeld in the slightest degree to any argument for their adoption.

It is interesting, therefore, to study the figures which Veniaminov gives us of the yield from these islands during that period extending down from 1817 to 1837 — study it in connection with his statement of what those attempts were, and which were being made, futile efforts by the old Company to build up the business, and yet continue sealing; until, finally, after seventeen years of continual diminution and repeated introduction of half way methods of restoration, the end came abruptly, and what ought to have been done at first, was finally forced in 1834 — the absolute rest of the rookeries in 1835 came, and practically continued, until 1846-'50; then a gradual rise above 10,000 " holluschickie " or young male fur-seals per annum began to be safely taken; and, by 1854, the exhausted and nearly ruined rookeries of St. Paul and St. George were able to yield 35,000 prime fur-seal pelts without the slightest injury to them, and by 1857-60 they were so numerous that the Russians ceased to regard them as objects of care: and there after governed their annual catch by the demands outside alone — taking as the market called for them anywhere from 40,000 to 80,000 annually.

As matters stand to day on the Seal Islands, the situation is very much the same as it was in 1834, then it was expected that 20,000 seals would be taken, but only 12,000 were secured with all possible exertion; this year it was expected that 60,000 fine skins would be taken; but only 21,000 have been secured with all possible exertion, nearly half of this catch being small, or 5 1/2 — 6 1/2 lb. skins — raking and scraping the rookery margins without a days intermission from the opening to the closing of the season; of this work of 1890, I give you in this report the fullest detail of its progression, day by day, to the merciful ending of it, ordered so happily by you.

It will be promptly observed from a study of this record of the Russians, which has been so plainly and so honestly given us by Veniaminov and Shaiesnickov, that the Russians during their control were faced at two periods with the prospect of a speedy extermination of these fur-seal rookeries of Alaska : in 1806 and 1807, they stopped all killing on these islands of St. Paul and St. George, but, began to kill again in 1810 — too soon; Veniaminov's record and account shows that from 1817, in spite of everything they could do, save stopping short of all killing, " only made matters worse. "

Finally in 1834, with the second and positive threat of swift extermination again facing them, the Russians reluctantly surrendered, and ordered a rest which lasted seven years, ere any beginning was fairly made to kill more than a few thousand young male seals annually. In the first year, only 100 of such animals were taken, the number being very slowly raised year after year until 1847-'50.

With reference to the preservation and conduct of this interesting and valuable industry, my study last summer of the subject has led me step by step to the following conclusions :

1st. That we restrict and prohibit all killing of fur-seals on the Pribxlov islands for tax and shipment of skins for the next seven years without reflection on the present lessees : the Government to assume entire control, care and supervision of the restoration of these interests during that period, since a division of responsibility will only provoke confusion and scandal and probably result in defeating the object in view.

2nd. This step on our part warrants us in asking the cooperation of Great Britain and Russia : in asking these powers to establish a close time for the protection of the fur-seals of Bering Sea during their breeding season, and that these regulations be agreed upon by a joint commission which shall consist of experts selected by the powers interested, and who shall visit the seal islands of Bering Sea next summer for that purpose : pending the settlement of these regulations and the report of this commission, all pelagic sealing in Bering Sea to be declared illegal, by the several powers interested.

In concluding this introduction to my work of the past season, and its results, I desire to say that have been exceedingly careful in gathering my data upon which I base all statement of fact, and opinion, and to secure these data I have literally live out upon the field itself, where those facts alone can be gathered honestly, or else had better not be gathered at all.

I now submit, most respectfully, my detailed report covering above mentioned heads, together with those field sketches and maps which I deem necessary to give a more distinct, clear and full idea of my meaning and understanding of the subjects treated : trusting that it will meet with your approval.

I am very respectfully your obedient servant,

HENRY W. ELLIOTT.

INTRODUCTION

GEOGRAPHICAL DISTRIBUTION OF THE FUR-SEAL AND ITS EXTERMINATION IN THE ANTARCTIC

Peculiarities of Distribution. — Our first thought in studying the distribution of the fur-seals throughout the high seas of the earth, is one of wonder. While they have been so widely spread over the Antarctic regions, yet, as we pass the equator going north, we find in the Atlantic above the tropics nothing that resembles them. Their range in the North Pacific is virtually confined to four islands in Bering sea, Saint-Paul and Saint-George of the Pribylov group, and Bering and Copper of the Commander Islands.

It should be observed that there is abundant reason, owing to constitution and the habit of *Callorhinus*, for this remarkable restriction in the northern hemisphere compared with its expansion to the south. It is, however, very singular, even in the light of all we know, that right on the equator itself a trifle to the southward of it, viz. on the Galapagos Islands, fur-seals are still found where they were first found a hundred years ago.

The remarkable discrepancy which we have alluded to may be better understood, when we consider that these animals require certain conditions of landing, breeding ground, and climate, all combined, for their perfect life and reproduction. In the North

INTRODUCTION.

Atlantic no suitable ground for their reception exists, or ever did exist; and really nothing in the North Pacific, beyond what we have designated in Bering sea will answer the requirements of the fur-seal. When we look over the Antarctic waters, we are surprised at what might have been done, and should have been done, in those southern waters. Hundreds of miles of the finest seal-breeding grounds on the western coast of Patagonia, the beautiful reaches of the Falkland islands, the great extent of Desolation island, together with the whole host of smaller islets, where these animals abounded in almost countless numbers when first discovered and should abound to-day — millions upon millions — but which have been, through nearly a century, the victims of indiscriminate slaughter, directed by most unscrupulous and most energetic men. It seems well-nigh incredible, but is true, nevertheless, that for more than fifty years a large fleet, numbering more than sixty sail, and carrying thousands of active men, traversed this coast and circumnavigated every island and islet, annually slaughtering right and left wherever the seal-life was found. Ships were laden to the water's edge with the fresh air-dried, and salted skins, and they were swallowed up in the marts of the world, bringing mere nominal prices — the markets glutted, but the butchery never stopping.

I will pass in brief review the seal-grounds of the southern hemisphere; taking at the outset those which are peculiar to the waters of the Western ocean. The Galapagos island come first to our notice; this scattered group of small rocks and islets, uninhabited and entirely arid, was, fifty years ago, resorted to by a very considerable number of these animals, *Arctocephalis australis*, together with many sea lions, *Otaria Hookeri;* great numbers were then taken by those sealers, who found to their sorrow, when the skins were inspected, that they were thin-furred and worthless. A few survivors, however, remains to this day.

Along and off the coast of Chili and Bolivia are the St. Felix, Juan Fernandez and Más-á-fuera islands, the later place being one of the most celebrated rookeries known to Arctic sealers. The west coast of Patagonia and a portion of that of Tierra del Fuego was, in those early days of seal-hunting, and is to-day, the finest connected range of seal-rookery ground in the south. Here was annually made the concentrated attack of that sealing fleet above referred to; and one can readily understand how thorough must have been its labor, as he studies the great extent and deep indentation of this coast, its thousand and one islands, and islets and when he sees to-day that there is scarcely a rookery of fur-seals known to exist there. The Falkland islands, just abreast of the straits of Magellan, were also celebrated, and a favorite resort, not only of the sealers, but of the whale fleets of the world. They are recorded, in the brief mention made by the best authority, as fairly swarming with fur-seals when they were opened up by Captain Cook. There are to-day, in the place of the millions that once existed, an insignificant number, taken notice of only now and then.

The Georgia islands and the Sandwich group, all a succession of rocky islands and reefs awash — the South Orkneys, the Shetlands the Auckland group, Campbell's island, Emerald island, and a few rocks lying just to the southward of New Zealand — have all been places of lively and continued butchery; the fur-seals ranging in desperation from one of those places to the other as the seasons progressed and the merciless search and slaughter continued. These pinnipeds, however, never went to the southward of 62° south latitude.

In considering the western Antarctic hemisphere, I must not forget also to mention, that the fur-seal was in early times found, up the coast of South America, here and there in little rookeries, as far north as Cape St. Roque; but the number was unimportant when brought into contrast with that belonging to those localities which we have designated. A small cliff-bound rookery to-day exists at cape Corrientes. This is owned and farmed out by the Argentine Republic, and we are informed that in spite of all their care and attention they have neither increased nor have they diminished from their original insignificance; from this rookery only three to five thousand were and are annually taken. Another small preserve on the Lobos islets, near the mouth of the River Plate is also protected and leased by the government of Uruguay, and from 12,000 to 15,000 skins are annually taken there.

When we look at our northern Atlantic waters we speedily recognize the fact, that between North America and Europe, across the Atlantic and into the Arctic, there is not a single island or islet or stretch of coast that the fur-seal could successfully struggle for existence on; therefore it has never been found there. It appears as if our fur-seals had originally passed to Bering sea from the parent stock of the Patagonia region, up along the coast of South America, a few tarrying at the dry and heated Galapagos island, the rest speeding on to the northward, disturbed by the clear skies and sandy beaches of the Mexican coast, on and up to the great fish-spawning shores of the Aleutian islands and Bering sea. There, on the Pribylov group and the bluffy Commander islands, they found that union of cool water, well-adapted landing, and moist foggy air which they had missed since they left the storm-beaten coasts far below.

In the Antarctic waters of the eastern hemisphere seals were found at Tristan da Cunha, principally on Little Nightingale island, the Crozets group, all small rocks, as it were, over which violent storms fairly swept; then we observe the great rookeries of Kerguelen land, or Desolation island where perhaps nine-tenths of all the oriental fur-seals congregated, thence over to a small and insignificant islet known as the Royal Company, south of Good Hope. This list includes all the known resting-places of the fur-seal in these waters.

In the North Pacific, during prehistoric times, a legend from Spanish authority states, that fur-seals were tolerably abundant on the Santa Barbara and Guadaloupe islands, off the coast of California, and the peninsula to the southward. A few were annually taken from these islands, up to 1835, and irregularly found there until 1874; an interregnum of some ten years and a few hundred skins were taken from there in 1885. None have been secured since. Also, fur-seals were wont to sport and rest on those celebrated rocks of the harbor of San Francisco, known as the Farralones; but no tradition locates a seal-rookery anywhere else on the northwest coast, or anywhere else in all Alaska and its islands, save the Pribylov group, while across and down the Asiatic coast only the Commander islands and a little rock islet know as Robben Reef (right under the lee of Saghalien Island, Okhotsk Sea) is known as the resort of this animal. The crafty savage of that entire region, the hairy Aino and the Japanese

INTRODUCTION.

themselves have searched in vain during the last hundred years for other ground frequented by these fur-seals.

In the light of the foregoing remarks, is it not natural when we reflect upon the immense area and the exceedingly favored conditions of ground and climate frequented by the fur-seals of the Southern ocean, to say that their number must have been infinitely greater as they were first apprehended, surpassing all adequate description, when compared to those which we did regard as the marvel and wonder of the age the breeding rookeries of the Pribylov group?

It is a great pity that this work of extermination and senseless destruction should have progressed as it has to the very verge of total extinction, ere any one was qualified to take note of and record the wonderful life thus eliminated. The Falkland islands and Kerguelen land, at least, might have been placed under the same restrictions and wholesome direction which the Russians established in the North seas, the benefits of which accrue to us to-day, and will forever, as matters are now conducted. Certainly is is surprising that the business thought, the hard headed sense, of those early English navigators, should not have been equal to that of the Russian Promyshlenik, who were renowned as the most unscrupulous and the greediest of gain-getters.

The Antarctic islands offered natural advantages of protection by land far superior to those found on the Pribylov or Commander groups. They had harbors and they lay outside of the track of commerce, advantages which are not all shared by our islands; at Desolation island, perhaps the difficulties were insuperable on account of the great extent of coast, which is practically inaccessible to men and nearly so to the seals; but the Falkland islands might have been farmed out by the British government at a trifling outlay and with exceeding good results, for millions upon millions of the fur-seals could rest there to-day, as they did a hundred years ago, and be there to-morrow, as our seals do and are in Bering sea. But the work is done. There is nothing down there, now valuable enough to rouse the interest of any government, still a beginning might be made, which possibly forty or fifty years hence would rehabilitate the scourged and desolated breeding ground of the South seas. We are selfish people, however, and look only to the present, and it is, without question, more than likely that should any such proposition be brought before the British Parliament it would be so ridiculed and exaggerated by demagogues as to cause its speedy suppression. Now we are brought in this season of 1890 face to face with the same danger on our own preserves which has destroyed these interests in the Antarctic. Shall we be equal to the occasion?

SECTION I

THE "ROOKERIES" OR BREEDING GROUNDS
OF THE FUR-SEAL ON THE PRIBYLOV ISLANDS OF ALASKA
THEIR AREA AND CONDITION IN 1872-74, 1890

SECTION I

THE "ROOKERIES" OR BREEDING GROUNDS OF THE FUR-SEAL ON THE PRIBYLOV ISLANDS OF ALASKA: THEIR AREA AND CONDITION IN 1872-74, 1890

The breeding grounds or " rookeries " of the Pribylov islands have altered very slightly in as far as their topographical features are concerned since the date of my last survey of them in 1874; but a marked change in the numbers of the fur seals that then repaired to these grounds has taken place.

On Saint Paul's Island in 1872 we saw the breeding herds of the fur-seal in the following form and numbers contrasted with the figures of to-day which are made in precisely the same time and method as those of 1872-74 were.

ANALYSIS OF THE BREEDING GROUNDS OF THE FUR-SEAL ON ST. PAUL ISLAND

(PRIBYLOV GROUP)

As surveyed, Seasons of 1872-1874.					As Surveyed, Season of 1890.				
ROOKERIES.	SEA MARGIN.	AVERAGE DEPTH solid massing.	SQUARE feet.	NUMBER of SEALS ♂ ♀ and ○	ROOKERIES.	SEA MARGIN	AVERAGE DEPTH solid massing.	SQUARE feet.	NUMBER of SEALS ♀ and ○
July 10, 1872. July 15, 1874. "Reef" had.	4,016 ft.	150 ft.	602,006	301,000	July 10, 1890. "Reef" has.	4,300 ft.	65 1/3 ft.	281,000	140,300
July 10, 1872. July 15, 1874. "Garbotch" had.	3,660 ft.	100 ft.	366,000	183,000	July 10, 1890. "Garbotch" has.	2,400 ft.	70 2/3 ft.	169,664	84,802
July 10, 1872. July 16, 1874. "Lagoon" had.	750 ft.	100 ft.	750,000	37,000	July 14, 1890. "Lagoon" has.	1,500 ft.	12 ft.	18,000	9,000
July 10, 1872. "Nah Speel" had.	400 ft.	40 ft.	16,000	8,000	July 14, 1890. "Nah Speel" has.	(Has disappeared.)			
July 15, 1872. July 19, 1874. "Lukannon" had.	2,270 ft.	130 ft.	340,000	170,000	July 11, 1890. "Lukannon" has.	2,050 ft.	60 1/2 ft.	145,000	72,500
July 14, 1872. July 19, 1874. "Ketavie" had.	2,200 ft.	150 ft.	330,000	165,000	July 11, 1890. "Ketavie" has.	1,700 ft.	34 ft.	56,000	28,000
July 15, 1872. July 6, 1874. "Tolstoi" had.	3,000 ft.	150 ft.	450,000	225,000	July 11, 1890. "Tolstoi" has.	2,800 ft.	44 1/2 ft.	124,800	62,400
July 16, 1872. July 16, 1874. Upper "Zapadnie" had. Lower	2,680 ft. 3,200 ft.	73 1/3 ft. 215 1/2 ft.	195,600 690,000	97,800 345,000	July 12, 1890. Upper "Zapadnie" has. Lower	4,500 ft. 2,700 ft.	45 2/3 ft. 63 1/2 ft.	70,000 175,440	35,300 85,705
July 17, 1872. July 18, 1874. "Polavina" had. Inc. "Little Polavina"	4,000 ft.	150 ft.	600,000	300,000	July 13, 1890. "Polavina" has. Inc. "Little Polavina."	2,255 ft.	124 1/2 ft.	284,500	142,250
July 18, 1872. July 18, 1874. "Norastoshnah" had	13,840 ft.	150 ft.	240,000	1,200,000	July 13, 1890. "Norastoshnah" has.	11,135 ft.	37 1/2 ft.	435,730	217,875
Grand Sum Total, Season of 1872.				3,030,000	Grand Sum Total, Season of 1890.				878,532
Showing a loss since 1872 on the Rookeries of St. Paul of.				2,151,468	Seals (Cows, pups and bulls) at this date, July 10th-14th, 1890.				

Without explanation, I may be considered as making use of paradoxical language by using these terms of description; for the inconsistency of talking of " pups ", with " cows ", and " bulls " and " rookeries ", on the breeding-grounds of the same, cannot fail to be noticed, but this nomenclature has been given and used by the American and English whaling and sealing parties for many years, and the characteristic features of the seals themselves so suit the naming, that I have felt satisfied to retain the style throughout as rendering my description more intelligible, especially so to those who are engaged in the business, or may be hereafter. The Russians are more consistent, but not so " pat ", they call the " bull " " see-catch ", a term implying strength, vigor, etc.; the cow " matkah ", or mother; the pups, " kotickie ", or little seals; the non-breeding males under six and seven years, " holluschickie " or bachelors. The name applied collectively to the fur-seal by them is " morskiekot ", or sea-cat.

The rookeries of Saint George's Island have suffered also, but not to so great an extent, only half their number of 1873-1874 is missing as we view them this season : the following statement tells the story.

ANALYSIS OF THE BREEDING GROUNDS OF THE FUR-SEAL ON ST. GEORGE ISLAND
(PRIBYLOV GROUP)

As surveyed, Seasons 1872-74.

ROOKERIES.	SEA MARGIN.	AVERAGE DEPTH solid massing.	SQUARE feet.	NUMBER of SEALS. ♂ ♀ and ○
July 12, 1873. July 10, 1874. "Zapadnie" had.	600 ft.	60 ft.	36,000	18,000
July 12, 1873. July 10, 1874. "Starry Arteel" had.	500 ft.	125 ft.	60,840	30,420
July 13, 1873. July 11, 1874. "North" had.	750 ft. / 2,000 ft.	150 ft. / 20 ft.	112,500 / 40,000	76,250
July 13, 1873. July 11, 1874. "Little East" had.	200 ft. / 550 ft.	100 ft. / 10 ft.	20,000 / 5,500	12,750
July 13, 1873. July 11, 1874. "Eaast" had.	200 ft. / 700 ft.	200 ft. / 15 ft.	40,000 / 10,500	25,250
Grand Sum Total of 1873				162,670
1890				80,923

Showing a loss since 1873 of the Rookeries of St. George of 81,547.

As surveyed, Season of 1890.

ROOKERIES.	SEA MARGIN.	AVERAGE DEPTH solid massing.	SQUARE feet.	NUMBER of SEALS. ♂ ♀ and ○
July 20, 1890. "Zapadnie" has.	1,250 ft.	20 ft.	25,000	12,000
July 20, 1890. "Starry Arteel" has.	800 ft.	20 ft.	32,000	16,000
July 19, 1890. "North" has.	2,066 ft. / 1,300 ft.	31 ft. / 10 ft.	64,046 / 13,000	38,523
July 20, 1890. "Little East" has.	800 ft. / 200 ft.	12 ft. / 30 ft.	9,600 / 6,000	4,800
July 20, 1890. "East" has.	2,040 ft. / 1,000 ft.	5 ft. (allowed 2)	10,200 / 2,000	9,100
Grand Sum Total of.				80,923

Seals: (Cows, pups and bulls) up to date, July 20th, 1890.

In the light of the foregoing tables, it will be seen that during 1872-74 the rookeries of St. Paul and St. George carried 3,192,670 breeding fur-seals and their young : that sixteen years later only 959,455 breeding seals and their young can be honestly said to exist thereon.

Great as this loss is, yet it is faint in comparison with that sustained on the hauling grounds as we find matters to-day — there not even hundreds can be seen now, where we saw thousands sixteen years ago : the young male seals have been directly between the drive, club and poacher since 1882, while the females have had but one direct attack outside of natural causes, they have been however the chief quarry of the pelagic sealer during the last five years. The slow elimination of that surplus young male life which was and is necessary for the continued support of these rookeries, and its abrupt curtailment entirely during the last two seasons, coupled with the deadly work of the open sea hunter throughou, the last five years, brings these renowned fields of fur-seal life into inmediate danger of speedy extermination as matters are to-day. In order that the full gravity of this statement may be appreciated, I deem it proper that the several steps should be retaken which I took in 1872-74 towards the determination of that number of seals I recorded then as existing in the Pribylov rookeries. I said then in my published Monograph under this particular head[1]. " Before I can intelligently and clearly present an accurate estimate of the aggregate number of fur-seals which appear upon those great breeding grounds of the Pribylov group, every season, I must take up in regular sequence, my surveys of these remarkable rookeries which I have illustrated in this memoir by the accompanying sketch-maps, showing topographically the superficial area and distribution assumed by the seal-life at each locality. "

It will be observed, that the sum total on St. Paul Island preponderates, and completely overshadows that which is represented at St. George. Before passing to the detailed discussion of each rookery, it is well to call attention to a few salient features in regard to the present appearance of the seals on these breeding grounds, which latter are of their own selection. Touching the

---

1. Pp. 48-50 Mon. Seal Islands. (Census Ed. 1881.)

location of the fur-seals to-day, as I have recorded and surveyed it, compared with their distribution in early times, I am sorry to say that there is not a single line on a chart, or a word printed in a book, or a note made in manuscript, which refers to this all-important subject, prior to my own work, which I present herewith for the first time to the public. The absence of definite information in regard to what I conceive to be of vital interest and importance to the whole business, astonished me; I could not at first believe it; and, for the last four or five years, I have been searching among the archives of the old Russian company, as I searched diligently when up there, and elsewhere in the territory of Alaska, for some evidence in contradiction of this statement which I have just made. I wanted to find, I hoped to discover, some old record, some clue, by which I could measure with authority and entire satisfaction to my own mind, the relative volume of seal-life in the past, as compared with that which I record in the present, but was disappointed. "

"I am unable, throughout the whole of the following discussion, to cite a single reliable statement which can give any idea as to the condition and numbers of the fur-seal on these islands, when they were discovered in 1786-87, or during the whole time of their occupation since, up to the date of my arrival. I mark this so conspicuously, for it is certainly a very strange oversight, a kind of neglect, which, in my opinion, has been, to say the least, inexcusable. "

" **Russian records.** — In attempting to form an approximate conception of what the seals were or might have been in those early days, as they spread themselves over the hauling and breeding-grounds of these remarkable islands, I have been thrown entirely upon the vague statements given to me by the natives and one or two of the first American pioneers in Alaska. The only Russian record which touches ever so lightly upon the subject[1]

1. Veniaminov : Zapieskie ob Oonalashkenskaho Otdayla, 2 vols. St. Petersburg, 1842. This work of Bishop Innocent Veniaminov is the only one which the Russians can lay claim to as exhibiting anything like a history of western Alaska, or of giving a sketch of its inhabitants and resources, that has the least merit of truth, or the faintest stamp of reliability. Without it we should be simply in the dark as to much of what the Russians were about during the whole period of their occupation and possession of that country. He served, chiefly as a priest and missionary, for 25 years,

contains the remarkable statement, which is, in the light of my surveys, simply ridiculous now, that is, that the number of furseals on St. George during the first years of Russian occupation, was nearly as great as that on St. Paul. The most superficial examination of the geological character portrayed on the accompanying maps of these two islands, will satisfy any unprejudiced mind as to the total error of such a statement. Why, a mere tithe only of the multitudes which repair to St. Paul, in perfect comfort, over the sixteen to twenty miles of splendid landing-ground found thereon, could visit St. George, when all of the coast-line fit for their reception at this island, is a scant two and a half miles; but for that matter there was, at the time of my arrival and incredible legends afloat in regard to the rookeries on St. Paul and St. George. Finding, therefore, that the whole work must be undertaken *de novo*, I set about it without further delay."

" Thus it will be seen that there is, frankly stated, nothing to guide to a fair or even approximate estimate as to the number of the furseals on these two islands, prior to my labour."

" **Manner of Computing the number of seals.**—After a careful study of the subject, during three entire consecutive seasons, and a confirmatory review of it in 1876, I feel confident that the following figures and surveys will, upon their own face, speak authoritatively as to their truthful character."

" At the close of my investigation, during the first season of my labour on the grounds, in 1873, the fact became evident that the breeding-seals obeyed implicitly an imperative and instinctive natural law of distribution; a law recognized by each and every

from 1814 to 1839, at Oonalashka, having the seal-islands in his parish, and was made bishop of all Alaska. He was soon after recalled to Russia, where he became the primate of the national church, ranking second to no man in the empire, save the czar. He must have been a man of fine personal appearance, judging from the following description of him, noted by Sir George Simpson, who met him at Sitka, in 1842, just as he was about to embark for Russia : " His appearance, to which I have already alluded, impresses a stranger with something of awe, while in further intercourse, the gentleness which characterizes his every word and deed, insensibly moulds reverence into love; and, at the same time, his talents and attainments are such as to be worthy of his exalted station. With all this, the bishop is sufficiently a man of the world to disdain anything, like cant. His conversation, on the contrary, teems with amusement and instruction, and his company is much prized by all who have the honour of his acquaintance ". Such is the portrait drawn of him by a governor of the Hudson's Bay Company. At the advanced age of 93 years, this much beloved and esteemed prelate died, in Moscow April 27, 1879.

SECTION I.

seal upon the rookeries, prompted by a fine consciousness of necessity to its own well-being. The breeding-grounds occupied by them were, therefore, invariably covered by the seals in exact ratio, greater or less, as the area upon which they rested was larger or smaller. They always covered the ground evenly, never crowding in at one place here, to scatter out there. The seals lie just as thickly together, where the rookery is boundless in its eligible area to their rear and unoccupied by them, as they do in the little strips which are abruptly cut off and narrowed by rocky walls behind. For instance, on a rod of ground, under the face of bluffs which hemmed it in to the land from the sea, there are just as many seals, no more and no less, as will be found on any other rod of rookery-ground throughout the whole list, great and small; always exactly so many seals, under any and all circumstances, to a given area of breeding-ground. There are just as many cows, bulls and pups on a square rod at Nah Speel, near the village, where, in 1874, all told, there were only seven or eight thousand, as there are on any square rod at North-east point, where a million of them congregate. "

" This fact being determined, it is evident that, just in proportion as the breeding-grounds of the fur-seal on these islands expand or contract in area from their present dimensions, the seals will increase or diminish in number ".

" The discovery, at the close of the season of 1872, of this law of distribution, gave me at once the clue I was searching for, in order to take steps by which I could arrive at a sound conclusion as to the entire number of seals herding on the island ".

" I noticed, and time has confirmed my observation, that the period for taking these boundaries of the rookeries, so as to show this exact margin of expansion at the week of its greatest volume, or when they are as full as they are to be for the season, is between the 10th and 20th of July of every year; not a day earlier, and not many days later. After the 20th of July the regular system of compact, even organisation breaks up. The seals then scatter out in pods or clusters, the pups leading the way, straying far back — the same number instantly covering twice and thrice as much ground as they did the day or week before, when they lay in solid masses and were marshaled on the rookery-ground proper. "

"There is no more difficulty in surveying these seal-margins during this week or ten days in July, than there is in drawing sights along and around the curbs of a stone-fence surrounding a field. The breeding-seals remain perfectly quiet under your eyes all over the rookery, and almost within your touch, everywhere on the outside of their territory that you may stand or walk. The margins of massed life, as I have indicated on the topographical surveys of these breeding-grounds of St. Paul and St. George, are as clean cut and as well defined against the soil and vegetation, as is the shading on my maps. There is not the least difficulty in making the surveys, and in making them correctly."

"Now, with a knowledge of the superficial area of these breeding-grounds, the way is clearly open to a very interesting calculation as to the number of fur-seals upon them. I am well aware of the fact, when I enter upon this discussion, that I cannot claim perfect accuracy, but, as shadowing my plan of thought and method of computation, I propose to present every step in the processes which have guided me to the result."

"**Rookery-space occupied by single seals.**—When the adult males and females, fifteen or twenty of the latter to every one of the former, have arrived upon the rookery, I think an area a little less than two square feet for each female may be considered as the superficial space required by each animal with regard to its size and in obedience to its habits; and this limit may safely be said to be over the mark. Now, every female, or cow, on this two square feet space, doubles herself by bringing forth her young; and in a few days or a week, perhaps, after its birth, the cow takes to the water to wash and feed, and is not back on this allotted space one-fourth of the time again during the season. In this way, is it not clear that the females almost double their number on the rookery-grounds, without causing the expansion of the same beyond the limits that would be actually required, did they not bear any young at all? For every 100,000 breeding-seals, there will be found more than 85,000 females, and less than 15,000 males; and in a few weeks after the landing of these females, they will show for themselves; that is, for this 100,000, fully 180,000 males, females, and young instead, on the same area of ground occupied previously to the birth of the pups.

SECTION I.

It must be borne in mind, that perhaps 10 or 12 per cent of the entire number of females were yearlings last season, and came up on to these breeding-grounds as virgins for the first time during this season — as two-year old cows; they of course bear no young. The males being treble and quadruple the physical bulk of the females, require about four feet square for their use of this same rookery-ground, but as they are less than one-fifteenth the number of the females, much less in fact, they therefore occupy only one-eight of the space over the breeding-ground, where we have located the supposed 100,000; this surplus area of the males is also more than balanced and equalized by the 15,000 or 20,000 virgin females which come on to this rookery for the first time to meet the males. They come, rest a few days or a week, and retire, leaving no young to show their presence on the ground.

" The breeding bulls average 10 feet apart by 7 feet on the rookery-ground — have each a space therefore of about 70 square feet for an average family of 15 cows, 15 pups and 5 virgin females, or 35 animals for the 70 feet — 2 square feet for each seal big or little : the virgin females do not lay out long and the cows come and go at intervals, never all being on this ground at one time; as the bull has plenty of room in his space of 70 feet for himself and harem. "

" Taking all these points into consideration, and they are features of fact, I quite safely calculate upon an average of two square feet to every animal, big or little, on the breeding-grounds as the initial point upon which to base an intelligent computation of the entire number of seals before us. Without following this system of enumeration, a person may look over these swarming myriads between South-west point and Novastoshnah, guessing vaguely and wildly, at any figure from one million up to ten or twelve millions, as has been done repeatedly. How few people know what a million really is; it is very easy to talk of a million, but it is a tedious task to count it off, and makes one's statements as to " millions " decidedly more conservative after the labor has been accomplished."

" Before summing up the grand total, I shall now in sequence, review each one of the several rookeries of St. Paul, taking them in their order as they occur, going north from the Reef point. The accompanying maps show the exact area occupied by the breeding-seals and their young in the season of 1874, which is the date of my latest field-work on the Pribylov Islands."

I may add that my method of surveying these breeding-grounds in 1872-74 was by means of measured base lines, taking my angles and cross-bearings with an azimuth compass: in 1890 I used a fine prismatic compass — otherwise precisely the same method was again employed. I made a careful land survey of each rookery on St. Paul Island between the 22nd May and 4th of June, so that when the females all arrived by the 10th of July, I was able to go there out upon each one of these rookeries with my finished plat of the land in hand; and upon it in the field again plat the massing of the breeding animals as they exhibited themselves, without a moment's delay, so as to properly and deliberately finish the entire work before the rutting season was over by the 20th July: by this time those rookeries are scattering and scattered as they always do by the lapse of that period, since the old bulls then relax their absolute control of their harems, and permit all to wander at will.

In this connection it is pleasant for me to say now, that in 1874, I was accompanied by Lieut. Washburn Maynard, U. S. N. who being also a trained topographer, aided me in verifying my surveys of 1872-73. He gave this subject close attention; he appreciated its importance and in his published report to the Secretary of the Navy in 1875, he uses the following language.

" It is of very great significance in this connection to know how many seals come annually to the islands, or rather to understand how many may be killed for their skins annually, without causing less to come hereafter than do at the present time. To determine how many there are with accuracy is a task almost on a par with that of numbering the stars. The singular motion of the animals when on shore. the great variety in size, colour, and position; the extent of surface over which they are spread, and the fact that it cannot be determined exactly what proportion of them, of their several classes, are on shore, at any given time; all these desiderata for comprehension make it simply impossible to get more than an approximation of their numbers. They have been variously estimated at from one to fifteen millions."

"I think the most accurate enumeration yet made is that by Mr. H. W. Elliott, special agent of the Treasury Department, in 1872. This calculation is based upon the hypothesis that the breeding seals are governed in hauling by a common and invariable law of distribution, which is, that the area of the rookery ground is directly proportional to the number of seals occupying it. He estimates that there is one seal to every two square feet of rookery surface. Hence the problem is reduced to the simple operation of obtaining half the sum of the superficial area of all the rookeries in square feet. He surveyed these breeding-grounds of both islands in 1872 and 1873, when at their greatest limit of expansion, and obtained the following results : Upon St. Paul island there were 6,060,000 feet of ground occupied by 3,030,000 breeding-seals and their young. On St. George island he announced 326,850 square feet of superficial rookery area occupied by 163,420 breeding seals and their young; a total for both islands of 3,193,420 breeding-seals and their young. The number of non-breeding seals cannot be determined in the foregoing manner, as they haul most irregularly, but it seems to me probable that they are nearly as numerous as the other class is. If so, it would give not far from 6,000,000 as the stated number of seals of all kinds which visited the Pribylov islands during the season of 1872."

"It is likely that these figures are not far from the truth, but I do not think it necessary myself to take into consideration the actual number of seals in order to decide the question of how many can be taken each year without injury to the fishery. The law that the size of the rookeries varies directly as the number of seals increases or diminishes, seems to me, after close and repeated observation, to be correct. All the rookeries, whether large or small, are uniform in appearance, alike compact, without waste of space, and never crowded. Such being the case, it is unimportant to know the actual number of seals upon the rookeries. For any change in the number of seals, which is the point at issue, increases or decreases in size, and the rookeries taken collectively, will show a corresponding increase or decrease in the number of breeding-seals; consequently changes in the aggregate of pups born annually upon which the extent and safety of the fisheries depends, can be observed accurately from year to year by following these lines of survey."

"If, then, a plan or map of each rookery be made every year, showing accurately its size and form, when at its greatest expansion, which is between the 10th and 25th of July annually, a comparison of this map will give the relative number of the breeding-seals as they increase or diminish from year to year. I submit with this report maps of St. Paul and St. George islands, showing the extended location of breeding-rookeries, and hauling grounds upon them. These maps are from surveys made in July, 1874, by Mr. Elliott and myself, and a map of each rookery on both islands drawn from careful surveys made by Mr. Elliott in 1872, show them now as they were in the season of 1874 as compared with that of 1872. I respectfully recommend that enlarged copies of these latter maps be furnished to the government agents in charge of the islands, and that they be required to compare them each year with the respective rookeries, and note what change in size and form, if any, exists upon them. This, if carefully done, will afford data, after a time, by which the seal fisheries can be regulated with comparative certainty, so as to produce the greatest revenue to the government, without injury to this valuable interest" (44th Cong. 1st Sess. H. R. Ex. Doc. No. 43), pp. 4, 5.

This finished work of 1872-74 I reproduce in the following maps of the several rookeries of St. Paul Island, and add the hauling grounds of St. George Island to the original survey of 1874: the smallness of the rookeries on the latter island permits this addition to these charts, but the hauling grounds of St. Paul for 1872-74 cannot be drawn upon so small a scale, and require a special general map of the entire island itself, to properly show them: this map appears under Section II, following. The hauling-grounds of St. George are so limited in area that a general map of this island to clearly show them would need an immensely enlarged scale. The general position however of the St. George rookeries and hauling grounds is clearly defined on my revised map of St. George Island under the head of Section II.

I pass to a description in detail of each rookery of the Pribylof Islands, giving first my published account of them as they appeared in 1872-1874, and each original description is supplemented by my notes and surveys of last summer : the accompanying maps are so tinted as to express clearly the status of 1872-1874 as compared with the condition of 1890 [1].

1872-74. " The Reef Rookery.— By reference first to the general map, it will be observed that this large breeding-ground, on that grotesquely-shaped neck which ends in the Reef point, is directly contiguous to the village, indeed it may be fairly said to be right under the lee of the houses on the hill. It is one of the most striking of all the rookeries, owing probably to the fact that on every side it is sharpy and clearly exposed to the vision, as the circuit is made in boats. A reach of very beautiful drifting sand, a quarter of a mile from the village hill to the Reef bluffs, separates the breeding-grounds proper from the habitations of the people. These Zoltoi sands are, however, a famous rendezvous for the " holluschickie ", and from them, during the season, the natives make regular drives, having only to step out from their houses in the morning and walk but a few rods to find their fur-bearing quarry".

" Passing over the sands on our way down to the point, we quickly come to a basaltic ridge or back-bone, over wich the sand has been drifted by the winds, and which supports a rank and luxuriant growth of the *Elymus* and other grasses, with beautiful flowers. A few hundred feet farther along, our course brings us in full view, as we look to the south, of one the most entrancing spectacles which seals afford to man. We look down upon and along a grand promenade-ground, wich slopes gently to the eastward and trends southward down to the water from the abrupt walls bordering on the sea on the west, over a parade-plateau as smooth as the floor of a ball room, 2,000 feet in length, from 500 to 1,000 feet in width, over which multidues of " holluschickie" are filing in long strings, or deploying in vast platoons, hundreds abreast, in an unceasing march and countermarch ; the breath which from a hundred thousand hot throats hangs like clouds of white steam rises into the cold air steam in the gray fog itself; indeed, it may be said to be a seal-fog peculiar to the spot, while the din, the roar arising over all, defies our description. "

1. This combination of the work of 1872-74 and 1890 upon one chart of each rookery is much better and more satisfactory than to publish the original survey by itself with a duplicate series of charts for 1890.

" We notice to our right and to our left, the immense solid masses of the breeding-seals at Gorbotch, and those stretching and trending around nearly a mile from our feet, far around to the Reef point below and opposite the parade-ground, with here and there a neutral passage left open for the " holluschickie " to go down and come up from the waves. "

" The adaptation of this ground of the Reef rookery to the requirements of the seal is perfect. It so lies that it falls gently from its high Zoltoi bay-margin on the west, to the sea on the east; and upon its broad expanse not a solitary puddle of mud-spotting is to be seen, though everything is reeking with moisture, and the fog even dissolves into rain as we view the scene. Every trace of vegetation upon this parade has been obliterated; a few tufts of grass, capping the summits of those rocky hillocks, indicated on the eastern and middle slope, are the only signs of botanical life which the seals have suffered to remain. "

" A small rock, "Seevitchie Kammin " five or six hundred feet high to the southward and out at sea, is also covered with the black and yellow forms of fur-seals and sea-lions. It is environed by shoal-reefs, rough, and kelp-grown, which navigators prudently avoid. "

" This rookery of the Reef proper has 4,016 feet of sea-margin, with an average depth of 150 feet, making ground for 301,000 breeding-seals and their young. Gorbotch rookery has 3,660 feet of sea-margin, with an average depth of 100 feet, making ground for 183,000 breeding-seals and their young; an aggregate for this great Reef Rookery of 484,000 breeding-seals and their young. Heavy as this enumeration is, yet the aggregate only makes the Reef rookery third in importance, compared with the others which we are yet to describe. "

1890. The Reef Rookery. — On the accompanying map of this breeding-ground, the area and position of the massed seal life as surveyed in 1872, is shown by a higher tint over which the reduced form and number of 1890 is sharply drawn, in dark relief; the ragged, scattered massing of to-day is also clearly shown by this survey : that solid uniform organization of 1872, is not more than suggested by it over the entire field : these curious, " jags " of breeding seals which show so plainly on the Gorbotch slope, form the most striking feature af that changed order of affairs, which declares a reduction of more than one-half of the females and fully nine-tenths of the males on this rookery.

Then that splendid parade-ground of 1872 is now fairly deserted, grass and mosses and lichens and even flowers are taking root everywhere over its polished surface of 1872; and Zoltoi sands, it has not been visited by young male seals this year during the sealing season, none left to come.

The whole of this Reef Neck in 1872, south of Grassy Summit and Fox Cliff was entirely bare of grass or any vegetation whatever, except lichens on inaccessible rocks to seals, and tufts of grass on the overhanging point and cliff edges of the west shore but, on the 9th of last August, as I stood overlooking the whole field from the summit of Fox Cliff, the interior of it was fairly green, and only struggling bands of a dozen seals here and a hundred there were hauling over it.

Eighteen years ago these slopes of " Garbotch " and the Reef Parade were covered with angry, eager lusty bulls, two and three weeks before the first cows even arrived : they came in by the 5th to 22nd May in such numbers as to fill the space at close intervals of from 7 to 10 feet apart, solidly from the shore line to the ridge summit, and over, even, so far that it required the vigorous use of a club before we could get upon " Old John Rock " from the rear : then too, at that time they were fighting in every direction under our eyes.

This season I do not observe a bull here, where I saw at least ten at this time 18 years ago. *Now, not a fight in progress anywhere here*, there are not bulls enough to quarrel, they are now scattered apart so widely over this same ground as to be a hundred and even a hundred and fifty feet apart over ground where in 1872 an interval of ten feet between them did not exist.

The labour of locating and maintaining a position on the rookery then was a serious business for those bulls which came in last; and it was so all the time to those males that occupied the water line of the breeding-grounds. A constantly-sustained fight between the newcomers and the occupants progressed morning, noon, and night, without cessation, frequently resulting in death to the combatants.

In 1874, I said "It appears, from my survey of these breeding-grounds, that a well-understood principle exists among the able-bodied bulls, to wit : that each one shall remain on his ground, which is usually about six to eight feet square; provided that at the start, and from that time until the arrival of the females, he is strong enough to hold this ground against all comers; inasmuch as the crowding in of the fresh arrivals often causes the removal of those which, though equally able-bodied at first, have exhausted themselves by fighting earlier and constantly; they are finally driven by these fresher animals back farther and higher up on the rookery; and sometimes off altogether."

"Many of these bulls exhibit wonderful strength and desperate courage. I marked one veteran at Garbotch, who was the first to take up his position early in May, and that position, as usual, directly at the water-line. This male seal had fought at least forty or fifty desperate battles, and fought off his assailants every time, perhaps nearly as many different seals which coveted his position, and when the fighting season was over (after the cows are mostly all hauled up), I saw him still there, covered with scars and frightfully gashed; raw, festering, and bloody, one eye gouged out, but lording it bravely over his harem of fifteen or twenty females, who were all huddled together on the same spot of his first location and around him."

In order that every step shall show which I have taken in making these surveys as presented, I submit the following detailed figures which taken in conjunction with the map, explain themselves and declare the method and manner of my work.

Detailed analysis of the Survey of "Reef Rookery"
July 10th, 1890.

Sea Margin of "Reef Rookery" beginning at foot of Fox Hill.   Sq. feet.

300 ft. sea margin beginning at foot of Fox Hill, with
    75 ft. average depth, massed   22,500
300 ft. from thence to "1st Point", with
    30 ft. average depth, massed   9,000
200 ft. from thence, with
    70 ft. average depth, massed   14,000

                          Carry forward. . . . 45,500

SECTION I.

	Sea Margin of "Reef Rookery" beginning at foot of Fox Hill.	Sq. feet.
	Brought forward . . .	45,500
100 ft. from thence, with 80 ft. average depth, massed		8,000
100 ft. from thence with 20 ft. average depth, massed		2,000
900 ft. from thence, with 75 ft. average depth massed		67,500
1,400 ft. from thence with 20 ft. average depth, massed		28,000
500 ft. from thence ("E" and "F" "Jags" included), with 30 ft. average depth, massed		15,000
200 ft. from thence ("G" "Jag" included), with 100 ft. average depth, massed		20,000
300 ft. from thence to end of "Reef Rookery", with 10 ft. average depth, massed		3,000
Jag "A" is 250 ft. deep above sea margin, with 60 ft. average width, massed		15,000
do. "B" is 400 ft. deep above sea margin, with 60 ft. average width, massed		24,000
Jag "C" is 400 ft. deep above sea margin, with 100 ft. average width, massed		40,000
do. "D" is 130 ft. deep above sea margin, with 100 ft. average width, massed		13,000
	Total square feet. . .	281,000

This makes ground for and declares the presence of 140,500 seals, ☿ ♀ and ○ (Bulls, Cows, and Pups).

Detailed analysis of the Survey of "Garbotch Rookery"
July 10, 1890

	Sea Margin of "Garbotch" Rookery beginning under "Cap".	Sq. feet.
800 ft. sea margin, beginning under "Cap" to "Blk. Bend" base with 15 ft. average depth, massed		12,000
300 ft. sea margin from "Black Bend" to Jag "O", with 60 ft. average depth, massed		18,000
1,100 ft. sea sea margin from Jag "O" to Jag "L", with 40 ft. average depth, massed		44,000
500 ft. sea margin from Jag "L" to Jag "J", with 30 ft. average depth, massed		15,000
700 ft. sea margin from Jag "J" to end of "Garbotch Ry" with 15 ft. average depth, massed		10,500
Jag "R" is 75 ft. deep above sea margin, with 75 ft. average width, massed		5,625
	Carry forward . . .	105,125

THE "ROOKERIES".

Sea Margin of "Garbotch Rookery" beginning under "Cap.	Sq. feet.
Brought forward...	105,125
Jag "Q" is 60 ft. deep above sea margin, with 200 ft. average width, massed........	12,000
Jag "O" is 70 ft. deep above sea margin, with 70 ft. average width, massed........	4,900
Jag "N" is 60 ft. deep above sea margin with 150 ft. average width, massed........	9,000
Jag "M" is 150 ft. deep above sea margin with 40 ft. average width, massed........	6,000
Jag "L" is 70 ft. deep above sea margin with 30 ft. average widht, massed........	2,100
Jag "K" is 250 ft. deep above sea margin, with 40 ft. average width, massed........	10,000
Jag "J" is 185 ft. deep above sea margin, with 80 ft. average width, massed........	14,800
Jag "I" is 185 ft. above above sea margin, with 20 ft. average width, massed........	3,700
Jag "H" is 100 ft. deep above sea margin, with. 20 ft. average width, massed..... ..	2,000
TOTAL SQUARE FEET......	169,625

Or ground for 84,802 seals, ♂ ♀ and ○ (Bulls, Cows and Pups). Briefly summed up, the "Reef Rookery" has, (July 10, 1890) 4,300 ft. sea margin with 65 1/3 ft. of average depth, making ground for 140,500 fur seals and "Garbotch Rookery" has (July 10, 1890) 2,400 ft. sea margin with 70 2/3 ft. of average depth, making ground for 84,802 fur seals and thus declaring a total for this Reef peninsula of only 225,302 seals against the total of 484,000 which existed here in 1872-74 and which were massed upon this ground as indicated on the accompanying map.

1872-74. "Lagoon Rookery. — We now pass from the Reef up to the village, where one naturally would not expect to find breeding-seals within less than a pistol-shot from the natives' houses; but it is a fact, nevertheless, for on looking at the sketch map of the Lagoon rookery herewith presented, it will be noticed that I have located a little gathering of breeding-seals right under the village hill to the westward of that place called "Nah Speel". This is in itself an insignificant rookery and never has been a large one, though it is one of the oldest on the island. It is only interesting, however, superficially so, on account of its position, and the fact that through every day of the season half the population of the entire village go and come to the summit of the bluff, which overhangs it, where they peer down for hours at a time upon the methods and evolutions of the " kautickie " below, the seals themselves looking up with intelligent appreciation of the fact that, though they are in the hands of man, yet he is wise enough not to disturb them there as they rest. "

" If at Nah Speel, or that point rounding into the village cove, there were any suitable ground for a rookery to grow upon or spread over, the seals would doubtless have been there long ago. There are, however, no such natural advantages offered them; what there is they have availed themselves of. "

" Looking, from the village across the cove and down upon the Lagoon, still another strange contradiction appears, at least it seems a natural contradiction to one's usual ideas. Here we see the Lagoon rookery, a reach of ground upon which some twenty-five or thirty thousand breeding-seals come out regularly every year during the appointed time, and go through their whole elaborate system of reproduction, without showing the slightest concern for or attention to the scene directly east of them and across that shallow slough not forty feet in width. There are the great slaughtering fields of St. Paul Island; there are the sand-flats where every seal has been slaughtered for years upon years back, for its skin; and even as we take this note, forty men are standing there knocking down a drove of two or three thousand " holluschickie " for the day's work, and as they labour, the whacking of their clubs and the sound of their voices must be as plain to those breeding-seals, which are not one hundred feet from them, as it is to us, a quarter of a mile distant. In addition to this enumeration of disturbances, well calculated to amaze, and dismay, and drive off every seal within its influence, are the decaying bodies of the last year's catch 75,000 or 85,000 unburied carcasses that are sloughing away into the sand, which two or three seasons from now, nature will, in its infinite charity, cover over with the greenest of all green grasses. The whitened bones and grinning skulls of over 3,000,000 seals have bleached out on that slaughtering spot, and are buried below its surface now. "

" Directly under the north face of the Village hill, where it falls to the narrow flat between its feet and the Cove, the natives have sunk a well. It was excavated in 1857, they say, and subsequently deepened to its present condition, in 1868. It is twelve feet deep, and the diggers said that they found bones of the sea-lion and fur-seal thickly distributed every foot down, from top to bottom, how much lower these osteological remains of prehistoric pinnipeds can be found, no one knows as yet; the water here on that account, has never been fit to drink, or even to cook with; but being soft, was and is used by the natives for washing clothes, etc. Most likely, it records the spot where the Russians, during the heyday of their early occupation, drove the unhappy visitors of Nah Speel to slaughter. There is no Golgotha known to man elsewhere in the world as extensive as this one of St. Paul."

"Yet, the natives say that this Lagoon rookery is a new feature in the distribution of the seals; that when the people first came there and located a part of the present village, in 1824 up to 1847, there never had been a breeding seal on that Lagoon rookery of to day; so they have hauled up here from a small beginning, not very long ago, until they have attained their present numerical expansion, in spite of all these exhibitions of butchery of their kind, executed right under their eyes and in full knowledge of their nostrils, while the groans and low moanings of their stricken species stretched out beneath the clubs of the sealers, must have been far plainer in their ears than they are in our own."

"Still they come, they multiply, and they increase knowing so well that they belong to a class which intelligent men never did molest; to-day at least they must know it, or they would not submit to these manifestations which we have just cited, so close to their knowledge."

"The Lagoon rookery, however, never can be a large one on account of the very nature of the ground selected by the seals; for it is a bar simply pushed up above the surf-wash of boulders, waterworn and rounded, which has almost inclosed and cut out the Lagoon from its parent sea. In my opinion, the time is not far distant when that estuary will be another inland lake of St. Paul, walled out from salt water and freshened by rain and melting snow, as are the other pools, lakes and lakelets on the island."

1890. Lagoon rookery. — There has been little or no change in the character of the topographical features of the Lagoon rookery since my survey of 1872, except that the sea-wall of boulders which separates the Lagoon from Bering Sea, this break-water has been shoved up still higher by ice-floes, some six or ten feet perhaps. This shoving up of these boulders which compose the Lagoon sea-wall on which the rookery is established has also resulted in shoaling the " Cove ". This village lagoon has been filling up very perceptibly since 1868, when Hutchinson and Morgan then were able to sail in a small sloop, drawing six feet of water, up to its head. To-day such a vessel could not come nearer than a mile to their anchorage of 1868. The principal shoaling takes place in a direct line here between Tolstoi Point and the Village Hill, where a rocky reef seems to be slowly rising, pushed up by ice fields. The sloop yacht " Jabez Howe ", which was wrecked in 1873 on Akootan, is probably the last sea-going vessel that has or ever will gain an entrance to the village lagoon, St. Paul Island; or swing at anchor in the Cove.

The singular location of this Lagoon Rookery, in close contact with the killing grounds where all the seals are slaughtered on St. Paul Island (save those killed at North-east point), and its immediate juxtaposition with the village, causes me to extend the lines of my survey of it so as to include the entire site of the town, the killing grounds, the salt-houses and contiguous territory. It illustrates a remarkable paradox.

The natives say that when the village was first established down here, it was placed under the southern slope of the Black Bluffs, on East Landing, in 1817 : but the need of utilizing a good landing in the Village Cove, finally became so urgent that, in spite of the present village site being then a large hauling-ground for seals with Nah Speel rookery in the foreground, the town was moved over, and the seals driven off in 1824 : this caused quite an exodus of breeding-seals from "Nah Speel" which established themselves then for the first time on the Lagoon sea-wall, across the Cove : prior to this date no fur-seals had ever hauled there to breed.

The little rookery of " Nah Speel ", has been gradually dwindling away since 1884; in 1886 only a few harems remained, and they disappeared altogether in 1887.

A detailed analysis of the survey of Lagoon Rookery, as it is presented on the accompanying map, is unnecessary, since the eye at once grasps a simple extension of 1500 feet of ragged sea-margin and an irregular scattered massing which is best expressed by allowing 12 feet of solid massing for the average depth : that gives ground for 9,000 seals ♂♀ and ○. July 12th 1890.

The survey of 1872 gave a total here of 37,000 ♂♀ and ○.

1872-1874. "Lukannon and Keetavie Rookeries. — The next rookeries in order can be found at Lukannon and Keetavie. "

" Here is a joint blending of two large breeding-grounds, their continuity broken by a short reach of sea-wall right under and at the eastern foot of Lukannon hill. The appearance of these rookeries is like all the others, peculiar to themselves. There is a rounded swelling hill, at the foot of Lukannon bay, which rises perhaps 160 or 170 feet from the sea, abruptly at the point, but swelling out, gently up from the sand-dunes in Lukannon bay, to its summit at the northwest and south. The great rookery rests upon the northern slope. Here is a beautiful adaptation of the finest drainage, with a profusion of those rocky nodules scattered everywhere over it, upon which the females so delight in resting."

" Standing on the bald summit of Lukannon hill, we turn to the south, and look over Keetavie point, where another large aggregate of breeding seals rests under our eye. The hill falls away into a series of faintly terraced tables, which drop down to a flat that again abruptly descends to the sea at, Keetavie point. Between us and the Keetavie rookery is the parade-ground of Lukannon, a sight almost as grand as is that on the Reef which we have feebly attempted to portray. The sand-dunes to the west and to the north are covered with the most luxuriant grass, abruptly emarginated by the sharp abrasion of the hauling seals : this is shown very clearly on the general map. Keetavie point is a solid basaltic shelf. Lukannon hill, the summit of it, is composed of volcanic tufa and cement, with irregular cubes and fragments of pure basalt scattered all over its flipper-worn slopes. Lukannon proper has 2,270 feet of sea-margin, with an average depth of 150 feet, making ground for 170,000 breeding-seals and their young. Keetavie rookery has 2,200 feet of sea-margin, with an average depth of 150 feet, making ground for for 165,000 breeding-seals and their young, a whole aggregate of 335,000 breeding-seals and their young. This is the point, down along the flat shoals of Lukannon bay, were the sand-dunes are most characteristic, as they rise in their wind-whirled forms just above the surf-wash. This also is where the natives come from the village during the early mornings of the season, for driving, to get any number of "holluschickie."

" It is a beautiful sight, glancing from the summit of this great rookery-hill, up to the north over that low reach of the coast to Tonkie Mees, where the waves seem to roll in with crests that rise in unbroken ridges for a mile in length each, ere they break so grandly and uniformly on the beach. In these rollers the "holluschickie" are playing like sea-birds, seeming to sport the most joyously at the very moment when the heavy billow breaks and falls upon them."

1890. Lukannon and Keetavie Rookeries. — The unusually heavy loss sustained by Keetavie Rookery, and the utter absence of the holluschickie or killable young male seals where they trooped in platoons of tens of thousands in 1872-74 upon the Lukannon parade ground, made the view from Lukannon Hill an exceedingly sad one at any time last summer. Grass is growing thickly down to the very water's edge over the parade grounds of 1872-74 and creeping into the rookery grounds also : this grass which springs up over an abandoned seal parade is quite different in fibre and colour from that which has never been disturbed and destroyed by the seals : it is quickly noted and marked as " seal grass " since it grows closer and thicker and softer than all surrounding grasses. There is no contradiction possible of its silent though eloquent testimony of the hour, of the absence of those swarming herds which so impressed me in 1872-74 as they restlessly swept hither and thither over these grassy grounds, deserted fields of 1890.

A careful survey of the area and position of the breeding seals on Lukannon and Keetavie Rookeries, July 10, 1890, gives the following figures.

Detailed analysis of the survey of "Lukannon Rookery"
July 10, 1890.

Sea margin of "Lukannon Rookery" beginning at "G", ending at "D".	Sq. feet.
1,550 ft. sea margin, between "G" and "F" with 70 ft. average depth, massed	108,050
350 ft. sea margin between "F" and "E" with 80 ft. average depth, massed	27,000
1,100 ft. sea margin from "E" to "D" too scattered and thin for an average depth	10,000
TOTAL SQUARE FEET.	145,050

Making ground for 72,525 seals ♂♀ and ○ (Bulls, Cows and Pups) against a total here in 1872-74 of 17,000 : a loss since then of 65 %.

Detailed analysis of the survey of "Keetavie Rookery"
July 10, 1890.

Sea margin beginning at "A" and ending at "D".	Sq. feet.
700 ft. sea margin between "A" and "B" with 30 ft. average depth, massed	21,000
1,000 ft. sea margin between "C" and "D" with 35 ft. average depth, massed	35,000
TOTAL SQUARE FEET.	56,000

Making ground for 28,000 seals ♂♀ and ○ (Bulls, Cows and Pups), against a total of 165,000 in 1872-70 a loss of 137,000 seals, or 85 % since then.

This rookery is one of the worst wrecks, in the general diminution it is the worst, having suffered a greater loss than any other on St. Paul or St. George for that matter.

On Lukannon this last summer, while there were two-fifths as many cows as in 1872, yet the bulls did not average more than one fifteenth of the number they showed in 1872. On Keetavie, it was no better, if anything a shade worse. No young bulls anywhere offering service or attempting to land. This undue proportion of the sexes and the general apathy and advanced age of the breeding bulls is characteristic of all the rookeries to-day as we view them on Pribylov Islands. Here and there at wide intervals we observe an alert, virile bull, while its companions all around are stretched out in somnolence, or regarding the incoming cows with positive indifference. In 1872 it was just the opposite; I made then the following note " Between the 12th and 14th of June, the first of the cow seals, as a rule come up from the sea; then the long agony of the waiting bulls is over, and they signalize it by a period of universal, spasmodic, desperate fighting among themselves. Though they have quarreled all the time from the moment they first landed, and continue to do so until the end of the season, in August, yet that fighting which takes place at this date is the bloodiest and most vindictive known to the seal. I presume that the heaviest percentage of mutilation and death among the old male from these brawls, occur in this week of the earliest appearance of the females.

A strong contrast now between the males and females looms up, both in size and shape, which is heightened by the air of exceeding peace and dove-like amiability which the latter class exhibit, in contradistinction to the ferocity and saturnine behaviour of the former."

1872-74. Tolstoi Rookery.—" Directly to the west from Lukannon, up along and around the head of the Lagoon, is the seal-path road over which the natives bring the "holluschickie" from Tolstoi. We follow this and take up our position on several lofty grass-grown dunes, close to and overlooking another rookery of great size : this is Tolstoi."

" We have here the largest hill-slope of breeding-seals, on either island, peculiarly massed on the abruptly sloping flanks of Tolstoi ridge, as it falls to the sands of English bay, and ends suddenly in the precipitous termination of its own name, Tolstoi point. Here the seals are in some places crowded up to the enormous depth of 500 measured feet, from the sea-margin of the rookery to its outer boundary and limitation; and when viewed as I view it in July, taking the angles and lines shown on the accompanying sketch-map, I considered it with the bluff terminating it at the south, and its bold sweep, which ends on the sands of English bay, to be the most picturesque, though it is not the most impressive rookery on the island, especially when that parade-ground, lying just back and over the point and upon its table-rock surface, is reached by the climbing seals."

"If the observer will glance at the map, he will see that the parade-ground in question lies directly over and about 150 feet above, the breeding-seals immediately under it. The sand-dune tracts which border the great body of the rookery seem to check the 'holluschickie' from hauling to the rear, for sand drifts here, in a locality so high and exposed to the full force of the wind, with more rapidity and consequently more disagreeable energy to the seals than anywhere else on the island."

"A comical feature of this rookery is the appearance of the foxes in the chinks under the parade-ground and interstices of the cliffs; their melancholy barking and short yelps of astonishment, as we walk about, contrast quite sensibly with the utter indifference of the seals to our presence."

"From Tolstoi at this point, sweeping around three miles to Zapadnie, is the broad sand-reach of English bay, upon which and back over its gently rising flats are the great hauling grounds of the 'holluschickie', which I have indicated on the general map, and to which I made reference in a previous section of this chapter looking at the myriads of "bachelor-seals" spread out in their restless hundreds and hundreds of thousands upon this ground, one feels the utter impotency of verbal description, and reluctantly shuts his note- and sketch-books to gaze upon it with renewed fascination and perfect helplessness."

"Tolstoi rookery has attained, I think, its utmost limit of expansion. The seals have already pushed themselves as far out upon the sand at the north as they can or are willing to go, while the abrupt cliffs, hanging over more than one-half of the sea margin, shut out all access to the rear for the breeding-seals. The natives said that this rookery had increased very much during the last four or five years prior to the date of my making the accompanying survey. If it continues to increase, the fact can be instantly noted, by checking off the ground and comparing it with the sketch-map herewith presented. Tolstoi rookery has 3,000 feet of sea margin, with an average depth of 150 feet, making ground for 225,000 breeding-seals and their young."

1890. Tolstoi Rookery. — My picture of this rookery as above drawn in 1872, forms a remarkable contrast when held up in view of the picture which Tolstoi made in the height of the sealing season last summer. The scant, scattered massing of the breeding animals as exhibited this year over those same areas of splendid congregation in 1872, where 500 feet deep from the sea margin, the breeding seals and their young lay in compact solid organization throughout the rutting season — this contrast between the condition of 1872 and 1890 was most vividly made here, since it is the only one of the St. Paul rookeries which can be seen in all of its extent from a single point of view. It also was an exceedingly attractive rookery to visit in 1872, because from its height, the vast sweep of those English Bay hauling-grounds lay under your eyes, and the tens of thousands of holluschickie which then hauled out there, in sport or in sleep, were always to be seen whenever you glanced that way.

Not even a faint suggestion of 1872 appeared on this hauling ground of English Bay last summer, and the shrivelled form of Tolstoi rookery in 1890 is best expressed by the figures which follow, explanatory of the accompanying map.

Detailed analysis of the survey of "Tolstoi Rookery" July 10, 1890.

Sea margin beginning at "A" and ending at "D". Sq. feet.

800 ft.	sea margin between "A" and "B", with 80 ft. average depth, massed............	64,000
400 ft.	sea margin between "B" and "C", with 60 ft. average depth, massed............	24,000
1,600 ft.	sea margin between "C" and "D" with 10 ft. average depth, massed............	16,000
Jag "E" has 300 ft. of. depth, with 40 ft. average width, massed......		12,000
Jag "F" has 100 ft. of depth, with 40 ft. average width, massed......		4,000
Jag "G" has 120 ft. of depth, with 40 ft. of average width, massed......		4,800
	TOTAL SQUARE FEET...	124,800

Making ground for 62,400 seals ♂♀ and ○ (Bulls, Cows and Pups) against a total of 225,000 in 1872-1874; these figures declare a decrease here of 162,600 seals since my earlier survey, or a loss of some 75 %.

While there appears to be a little more than one-fourth only of the females here as compared with their number of 1872 yet the proportion of loss in males is still more startling — there is not one-fifteenth of the showing made by the bulls in 1872-1874, and not a single young bull seen upon the ground offering service — not one even attempting to land at the water's edge : the half dozen that I did see on the outskirts of the rookery were evidently dropped from sealing " drives ", broken-spirited and utterly worthless.

The topographical features of this ground are wholly unchanged since my survey of 1872 : the sands still drift with their accustomed disagreeable energy backwards and forwards between Middle Hill and the base of the rookery; but being bare of seal life last summer, they seem to aid in the expression of a deeper air of desolation than that given to any other one spot on the islands save Keetavie.

1872-1874. "Zapadnie Rookery. — From Tolstoi, before going north, we turn our attention directly to Zapadnie on the west, a little over two miles as the crow flies, across English Bay, which lies between them. Here again we find another magnificent rookery, with features peculiar to itself, consisting of great wings separating, one from the other, by a short stretch of five or six hundred feet of the shunned sand-reach which makes a landing and a beach just between them. The northern Zapadnie lies mostly on the gently sloping, but exceedingly rocky, flats of a rough volcanic ridge which drops there to the sea; it, too, has an approximation to the Tolstoi depth, but not to such a solid extent, it is the one rookery which I have reason to believe has sensibly increased since my first survey in 1872. It has over-flowed from the boundary which I laid down at that time, and has filled up for nearly half a mile, a long ribbon-like strip of breeding-ground to the north-east from the hill-slope, ending at a point where a few detached rocks jut out, and the sand takes exclusive possession of the rest of the coast. These rocks aforesaid are called by the natives " Nearhpahskie Kammen ", because it is a favorite resort for the hair-seals. Although this extension of a very decided margin of breeding-ground, over half a mile in length, between 1872-1876, does not in the aggregate, point to a very large increased number, still it is a gratifying evidence that the rookeries, instead of tending to diminish in the slightest, are more than holding their own ".

" Zapadnie, in itself, is something like the Reef plateau on its eastern face, for it slopes up gradually and gently to the parade-plateau on top — a parade-ground not so smooth, however, being very rough and rocky, but which the seals enjoy. Just around the point, a low reach or rocky bar and beach connects it with the ridge walls of South-west point : a very small breeding-rookery, so small that it is not worthy of a survey, is located here; I think probably, on account, of the nature of the ground, that it will never hold its own, and is more than likely abandoned by this time ".

" One of the prehistoric villages, the village of Pribylov's time, was established here between the point and cemetery ridge, on which the northern wing of Zapadnie rests. The old burying ground, with its characteristic Russian crosses and faded pictures of the saints, is plainly marked on the ridge. It was at this little bight of sandy landing that Pribylov's men first came ashore and took possession of the island, while the others in the same season proceeded to North-east point and to the north shore, to establish settlements of their own order. When the indiscriminate sealing of 1868 was in progress, one of the parties lived here, and a salt-house which was then erected by them still stands; it is in a very fair state of preservation, although it has never been since occupie, except by the natives who come over here from the village in the summer to pick the berries of the *Empetrum* and *Rubus*, which abound in the greatest profusion around the rough and rocky flats that environ the little lake adjacent. The young people of St. Paul are very fond of this berry-festival, so called among themselves, and they stay here every August, camping out a week or ten days at a time, before returning to their homes in the village "·

" Zapadnie rookery, has, the two wings included, 5,880 feet of sea margin, with an average depth of 150 feet, making ground for 441,000 breeding-seals and their young, being the second rookery on the island as to size and importance. "

" The ' holluschickie ' that sport here on the parade-plateau, and indeed over all of the western extent of the English Bay hauling-grounds, have never been visited by the natives for the purpose of selecting killing drives since 1872, inasmuch as more seals than were wanted have always been procured from Zoltoi, Lukannon, and Lower Tolstoi points, which are all very close to the village. I have been told, since making this survey, that during the past year the breeding-seals of Zapadnie have overflowed, so as to occupy all of the sand-strip which is vacant between them on the accompanying map".

1890. Zapadnie Rookery. — It is impossible to convey the full sense of utter desolation wich the vacant seal area of 1872 on this fine rookery aroused in my mind last July while then making my survey of it. Grass and flowers springing up over those broad areas back of the breeding-grounds here, where in 1872-1874, thousand upon thousands of young male seals hauled out and over, throughout the entire season, and were undisturbed by any man, not even visited by any one except myself! No one then, even thought of such a thing as coming over from the village to make a killing at Zapadnie, more seals than wanted were close by, at Tolstoi, Lukannon, and Zoltoi sands. This not alone, but that splendid, once clean-swept expanse of hauling ground in English Bay between the Zapadnies and Tolstoi, is all grass-grown to-day except over its areas of drifting sand, with mosses, lichens and flowers interspersed : it is entirely bare of seals, save a lonely pod under Middle Hill.

Lower Zapadnie is certainly the roughest-surfaced breeding-ground peculiar to the Seal Islands, and it is a curious place on which to view the seals as they locate themselves, for as you walk along they suddenly appear and disappear as they lie in those queer little valleys and cañons here which have been formed by lava bubbles of the geological time of that elevation of St. Paul Island from the sea. But to-day so scant is the massing of the breeding-seals, here that that unbroken uproar which boomed out from them in 1872, is wholly absent — it is positively quiet save the subdued sheep-like[1] calling of the females, and the lamb-like answer of their offspring.

---

1. Indeed, so similar is the sound, that I noticed that a number of sheep which the Alaska Commercial Company had brought up from San Francisco to St. George island, during the summer of 1873 were constantly attracted to the rookeries, and were running in among the " holluschickie " so much so, that they neglected the good pasturage on the uplands beyond, and a small boy had to be regularly employed to herd them where they could feed to advantage. These transported Ovidæ, though they

As this breeding-ground of Zapadnie was the second one in size and importance on St. Paul in 1872, the figures which my survey of last July warrant, show an extraordinary decrease here, and make a melancholy exhibit.

Detailed analysis of the survey of "Lower Zapadnie Rookery" July 11, 1890.

Sea margin beginning at " O " and ending at " Zapadnie Point".   Sq. feet.

2,700 ft. sea margin between "O" and "Zapadnie Point", with
       20 ft. average depth, massed............ 54,000
Jag "A" is 400 ft. deep above sea margin, with
       50 ft. average width, massed......'... 20,000
Jag "B" is 300 ft. deep above sea margin, with
       60 ft. average width, massed........ 18,000
Jag "C" is 380 ft. deep above sea margin, with
       35 ft. average width, massed........ 13,300
Jag "D" is 200 ft. deep above sea margin, with
       75 ft. average width, massed........ 15,000
Jag "E" is 175 ft. deep above sea margin, with
       75 ft. average width, massed........ 13,125
Jag "F" is 350 ft. deep above sea margin, with
       60 ft. average width, massed........ 21,000
Jag "G" is 200 ft. deep above sea margin, with
       60 ft. average width, massed........ 12,000
Jag "H" is 125 ft. deep above sea margin, with
       40 ft. average width, massed........ 5,000

                 TOTAL SQUARE FEET. . . 171,425

Making ground for 85,705 seals ♂ ♀ and ○. (Bulls, Cows and Pups) against a total of 345,000 in 1872.

The figures for " Upper Zapadnie " are not much better — I regard it as part and parcel of one rookery *i.e.* Zapadnie, but for clearness of definition in survey, separate the wings.

could not possibly find anything in their eyes suggestive of companionship among the seals, had their ears so charmed by the sheep-like accents of the female Pinnipeds, as to persuade them against their senses of vision and smell.

The sound which arose in 1872 from these great breeding-grounds of the fur-seal when thousands upon tens of thousands of angry, vigilant bulls were roaring, chuckling, and piping, and multitudes of seal-mothers were calling in hollow, blasting tones to their young, that in turn responded incessantly, is simply defiance to verbal description. It was, at a slight distance, softened into a deep booming, as of a cataract; and I have heard it, with a light fair wind to the leeward, as far as six miles out from land on the sea; and even in the thunder of the surf and the roar of heavy gales, it would rise up and over to your ear for quite a considerable distance away.

**Detailed Analysis of the Survey of "Upper Zapadnie Rookery"
July 11th, 1890.**

Sea margin beginning at "Q", ending at "V" resumed at "W" and ending at "R". Sq. feet.

1,200 ft. sea margin between "O" and "V", with
    40 ft. average depth, massed. 48,000
2,300 ft. sea margin, (beach) between "W" and "R", with
    10 ft. average depth, massed. 23,000

                                  TOTAL SQUARE FEET. . . 71,000

Making ground for 35,500 seals ♂ ♀ and ○. (Bulls, Cows and Pups) against a total of 97,800 in 1872; or a total to-day of 121,205 for Zapadnie, entire, against 442,800 in 1872.

1872-1874. " Polavina Rookery. — Half-way between the village and North-east point lies Polavina, another one of the seven large breeding-grounds on this island. The conspicuous cone-shaped head of Polovina Sopka rises clearly cut and smooth from the plateau at its base, which falls two miles to the eastward and south-eastward, sharp off into the sea, presenting a bluff margin over a mile in length, at the base of which the sea thunders incessantly. It exhibits a very beautiful geological section of the simple structure of St. Paul. The ringing, iron-like basaltic foundations of the island are here setting boldly up from the sea to a height of 40 or 50 feet — black and purplish-red, polished like ebony by the friction of the surf, and worn by its agency into grotesque arches, tiny caverns, and deep fissures. Surmounting this lava-bed is a cap of ferruginous cement and tufa from three to ten feet in thickness, making a reddish floor, upon which the seals patter in their restless, never-ceasing evolutions, sleeping or waking on the land. It is as great a single parade-plateau of polished cement as that of the Reef, but we are unable from any point of observation to appreciate it, inasmuch, as we cannot stand high

---

It was the monitor which the sea-captains anxiouly strained their ears for, when they ran their dead reckoning up, and were laying to for the fog to rise, in order that they might get their bearings of the land; once heard, they held on to the sound and felt their way in to anchor. The seal-roar at " Novastoshnah " during the summer of 1872, saved the live of the surgeon and six natives belonging to the island, who had pushed out on an egging-trip from North-east point to Walrus island. I have sometimes thought, as I have listened through the night to this volume of extraordinary sound, which never ceases with the rising or the setting of the sun throughout the entire season of breeding, that it was fully equal to the churning boom of the waves of Niagara. Night and day, throughout the season of 1872, this din upon the rookeries was steady and constant.

enough to overlook it, unless we ascend Polavina Sopka, and then the distances, with the perspective fore-shortening, destroy the effect. "

" The rookery itself occupies only a small portion of the seal-visited area at this spot. It is placed at the southern termination, and gentle sloping of the long reach of bluff wall, which is the only cliff between Lukannon and Novastoshnah. It presents itself to the eye, however, in a very peculiar manner, and with great scenic effect, when the observer views it from the extreme point of its mural elevation; viewed from thence, nearly a mile to the northeast, it rises as a front of bi-coloured lava-wall, high above the sea that is breaking at its base, and is covered with the infinite detail of massed seals in reproduction : at first sight, one wonders how they got there. No passages whatever can be seen, down or up. A further survey, however, discloses the common occurence of rain-water runs between surf-beaten crevices, which make many stairways for the adhesive feet of *Callorhinus* amply safe and confortable. "

" For the reason cited in a similar example at Zapadnie, no " holluschickie " have been driven from this point since 1872, though it is one of the easiest worked. It was in the Russian times a pet sealing-ground with them. The remains of the old village have nearly all been buried in the sand near the lake, and there is really no mark of its early habitation, unless it be the singular effect of a human grave-yeard being dug out and despoiled by the attrition of seal bodies and flippers. The old cemetery just above and to the right of the barrabkie, near the little lake, was originally established, so the natives told me, far away from the hauling of the " holluschickie "; it was, when I saw it in 1876, in a melancholy state of ruin — a thousand young seals at least moved off from its surface as I came up, and they had actually trampled out many sandy graves, rolling the bones and skulls of Aleutian ancestry in every direction. Beyond this old barrabkie, which the present natives established as a house of refuge during the winter, when they were trapping foxes, looking to the west over the lake, is a large expanse of low, flat swale and tundra, which is terminated by the rocky ridge of Kaminista; every foot of it has been placed there subsequent to the original elevation of the island by the action of the sea, beyond all question. It is covered with a thick growth of the rankest sphagnum, which quakes and trembles like a bog under one's feet, but over which the most beautiful mosses ever and anon crop out, including the characteristic floral display before referred to in speaking of the island; most of the way from the village up to North-east point, as will be seen by a cursory glance at the map, with the exception of this bluff of Polavina and the terraced table setting back from its face to Polavina Sopka, the whole land is slightly elevated above the level of the sea, and its coast-line is lying just above and beyond the reach of the surf where great ledges of sand have been piled by the wind, capped with sheafs and tufts of rank-growing *Elymus.* "

" There is a small rookery, which I call, " Little Polavina ", indicated here, which does not promise much for the future ; the sand cuts it off on the north, sand has blown around so at its rear, as to make all other ground not now occupied by the breeding-seals there quite ineligible. Polavina rookery has 4,000 feet sea-margin, including Little Polavina, with 150 feet average depth, making ground for 300,000 breedings-seals and their young."

1890. Polavina Rookery. — My survey, July 13, 1890, of this breeding ground shows it to be one of the two rookeries only which have suffered on St.-Paul island no greater loss than from 50 °/₀ to 55 °/₀ of their general form and number, as recorded in 1872. Yet I cannot avoid the conclusion, however, that this rookery has been hard driven from during the last eight years, since the chief hauling-grounds lay directly up in the rear of the breeding lines, therefore, when the shrinking of the supply of holluschickie began, the driving of the killable seals here involved a regular scraping of the large semi-circular edge of Polavina Rookery whenever a drive was made: illustrative of this, a drive made here on the 18th July, brought in out of a total of 1541 animals 172 old breeding bull's, which had been scraped up on the rookery margin by the native drivers, who were obliged to take these old fellows along, or lose the handful of killable young male seals that they were after. I witnessed this driving, and saw not only these old bulls, but cows swept up into the stampeded herd, their pups left bruised and helpless behind to starve and to otherwise perish.

SECTION I.

This is a locality where, until 1872 [1882?] like the Zapadnie and South-west Point areas, the fur-seals on St. Paul island had been undisturbed by the sealers, since 1857 : therefore the holluschickie and the breeding seals had polished the whole surface of that high plateau laying gently back from the bluffs a mile of sea-margin, way back entirely free from vegetation, 1,000 to 2,000 feet : every vestige of vegetable growth utterly eliminated by their flippers. The reddish to blood-red breccia and cinders which compose the floor of this parade ground of Polavina was literally powdered by the attrition of seal flippers into an impalpable red dust, which during every windy dry day would rise in columns and clouds to betray the locality to your eye from all points of the island, and often has suggested to sailors at sea, the idea of a steamer under way within lee of the land. During misty, foggy and wet days, this soil would and does now resolve itself into the condition of a rich moist humus, and after heavy rains, a thick paste, if puddled by the seals.

The natives, in Russian times, had a small village on the lake shore near by this rookery, and regularly worked this field, especially severe up to that season of utter diminution which ended in 1834, by the stopping of all killing for shipment on St. Paul and St. George. When that Zapooska was ordered, the settlement at Polavina was abandoned, and the people removed to the present location which was established in 1824 ; also, the Northeast point village was brought down at this time to the existing town site, and the consolidation was final.

Since that time, up to 1882, beyond a few small drives made early in June, (driven for food) no seals have been drawn from the hauling grounds of Polavina, from Zapadnie or South-west point. But as the regular source of abundant supply near the village, became exhausted, then in 1882 the draft upon these five reserves of Polavina and Zapadnie, became sudden and steady, and every killable seal scraped up, easily at first and ruggedly during the last two years, and I may add with great severity during 1889 and also the present season of of 1890.

So, when I regard this ground to-day after an interval of sixteen years since my last survey, I find a square declaration from the ground itself of loss to this rookery of one-half of its female life while its breeding-bulls are not equal to one fifteenth of their number here in 1872 : then too the utter absence of a young bull on the vacant spaces in the rookery or in the water at sea margin ; — and, still more remarkable in contrast, that pronounced utter absence of the holluschickie from their grand parade ground here; — that, silent empty space before me on which at this time in 1872, anywhere from 75,000 to 100,000 young male seals were trooping in and out from the water frolicing in tireless antics one with another or wrapped in profound sleep : — this deserted parade ground of Polavina, like unto all the others on both islands, speaks most eloquently and truthfully of the present order and condition of the interests of our Government : my survey as exibited on the accompanying chart gives the following figures :

Detailed analysis of the survey of "Polavina Rookery", July 13, 1890

	Sq. feet.
Sea margin beginning at "E" and ending at "D"	
150 ft. sea margin from "D" to "D", with 100 ft. average depth massed.	15,000
900 ft. sea margin from "D" to "E" with 200 ft. average depth, massed	180,000
150 ft. sea margin from "E" to "E", with 100 ft. average depth, massed	15,000
Jags "1", "2", "3" and "4" have 400 ft. of sea margin, with 100 ft. of average, with	40,000
TOTAL SQUARE FEET. . .	250,000

Making ground for 135,000 seals ♂ ♀ and ○ (Bulls, Cows and Pups) against a total of 210,000 in 1872.

Detailed analysis of the survey of "Litle Polavina Rookery" July 13, 1890

	Sq. feet
Sea margin beginning at "C" and ending at "D"	
175 ft. sea margin from "C" to "b", with 20 ft. average depth, massed.	3,500
280 ft. sea margin from "b" to "a", with 100 ft. average depth, massed	28,000
100 ft. sea margin from "a" to "d", with 30 ft. average depth, massed.	3,000
TOTAL SQUARE FEET. . .	34,500

Making ground for 17,250 seals ♂ ♀ and ○ (Bulls, Cows and Pups) against a total of 60,000 in 1872. This survey gives a total for the Polavinas of 142,250 for 1890 against the total they possessed of 300,000 in 1872-74.

1872-74. " **North-east Point or Novastoshnah Rookery.** — Though this is the last of the St. Paul rookeries which I notice, yet it is so much greater than any other one on the island, or two others for that matter, that it forms the central feature of St. Paul, and in truth presents a most astonishing and extraordinary sight. It was a view of such multitudes of amphibians, when I first stood upon the summit of Hutchinson hill, and looked at the immense spread around me, that suggested to my mind a doubt whether the accurate investigation which I was making would give me the courage to maintain the truth in regard to the subject. "

" The result of my first survey here presented such a startling array of superficial area massed over by the breeding-seals, that I was fairly disconcerted at the magnitude of the result. It troubled me so when my initial plottings were made, and I had worked them out so as to place them tangibly before me, that I laid the whole preliminary survey aside, and seizing upon the next favourable day, went over the entire field again. The two plats then, laid side by side, substantially agreed, and I now present the great rookery to the public. It is in itself, as the others are, endowed with its own particular physionomy, having an extensive sweep, everywhere surrounded by the sea, except at that intersection of the narrow neck of land which joins it to the island. Hutchinson Hill is the foundation of the point — a solid basaltic floor, upon which a mass of breccia has been poured at its north-west corner, which is so rough, and yet polished so highly by the countless pattering flippers of its visitors, as to leave it entirely bare and bald of every spear of grass or trace of cryptogamic life. The hill is about 120 feet high; it has a rounded summit flecked entirely over by the " holluschickie ", while the great belt of breeding-rookery sweeps high up on its flanks, and around right and left, for nearly three and a half miles unbroken — an amazing sight in its aggregate, and infinite in its detail. "

" A picturesque feature, also, of the rookery here, is the appearance of those tawny, yellowish bodies of several thousand sea-lions, which lay in and among the fur-seals at the several points designated on the sketch-map, though never far from the water. Sea-lion neck, a little tongue of low basaltic jutting, is the principal corner where the natives take these animals from when they capture them in the fall for their hides and sinews[1]. "

" Cross, or St. John's hill, which rises near the lake, to a height of 60 or 70 feet, and is quite a land-mark itself, is a perfect cone of sand entirely covered with a luxuriant growth of *Elymus*; it is growing constantly higher by the fresh deposit brought by wind, and its retention by the annually rising grasses. "

" At this point, it will be noticed, there is a salt-house, and here is the killing-ground for North-east point, where nineteen or twenty thousand " holluschickie " are disposed of for their skins every season; their carcasses being spread out on the sand-dunes between the foot of Cross hill and Webster's house; a squad of sealers live there during the three or four weeks that they are engaged in the work. The " holluschickie " are driven from the large hauling grounds on the sand-flats immediately adjacent to the killing-grounds, being obtained without the slightest difficulty. "

" Here also was the site of a village, once the largest one on this island ere its transfer to the sole control and charge of the old Russian-American Company, ten years after its discovery in 1787. The ancient cemetery and the turf lines of the decayed barrabaras are still plainly visible. "

" The company's steamer runs up here, watching her opportunity, and drops her anchor, as indicated on the general chart, right south of the salt-house, in about four fathoms of water; and the skins are invariably hustled aboard, no time being lost, because it is an exceedingly uncertain place to safely load the vessel. "

" The " podding " of these young pups in the rear of the great rookeries of St Paul, is one of the most striking and interesting phases of this remarkable exhibition of highly-organized life. When they first bunch together, they are all black, for they have not begun to shed the natal coat : they shine with an unctuous, greasy reflection, and grouped in small armies or great regiments on the sand-dune tracts at North-east point, they present a most extraordinary and fascinating sight. Although the appearance of

---

1. The sea-lions breed on no one of the other rookeries at the island, the insignificant number that I noticed on Seevitchie Kammen excepted. At South-west point, however, I found a small sea-lion rookery, but there are no breeding fur-seals there. A handful of *Eumetopias* used to breed on Otter island, but do not now, since it has been necessary to station government agents there, for the apprehension of fur-seal pirates, during the sealing season.

the " holluschickie " at English Bay fairly overwhelms the observer with the impression of its countless multitudes, yet I am free to declare, that at no one point in this evolution of the seal-life, during the reproductive season, have I been so deeply stricken by the sense of overwhelming enumeration, as I have, when standing on the summit of Cross Hill, I looked down to the southward and westward over a reach of six miles of alternate grass and sand-dune stretches, mirrored upon which were hundreds of thousands of these little black pups, spread in sleep and sport within this restricted field of vision. They appeared as countless as the grains of sand upon which they rested. "

" There is no impression in my mind really more vivid, than is the one which was planted there during the afternoon of that July day, when I first made my survey of this ground; indeed, whenever I pause to think of the subject, the great rookery of Novastoshnah rises promptly to my view, and I am fairly rendered voiceless as I try to speak in definition of the spectacle. In the first place, this slope from Sea-lion neck to the summit of Hutchinson Hill is a long mile, smooth and gradual from the sea to the hill-top; the parade-ground lying between is also nearly three-quarters of a mile in width, sheer and unbroken. Now, upon that area before my eyes, this day and date of which I have spoken were the forms of not less than three-fourths of a million seals—pause a moment—think of the number—three-fourths of a million seals moving in one solid mass from sleep to frolicsome gambols, backward, forward, over, around, changing and interchanging their heavy squadrons, until the whole mind is so confused and charmed by the vastness of mighty hosts, that it refuses to analyze any further. Then, too, I remember that the day was one of exceeding beauty for that region; it was a swift alternation over head of those characteristic rain fogs, between the succession of which the sun breaks out with transcendent brilliancy through the misty halos about it; this parade-field reflected the light like a mirror and the seals, when they broke apart here and there for a moment, just enough to show its surface, seemed as though they walked, upon the water. What a scene to put upon canvas—that amphibian host involved in those alternate rainbow lights and blue-gray shadows of the fog! "

1890. Novastoshnah. — As this great rookery was the object of my chief admiration in 1872, now it in 1890 becomes the again main idea of my concern, not admiration to-day but commiseration, for this breeding-ground has suffered a startling loss of life during the last eight years : it presents the deepest shadows now that that sunshine which I saw it in, eighteen years ago. I have walked around and over it as I surveyed the ground last summer as one would pass thus, a grave-yard, and not even a suggestion of the massed life of 1872, have I been unable to see within its desolate area. That ground, which I described above, as covered with hosts of amphibians in 1872-74 is again before me to-day with not a single herd of seals upon it — actually green with upspringing grass and tinted and flecked with varied flowers!

The accompanying map with the tinted massing of 1872-74, contrasted with that of 1890, speaks for itself — the great rookery of Novastosnah is a mere wreck to-day, and the chart rudely, but forcibly declares it.

Detailed analysis of the survey of "Novastoshnah Rookery"
July 13th, 1890.

Sea margin extending from "A" in the S.E. to "B" in the S.W. 11,435 ft.						Sq. feet.
"A" to "B" 700 ft. sea margin, 35 ft. deep, massed.						24,500
Sea-lion Neck, harems scattered among Sea-lions, an estimate only.						6,000
"C"	to "D"	300 ft.	sea margin, 200 ft. deep, massed		. . . .	60,000
"D"	to "E"	400 ft.	—	10 ft.	—	4,000
"F"	to "G"	200 ft.	—	35 ft.	—	7,000
"G"	to "H"	550 ft.	—	18 ft.	—	6,600
"H"	to "I"	400 ft.	—	35 ft.	—	14,000
"I"	to "J"	500 ft.	—	10 ft.	—	5,000
"J"	to "K"	400 ft.	—	35 ft.	—	14,000
"K"	to "L"	200 ft.	—	10 ft.	—	2,000
"L"	to "M"	700 ft.	—	20 ft.	—	14,000
"N"	to "O"	2,100 ft.	—	60 ft.	—	126,000
"P"	to "Q"	420 ft.	—	30 ft.	—	12,000
"R"	to "S"	425 ft.	—	20 ft.	—	8,500
"S"	to "T"	350 ft.	—	10 ft.	—	3,500
"T"	to "U"	550 ft.	—	30 ft.	—	16,500
"U"	to "V"	500 ft.	—	100 ft.	—	50,000
"W"	to "S"	225 ft.	—	20 ft.	—	5,500
"S"	to "X"	350 ft.	—	10 ft.	—	3,500
				Carry forward.	. . .	382,100

SECTION I.

Sea margin extending from " A " in the S. E. to " B " in the S. W. 11,435 ft.						Sq. feet.
				Brought forward.		382,100
"Y" to "Z"	710 ft. sea margin.		10 ft. deep. massed			7,100
"Z" to "Z²"	350 ft.	—	20 ft.	—	. . . .	7,000
"Z²" to "A²"	125 ft.	—	10 ft.	—	. . . .	1,250
"A²" to "A³"	500 ft.	—	40 ft.	—	. . . .	20,000
"A³" to "B¹"	480 ft.	—	15 ft.	—	. . . .	7,200
			TOTAL SQUARE FEET.		. . .	435,750

Making ground for 217,875 seals ♂ ♀ and o (Bulls, Cows and Pups) against a total of 1,200,000 in 1872-74.

With this enumeration of Novastoshnah we close the list of St. Paul Island, and now turn to the breeding-grounds of St. George, merely mentioning the fact as we do so, that no fur-seals breed on Otter Island, or Walrus Islet, which are near by. The method in vogue here during the last six or seven years, of scraping the margins of the rookeries for killable seals has so harassed and broken up the compact organization at the Reef rookery, as to cause quite a hauling out of breeding seals or Scevitchie Kammen, a small islet less than 900 feet in greatest length with an average width of less than 200 ft; this rock as may be seen on my detailed chart of the Reef rookery lies just south south-east of the Reef point, a few hundred yards (abt. 2,500 feet). It is a bad place for the location of even a small rookery since most of its elevation is only slightly above surf-wash in moderate weather, and a storm in the summer or fall would destroy nearly every pup born upon it : it is a small crescentic splintered rock and reef-bar' with a little shoulder of gray basalt in its centre some 25 or 40 feet only above tide-water. The " ears " or wings which make that odd half-moon shape of this islet, are simply ice-ground and pushed basaltic boulders, over which the surf of every storm from the South-west backing around and to the North-east rolls and breaks completely. In 1872 the fur-seal did not breed here; its instinct warned it of this danger to its offspring from sea storms : but since then so harassed has it been, that a few hundred families or harems have preferred to risk the chance of a quiet living there rather than to longer submit to that hustling of these sealing gangs all along the margin of the breeding grounds on the Reef point.

I estimate that some six or seven thousand breeding seals and their young were hauled out in Seevitchie Kammen this last season. of 1890

1873-74. "**St. George.** — St. George is now in order, and this island has only a trifling contribution for the grand total of the seal-life; but small as it is, it is of much value and interest. Certainly Pribylov, not knowing of the existence of St. Paul, was as well satisfied as if he had possessed the boundless universe, when he first found it. As in the case of St. Paul island, I have been unable to learn much here in regard to the early status of the rookeries, none of the natives having any real information. The drift of their sentiment goes to show that there never was a great assemblage of fur-seals on St. George; in fact, never as many as there are to-day, insignificant as the exhibit is, compared with that of St. Paul. They say that, at first the sea-lions owned this island, and that the Russians, becoming cognizant of the fact, made a regular business of driving off the seevitchie in order that the fur-seals might be encouraged to land. Touching this statement, with my experience on St. Paul, where there is no conflict at all between the five or ten thousand sea-lions which breed around on the outer edge of the seal rookeries there, and at Southwest point, I cannot agree to the St George legend. I am inclined to believe however, indeed it is more than probable, that there were a great many more sea-lions on and about St. George before it was occupied by men — a hundred-fold greater, perhaps, than now; because a sea-lion is an exceeding timid, cowardly creature when it is in the proximity of man, and will always desert any resting place where it is constantly brought into contact with him[1]. "

---

[1]. This statement of the natives has a strong circumstantial backing by the published account of Choris, a French gentleman of leisure, and amateur naturalist and artist, who landed at St. George in 1820 (July); he passed several days and on the Island he wrote at short length in regard to the sea-lion, saying " that the shores were covered with innumerable troops of sea-lions. The odour which arose from them was insupportable. These animals were all the time rutting ", etc., yet nowhere does he speak in the chapter, or elsewhere in his volume, of the fur-seal on St. George, but incidently remarks that over on St. Paul it is the chief animal and most abundant. — Voyage Pittoresque autour du Monde, Iles Aleoutiennes, pp. 12, 13, pl. vix. 1822.

Although this writing of Choris in regard to the subject is brief, superficial, and indefinite, yet I value the record he made. because it is *prima facie* evidence, to my mind, that had the fur-seal been nearly as numerous on St. George then as it was on St. Paul, he would have spoken of the fact surely, inasmuch, as he was searching, for

The scantiness of the St. George rookeries, is due to the configuration of the island itself. There are five separate, well-defined rookeries on St. George, as follows : -

1873-74 " Zapadnie Rookery ". — Directly across the island from its north shore to Zapadnie bay, a little over five miles from the village, is a point where the southern bluff-walls of the island turn north, and drop quickly down from their lofty elevation in a succession of heavy terraces, to an expanse of rocky flat, bordered by a sea sand-beach; just between the sand-beach, however, and these terraces, is a stretch of about 2,000 feet of low, rocky shingle, which borders the flat country back of it, and upon which the surf breaks free and boldly. Midway between the two points is the rookery, and a small detachment of it rests on the direct sloping of the bluff itself, to the southward; while in and around the rookery, falling back some distance, the " holluschickie " are found. "

" A great many confusing statements have been made to me about this rookery — more than in regard to any other on the islands. It has been said, with much positiveness, that, in the times of the Russian rule, this was an immense rookery for St. George; or, in other words, it covered the entire ground between that low plateau to the north and the high plateau to the south, as indicated on the map; and it is also cited in proof of this that the main village of the island, for many years, thirty or forty, was placed on or near the limited drifting sand-dune tracts just above the plateau, to the westward. Be the case at is may, it is certain that for a great many years back, no such rookery has ever existed here. When seals have rested on a chosen piece of ground to breed, they wear off the sharp edges of fractured basaltic boulders, and polish the breccia and cement between them so thoroughly and so finely that years and years of chiseling by frost, and covering by lichens and creeping of mosses, will be required to efface that record. Hence I was able, acting on the suggestion of the natives

just such items with which to illumine his projected book of travels. The old Russian record as to the relative number of fur-seals on the two islands of St. George and St. Paul is clearly as palpably as erroneous for 1820; as I found it to be in 1872, 1873. No intelligent steps towards ascertaining that ratio were ever taken until I made my survey.

of St. Paul, to trace out those deserted fur-seal rookeries on the shores of that island. At Maroonitch, which had, according to their account, been abandoned for over sixty years by the seals, still, at their prompting, when I searched the shore, I found the old boundaries tolerably well defined; I could find nothing like them at Zapadnie ".

" Zapadnie Rookery in July 1873. had 600 feet of sea margin, with 60 feet of average depth; making ground for 18,000 breeding seals and their young. In 1874, I re-surveyed the field and it seemed very clear to me that there had been a slight increase, perhaps to the number of 5,000, according to the expansion of the superficial area over that of 1873 ".

" From Zapadnie we pass to the north shore, where all the other rookeries are located, with the village at a central point between them on the immediate border of the sea. And, in connection with this point, it is interesting to record the fact that every year, until recently, it has been the regular habit of the natives to drive the " holluschickie " over the two and a half or three miles of rough basaltic uplands which separate the hauling ground of Zapadnie from the village; driving them to the killing grounds there, in order to save the delay and trouble generally experienced in loading these skins in the open bay. The prevailing westerly and northwesterly winds during July and August, make it, for weeks at a time, a marine impossibility to effect a landing at Zapadnie, suitable for the safe transit of cargo to the steamer ".

" This five[1] miles of the roughest of all rough walks that can be imagined, is made by the fur-seals in about fourteen[2] to sixteen hours, when driven by the Aleuts; and the weather is cool and foggy. I have known one Treasury agent, who, after making the trip from the village to Zapadnie, seated himself down in the barrabkie there, and declared that no money would induce him to walk back the same way that same day, so severe is the exercise to one not accustomed to it; but it exhibits the power of land-locomotion possessed by the ' holluschickie[3] '.

1. Three in original. Ed.
2. Seven to eight in original. Ed.
3. The peculiarly rough character to this trail is given by the large, loose, sharp-edged basaltic boulders, which are strewn thickly over all those lower plateau that bridge the island between the bluffs at Starry Arteel and the slopes of Ahluckeyak hill.

1890. Zapadnie Rookery. — The St. George "Zapadnie" was a very small edition of the St. Paul "Zapadnie" in 1872 : it is still a small rookery, but relatively has held its own much better than its big namesake has during the last seventeen years. I often wondered in 1873, why this little rookery way over here, and all by itself on the south shore, should be the mark of the best hauling of the holluschickie on St. George island : I now believe that its location is the cause, since the scent and noise of the breeding seals must appeal strongly to the upward-bound bands of holluschickie, as they come en route from the Aleutian passes for St. Paul island : the south shore of St. George would be the first land met by them, hence, the largest and best drives on St. George can always be made here although the rookery itself is and always has been one of the smallest.

Yet, it is the finest lay of seal landing for a breeding ground on the island, since the polished, flat basaltic shelves and cubes that are its chief topographical characteristics could easily receive ten times as many seals as I found there in 1873, or to-day, July 20, 1890. But, for some reason or other the eligible rookery ground here has never been occupied beyond the beach belt or sea margin : the area in the rear is a superb rocky slope, nearly flat but well drained; it never has been occupied prior to 1872-1873 in so far as I can trace the record, and certainly has not been since.

Upon the accompanying map of this rookery, I have also added the hauling grounds, which are all confined to this single spot on the south shore of St. George —there are none on the east shore, and there is no west shore to speak of, owing to the peculiar shape of this island; each rookery map belonging to St. George must carry also the hauling grounds adjacent and continguous, since these seal fields over here are on too small a scale to show clearly

---

The summits of the two broader, higher plateaus, east and west respectively, are comparatively smooth and easy to travel over; and so is the sea-level flat at Zapadnie itself. On the map of St. George, a number of very small ponds will be noticed; they are the fresh-water reservoirs of the island. The two largest of these are near the summit of this rough divide; the seal-trail from Zapadnie to the village runs just west of them, and comes out on the north shore, a little to the eastward of the hauling grounds of Starry Arteel, where it forks and unites with that path. The direct line between the village and Zapadnie, though nearly a mile shorter on the chart, is equal to five miles more of distance by reason of its superlative rocky inequalities.

on a general map of this island unless drawn on a vastly larger scale than that which can be successfully employed for St. Paul island.

Detailed analysis of survey of "Zapadnie" (St. George) Rookery July 20th, 1890.

Sea Margin extending from "A" to "B" and "C" to "D" 1,250 ft.   Sq. feet.

1,250 ft. sea margin from "A" to "B" — "C" to "D", with 20 ft. average depth, massed.   25,000

Making ground for 1,500 seals ♂ ♀ and ○. (Bulls, Cows and Pups) against total of 18,000 in 1873-74.

It will be observed by my tinting on this map of 1890, that in 1873, there was but 600 feet of sea margin to this rookery but that it had the greater depth of 60 feet which threw a third more seals into the field then than is now seen to-day with a sea margin twice as great, but no backing to speak of. This great scattering of these breeders along the sea margin here, instead of massing solidly as in 1873, is due to that rough driving by the sealing gangs along the rookery margins during the last six or seven years; this scraping there has the decided effect of forcing the outside harems, laying farthest back from the water, down along the edges of the rookery to a spot less exposed to the hustling of the native drivers : this steadily kept up, spreads the rookery out along the waters edge : this again operates badly in still another very significant, manner; the doubled extension of the sea margin of a small rookery like Zapadnie here, brings an unduly increased numbers of the pups born here every year, within the danger line of heavy surf, in August and September, before these little fellows can swim well : — therefore the method of driving as practiced to-day is actually forcing the exposure of a decreasing life to a new and an unwarranted increasing danger of destruction which every August and September gale will surely visit upon it; such storms are not lacking, and when they do prevail, thousands and tens of thousands of pups within the reach of the surf-washing violence, are destroyed.

1. " Starry Arteel " or " Old Settlement "; a few hundred yards to the eastward of the rookery, is the earthen ruins of one of the pioneer settlements in Pribylov's

SECTION I.

1873-1874. " **Starry Arteel.** — This rookery is the next in order, and it is the most remarkable one on St. George, lying as it does in a bold sweep from the sea, up a steeply inclined slope to a point where the bluffs bordering it seaward are over 400 feet high; the seals being just as closely crowded at the summit of this lofty breeding plat as they are at the water's edge; the whole oblong oval on the side-hill, as designated by the accompanying survey, is covered by their thickly covered forms. It is a strange sight also, to sail under these bluffs with the boat, in fair weather, for a landing; and, as you walk the beach, over which the cliff wall froms a sheer 500 feet, there, directly over your head the craning necks and twisting forms of the restless seals, ever and anon, as you glance upward, appear as if ready to launch out and fall below, so closely and boldly do they press to the very edge of the precipice. There is a low, rocky beach to the eastward of this rookery, over which the " holluschickie " haul in proportionate numbers, and from which the natives make their drives, coming from the village for this purpose, and directing the seals back, in their tracks[1]. Starry Arteel has 500 feet of sea and cliff margin,

time and which, the natives say, marks the first spot selected by the Russians for their villages after the discovery of St. George, in 1786.

1. Driving the " holluschickie " on St. George, owing to the relative scantiness of hauling area for those animals there, and consequent small numbers found upon these grounds at any one time, is a very arduous series of daily exercices on the part of the natives who attend to it. Glancing at the map, the marked considerable distance, over an exceedingly rough road, will be noticed between Zapadnie and the village; yet, in 1872, eleven different drives across the island, of 400 to 500 seals each, were made in the short four weeks of that season.

The following table shows plainly the striking inferiority of the seal-life, as to aggregate number even as far back as 1872 on this island, compared with that of St. Paul.

ROOKERIES OF ST. GEORGE.

	Number of drives made in 1872	Number of seals driven
" Zapadnie " (Between June 14 and July 28)	11	5,194
" Starry Arteel " (between June 6 and July 29)	14	5,374
" North Rookery " (between June 1 and July 27)	16	4,818
" Little Eastern "		
" Great Eastern " (between June 5 and July 28)	16	9,713

The same activity then in " sweeping " the hauling-grounds of St. Paul, would have brought in ten times as many seals and the labor have been vastly less; the driving at St. Paul was generally done with an eye to securing each day of the season only as many as could be well killed and skinned on that day, according as it was warmish or cooler.

with 125 feet of average depth, making ground for 30,420 breeding-seals and their young."

1890. Starry Arteel Rookery. — This rookery, I am inclined to believe, is the only one on St. George island that really did increase in size, since my work of 1873 : the natives all unite in saying that it "grew larger and larger" until 1878 : then it ceased to expand, and during the last four years, it has gone into a rapid decline — " worse than any other here, except the East Rookery, — nothing, really nothing there". In 1874 when on this rookery, in reviewing my survey of 1873 I could not detect any increase, or change worthy of note whatever, but at Zapadnie, I thought I found ground for a small increase there of nearly 5,000, but I was not wholly certain of it inasmuch as the day was very foggy — and I could not entirely trust my compass bearings.

Here, as at Zapadnie is that undue extension of sea-margin for the number of seals occupying the ground, caused by that peculiar driving which has been in vogue on each island here ever since the shrinking of the supply of killable seals in 1882. In 1873 this breeding ground of Starry Arteel was a compact oblong-oval mass of breeding seals resting on that steep hill slope of volcanic breccia and cement, which these seals seem to love so well (happy as it is as to drainage, and always free from mud and dust) : then it had but 500 feet of sea and cliff margin, but had an average depth of 125 feet : within these lines 30,000 breeding seals and young were easily located : to-day it presents a straggling belt of 800 feet of cliff and sea margin with a scant 40 feet of average depth upon which a very liberal estimate cannot place more than 16,000 animals, old and young.

**Detailed analysis of the survey of " Starry Arteel " Rookery
July 20th, 1890.**

	Sq. feet.
Sea and cliff margin beginning at "O" and ending at "G" 800 ft.	
800 ft. sea and cliff margin between "G" and "O", with 40 ft. average depth, massed.	32,000

Making ground for 16,000 seals ♂ ♀ and ○. (Bulls, Cows, and Pups) against a total in 1873 of 30,420.

This rookery, East and Zapadnie are the only ones on St. George which have thus far been landed upon and raided by seal pirates, three attempts have been made here, and one only at Zapadnie, the damage done was insignificant, since the marauders were detected before they had fairly got to work, and driven off by the natives and officers of the Government.

1873-1874. "**North Rookery.** — Next in order, and half a mile to the eastward, is this breeding-ground, which sweeps for 2,750 feet along and around the sea front of a gently sloping plateau[1], being in full sight of and close to the village. It has a superficial area occupied by 77,000 breeding-seals and their young. From this rookery to the village, a distance of less than a quarter of a mile, the "holluschickie" are driven which are killed for their skins, on the common track or seal-worn trail, that, not only the "bachelors" but ourselves travel over *en route* to and from Starry Arteel and Zapadnie; it is a broad, hard-packed erosion through the sphagnum and across the rocky plateaux — in fact a regular seal-road, which has been used by the drivers and victims during the last eighty or ninety years. The fashion of St. George, in this matter of driving seals, is quite different from that on St. Paul. To get their maximum quota of 25,000 annually, it is necessary for the natives to visit every morning the hauling-ground of each one of these four rookeries on the north shore, and bring what they may find back with them for the day[1]."

1. The original text of the existing law for the protection of the seal-islands, provides that 100,000 seals which may be annually taken from them shall be proportioned by killing 75,000 on St. Paul and 25,000 on St. George. This ratio was based evidently upon the published tables of Veniaminov, which, if accurate, would clearly show that fully one third as many seals repaired to the smaller island as to the larger one, and until I made my surveys, 1872-74, it was so considered by all parties interested. The fact, however, which I soon discovered, is that St. George receives only one-eighteenth of the whole aggregate of fur-seal visitation peculiar to the Pribylov islands, St. Paul entertaining the other seventeen parts.

This amazing difference, in the light of prior knowledge and understanding, caused me, on returning to Washington in October 1873, to lay the matter before the Treasury Department, and ask that the law be so modified that, in the event of abnormally warm killing seasons, for other reasons a smaller number might be taken from St. George, with a corresponding increase at St. Paul; for unless this was done, it might become at any season a matter of great hardship to secure 25,000 killable seals on St. George, in the short period allotted by law. The Treasury Department, while fully concurring in my representations, seemed to doubt its power to do so; then, with its sanction, I carried the question before Congress January, 1874, and secured from that body an amendment of the act of July 1, 1870, (act, etc., approved March 24, 1874), which gives the Secretary of the Treasury full discretion in the matter, and

1890. North Rookery. — I came upon this breeding-ground to-day, July 19, 1890, after an absence of just sixteen years. I find the topography unchanged : the hauling grounds all grass-grown, and the usual flowering plants which seem to follow (on all of these declining rookeries), the abandonment of hitherto polished rock and hard-swept soil travelled over and laid upon by the seals; the breeding animals on the several areas of this rookery are in the usual form, and characteristic of those which I have described on St. Paul — the same scanty supply of old bulls — no young bulls on the rookery or outside at the waters edge : — large scattered harems and every evidence of imperfect service — in all these forms, precisely as they are over on St. Paul.

But, this, the chief rookery of St. George, which held 76,250 breeding animals and their young in 1874, has suffered a loss of only one half of its cows and pups; but, the bulls, fully five sevenths of them are missing. This rookery was the largest on St. George in 1874 : it has been so ever since and is to-day : but large as it was, there was only one on St. Paul smaller in 1874. The " Lagoon " rookery (" Nah Speel " we cannot, count). But to-day there is still another one on St. Paul smaller, and that is Keetavie, though it was twice as large as this North rookery in 1874 :

It is an admirable point of seal ground, well drained, and free from muddy pools during rain storms : it is in full sight of the village, and only a short half mile walk away.

---

fixes the hitherto inflexible ratio of killing on each island upon a sliding scale, as it were, for adjustment from season to season upon a more intelligent understanding of the subject; and, also, this amendatory act gives the Secretary of the Treasury the power to fix the legal limit of killing as the case may require.

As the law is now amended, the killing on the two islands can be sensibly adjusted each season, by the relative number of seals on the two islands, which will vary so markedly on St. George according as it may be abnormally dry and warm when the period for driving the " holluschickie " is at hand, or other causes.

Detailed analysis of the survey of North Rookery
July 19, 1890.

	Sea margin begins at "a" and ends at "1", 3,366 ft.	Sq. feet.
150 ft.	sea margin from "a" to "b" with 15 ft. average depth, massed.	2,250
300 ft.	sea margin "b" to "c" with 60 ft. average depth, massed.	18,000
95 ft.	sea margin from "c" to "d", with 0 ft. sea (nothing there)	
245 ft.	sea margin from "d" to "e", with 60 ft. average depth, massed	20,700
250 ft.	sea margin from "e" to "f", with 10 ft. average depth, massed	2,500
186 ft.	sea margin from "f" to "g", with 12 ft. average depth, massed	2,232
220 ft.	sea margin from "g" to "h", with 60 ft. average depth, massed	13,200
240 ft.	sea margin from "h" to "i", with 12 ft. average depth, massed	2,880
280 ft.	sea margin from "i" to "j", with 12 ft. average depth, massed	3,360
1,300 ft.	sea margin from "j" to "l", with 10 ft. average depth, massed	13,000
	TOTAL SQUARE FEET. . .	77,122

Making ground for 38,561 ♀ ♂ and ○. (Bulls, Cows and Pups) against a total of 76,250 in 1873-1874.

1873-74. " **Little Eastern Rookery.**[1] — From the village to the eastward, about half a mile, again, is a little eastern rookery, which lies on a low, bluffy slope, and is not a piece of ground admitting of much more expansion. It has superficial area for the reception of nearly 13,000 breeding seals and their young. "

1890. Little Eastern Rookery. — This was not much of a rookery in 1873-74 and although it has fallen away in accord with the general diminution of the seal life on these islands, yet it has held its own proportionately, much better than many others. The

---

1. The site of this breeding-ground and that of the marine slope of the killing-grounds to the east of the village, on this island, is where sea-lions hold exclusive possession prior to their driving off by the Russians — so the natives affirm — the only place on St. George now where the *Eumetopias* breeds, is that one indicated on the general chart, between Garden cove and Tolstoi Mees.

most striking evidence of desolation is the grassing solidly over rank and luxuriant, of the hauling-grounds in its rear, and to the eastward, which were so well polished off by the restless flippers of young male seals in 1873-74 : then these hauling grounds were not driven from much the seals were practically undisturbed here and when a drive was made, the seals were always merged into the larger drive from the Great Eastern.

Detailed analysis of the survey of Little Eastern Rookery, July 20th, 1890.

Sea margin beginning at "A"and ending at "B" — 800 feet.   Sq. feet.
800 ft. sea margin from "A" to "B",. with 12 ft. average depth, massed.. 9,600

Making ground for 4,800 seals ♂♀ and ○. (Bulls, Cows and Pups) against a total of 13,000 in 1873-74.

1873-74. "The Great Eastern. — This is the fifth and last rookery that we find on St. George. It is an imitation, in miniature of Tolstoi on St. Paul, with the exception of there being no parade ground in the rear, of any character whatever. It is from the summit of the cliffs, overlooking the narrow ribbon of breeding-seals right under them, that I have been able to study the movements of the fur seal in the water to my heart's content; for out and under the water, the rocks, to a considerable distance, are covered with a whitish algoid growth, that renders the dark bodies of the swimming seals and sea-lions as conspicuous as is the image thrown by a magic lantern of a silhouette on a screen prepared for its reception[1]. The low rocky flats around the pool to the west-

[1]. The algoid vegetation of the marine shores of these islands is one that adds a peculiar charm and beauty to their treeless, sunless coasts. Every kelp bed that floats raft-like in Bering sea, or is anchored to its rocky reefs, is fairly alive with minute sea-shrimps, tiny crabs, and little shells which cling to its masses of interwoven fronds or dart in ceaseless motion through yet within its interstices. It is my firm belief that no better base of operations can be found for studying marine invertebrata than is the post of St. Paul or St. George; the pelagic and the littoral forms are simply abundant beyond all estimation within bounds of reason. The phosphorescence of the waters of Bering sea surpasses in continued strength of brilliant illumination, anything that I have seen in southern and equatorial oceans. The crests of the long unbroken line of breakers on Lukannon beach looked to me, one night in August, like an instantaneous flashing, of lightning, between Tolsti Mees and Lukannon head, as the billows successively rolled in, and broke; the seals swimming under the water, here on

ward and north-west of the rookery seem to be filled up with a muddy alluvial wash that the seals do not favor; hence nothing but holluschickie range round about them ".

1890. The Great Eastern Rookery.—In 1873-74 this breeding-ground ranked third in the list of five that belong to this island of St. George. To day it seems to have been the heaviest loser over here — it has literally dropped down to a mere skeleton of its form in my early survey, that extended rocky flat from which the rookery ground proper gently rises on the hill slope, was one of the most attractive hauling-grounds for the holluschickie on St. George sixteen years ago : now its surface is covered with a most luxuriant turf — it looks like a Kentucky blue grass meadow.

I observed here in 1873-74 a good many sea-lions hauled out on the beach curve right under the rookery bluffs : these animals are very much more numerous now than then, not less than five hundred of them being lazily extended just above surf-wash here as I made my survey (July 20th, 1890), their huge yellow bodies hauled out like Mississippi river steamboats on the levee at St. Louis.

Detailed analysis of the survey of Great Eastern Rookery July 20th, 1890.

Sea margin beginning at "b" and ending at "a" 2,040 ft.   Sq. feet.

2,040 ft. sea margin "a" to "b" with a straggling average depth of
    5 ft. (a very liberal estimate). 10,000
200 ft. sea margin "f" to "g", with
    30 ft. average depth, massed.   6,000
1,000 ft. sea margin, "g" to "e", with a straggling average depth too
    thin for calculation allowed.   2,000
                                  TOTAL SQUARE FEET. . . 18,000

Making ground for 9,000 seals, ♂ ♀ and ○ (Bulls, Cows and Pups) against a total of 25,250 in 1873-74.

I think that this rookery presents the most eloquent illustration of that ruin and demoralization wrought by the present order of scraping the breeding lines on all the rookeries in getting the daily " drives " of killable seals : it presents itself in this plain

St. George and beneath the Black Bluffs, streaked their rapid course like comets in the sky; and every time their dark heads popped above the surface of the sea, they were marked by a blaze of scintillant light.

manner; — in 1873, *there was only* 900 *feet of rookery sea margin here:* 200 feet of this total was a solid massing of breeding-seals from the water up on the hillside as shown by the 1874 tint on the accompanying map; it was 200 feet deep, and contained 20,000 of the 25,000 seals all told that then existed at this point.

To day, there is 3,275 *feet of rookery sea margin here!* a straggling, ragged belt, not even a full harem's width in depth! except under that side hill expansion between " g " and " f " where there is instead of the 200 feet of massing cited above, only 30 feet of average depth.

Thus it becomes entirely plain upon the least study of this subject that the present order of raking and dinning by which the holluschickie are started out from the shelter of these breeding grounds also starts the outlying cows and bulls and hustles them of and down to the waters edge : this repeated day after day has created that long extension of over 3,000 feet to my sea margin of 1873-74 on this rookery, while the seals themselves, are barely one third the number that they were at first record.

Recapitulation of the estimates of numbers of seals. — Below is a brief recapitulation of those figures made from my surveys of the area and position of the breeding-grounds of St. Paul island, between the 10th and 18th of July 1872, confirmed and revised to that date in 1874. On St. George Island, July 12th to 15th, 1873 confirmed and revised to that date in 1874. Opposed to these tables are my figures made July 10th to 16th 1890, — on St. Paul Island, and July 19th-20th 1890 on St. George.

**Breeding-grounds of the fur-seal, on St. Paul Island
July 10th-18th 1872-1874.**

	Number of seals, male, female, and young.
" Reef rookery " has 4,016 feet of sea-margin, with 150 feet of average depth, making ground for.	301,000
" Garbotch rookery " has 3,660 feet of sea-margin, with 100 feet of average depth, making ground for.	183,000
" Lagoon rookery " has 750 feet of sea-margin, with 100 feet of average depth, making ground for.	37,000
Carry forward. . .	521,000

	Number of seals, male, female and young.
Brought forward.	521,000
" Nah Speel rookery " has 400 feet of sea-margin, with 40 feet of average depth, making ground for.	8,000
" Lukannon rookery " has 2,270 feet of sea-margin, with 150 feet of average depth, making ground for.	170,000
" Keetavie rookery " has 2,200 feet of sea-margin, with 150 feet of average depth, making ground for.	165,000
" Tolstoi rookery " has, 3,000 feet of sea-margin, with 150 feet of average depth, making ground for.	225,000
" Zapadnie rookery " has 5,880 feet of sea-margin, with 150 feet of average depth, making ground for.	441,000
" Polavina rookery " has 4,000 feet of sea-margin, with 150 feet of average depth, making ground for.	300,000
" Novastoshnah, or Northeast Point " has 15,840 feet of sea-margin, with 150 feet of average depth, making ground for. . .	1,200,000
A grand total of breeding-seals and young for St. Paul Island in 1874 of	3,030,000

Breeding-grounds of the fur-seal on St. Paul Island
July 10th-16th, 1890.

	Number of seals, male, female and young.
" Reef rookery " has 4,300 feet of sea-margin, with 65 1/3 ft. average depth, making ground for.	140,500
" Garbotch rookery " has 2,400 feet of sea-margin, with 70 2/3 ft. average depth, making ground for.	84,802
" Lagoon rookery " has 1,500 feet of sea-margin, with 12 ft. average depth, making ground for.	9,000
" Nah Speel " has disappeared.	
" Lukannon rookery " has 2,050 feet of sea-margin, with 60 1/2 ft. average depth, making ground for.	72,500
" Keetavie rookery " has 1,700 feet of sea-margin, with 34 ft. average depth, making ground for.	28,000
" Tolstoi rookery " has 2,800 feet of sea-margin, with 44 1/2 ft. average depth, making ground for.	62,400
" Zapadnie rookery " has 7,200 feet of sea-margin, with 33 1/2 ft. average depth, making ground for. . . . . . »	121,200
" Polavina rookery " has 2,255 feet of sea-margin, with 126 1/3 ft. average depth, making ground for.	142,250
" Novosthoshnah " or Northeast Point ", has 11,435 ft. of sea-margin with 37 1/2 ft. of average depth, making ground for.	217,875
A grand total of breeding-seals and young for St. Paul Island in 1890 of.	878,532

**Breeding-Grounds of the fur-seal on St. George Island.
July 12th-15th, 1873-1874.**

	Seals ♂.♀.○
"Zapadnie rookery" has 600 feet of sea-margin, with 60 feet of average depth, making ground for.	18,000
"Starry Arteel rookery" has 500 feet of sea-margin, with 125 feet of average depth, making ground for.	30,420
"North rookery" has 750 feet of sea-margin, with 150 feet of average depth, and 2,000 feet of sea-margin, with 25 feet of average depth; making ground in all for.	77,000
"Little Eastern rookery" has 750 feet of sea-margin, with 40 feet of average depth, making ground for.	13,000
"Great Eastern rookery" has 900 feet of sea-margin, with 60 feet of average depth, making ground for.	25,000
A grand total of the seal-life for St. George Island, breeding-seals and young, of.	163,420
Grand total for St. Paul Island, brought down, breeding-seals and young, of.	3,030,000
Grand sum total for the Pribylov islands (season of 1872-1874) breeding-seals and young.	3,193,420

**Breeding-Grounds of the fur-seal on St. George Island
July 19th-20th, 1890**

	Seals. ♂.♀.○
"Zapadnie rookery" has 1,250 feet of sea-margin, with 20 ft. average depth, making ground for.	12,250
"Starry Arteel rookery" has 800 feet of sea-margin, with 40 ft. average depth, making ground for.	16,000
"North Rookery" has 2,066 feet of sea-margin, with 31 ft. average depth and 1,300 feet of sea-margin with 10 ft. of average depth, making ground for	38,561
"Little Eastern rookery" has 800 feet of sea-margin, with 12 ft. average depth, making ground for..	4,800
"Great Eastern rookery" has 200 feet of sea-margin, with 30 ft. average depth, 2,040 feet of sea-margin with 5 ft. average depth, making ground for..	9,000
A grand total of the breeding seals and young for St. George Island for 1890, of..	80,861
Grand total for St. Paul Island, brought down, breeding-seals and young, of	878,532
Grand sum total for the Pribylov islands, season of 1890, breeding-seals and young	959,393

SECTION I.

The foregoing figures, presented step by step as they were made, declare the fact that in 1890 there are in round numbers only one third of that number of the breeding seals and young on the Pribylov rookeries, which existed upon them in 1872-74.

Following my figures, published in 1874, I made this detailed explanation of my understanding of the question as to number and condition; it is perfectly applicable to the present order of affairs.

"The figures above thus show a grand total of 3,193,420 breeding-seals and their young. This enormous aggregate is entirely exclusive of the great numbers of the non-breeding-seals, that, as we have pointed out, are never permitted to come upon those grounds which have been surveyed and epitomized by the table just exhibited. That class of seals, the ' holluschickie ', in general terms, all males, and those to which the killing is confined, come upon the land and sea-beaches, between the rookeries, in immense straggling droves, going to and from the sea at irregular intervals from the beginning to the closing of the entire season. The method of the ' holluschickie ' on these hauling-grounds is not systematic — it is not distinct, like the manner and law prescribed and obeyed by the breeding-seals, which fill up those rookery grounds to the certain points as surveyed, and keep these points intact for a week or ten days, at a time, during the height of every season in July and August; but, to the contrary, upon the hauling-grounds to-day an immense drove of 100,000 will be seen before you at English Bay, sweeping hither and surging thither over the polished surface which they have worn with their restless flippers, tracing and retracing their tireless marches; to-morrow, if a heavy rain has fallen in the meantime, or it has changed to an unusual warm dry day, you will scarcely find ten thousand there or here where you saw legions yesterday : consequently the amount of ground occupied by the ' holluschickie ' is vastly in excess of what they would require did they conform to the same law of distribution observed by the breeding-seals; and this ground is therefore wholly untenable for any such definite basis and satisfactory conclusion as is that which I have surveyed on the rookeries. Hence, in giving an estimate of the aggregate number of ' holluschickie ' or non-breeding seals, on the Pribylov Islands, embracing, as it does, all the males under six one and seven years of age and all the yearling females, it must, necessarily, be a simple opinion of mine founded upon nothing better than my individual judgment. This is my conclusion. "

" The non-breeding seals seem nearly equal in number to that of the adult breeding-seal; but without putting them down at a figure quite so high, I may safely say that the sum total of 1,500,000, in round numbers, is a fair enumeration, and quite within bounds of fact. This makes the grand sum total, of the fur-seal life on the Pribylov Islands, over 4,700,000. "

My estimate as above cited of 1,500,000 non-breeding seals (*i. e.* all males under seven years and the yearlings of both sexes), as existing and hauling on the Pribylov Islands during the seasons of 1872-74, was a very conservative one, far more conservative and less liberal than the one I am about to make for the number of holluschickie and yearlings which have survived and appear in 1890 upon these hauling grounds of he Seal Islands of Alaska, and which calculation appears in all detail in the following Section (Sec. II) of this report: briefly stated here, it is an extremely liberal estimate of mine when I admit the existence to day (July 34, 1890) upon these islands of 80,000 ' holluschickie ' and ' polseacatchie ' *i. e.* male fur-seals from 1 year old up to 6 years old.

Naturally enough, when summing up my work of 1872-74, the thought arose as to the probable future of those wonderful exhibitions of massed animal life which I saw before me then upon the Pribylov rookeries : as to the subject of their increasing, I said then.

" I am free to say that it is not within the power of human management to promote this end to the slightest appreciable degree over its present extent and condition as it stands in the state of nature, heretofore described. It cannot fail to be evident, from my detailed narration of the habits and life of the fur-seal on these islands during so large a part of every year, that could man have the same supervision and control over this animal during the whole season which he has at his command while they visit the land he might cause them to multiply and increase, as he would so many cattle, to an indefinite number — only limited by time and the means of feeding them. But the case in question, unfortunately, is one where the fur-seal is taken, by demands for food, at least six months out of every year, far beyond the reach or even cognizance of any man, where it is all this time exposed to many known powerful and destructive natural enemies, and probably many others, equally so, unknown, which prey upon it, and, in accordance with that well-recognized law of nature, keeps this seal-life at a certain number — at a figure which has been reached, for ages past, and will continue to be in the future, as far as they now are, — their present maximum limit of increase, namely, between four and five million seals, in round numbers. This law holds good everywhere throughout the animal kingdom, regulating and preserving the equilibrium of life in the state of nature; did it not hold good, these seal-islands and all Bering Sea would have been literally covered, and have swarmed like the *Medusæ* of the waters, long before the Russians discovered them. But, according to the silent testimony of the rookeries, which have been abandoned by seals, and the noisy, emphatic assurance of those now occupied, there were no more seals when first seen here by human eyes in 1786 and 1787, than there are now in 1881, as far as all evidence goes."

"From my calculations, given above, it will be seen that 1,000,000 pups, or young seals, in round numbers, are born upon these islands of the Pribylov group every year; of this million, one-half are males. These 500,000 young males, before they leave the islands for sea, during October and November, and when they are between five and six months old, fat and hardy, have suffered but a trifling loss in numbers, say one per cent., while on and about the islands of their birth, surrounding which, and upon which, they have no enemies whatever to speak of; but, after they get well down to the Pacific, spread out over an immense area of watery highways in quest of piscatorial food, they form the most helpless of their kind to resist or elude the murderous teeth and carnivorous attacks of basking sharks and killer-whales. By these agencies, during their absence from the islands until their reappearance in the following year, and in July, they are so perceptibly diminished in number, that I do not think, fairly considered, more than one-half of the legion which left the ground of their birth, last October, came up the next July to these favorite landing-places; that is, only 250,000 of them return out of the 500,000 born last year. The same statement, in every respect, applies to the going and the coming of the 500,000 female pups, which are identical in size, shape, and behaviour ".

" As yearlings, however, these 250,000 survivors, of last year's birth, have become strong, lithe and active swimmers; and when they again leave the hauling grounds as before, in the fall, they are fully as able as are the older class to take care of themselves; and when they reappear next year, at least 225,000 of them safely return in the second season after birth; from this on I believe that they live out their natural lives of fifteen to twenty years each; the death-rate now caused by the visitation of marine enemies affecting them, in the aggregate, but slightly. And, again, the same will hold good touching the females, the average natural life of which, however, I take to be only nine or ten years each. "

" Out of these 325,000 young males, we are required to save only one-fifteenth of their number to pass over to the breeding-grounds, and meet there the 225,000 young females; in other words, the polygamous habit of this animal is such that, by its own volition, I do not think that more than one male annually out of fifteen born is needed on the breeding-grounds in the future; but in my calculations, to be within the margin and to make sure that I save two-year old males enough every season, I will more than double this proportion, and set aside every fifth one of the young males in question; that will leave 180,000 seals, in good condition, that can be safely killed every year, without the slightest injury to the perpetuation of the stock itself forever in all its original integrity[1]. "

[1]. When regarding the subject in 1872-73, of how many surplus young males could be wisely taken from the Pribylov stock, I satisfied myself that more than 100,000 could be drawn upon annually for their skins, and hence was impressed with the idea that the business might be safely developed to a greater maximum; since then, however, I have been giving attention to the other side of the question, which involves the market for the skins and the practical working of any sliding scale of increased killing, such as I then recommended. A careful review of the whole matter modified my original idea and caused me to think that, all things considered, it is better to "let well enough alone". Although it would be a most interesting commercial experiment to develop the yield of the Pribylov Islands to their full capacity, yet, in view of the anomalous and curious features of the case, it is wiser to be satisfied with the assured guarantee of perpetuation in all original integrity, which the experience of the last ten years gives us on present basis of 100,000 than to risk it by possibly doubling the revenue therefrom. Therefore, I am not now in favour of my earlier proposition of gradually increasing the killing, until the maximum number of surplus "holluschickie" should be ascertained.

SECTION I.

" In the above showing I have put the very extreme estimate upon the loss sustained at sea by the pup-seals too large, I am morally certain; but, in attempting to draw this line safely, I wish to place the matter in the very worst light in which it can be put, and to give the seals the full benefit of every doubt. Surely I have clearly presented the case, and certainly no one will question the premises after they have studied the habit and disposition of the rookeries; hence, it is a positive and tenable statement, that no danger of the slightest appreciable degree of injury to the interests of the government on the seal-islands of Alaska, exists as long as the present law protecting it, and the management executing it, continues."

Upon this same basis of estimation, less than 300,000 pups were born upon the Pribylov rookeries, last year 1889; but not more than 70,000 to 80,000 of them returned to these islands in 1890, since their natural enemies are as numerous and as active as ever in the sea, while the surplus store of seal-life upon which these enemies drew in 1872, as they draw now, has been rapidly diminishing during the last six years; touching this question in 1874 I said then: "These fur-seals of the Pribylov group, after leaving the islands in the autumn and early winter, do not visit land again until the time of their return, in the following spring and early summer, to these same rookery-and hauling-grounds, unless they touch, as they are navigating their lengthened journey back, at the Russian, Copper and Bering islands, 700 miles to the westward of the Pribylov group. They leave the islands by independent squads, each one looking out for itself; apparently all turn by common consent to the south, disappearing toward the horizon, and are soon lost in the vast expanse below, where they spread themselves over the entire North Pacific as far south as the 48th and even the 47th parallels of north latitude. Over the immense area between Japan and Oregon, doutless, many extensive submarine fishing shoals and banks are known to them; at least, it is definitely understood that Bering sea does not contain them long when they depart from the breeding-rookeries and the hauling-grounds therein. While it is carried in mind that they sleep and rest in the water with soundness and with greatest comfort on its surface, and that even when around the land, during the summer, they frequently put off from the beaches to take a bath and a quiet snooze just beyond the surf, we can readily agree that it is no inconvenience whatever, when the reproductive functions have been discharged, and their coats renewed, for them to stay the balance of the time in their most congenial element — the briny deep."

"That these animals are preyed upon extensively by killer-whales [1] (*Orca gladiator*), in especial, and by sharks [2], and probably other submarine foes now unknown, is at once evident; for, were they not held in check by some such cause, they would, as they exist to-day on Saint Paul, quickly multiply, by arithmetical progression, to so great an extent that the island, nay, Bering Sea itself, could not contain them. The present annual killing of 100,000 out of a yearly total of over a million males does not, in an appreciable degree, diminish the seal-life, or interfere in the slightest with its regular, sure perpetuation on the breeding-grounds every year. We may, therefore properly look upon this aggregate of four or five millions of fur-seals, as we see them every season on these Pribylov islands, as the maximum limit of increase assigned to them by natural law. The great equilibrium, which

---

1. *Orca gladiator.* While revolving this particular line of inquiry in my mind when, on the ground and among the seals, I involuntarily looked constantly for some sign of disturbance in the sea which would indicate the presence of an enemy; and, save seeing a few examples of the Orca, I never detected anything; but the killer-whale is common here, it is patent to the most casual eye, because it is the habit of this ferocious cetacean to swim so closely at the surface as to show its peculiar sharp, dorsal fin high above the water; possibly a very superficial observer could and would confound the long, trenchant fluke of the Orca with the stubby node upon the spine of the humpback whale, which that animal exhibits only when it is about to dive. Humpbacks feed around the islands, but not commonly — they are the exception; they do not, however, molest the seals in any manner whatever; and little squads of these pinnipeds seem to delight themselves by swimming in endless circles around and under the huge bodies of those whales, frequently leaping out and entirely over the cetacean's back, as witnessed on one occasion by myself and the crew of the "Reliance", off the coast of Kadiak, June, 1874.

2. *Somniosus microcephalus.* Some of these sharks are of very large size, and when caught by the Indians of the northwest coast basking or asleep on the surface of the sea, they will, if transfixed by the native's harpoons, take a whole fleet of canoes ntow and run swiftly with them several hours before exhaustion enables the savages to finally dispatch them. A Hudson Bay trader, William Manson (at Ft. Alexander, in 1865), told me that his father had killed one in the smooth waters of Millbank sound, which measured 24 feet in length, and its liver alone yielded 36 gallons of oil. The Somniosus lays motionless for long intervals in calm waters of the Nort Pacific, just under and at the surface, with its dorsal fin clearly exposed above; what havoc such a carnivorous fish would bel likely to effect in a "pod" of young fur-seals, can be better imagined than described.

nature holds in life upon this earth, must be sustained at St. Paul as well as elsewhere."

"Think of the enormous food consumption of these rookeries and hauling-grounds; what an immense quantity of finny prey must pass down their voracious throats as every year rolls by. A creature so full of life, strung with nerves, muscles like bands of steel, cannot live on air, or absorb it from the sea. Their food is fish, to the practical exclusion of all other diet. I have never seen them touch, or disturb with the intention of touching it, one solitary example in the flocks of water-fowl which rest upon the surface of the water all about the islands. I was especially careful in noting this, because it seemed to me that canine armature of their mouths must suggest flesh for food at times as well as fish; but fish we know they eat. Whole windrows of the heads of cod and wolf fishes, bitten off by these animals at the nape, were washed up on the south-shore of St. George during a gale in the summer of 1873; this pelagic decapitation evidently marked the progress and the appetite of a band of fur-seals to the windward of the island, as they passed into and through a stray school of these fishes."

"How many pounds per diem is required by an adult seal, and taken by it when feeding, is not certain in my mind. Judging from the appetite, however, of kindred animals, such as sea-lions fed in confinement at Woodward's gardens, San Francisco, I can safely say that forty pounds for a full grown fur-seal is a fair allowance, with at least ten or twelve pounds per diem to every adult female, and not much less, if any, to the rapidly growing pups and young 'holluschickie'. Therefore, this great body of four and five millions of hearty, active animals which we know on the seal-islands, must consume an enormous amount of such food every year. They cannot average less than ten pounds of fish each per diem, which gives the consumption, as exhibited by their appetite, of over six million tons of fish every year. What wonder, then, that nature should do something to hold these active fishermen in check[1]."

---

1. When, however, the fish retire from spawning here, there, and everywhere over these shallows of Alaska and the northwest coast, along by the end of September to 1st of November, every year, I believe that the young fur-seal, in following them into the depths of the great Pacific, must have a really arduous struggle for existence — unless it knows of fishing banks unknown to us. The yearlings, however, and all

"During tho winter solstice—between the lapse of the autumnal, and the verging of the vernal equinoxes—in order to get this enormous food supply, the fur-seals are necessarily obliged to disperse over a very large area of fishing ground, ranging throughout the North Pacific, 5,000 miles across between Japan and the Straits of Fuca. In feeding, they are brought to the southward all this time; and, as they go, they come more and more in contact with those natural enemies peculiar to the sea of these southern latitudes, which are almost strangers and are really unknown to the waters of Bering sea; for I did not observe, with the exception of ten or twelve perhaps, certainly no more, killer-whales, a single marine disturbance, or molestation, during the three seasons which I passed upon the islands that could be regarded in the slightest degree inimical to the peace and life of the *Pinnipedia;* and thus, from my observation, I am led to believe that it is not until they descend well to the south of the Aleutian islands, and in the North Pacific, that they meet with sharks to any extent, and are diminished by the butchery of killer-whales."

"The young fur-seals going out to sea for the first time and following in the wake of their elders, are the clumsy members of the family. When they go to sleep on the surface of the water, they rest much sounder than the others; and their alert and wary nature, which is handsomely developed ere they are two seasons old, is in its infancy. Hence, I believe that vast numbers of them are easily captured by marine foes, as they are stupidly sleeping, or awkwardly fishing."

"With reference to the amount of ground covered by the seals, when first discovered by the Russians, I have examined every foot of the shore line of both islands where the bones, and polished

---

above that age, are endowed with sufficient muscular energy to dive rapidly in deep soundings, and to fish with undoubted success. The pup, however, when it goes to sea, five or six months old, is not lithe and sinewy like the yearling; it is podgy and fat, a comparative clumsy swimmer, and does not develop, I believe, into a good fisherman until it has become pretty well starved after leaving the Pribylov.

I must not be understood as saying that fish alone constitute the diet of the Pribylov pinnipeds; I know that they feed to a limited extent, upon crustaceans and upon the squid (Loligo), also, eating tender algoid sprouts; I believe that the pup-seals live for the first five or six months at sea largely, if not wholly, upon crustaceans and squids; the are not agile enough, in my opinion, to fish successfully in any great degree, when they first depart from the rookeries.

rocks, etc., might be lying on any deserted areas. Since then, after carefully surveying the new ground now occupied by the seals, and comparing this area with that which they have deserted, I feel justified in stating that for the last twelve or fifteen years, at least, the fur-seals on these islands have not diminished, nor have they increased as a body to any noteworthy degree ; and throughout this time the breeding-grounds have not been disturbed except at that brief but tumultuous interregnum during 1868 ; and they have been living since in a perfectly quiet and natural condition. "

" **Can the number be increased?** — What can be done to promote their increase ? We cannot cause a greater number of females to be born every year than are born now ; we do not touch or disturb these females as they grow up and live ; and we never will if the law and present management is continued. We save double — we save more than enough males to serve; nothing more can be done by human agency; it is beyond our power to protect them from their deadly marine enemies as they wander into the boundless ocean searhing for food. "

" In view, therefore, of all these facts, I have no hesitation in saying, quite confidently, that under the present rules and regulations governing the sealing interests on these islands, the increase or diminution of the seal-life thereon will amount to nothing in the future ; that the seals will exist, as they do exist, in all time to come at about the same number and condition recorded in this monograph. To test this theory of mine, I here, in the record of my surveys of the rookeries, have put stakes down which will answer, upon those breeding-grounds, as a correct guide as to their present, as well as to their future, condition, from year to year. "

The theory has been well tested : I was right in then assuming that no increase could be noted over the record of 1872-74 ; but I was wrong in then believing that no injury to the regular supply of young male life necessary for the full support of the breeding grounds, would follow from the driving and killing of the holluschickie as conducted : also, the daily work of the pelagic sealer was not suggested in any serious sense sixteen years ago, and I did not take it into calculation. I have given, in my letter of introduction, the reason why this driving of the holluschickie, has been so destructive to young male seal life — a reason which I could not grasp in 1872-74 since it required time and experience to develop the fact beyond argument and contradiction. It is easy to see now in the clear light of the record that had there been no poaching at sea and had every young male seal been taken in every drive made from the outset in 1871, over one year old and under five, the annual quota of 100,000 would have been easily filled without injury whatsoever in less than twenty working days from the 14th of every June, with only one quarter of the driving necessary under the past and present order of culling out the largest seals for slaughter, and releasing the smaller ones from each drive, when on the killing grounds; — in other words, taking all the young male seal as driven, over one year old and under five years would have saved on an average for every year the lives of at least 50,000 to 60,000 holluschickie, which those spared from the club annually, during the last 20 years have nevertheless, perished or surviving, yet were rendered worthless for rookery service from the immediate or subsequent effect of severe overland driving.

It is a fact now plainly established, that, hereafter, should seals ever be driven for tax and shipment of their skins again on these islands, *that no culling of the " drives " be Permitted*. The market for the skins will promptly adjust itself to the several ages, sizes and their value : the rookeries however, will not, cannot endure any further adjustment of that scale of sizes on the killing grounds, if it is resumed, then, the extermination of the fur-seal is right at hand, in so far as its life on the Pribylov Islands is concerned.

I searched for danger to these interests, on every side in 1872-74. I could detect no disease whatever, even of the most trifling character in the vast herds, and no legend even, much less statement, of any sickness among the seals was extant [1].

---

1. The thought of what a deadly epidemic would effect among these vast congregations of Pinnepedia was one that was constant in my mind when on the ground and among them. I have found in the British Annals (Fleming's) on page 17, an extract from the notes of Dr. Trail : " In 1833 I inquired for my old acquaintances, the seals of the Hole of Papa Westray, and was informed that about four years before they had totally deserted the island, and had only within the last few months begun to reappear. About fifty years ago multitudes of their carcasses were cast ashore in every

But the importance of making an accurate record of the areas and position of these great breeding grounds as I found them in 1872-74 was not lost on me; — it impressed me deeply: and these surveys were made then of each rookery. In order that the officers of the Goverment who came after me, charged with the care and protection of these interests, might understand the feasibility of annually surveying these breeding grounds without disturbing the animals in the least degree, I said then — " During the first week of inspection of some of those earliest arrivals, the 'seecatchie', which I have described, will frequently take to the water when approached; but these runaways quickly return. By the end of May, however, the same seals will hardly move to the right or left when you attempt to pass through them. Then two weeks before the females begin to come in, and quickly after their arrival, the organization of the fur-seal rookery is rendered entirely indifferent to man's presence on visits of quiet inspection, or to anything else, save their own kind, and so continues during the rest of the season. "

" I have called attention to the singular fact, that the breeding-seals upon the rookeries and hauling grounds are not affected by the smell of blood or carrion arising from the killing-fields or of the stench of blubber fires which burn in the native villages. This trait is conclusively illustrated by the attitude of these two rookeries near the village of St. Paul; for the breeding-ground on this spot, at the head of the lagoon, is not more than forty yards from the killing-ground to the eastward; being separated from those spots of slaughter, and the seventy or eighty thousand rotting carcases thereon, by a slough not more than ten yards wide. These seals can smell the blood and carcasses, upon this field, from the time they land in the spring until they leave in the autumn; while the general southerly winds waft to then the odour and sounds of the village of St. Paul, not over 200 rods south of them, and above them, in plain sight. All this has no effect upon the seals — they know that they

bay in the north of Scotland, Orkney, and Shetland, and numbers were found at sea in a sickly state. " This note of Trail is the only record which I can find of a fatal epidemic among the seals; it is not reasonable to suppose that the Pribylov rookeries have never suffered from distempers in the past, or are not to, in the future, simply because no occasion seems to have arisen during the comparatively brief period of their human domination.

are not disturbed— and the rookery, the natives declare, has been slightly but steadily increasing. Therefore, with regard to surveying and taking those boundaries assumed by the breeding-seals every year, at that point of high tide, and greatest expansion, which they assume between the 8th and 15th of July, it is an entirely practicable and simple task. You can go everywhere on the skirts of the rookeries almost within reaching distance, and they will greet you with quiet, inoffensive notice, and permit close, unbroken observation, when it is subdued and undemonstrative, paying very little attention to your approach."

"**Yearly changes in the Rookeries.** — I believe the agents of the government there, are going to notice, every year, little changes here and there in the area and distribution of the rookeries; for instance, one of these breeding-grounds will not be quite as large this year as it was last, while another one, opposite, will be found somewhat larger and expanded over the record which it made last season. In 1874, it was my pleasure and my profit to retraverse all these rookeries of St. George and St. Paul, with my field notes of 1872 in my hand, making, careful comparisons of their relative size as recorded then, and now. To show this peculiarity of enlarging a little here, and diminishing a little there, so characteristic of the breeding-grounds, I reproduce the following memoranda of 1874 : "

Northeast Point, July 18, 1874.

Contrast on St. Paul between 1872 and 1874. — Quite a strip of ground near Webster's house has been deserted this season; but a small expansion is observed on Hutchinson's hill. The rest of the ground is as mapped in 1872, with no noteworthy increase in any direction. The condition of the animals and their young, excellent; small irregularities in the massing of the families, due to the heavy rain this morning; sea-lions about the same; none, however, on the west of the point.

The aggregate of life on this great rookery is, therefore, about the same as in 1872; the "holluschickie" or killable seals, hauling as well and as numerously as before. The proportions of the different ages among them of two, three, and four-year-olds, pretty well represented.

Polavina, July 18, 1874.

Stands as it did in 1872; breeding-and hauling-grounds in excellent condition; the latter, on Polavina, are changing from the uplands down upon Polavina sand beach, trending for three miles toward Northeast point. The numbers of the " holluschickie " on this ground of Polavina where they have not been disturbed for some five years, to mention, in the way of taking, do not seem to be any greater than they are on the hauling grounds adjacent to Northeast point and the village, from which they are driven almost every day during this season of killing. I notice also this remarkable characteristic of the " holluschickie "; no matter how cleanly the natives may drive the seals off a given piece of haulingground this morning, if the weather is favourable, to-morrow will see it covered again just as thickly; and, thus they drive in this manner from Zoltoi sands almost every day during the killing-season, generally finding on the succeeding, morning more, or as many, seals as they drove off the previous dawn. This seems to indicate that the " holluschickie " recognize no particular point as favoured over another at the island when they land, which is evidently in obedience to a general desire of coming ashore at such a suitable place as promises no crowding and no fighting.

Lukannon and Keetavie, July 19, 1874.

Not materially changed in any respect from its condition at this time in 1872.

Garbotch, July 19, 1874.

Just the same. Condition excellent.

Reef, July 19, 1874.

A slight, contraction on the south sea-margin of this ground compensated for by fresh expansion under the bluffs on the northwest side, not noteworthy in either instance. Condition excellent.

Nah Speel, July 20, 1874.

A diminution of one-half at least. Very few here this year. It is no place for a rookery; not a pistol-shot from the natives houses, and all the natives children fooling over the bluffs.

Lagoon, July 20, 1874.

No noteworthy change; if any, a trifling increase. Condition good. Animals clean and lively.

Tolstoi, July 21, 1874.

No perceptible change in this rookery from its good shape of 1872. The condition excellent.

Zapadnie, July 22, 1874.

A remarkable extension or increase I note here, of 2,000 feet of shore line, with an average depth of 50 feet of breeding-ground, which has been built on to Upper Zapadnie, stretching out toward Tolstoi; the upper rookery proper has not altered its bearings or proportions; the sand beach belt between it and Lower Zapadnie is not occupied by breeding-seals; and a fair track for the " holluschickie ", 500 feet wide, left clear, over which they have travelled quite extensively this season, some 20,000 to 25,000 of them, at least, lying out around the old salt-house to-day. Lower Zapadnie has lost in a noteworthy degree about an average of 20 feet of its general depth, which, however, is more than compensated for by the swarming on the upper rookery. A small beginning had been made for a rookery on the shore just southwest from Zapadnie lake, in 1872, but this year it has been substantially abandoned.

Contrast on St. George beetwen 1873 and 1874. — An epitome of my notes for St. George, gives, as to this season of 1874, the following data for comparison with that of 1873 :

Zapadnie, July, 8, 1874.

This rookery shows a slight increase upon the figures of last year, about 5,000. Fine condition.

Starry Arteel, July 6, 1874.

No noteworthy change from last year.

North Rookery, July 6, 1874.

No essential change from last year. Condition very good.

Little Eastern, July 6, 1874.

A slight diminution of some 2,000 or so. Condition excellent.

Eastern Rookery, July 7, 1874.

A small increase over last year of about 3,000, only trifling, however; the aggregate seal-life here similar to that of last season, with the certainty of at least a small increase. The unusually early season, this year, brought the rookery " seecatchie " on the ground very much in advance of the general time ; they landed as early as the 10th of April, while the arrival of the cows was as late as usual, corresponding to my observations during the past seasons.

SECTION I.

The general conditions of the animals of all classes on St. George is most excellent, — they are sleek, fat, and free from any disease.

In this way it is plain that, practically, the exact condition of these animals can be noted every season; and should a diminution be observed, due to any cause, known or unknown, the killing can be promptly regulated, or stopped, to any required quota.

Had such supervision of these rookeries and hauling-grounds been maintained in this manner and method above pointed out as essential to a correct understanding of their condition, as it is, then in 1882 the killing would have been "promptly regulated, or stopped", as it should have been, and the erroneous idea of an increase of seals since my record af 1872-74 would not have been entertained for a moment, unless dishonestly stimulated.

The arrival of the Breeding seals, 1872-1890. In view of the changed condition of the rookeries of St. Paul and St. George last summer, I took great care in noting the daily arrival of the breeding-seals and methods constrasting these notes with those taken eighteen years earlier : I can truthfully assert that they come as they came in 1872, in the same time, same manner, and in every respect comport themselves as they did, save in two characteristics; the old bulls are disproportionately scant in number, exceedingly so, and the young male life fit to take their places, is virtually extinct. I reviewed in 1874 my studies of this topic in the following language :

" I found it an exceedingly difficult matter to satisfy myself as to a fair general average number of cows to each bull on the rookery; but, after protracted study, I think it will be nearly correct when I assign to each male a general ratio of from fifteen to twenty females at the stations nearest the water; and for those back in order from that line to the rear[1], from five to twelve; but there

---

1. At the rear of all these rookeries there is invariably a large number of able-bodied males which have come late, but wait patiently, yet in vain, for families; most of them having had to fight as desperately for the privilege of being there as any of their more fortunately-located neighbors, who are nearer the water, and in succession from there to where they are themselves; but the cows do not like to be in any outside position. They cannot be coaxed out where they are not in close company with their female mates and masses. They lie most quietly and contendedly in the largest harems, and cover the surface of the graind so thickly that there is hardly moving or turning room until the females cease to come from the sea. The inaction on the part of the males in the rear during the breeding-season only serves to qualify them to move into the places which are necessarily vacated by those males that are, in the mean-time, obliged to leave from virile exhaustion, or incipient wounds. All the sur-

are so many exceptional cases, so many instances where forty-five and fifty females are all under the charge of one male ; and then, again where there are two or three females only, that this question was and is not entirely satisfactory in its settlement to my mind. "

" Near Ketavie point, and just above it to the north, is an odd wash-out of the basalt by the surf, which has chiselled, as it were, from the foundation of the island, a lava table, with a single roadway or land passage to it. Upon the summit of this footstool I counted forty-five cows, all under the charge of an old veteran. He had them penned up on this table-rock by taking his stand at the gate, as it were, through which they passed up and passed down — a Turkish brute typified. "

Thus in 1872, when the rookeries were carefully observed with reference to this question, I found a general average of fifteen cows to each bull : (without taking into consideration the virgin females) : in 1890, a general average of forty to fifty cows to each old bull (no young ones about), is the result of careful investigation : and single harems in which I have counted over one hundred cows each in the flimsy charge of an old and weary " sea-catch "; such harems were not uncommon : this unnatural disproportion of the sexes on these breeding-grounds to-day renders the service there of reproduction quite lifeless — almost impotent, wholly so in a vast aggregate of cases.

Therefore, with full knowledge of this state of the Pribylov rookeries, I say that their condition will be still worse next year, will be no better for the next four or five years ; indeed it will not, cannot mend until fresh male blood matures and comes upon these fields : these animals must grow up from the pups of last year and those born this season ; the others are either dead or worthless, if alive, and it will take at least seven years for them to do so, and prove their power to check and hold these demoralized and diminished herds from their downward grade of the present hour.

The young male seals on the Islands must have a rest, a full and

plus able-bodied males, that have not been successful in effecting a landing on the rookeries, cannot at any one time during the season be seen here on this rear line. Only a portion of their number are in sight : the others are either loafing at sea adjacent, or are hauled out in morose squads between the rookeries on the beaches.

earnest opportunity to mature and go unshorn of their virility upon these dwindling rookeries : if they are not at once spared and substantially undisturbed for at least six or seven years to come with a prompt suppression of pelagic sealing on the other hand, then it is idle to talk of or plan for the restoration of the seal-life on our islands in Bering Sea, and its preservation.

Then, when it shall be proper and safe to again kill surplus male fur-seals for their skins as a matter of revenue and profit, an entirely new set of regulations as to the manner of driving and killing must be enforced ; and these regulations must be, will be, quite different from those which have been the law up there during the last 21 years; that experience however, so dearly bought since 1882, now gives us full knowledge of the disease, and understanding of its course.

In 1874, I made the following analysis of a detailed description of the seals on the breeding-grounds.

" **Review of statements concerning life in the Rookeries.** — To recapitulate and sum up the system and regular method of life and reproduction on these rookeries of St. Paul and St. George, as the seals seem to have arranged it, I shall say that : "

"*First*. The earliest bulls land in a negligent, indolent way, at the opening of the season. soon after the rocks at the water's edge are free from ice, frozen snow, etc. This is, as a rule, about the 1st to the 5th of every May. They land from the beginning to the end of the season in perfect confidence and without fear; they are very fat, and will weigh at an average 500 pounds each ; some stay at the water's edge, some go to the tier back of them again, and so on until the whole rookery is mapped out by them, weeks in advance of the arrival of the first female."

"*Second*. That by the 10th or 12th of June, all the male stations on the rookeries have been mapped out and fought for, and held in waiting by the " see-catchie ". These males are, as a rule, bulls rarely ever under six years of age; most of them over that age, being sometimes three, and occasionally doubtless four, times as old."

"*Third*. That the cows make their first appearance, as a class, on or after the 12th or 15th of June, in very small numbers; but rapidly after the 23d and 25th of this month, every year, they begin to flock up in such numbers as to fill the harems very perceptibly; and by the 8th or 10th of July, they have all come as a rule a few stragglers excepted. The average weight of the female now will not be much more that 80 to 90 pounds each."

"*Fourth.* That the breeding-season is at its height from the 10th to the 15th of July every year, and that it subsides entirely at the end of this month and early in August: also, that its method and system are confined entirely to the land, never effected in the sea."

"*Fifth.* That the females bear their first young, when they are three years old, and that the period of gestation is nearly twelve months, lacking a few days only of that lapse of time."

"*Sixth.* That the females bear a single pup each, and that this is born soon after landing; no exception to this rule has ever been witnessed or recorded."

"*Seventh.* That the " see-catchie " which have held the harems from the beginning to the end of the season, leave for the water in a desultory and straggling manner at its close, greatly emaciated and do not return, if they do at all, until six or seven weeks have elapsed, when the regular systematic distribution of the families over the rookeries is at an end for this season. A general medley of young males now are free, which come out of the water, and wander all over these rookeries, together with many old males, which have not been on seraglio duty and great numbers of females. An immense majority over all others present are pups, since only about 25 per cent. of the mother-seals are out of the water now at any one time."

"*Eight.* That the rookeries lose their compactness and definite boundries of true breeding limit and expansion by the 25th to the 28th of July every year; then, after this date, the pups begin to haul back, and to the right and left, in small squads at first, but as the season goes on, by the 18th of August, they depart without reference to their mothers; and when thus scattered, the males, females, and young swarm over more than three and four times the area occupied by them when breeding and born on the rookeries. The system of family arrangement and uniform compactness of the breeding classes breaks up at this date."

"*Ninth.* That by the 8th or 10th of August the pups born nearest the water first begin to learn to swin; and that by the 15th or

20th of September they are all familiar, more or less, with the exercise."

"*Tenth.* That by the middle of September the rookeries are entirely broken up; confused, straggling bands of females are seen among the bachelors, pups, and small squads of old males, crossing and recrossing the ground in an aimless, listless manner. The season now is over."

"*Eleventh.* That many of the seals do not leave these grounds of St. Paul and St. George before the end of December, and some remain even as late as the 11th of January; but that by the end of October and the beginning of November every year, all the fur-seals of mature age five and six years, and upward have left the islands. The younger males go with the others: many of the pups still range about the islands, but are not hauled to any great extent on the beaches or the flats. They seem to prefer the rocky shore-margin, and to lie as high up as they can get on such bluffy rookeries as Tolstoi and the Reef. By the end of this month, November, they are, as a rule, all gone."

In precisely the same time and the same manner as above, did the breeding seals arrive and behave on the Pribylov rookeries this season of 1890. I know this by daily verification up to the 11th of August: the seals are not " coming later ", nor are they changed in any respect except as to sadly diminished numbers, and the practical extinction of effective male life on the breeding grounds. Illustrative of the extreme regularity of the arrival of these animals every season throughout a period of 20 consecutive years I present the following statement of the annual dates of first arrivals of fur-seals for each year from 1870 to 1890 inclusive: these dates are taken from the Treasury Agent's journal, on the Seal islands.

First appearance of Bulls and Cows on the Rookeries of St. Paul and St. George Islands, Pribilof Group, Alaska.

	Island of St. Paul. Bulls.		Cows.	Island of St. George. Cows.			Bulls.
1870	May	2	June 4 to 6		1870	May	1st
1871	—	4	— 4 5		1871	—	4
1872	—	5	— 6-8	June 4-5	1872	—	6
1873	April	24	— 6-7	— 6-7	1873	—	12
1874	—	23	— 4-6	— 6-8	1874	April	30
1875	—	28	— 4-8	— 3-8	1875	May	5

THE " ROOKERIES ".

ISLAND OF ST. PAUL.			ISLAND OF ST. GEORGE.		
	Bulls.	Cows.	Cows.		Bulls.
1876	May 3	June 6-8	June 4-6	1876	April 28
1877	— 17	— 4-6	— 4-6	1877	May 17
1878	— 6	— 6-8	— 4-6	1878	— 9
1879	April 29	— 4-6	— 4-6	1879	— 10
1880	— 30	— 6-8	— 3-6	1880	— 11
1881	May 5	— 2-6	— 3-6	1881	— 6
1882	April 26	— 4-8	— 3-7	1882	— 6
1883	May 6	— 5-6	— 4-6	1883	— 7
1884	April 30	— 4-8	— 4-8	1884	— 3
1885	— 27	— 6-8	— 4-6	1885	April 29
1886	— 16	— 4-6	— 3-4	1886	May 1
1887	May 1	— 3-7	— 4-6	1887	— 7
1888	— 1	— 4-6	— 3-6	1888	— 8
1889	— 3	— 4-6	— 4-6	1889	— 5
1890	April 28	— 6-8	— 4-6	1890	— 26

The first " drives " for food each year on St. Paul island have been made with great regularity between the 15th and 21st of May annually throughout the time specified above : and also on St. George island. The bulls all arrived prior to, and by the 1st of June : the cows all arrived prior to and by the 20th of July of every year.

As to the cause for this decrease on the Pribilov Rookeries. — This point of enquiry does not require elaboration : — the reason is plain; the cause fairly asserts itself : overdriving since 1882 on land, together with the bullet and buck-shot of the pelagic scaler since 1886 : the overdriving has chiefly robbed the rookeries of that supply of fresh male life absolutely required every season, and the seal pirate has destroyed the females with unborn and born young[1]. It is needless to speculate as to other causes,

---

[1]. " Out of 77 fur seal skins seized on the " Mattie T. Dyer " (schooner) only 6 of them came from animals without pups, (i. e. 71 were pregnant females.) They (the scalers) had little black pup skins fresh cut out from the womb — womb moist — 17 fresh female fur seal skins, and every one of these bodies had a pup in them. These men declared that they got only 1 out of every 5 that they shot, that is for the 7 hit, they only got 1 of them: the number of shots fired they did not count : but of the 5 seals that they undertook to get that they hit they usually got but 1 of them ".

U. S. COLLECTOR, EMMONS,

Oonalashka, Augt. 14, 1890.

In Section VIII of this report will be found the best arrangement of notes bearing upon this subject which I have been able to make

for the two cited above are full and ample reasons for the existing diminution, were they not so patent, we might speculate as I did in 1872-'74 in the following tone.

"**Thoughts upon the possible movements of the fur seals in the future.** — As these animals live and breed upon the Pribylov islands, the foregoing studies of their habit declare certain natural conditions of landing-ground and climate to be necessary for their existence and perpetuation. From my surveys made upon the islands to the north, St. Matthew and St. Lawrence, together with the scientific and corroborating testimony of those who have visited all of the mainland coast of Alaska, and the islands contiguous, including the peninsula and the great Aleutian archipelago, I have no hesitation in stating that the fur-seal cannot breed, or rest for that matter, on any other land than that now resorted to, which lies within our boundary lines; the natural obstacles are insuperable."

"Therefore, so far as our possessions extend, we have, in the Pribylov group, the only eligible land to which fur-seal can repair for breeding; and on which at St. Paul Island alone, there is still room enough of unoccupied rookery-ground for the accommodation of twice as many seals as we find there to-day. But we must not forget a very important prospect; for we know that to the westward, only 700 miles, and within the jurisdiction of Russia, are two other seal-islands — one very large, on which the fur-seal regularly breeds also; and though from the meagre testimony in my possession, compared with St. Paul, the fur-seal life upon them is small, still, if that land within the pale of the czar's dominion be as suitable for the reception of the rookeries as is that of St. Paul, then what guarantee have we that the seal-life on Copper and Bering islands, at some future time, may not be greatly augmented by a corresponding diminution of our own, with no other than natural causes operating? Certainly, if the ground on either Bering or Copper island, in the Commander group, is as well suited for the wants of the breeding fur-seal as is that exhibited by the Pribylov islands, then I say confidently that we may at any time note a diminution here and find a corresponding augmentation there, for I have clearly shown, in my chapter on the habits of these animals, that they are not so particularly attached to the respective places of their birth, but that they rather land with an instinctive appreciation of the fitness of that ground as a whole. "

"**Need of more definite knowledge concerning the Russian seal-Islands.** — If we, however, possess all the best suited ground, then we can count upon retaining the seal-life as we now have it by a vast majority, and, in no other way; for it is not unlikely that some season may occur when an immense number of the fur-seals, which have lived during the last four or five years on the Pribylov islands, should be deflected from their usual feeding-range at sea by the shifting of schools of fish, and other abnormal causes, which would bring them around quite close to the Asiatic seal-grounds, in the spring; and the scent from those rookeries would act as a powerful stimulant and attraction for them to land there, where the conditions for their breeding may be just as favorable as they desire. Such being the case, this diminution, therefore, which we would notice on the Pribylov group, might be the great, increase observed at the Commander islands, and not due to any mismanagement on the part of the men in charge of these interests. Thus, it appears to me necessary that definite knowledge concerning the Commander islands and the Kuriles should be gathered. "

" If we find, however, that the character of this Russian seal land is restricted to narrow beach-margins, under bluffs, as at St. George, then we shall know that a great body of seals will never attempt to land there when they could not do so without suffering, and in violation of their laws, during the breeding-season. Therefore, with this correct understanding to start on, we can then feel alarmed with good reason, should we ever observe any diminution, to a noteworthy degree, on our seal-islands of Bering sea. "

" **Possible Deflection of Seals in Feeding.** — I do not call attention to this subject with the slightest idea in my mind, as I write, of any such contingency arising, even for an indefinite time to come; but still I am sensible of the fact that it is possible for it to occur any season. But the seals undoubtedly feed on their pelagic fields in systematic routine of travel, from the time they leave the Pribilov islands until that of their return; therefore, in all probability, unless the fish upon which they are nourished suddenly become scarce in our waters and soundings, the seals will not change their base, as matters now progress; but it is possible for the finny shoals and schools to be so deflected from their migration to and from their spawning beds, as to carry this seal-life with it, as I have hinted above. Thus it cannot be superfluous to call up this question, so that it shall be prominent in discussion, and suggestion for future thought. "

" **Need of careful yearly examination.** — In the meantime the movements of the seals upon the great breeding-rookeries of St. Paul and those of St. George should be faithfully noted and recorded every year; and as time goes on this record will place the topic of their increase or diminution beyond all theory or cavil. "

Since writing and publishing the above, I have learned that the Russian seal islands have been steadily increasing their rookery areas from 1870 up to 1879-80; and since that time, the yield of the hauling grounds over there was trebled in 1889 over the catch of 1876 : whether or no these Slavonian rookeries will stand this driving so as to annually get 62,000 young males hereafter, as was done last year (1889) or fail to do so in a few years to come, I can, at this distance, only conjecture. But our seals have not gone over there — they have been destroyed in plain view on this side.

The following salient points of change can be clearly stated in so far as the Pribylow Rookeries exist his season of 1890 accompanied with their condition of 1872.

STATUS OF 1872.	STATUS OF 1890.
1. On the rookery ground the BULLS were all by June 1st.	1. On the rookery ground the BULLS were all by June 1st.
2. Located on this ground then no further apart than 6 to 10 feet, and	2. Located on this ground, now from 15 to 150 feet apart and are inert and
3. were very active, incessantly fighting with one another and with the	3. somnolent : I have not seen a single fight between the bulls yet.
4. thousands upon tens of thousands of "1/2 bulls" or polseacatchie, which were then trying to land upon the breeding belt of sea-margin, provoking and sustaining a constant fight	4. Not a single " 1/2 bull " or polseacatchie attempting to land and serve the cows — not a single one have I been able to observe — in fact there are none left : those that exist have been ruined

STATUS OF 1872	STATUS OF 1890
and turmoil there, but being almost invariably whipped off by the old bulls, stationed there.	as breeders from the effects of driving: and several thousand of these broken spirited bulls, old and young now loafing on the outskirts of these rookeries, and hauling out with the small holluschickie on the sand and rock margins
5. COWS began to arrive on the breeding grounds by 4th to 6th of June : and all arrived in good form by July and were	5. COWS began to arrive on the breeding grounds by 4th to 6th of June, all arrived as a rule by July 10, and were
6. located on the breeding-ground in compact solid masses uniformly distributed over a given area of ground no matter how large or how small.	6. located on the breeding grounds in scattered harems, solidly here, one or two harems, then a dozen or so families scattered over twice and thrice as much ground as they should occupy if massed as in 1872-74. The scanty supply of, and wide stations and feebleness of the bulls is undoubtedly the reason for this striking change in their distribution as they ordered it in 1872-74.
7. A general average of 15 cows to 1 bull was the best understanding : once in a while a peculiar configuration of the breeding ground enabled one bull the chance to pen up 35 or 45 cows, but it was seldom witnessed.	7. A general average of 45 or 50 cows to 1 bull is the best estimate that can be made to-day : there are so many harems of 60 and 75 cows in charge of one bull to each, and frequently single harems of 108 to 120: cows that, it makes the general average of 45 or 50 very conservative.
8. Cows all promptly and efficiently served when in heat : never witnessed a failure.	8. Cows, many of them not served even when persistly solicitous early in the season. Vigorous willing service seems to be the exception not the rule. Bulls not one tenth as numerous as in 1872, and only one third of the cows here as a rule; and no new young male blood mature enough to take its station on these rookeries.

In regard to the probable number of breeding bulls on each rookery, in 1872-'74, I made the following note and tabulation : " St. George Island. North Rookery : July 12 1873. I think now that this is a safe and equitable basis for beginning my calculation : ... Every 100 feet of sea margin will have 10 bulls on it : and for every 100 feet of depth from the margin, we will have a bull for every 7 feet of that depth : ... they fight so desperately on the sea margin, that the average is widest there uniformly : but it will average up right the 7 × 10 very honestly, " ...

On the Rookeries : St Paul Island.

BASIS FOR ESTIMATION OF BULLS : IN 1872-74
WITH AN AVERAGE OF 15 COWS, 15 PUPS, AND 5 V. F. TO EACH BULL.

" Reef " has 4,016 ft. sea margin with 1 Bull on every 10 ft. sea margin 150 ft. average depth and 1 Bull for every 7 ft. average depth, gives 402 bulls × 21 1/2 bulls, or about 8,642 bulls.

On this basis and method of calculation, therefore :

" Garbotch " has about..............	5,207 bulls.	
" Lagoon " —	580	—
" Lukannon " —	4,880	—
" Keetavie " —	4,730	—
" Tolstoi " —	6,450	—
" Zapadnie " has about. { Upper wing. 2,814 } { Lower — . 9,700 }	12,514	—
" Polavina " has about...............	8,600	—
" Novashoshnah " has about...........	34,006	—
TOTAL BULLS FOR ST. PAUL.	85,609 bulls.	

On the Rookeries : St George Island.

" Zapadnie " has about.............	599 bulls.	
" Starry Arteel " has about...........	975	—
" North " —	2,302	—
" Little Eastern " —	112	—
" Great Eastern " —	714	—
TOTAL BULLS FOR ST. GEORGE.	4,702 bulls.	

Or, in round numbers, a grand total of 90,000 breeding bulls on the rookeries of both islands.

The wide and scanty hauling of the bulls on these breeding grounds for this season of 1890, together with the strange massing of immense harems around single bulls, while the others immediately around have no part in the service, render such a tabulation on the basis of 1872-'74 as above given, quite out of the question, as a measure of just contrast, I therefore will not attempt it, since the comparison cannot be well made in this respect.

In concluding my observations under this head, it is perhaps not superfluous to anticipate and reply to the following generalizations which will naturally arise to the mind of the general reader.

It seems from the foregoing surveys that at the close of the season of 1890, there are still existing upon the Pribylov rookeries 959,000 seals, old and young and pups of this year's birth, or about one third of the whole number of breeding seals and young recorded as being there in-74, how then can they be so near the danger of extermination, though they are in danger of it?

The explanation is as follows :

1. There is but one breeding bull now upon the rookery ground where there were fifteen in 1872 : and the bulls of to-day are nearly all old and many positively impotent.

2. This decrease of virile male life on the breeding grounds causes the normal ratio of 15 or 20 females to a male as in 1872-74 now to reach the unnatural ratio of 50 to even 100 females to an old and enfeebled male.

3. There is no appreciable number of young males left alive to-day on these " hauling " or non-breeding grounds to take their places on the breeding grounds, which are old enough for that purpose, or will be old enough if not disturbed by man, even if left alone for the next five years.

4. Meanwhile the natural enemies of the fur-seal are just as numerous in the sea and ocean as they ever were — the killer-whale and the shark are feeding upon them just as they did in 1872-74.

5. Therefore, we have destroyed by land and by sea the equilibrium which nature had established in 1868 on these rookeries, and we must now restore it, or no other result can follow save that of swift extermination.

6. That condition of 1872, being restored, then that surplus male life can be taken again under better regulations than those of 1870, and the pelagic sealing can be restricted to proper limits, so as to enable the fur-markets of the world to have a regular supply for all time to come.

SECTION II

THE " HAULING-GROUNDS " OF THE FUR-SEAL
ON THE PRIBILOV ISLANDS OF ALASKA;
THEIR AREA,
POSITION AND CONDITION IN 1872-74, 1890

SECTION II

THE " HAULING-GROUNDS " OF THE FUR-SEAL ON THE PRIBILOV ISLANDS OF ALASKA, THEIR AREA, POSITION AND CONDITION IN 1872-74, 1890

In 1872-74, these fields of seal life on the Pribylov Islands were in themselves quite as impressive and interesting as the great rookeries then were; to-day, (1890) it is a difficult matter to say where a single well defined hauling ground on either island exists of more than the least extent in superficial area; these broad acres upon which not even a vestige of vegetable growth could live, owing to the tireless pattering of fur-seal flippers, — those clean swept fields are now mossy, grass-grown and flecked with indigeneous flowering plants, clear down to the water's edge or to the very margins of the rookery grounds, where a scanty remnant of that swarming host of surplus male seal-life which so astonished me in 1872, now hauls; it hauls there now for quiet and protection instinctively to its last stand for self-preservation left for it on these islands, during the past six years.

In 1872 there was a marked distinction between the " rookeries "[1] or breeding-grounds, and the " ezvairie "[2] or hauling-grounds; not in name, not on paper as it literally is to-day, but in reality then of the testimony of those grounds and life thereon

1. " Rookery ", an old sealer's term derived from the swarming noisy rools of the rook-bird in England.
2. " Ezvairie ", a Russian equivalent of " hauling up "; means literally a " coming out ", or " coming up ". The natives call the rookeries " laying out " places or " laasbustchie " and the hauling grounds, " ezvairie ".

itself. I gave the following description of the Pribylov hauling-grounds and of that life characteristic of them in 1874.

"**The hauling-grounds and their occupants.** — I now call the attention of the reader to another very remarkable feature in the economy of the seal-life on these islands. The great herds of ' holluschickie ',¹ numbering about one-third perhaps, of the whole aggregate of near 5,000,000 seals known to the Pribylov group, are never allowed by the ' see-catchie ', under the pain of frightful mutilation or death, to put their flippers on or near the rookeries."

" By reference to my map, it will be observed that I have located a large extent of ground, markedly so on St. Paul, as that occupied by the seals' ' hauling-grounds '; this area, in fact, represents those portions of the island upon which the ' holluschickie' roam in their heavy squadrons, wearing off and polishing the surface of the soil, stripping every foot, which is indicated on the chart as such, of its vegetation and mosses, leaving the margin as sharply defined on the bluffy uplands and sandy flats as it is on the map itself."

"The reason that so much more land is covered by the 'holluschickie' than by the breeding seals, ten times as much at least, is due to the fact, that though not as numerous, perhaps, as the breeding-seals, they are tied down to nothing so to speak are, wholly irresponsible, and roam hither and thither as caprice and the weather may dictate. Thus they wear off and rub down a much larger area than the rookery-seals occupy; wandering aimlessly, and going back, in some instances, notably at English Bay, from one-half to a whole mile inland, not travelling in desultory files along winding, straggling paths, but sweeping in solid platoons, they obliterate every spear of grass and rub down nearly every hummock in their way."

Definition of ' Holluschickie '. — All the male seals, from six years of age, are compelled to herd apart by themselves and away from the breeding-grounds, in many cases far away; the large hauling-grounds at South-west Point being about two miles from the nearest rookery. This class of seals is termed ' hollus-

---

1. The Russian term " hollusckickie " or " bachelors " is very appropriate, and is usually employed.

chickie' or thus 'bachelor' seals by the people, a most fitting and expressive appellation.

The seals of this great subdivision are those with which the natives on the Pribylov group are the most familliar; naturally and especially so, since they are the only ones, with the exception of a few thousand pups and occasionally an old bull or two, taken late in the fall for food and skins, which are driven up to the killing-grounds at the village for slaughter. The reasons for this exclusive attention to the 'bachelors' are most cogent, and will be given hereafter when the 'business' is discussed.

"**Locating the hauling-grounds : Paths through the Rookeries.** — Since the 'holluschickie' are not permitted by their own kind to land on the rookeries, and stop there, they have the choice of two methods of locating, one of which allows them to rest in the rear of the rookeries, and the other on the free beaches. The most notable illustration of the former can be witnessed on Reef Point, where a pathway is left for their ingress and egress through a rookery, a path by common consent, as it were, between the harems. On these trails of passage they come and go in steady files all day and all night during the season, unmolested by the jealous bulls which guard the seraglios on either side as they travel; all peace and comfort to the young seal if he minds his business and keeps straight on up or down, without stopping to nose about right or left; all woe and desolation to him, however, if he does not, for in that event he will be literally torn in bloody griping, from limb, by the vigilant old 'see-catchie'."

"Since the two and three-year old 'holluschickie' come up in small squads with the first bulls in the spring, or a few days later, such common highways as those between the rookery-ground and the sea are travelled over before the arrival of the cows, and get well defined. A passage for the 'bachelors', which I took much pleasure in observing day after at Polavina, another at Tolstoi, and two on the Reef, in 1872, were entirely closed up by the 'see-catchie' and obliterated, when I again searched for them in 1874. Similar passages existed, however, on several of the large rookeries of St. Paul; one of these at Tolstoi exhibits this feature very finely, for here the hauling-ground extends around from English Bay, and lies up back of the Tolstoi rookery, over a flat and rolling summit from 100 to 120 feet above the sea-level. The young males, and yearlings of both sexes, come through and between the harems, in the height of the breeding-season, on two of these narrow pathways, and before reaching the ground above, are obliged to climb up an almost abrupt bluff, which they do by following and struggling in the water-runs and washes that are worn into its face. As this is a large hauling-ground, on which, every favorable day during the season, fifteen or twenty thousand commonly rest, the sight of skilful seal-climbing can be witnessed here at any time during that period; and the sight of such climbing as this of Tolstoi is exceedingly novel and interesting. Why, verily, they ascend over and upon places where an ordinary man might, at first sight, with great positiveness say that it was utterly impossible for him to climb. "

"Hauling-grounds on the beaches. — The other method of coming ashore, however, is the one most followed and favored. In this case they avoid the rookeries altogether, and repair to the unoccupied beaches between them, and then extend themselves out all the way back from the sea, as far from the water, in some cases, as a quarter and even half of a mile. I stood on the Tolstoi sand-dunes one afternoon, toward the middle of July, and had under my eyes, in a straightforward sweep from my feet to Zapadnie, a million and a half of seals spread out on those hauling-grounds. Of these, I estimated that fully one-half, at that time, were pups, yearlings, and ' holluschickie '. The rookeries across the bay, though plainly in sight, were so crowded, that they looked exactly as I have seen surfaces appear upon which bees had swarmed in obedience to that din and racket made by the watchful apiarian, when he desires to hive the restless honey-makers. "

" The great majority of yearlings and ' holluschickie ' are annually hauled out and packed thickly over the sand-beach and upland hauling-grounds, which lay between the rookeries on St. Paul Island. At St. George there is nothing of this extensive display to be seen, for there is only a tithe of the seal-life occupying St. Paul, and no opportunity whatever is afforded for an amphibious parade. "

"Gentleness of the seals. — Descend with me from this sand-dune elevation of Tolstoi, and walk into that drove of ' holluschickie' below us; we can do it; you do not notice much confusion or dismay as we go in among them; they simply open out before us and close in behind our tracks, stirring, crowding to the right and left as we go, twelve or twenty feet away from us on each side. Look at this small flock of yearlings, some one, others two, and even three years old, which are coughing and spitting around us now, staring up at our faces in amazement as we walk ahead; they struggle a few rods out of our reach, and then come together again behind us, showing no further sign of notice of ourselves. You could not walk into a drove of hogs, at Chicago, without exciting as much confusion and arousing an infinitely more disagreeable tumult; and as for sheep on the plains, they would stampede far quicker. Wild animals indeed; you can now readily understand how easy it is for two or three men, early in the morning, to come where we are, turn aside from this vast herd in front of and around us two or three thousand of the best examples, and drive them back, up, and over to the village. That is the way they get the seals; there is not any ' hunting ' or ' chasing ' or ' capturing ' of fur-seals on these islands. "

" **Holluschickie** ' **do not fast.** — While the young male seals undoubtedly have the power of going for lengthy intervals without food, they, like the female seals on the breeding-grounds, certainly do not maintain any long fasting periods on land; their coming and going from the shore is frequent and irregular, largely influenced, by the exact condition of the weather from day to day; for instance, three or four thick, foggy days seem to call them out from the water by hundreds of thousands upon the different hauling-grounds, (which the reader observes recorded on my map). In some cases, I have seen them lie there so close together that scarcely a foot of ground, over whole acres, is bare enough to be seen; then a clear and warmer day follows, and this seal-covered ground, before so thickly packed with animal life, will soon be almost deserted : comparatively so at least, to be filled up immediately as before, when favorable weather shall again recur. They must frequently eat when here, because the first yearlings and ' holluschickie ' that appear in the spring are no fatter, sleeker, or livelier than they are at the close of the season ; in other words, their condition, physically, seems to be the same from the beginning to the end of their appearance here during the summer and fall. It is quite different, however, with the ' see-catch '; we know how and where it spends two to three months, because we find it on the grounds at all times, day or night, during that period.

Sports and pastimes of the young ' bachelor'. — A small flock of the young seals, one to three years old, generally, will often stray from these hauling-ground margins, up and beyond, over the fresh mosses and grasses, and there sport and play one with another, just as little puppy-dogs do; and when weary of this gamboling a general disposition to sleep is suddenly manifested, and they stretch themselves out, and curl up in all the positions and all the postures that their flexible spines and ball-and-socket joints will permit. They seem to revel in the unwonted vegetation, and to be delighted with their own efforts in rolling down and crushing the tall stalks of the grasses and umbelliferous plants; one will lie upon its back, hold up its hind-flippers, and lazily wave them about, while it scratches, or rather rubs, its ribs with the fore-hands alternately, the eyes being tightly closed during the whole performance; the sensation is evidently so luxurious that it does not wish to have any side-issue draw off its blissful self-attention. Another, curled up like a cat on a rug, draws its breath, as indicated by the heaving of its flanks, quickly but regularly, as though in heavy sleep; another will lie flat upon its stomach, its hind-flippers covered and concealed, while it tightly folds its fore-feet back against its sides just as a fish carries its pectoral fins, and so on to no end of variety, according to the ground and the fancy of the animals. "

" These ' bachelor ' seals are, I am sure, without exception, the most restless animals in the whole brute creation, which can boast of a high organization. They frolic and lope about over the grounds for hours, without a moment's cessation, and their sleep, after this, is exceedingly short, and it is ever accompanied with nervous twitchings and uneasy muscular movements; they seem to be fairly brimful and overrunning with spontaneitys to be surcharged with fervid, electric life. "

"Another marked feature which I have observed among the multitudes of " holluschickie ", which have come under my personal observation and auditory, and one very characteristic of this class, is, that nothing like ill-humor appears in all of their playing together; they never growl or bite or show even the slightest angry feeling, but are invariably as happy, one with another, as can be imagined. This is a very singular trait; they lose it, however, with astonishing rapidity, when their ambition and strength develops and carries them, in due course of time, to the rookery. "

" The pups and yearlings have an especial fondness for sporting on the rocks which are just at the water's level and awash, so as to be covered and uncovered as the surf rolls in. On the bare summit of these wave-worn spots, they will struggle and clamber in groups of a dozen or two at a time throughout the whole day, in endeavoring to push off that one of their number which has just been fortunate enough to secure a landing; the successor has, however, but a brief moment of exultation in victory, for the next roller that comes booming in, together with the pressure by its friends, turns the table, and the game is repeated, with another seal on top. Sometimes, as well as I could see, the same squad of ' holluschickie ' played for a whole day and night, without a moment's cessation, around such a rock as this, off ' Nah Speel ' rookery; but in this observation I may be mistaken, because the seals cannot be told apart. "

" **Seals among the Breakers.** — The graceful unconcern with which the fur-seal sports safely in, among, and under booming breakers, during the prevalence of the numerous heavy gales at the islands, has afforded me many consecutive hours of spell-bound attention to them, absorbed in watching their adroit evolutions within the foaming surf, that seemingly, every moment, would, in its fierce convulsions, dash these hardy swimmers, stunned and lifeless, against the iron-bound foundations of the shore, which alone checked the furious rush of the waves. Not at all. Through the wildest and most ungovernable mood of the roaring tempest and storm-tossed waters attending its transit, I never failed, on creeping out, ant peering over the bluffs, in such weather, to see squads of these perfect watermen, the most expert of all amphibians, gamboling in the seething, creamy wake of mighty rollers, which constantly broke in thunder tones over their alert, dodging heads. The swift succeeding seas seemed, every instant, to poise the seals at the very verge of death. Yet the *Callorhinus*, exulting in his skill and strength, bade defiance to their wrath, and continued his diversions.

"**Swimming feats of the 'Bachelors'**. — The 'holluschickie' are the champion swimmers of all the seal-tribe; at least, when in the water around the islands, they do nearly every fancy tumble and turn that can be executed. The grave old males and their matronly companions seldom indulge in any extravagant display, as do these youngsters, jumping out of the water like so many dolphins describing beautiful elliptic curves sheer above its surface, rising three and even four feet from the sea, with the back slightly arched, the fore-flippers folded tightly against the sides, and the hinder ones extended and pressed together straight out behind, plumping in head first, to re-appear in the same manner, after an interval of a few seconds of submarine swimming, like the flight of a bird, on their course. Sea-lions and hair-seals never jump in this manner."

All classes will invariably make these dolphin-jumps, when they are surprised or are driven into the water, curiously turning their heads while sailing in the air, between the 'rises' and 'plumps', to take a look at the cause of their disturbance. They all swim rapidly, with the exception of the pups, and may be said to dart under the water with the velocity of a bird on the wing; as they swim they are invariably submerged, running along horizontally about two or three feet below the surface, guiding their course with the hind-flippers as by an oar, and propelling themselves solely by the fore-feet, rising to breathe at intervals which are either very frequent or else so wide apart that it is impossible to see the speeding animal when he rises a second time."

"How long they can remain under water without taking a fresh breath, is a problem which I had not the heart to solve, by instituting a series of experiments at the island; but I am inclined to think, that if the truth were known in regard to their ability of going without rising to breathe, it would be considered astounding. On this point, however, I have no data worth discussing, but will say that, in all their swimming which I have had a chance to study, as they passed under the water, mirrored to my eyes from the bluff above by the whitish-colored rocks below the rookery waters, at Great Eastern rookery, I have not been able to satisfy myself how they used their long, flexible hind-feet, other than as steering media. If these posterior members have any perceptible motion, it is so rapid that my eye is not quick enough to catch it; but the fore-flippers, however, can be most distinctly seen, as they work in feathering forward and sweeping flatly back, opposed to the water, with great rapidity and energy. They are evidently the sole propulsive power of the fur-seal in the water, as they are its main fulcrum and lever combined, for progression on land. I regret that the shy nature of the hair-seal never allowed me to study its swimming motions, but is seems to be a general point of agreement among authorities on the *Phocide*, that all motion in water by them arises from that power which they exert and apply with the hind-feet. So far as my observations on the hair-seal go, I am inclined to agree with this opinion. "

" All their movements in water, whether they are traveling to some objective point or are in sport, are quick and joyous; and nothing is more suggestive of intense satisfaction and pure physical comfort, than is that spectacle which we can see every August, a short distance out at sea from any rookery, where thousands of old males and females are idly rolling over in the billows side by side, rubbing and scratching with their fore-and hind-flippers which are here and the there stuck up out of the water by their owners like the lateen-sails of the Mediterranean feluccas, or, when the hind-flippers are presented, like a ' cat-o'-nine tails '. They sleep in the water a great deal, too, more than is generally supposed, showing that they do not come on land to rest; very clearly not. "

The foregoing description of the hauling-grounds and their occupants, or the killable seals, as they were in 1872-'74 on the Seal Islands of Alaska was very soberly drawn from the bright view which they then presented; but, moderate as the simple truth of it is, it reads like a romance when contrasted with the condition of these fields and life as it is to-day.

While the diminution of the area and the life on the breeding-grounds of St. Paul is such as to show a trifle more than one-third of its extent and volume to-day compared with what existed in 1872, yet the discrepancy betwen the area of the hauling-grounds on this island and number of occupants as presented in 1872, and again in 1890 is something positively startling, — is almost unreal — but the truth easily asserts its strange reality on the accompanying map of these hauling grounds of St. Paul Island : the tint of 1872 seems an almost fabulous expanse when contrasted with the microscopic shade of 1890.

The loss is much greater here than on the rookeries for the following reasons :

Ever since 1879-'82 the surplus young male seal life has been sensibly feeling the pressure of the overland death drive, and the club; harder and harder became this wretched driving to get the quota in 1883-'84; finally when 1886 arrived, every nook and cranny on these islands that had hitherto been visited by the " holluschickie " in peace was now daily searched out, — close up back of, and against the breeding rookeries, under every cliff wall by the sea, over to South-West Point, and to Otter Island, and even the little islet, Seevitchik Kamman, under the lee of the Reef was regularly hunted out.

Every three-year old, every four-year old and every well-grown two-year old male seal has been annually taken here during the last two years within a day or two at the latest after it showed up on the beaches, and in the rear of rookeries, prior to the 26th-31st, July.

In 1872 the killable seals were permitted to " haul up " in every sense of the word; they hauled out far inland from the sea; in 1890, the few killable seals that appeared never had time in which to " haul up " over the land, — they simply landed, and at the moment of landing were marked and hustled into a drive; up to the 20th of July last summer, from the day of their first general hauling as a body in June, this class of seals never had an opportunity to get wonted or accustomed to the land, — never were permitted to rest long enough to do so after landing.

Order and time of the hauling of the " holluschickie ". — A careful comparison day by day of the arrival of the killable seals last season (1890) with my field notes of 1872-'74, declares that the " holluschickie " are hauling to-day in the same time and order of arrival from the beginning of the season in May until its close by the end of July; but their vastly reduced numbers, and the rigorous driving to which this remnant is subjected have caused them to abandon the hauling-grounds of 1872-'74 entirely, with the solitary exception of that sandbeach under Middle Hill, English Bay, on St. Paul; they now haul close into the rear of the breeding seals on the several rookery-grounds of both islands, — hauling there, as I have said before, for shelter and protection.

When the old bulls first appear for the season at the rookery-grounds, early in May of every year, as a rule, only a few squads of " holluschickie " accompany them; while these early bulls land promptly by the 4th to 6th of that month and all of them arrive and land by the close of it, yet the " holluschickie " do not come ashore until the 15th or 20th of May as a rule; sometimes a few days earlier, and sometimes a few days later; only a few hundred of these young males land at any one place or time as early as the 15th of May.

But after this date, rapidly after the 25th to 31st, May, the "holluschickie" of the largest growth, i. e., the 5-, 4-, 3-, and many 2-year old males begin to haul. By the 14th-20th June, they then appear in their finest form and number for the season, being joined now by the great bulk of the 2-year olds, and quite a number of yearling males. By the 10th of July their numbers are beginning to largely increase owing to the influx now at this time of that great body of the last year's pups or yearlings; by the 20th July, the yearlings have put in their appearance for the season in full force. Very few yearling females make their appearance until the 15th of July, but by the 20th they literally swarmed out, in 1872-'74, and mixed up completely with the young and older males and females as the rookeries relax their discipline and " pod " or scatter out.

By the 20th July annually, therefore, the seals of all ages have arrived, that are to arrive; it was so in 1872; it was so last season, 1890.

If it were true, as the idea of some sealers would have it, that the young male seals all haul on the ground contiguous to the rookery where they were born, it would be very puzzling to account for several marked exceptions to that rule : but it is not true : young male seals born upon St. Paul Island have been repeatedly marked as they left for the season, and these marked pups have been taken up in St. George drives as yearlings, 2-year olds, and even 4-year-olds during the following season or seasons.

This experiment was repeatedly made by the Russians[1], and has been made once by us.

I now know that the "holluschickie" haul on either St. George or St. Paul island indifferently as they go and come throughout the sealing season; the proportion of St. Paul bred "holluschickie" must be quite large on St. George, since that island lays directly in the path of the incoming and outgoing seals, as they first arrive from the south at the opening of the season, and thereafter sally

---

[1]. It is entertaining to note in this connection that the Russians themselves, with the object of testing this mooted query, during the later years of their possession of the islands, drove up a number of young males from Lukannon, cut off their ears, and turned them out to sea again. The following season, when the droves came in from the "hauling-grounds" to the slaughtering-fields quite a number of those cropped seals were in the drives, but instead of being found all at one place — the place from whence they were driven the year before — there were scattered examples of croppies from every point on the island. The same experiment was again made by our people in 1870 (the natives having told them of this prior undertaking), and they went also to Lukannon, drove up 100 young males, cut off their left ears, and set them free in turn. Of this number, during the summer of 1872, when I was there, the natives found in their driving of 75,000 seals from the different hauling-grounds of St. Paul up to the village killing-grounds, two on Novastoshnah rookery, 10 miles north of Lukannon, and two or three from English Bay and Tolstoi rookeries, 6 miles west by water; one or two were taken on St. George Island, 36 miles to the south-east, and not one from Lukannon was found among those that were driven from there; probably, had all the young males on the two islands this season been examined, the rest of the croppies that had returned from the perils of the deep, whence they sojourned during the winter, would have been distributed quite equally about the Pribilof hauling-grounds. Although the natives say that they think the cutting off of the animal's ear gives the water such access to its head as to cause its death, yet I noticed that those examples which we had recognized by this auricular mutilation, were normally fat and well developed. Their theory does not appeal to my belief, and it certainly requires confirmation.

These experiments would tend to prove very cogently and conclusively, that when the seals approach the islands in the spring, they have nothing in their minds but a general instinctive appreciation of the fitness of the land, as a whole; and no special fondness or determination to select any one particular spot, not even the place of their birth. A study of my map of the distribution of the seal-life on St. Paul, clearly indicates that the landing of the seals on the respective rookeries is influenced greatly by the direction of the wind at the time of their approach to the islands in the spring and early summer. The prevailing airs, blowing as they do at that season, from the north and north-west, carry far out to sea the odor of the old rookery-flats, together whith the fresh scent of the pioneer bulls which have located themselves on these breeding-grounds, three or four weeks in advance of their kind. The seals come up from the great North Pacific, and hence it will be seen that the rookeries of the south and southeastern shores of St. Paul Island receive nearly all the seal-life, although there are miles of perfectly eligible ground at Nahsayvernia, or north shore. To settle this matter beyond all argument, however, I know is an exceedingly difficult task, for the identification of individuals, from one season to another, among the hundreds of thousands, and even millions, that come under the eye on one of these great rookeries, is well-nigh impossible.

forth from the St. Paul hauling-grounds during the summer at frequent intervals to fish and search for similar food; the greatest cod and herring schools and salmon runs of Behring Sea lie to the eastward and south-eastward of St. Paul, and St. George — is squarely in the road.

These hauling grounds of St. George Island which were never, by the nature of the land, as broad or extended as those of St. Paul, were, however, in 1872, polished very brightly by the "holluschickie", but now, in 1890, the same utter desolation which prevails over them on St. Paul, also exists here; the hauling grounds at "Zapadnie" are simply grass-grown, also those of "Starry Ateel" while the "Great Eastern" parade is a mere suggestion, and the fine sweep of the "North" rookery looks like a soft green lawn from the village; as for the "Little Eastern", not a single drive has been made from there this year : at no time was there more than 12 to 15 "holluschickie" upon its grassy borders.

As for St. Paul, I have walked day after day last summer over the grass-grown deserted hauling grounds of Southwest Point, of "Zapadnie", of "English Bay", "Lukannon", "Ketavie", "Polavina", and "Novastoshnah" with the same feeling I should have were I to enter upon and walk over the abandoned and grass-grown streets of a once populous and busy city which I had previously visited in all its prosperity, only sixteen years ago.

In order that a clear, sharp contrast may be drawn between the appearance and condition of these hauling grounds and their occupants, as they were in 1872-74, and are to-day, 1890, I have arranged the following epitome. I do not carry the parallel column beyond St. Paul, since the status of St. George is precisely similar.

Condition of the "hauling-grounds" St. Paul Island, Pribilov Group.

From my field-notes made in 1872-74, and published in 1874, and again in 1881.	From my field-notes as per date, made last summer.
THE STATUS OF 1872-74.	THE STATUS OF 1890.
Zoltoi, June 19, 1872, pp. 50, 51.	*Zoltoi*, Thursday, May 22, 1890.
" These Zoltoi sands are however a famous rendezvous for the hollus-	" The sand has drifted very slightly from its boundaries during the last 18 years. "

SECTION II.

THE STATUS OF 1872-74.

chickie, and from them during the season, the natives make regular drives, having only to step out from their houses in the morning, and walk back a few rods to find their fur-bearing quarry."

June 20, 1872, p. 71.

..... "If the weather was favorable for landing, i.e., cool, moist and foggy the fresh hauling of the 'holluschickie' would cover the bare grounds again in a very short space of time, sometimes in a few hours after the driving of every seal from Zoltoi Sands over to the killing fields adjacent, those dunes and the beach in question would be swarming anew with fresh arrivals."

July 20, 1874, p. 72.

"As matters are to-day 100,000 seal alone can be taken and skinned in less than forty working days within a radius of one mile and a half from the village, ... hence the driving with the exception of two experimental drives ..... has never been made from longer distances than Tolstoi to the westward, Lukannon to the northward, and Zoltoi to the southward of the killing grounds at St. Paul village."

Tolstoi, p. 53.

"Directly to the west from Lukannon, up along and around the head of the Lagoon, is the seal path road over which the natives bring the holluschickie from Tolstoi."

July 20, 1874, p. 72.

"As matters are to-day 100 000 seals alone on St. Paul can be taken and skinned in less than forty working days, within a radius of one mile and a half from the village and from the salt house of North East Point; hence the driving with the exception of two experimental drives, which I witnes-

THE STATUS OF 1890.

June 19, 1890.

"Not a single holluschak of any age whatever on "Zoltoi" this day, and there has not been a killable seal there, thus far, this season:"

June 22, 1890.

"Fine weather for seals to haul continues, but the seals do not haul, not a single seal on Zoltoi Sands this morning, has not been a holluschak there yet, and this was the never-failing resort of the natives in 1872-76. Therefore this vacancy on Zoltoi makes a deep impression on one who has stood there in 1872-74 and observed the swarming platoons of hauling holluschickie now entirely vanished."

July 19, 1890,

"Not a single holluschak on Zoltoi Sands this morning and not one has hauled there thus far this season."

Tolstoi, June 15, 1890.

"During the last ten days while inspecting the several breeding grounds of this island, I have paid careful attention to every squad of holluschickie that has appeared, *and, except as to numbers*, I do not observe any change up to date in their habit of hauling early in the season. These early squads appear just above the surf margin at Tolstoi, in English Bay, ... precisely as they did in 1872, only the number is smaller."

June 19, 1890.

..... "I had a full sweep of English Bay, — a small squad of perhaps 150 holluschickie at Middle Hill and another small pod at the intersection of the beach with Tolstoi Rookery."

Tolstoi, June 22, 1890.

..... "At this time in 1872-74, inclusive, I never glanced over at Zoltoi, but I saw holluschickie coming

sed in 1872, has never been made from longer distances than Tolstoi to the westward, Lukannon to the northward and Zoltoi to the southward of the killing grounds at St. Paul village."

THE STATUS OF 1872-74.

Lukannon, June 20, 1872.

" The sand-dunes to the west and to the north are covered with the mostluxuriant grass, abruptly emarginated by the sharp abrasion of the hauling seals; this is shown very clearly on the general map. ..... This is the point down along the flat shoals of Lukannon Bay where the sand dunes are most characteristic as they rise in their wind-whirled forms just above the surf-wash. This, also, is where the natives come from the village during the early mornings of the season, for driving, to get any number of hollus chickie."

July 12, 1872.

" The task of getting up early in the morning, and going out to the several hauling grounds closely adjacent, is really all there is of there labour involved in securing the number of seals required for the day's work on the killing grounds. The two, three or four natives upon whom, in rotation, this duty is devolved, by the order of their chief, rise at first glimpse of dawn between 1 and 2 o'clock, and hasten over to Lukannon, Tolstoi, or Zoltoi, as the case may be, " walk out " their " holluschickie " and have them ready on the slaughtering field before 6 or 7 o'clock, as a rule, in the morning. In favorable weather the ' drive ' from Tolstoi consumes two and a half to three hours time; from Lukannon, about two hours and is often done in an hour and a half;

and going from and to the sea in steady files and platoons. I never looked over the broad sweep of English Bay beach from the high sand dunes of Tolstoi, but to see the same sight only in vastly greater form and numbers ..... I do not see to-day, except at Middle Hill, the least suggestion of the past. Will it improve? "

Tolstoi, July 12, 1890.

..... " When it is borne in mind that in the very height of the season, after 5 days rest, or non attention, only 633 medium fur seal skins, mostly 5 1/3 lbs. clean skins, of 2-year olds, can be secured from the combined scraping of everything in English Bay (on Zapadnie we know there is nothing) Middle Hill, Tolstoi, Lukannon, and Ketavie, the extraordinary condition of these interests can be well understood in a general way. Such a driving in 1872, at this time and circumstance of weather would have brought, 100,000 holluschickie up here, instead of the 5,150 to-day 3 cows in this drive."

THE STATUS OF 1890.

Lukannon. June 19, 1890.

" I ascended the basaltic ridge beween Lukannon Sands and the villages late this morning between 8 and 9 o'clock, — not a single seal, old or young on these hauling grounds and lands of Lukannon."

June 21, 1890.

" From the volcanic ridge I had a clear view of Lukannon beach and hauling grounds, — not a seal upon it of any age, and the weather superb for seals to haul in, cool, moist and foggy."

June 24, 1890.

..... " In the afternoon I took a survey of Lukannon Bay, and hauling

while Zoltoi is so near by that the time is merely nominal. "

July 20, 1872.

" As matters are to-day, 100,000 seals alone on St. Paul can be taken and skinned within a radius of one mile and a half from the village, ... hence the driving .... has never been made from longer distances than Tolstoi to the westward, Lukannon, to the northward, and Zoltoi to the southward of the killing grounds at St. Paul village. "

THE STATUS OF 1872-74.

Zapadnie, July 14, 1874.

" The holluschickie that sport here on the parade plateau, and indeed over all of the western extent of the English Bay hauling grounds have never been visited by the natives for the purpose of selecting killing drives, since 1872, inasmuch as more seals than were wanted have always been procured from Zoltoi, Lukannon, and Lower Tolstoi points, which are all very close to the village. "

July 4, 1872.

"I stood on the Tolstoi sand dunes one afternoon, toward the middle of July, and had under my eyes in one straight forward sweep from my feet to Zapadnie a million and a half of seals spread out on those hauling (and breeding) grounds. Of those I estimated fully one half at that time were pups, yearlings and holluschickie. The rookeries across the bay were plainly in sight and so crowded, that they looked exactly as I have seen surfaces appear upon which bees had swarmed in obedience to that din and racket made by the watchful apiarian when he desires to hive the restless honey-makers. "

grounds, — not a seal on the beach except a half-dozen " 1/2 " bulls abreast of the volcanic ridge. ..... "

July 1, 1890.

" Not a seal on the hauling ridge and sands of Lukannon Bay, and none on Ketavie. "

July 8, 1890.

" I came down on the sand beach between Tonkie Nees and Lukannon; not a seal has hauled there yet this year, — a place where thousands upon tens of thousands were to be seen at this time in 1872. "

July 13, 1890.

" Along the entire spread of Lukannon, Polavina, and N. E. Point sand beach, 8 miles, nearly, I did not see a single young seal, — only a dozen or two old worthless bulls scattered here and there at wide intervals; over this extent and at this time in 1872, such a walk as mine this morning would have brought me in contact with and in sight of 50,000 to 100,000 holluschickie; and the weather simply superb hauling weather, — all day yesterday, last night, and this morning. "

THE STATUS OF 1890.

Zapadnie, July 3, 1890.

"These drives at Zapadnie are made just as they are made at all the other rookeries this season, — just swept up from the immediate skirts of the breeding seals cows, pups, and bulls: — This method of driving was not even suggested in any time of 1872-74. Such a proceeding would have been voted abominable then; it is still more so now; it sweeps every young male seal that is 4, 3, and 2 years old into death as soon as it hauls to-day : nothing escapes except that which old age

July 22, 1874.

"And a fair track for the 'holluschickie', 500 feet wide left clear over which they have travelled quite extensively this season, some 20,000 to 25,000 of them, at least, lying out around the old salt house to-day."

July 18, 1890.

"This last scrape made here to-day was opened by the appearance of only 1192 animals on the grounds after a rest of 9 days since the last drive from this place; 115 of these 1192 were old bulls, all over 6 years, and the balance outside of the catch (241), are yearlings, 'runty' 2-year olds, 'bitten' 4-year olds, and a few 5-year old 'wigs'. Every 4-year old 'wig' was taken, — taken here as at Polavina yesterday, for the first time this season, — every 'smooth' 4 year old was taken in the first drives, and now the dregs are drawn also."

THE STATUS OF 1872-74.

Polavina, July 20, 1874.

"Surmounting this lava bed is a cap of ferrugineous cement and tufa, from three to ten feet in thickness, making a reddish floor upon which the seals patter in their restless, never ceasing evolutions, sleeping or waking on the land. It is as great a single-parade plateau of polished cement as that of the Reef, but we are unable from any point of observation to appreciate it, inasmuch as we cannot stand high enough to overlook it.

The rookery itself occupies only a small portion of the seal-visited area at this spot."

For the reasons cited in a similar example at Zapadnie, no holluschickie have been driven from this point since 1872, though it is one of the easiest

or extreme youth saves, — or in other words, the high tax of $10.22 saves.

July 9, 1890.

"I went over to Zapadnie early this morning with the natives, and witnessed their driving; most of the scanty drive was taken from the borders of upper Zapadnie Rookery, the whole sweep of Lower Zapadnie did not yield over 200 holluschickie, which had hauled in at several places just upward above the breeding seals."

"All that large space up above the rookery on Lower Zapadnie which was literally alive with trooping platoons of holluschickie in 1872, is to-day, *entirely vacant*, — not a seal on it, and the natives peering over the high bluffs on the south side of and to the westward of the 'Point' trying to find a few seal skulking down there on the rocks awash: their eager search with their backs turned to this silent parade ground of 1872, made me decidedly thoughtful."

THE STATUS OF 1890.

Polavina, June 16, 1890.

"I came down on foot to the village, giving Polavina a survey down outside so as to see the old and new seal grass on that famous parade, it is somewhat too soon to arrive at a conclusion, but what I saw and noted causes surprise."

"Suppose you had, fourteen or sixteen years ago, stood upon an eminence overlooking a sheep pasture or fold, some 3/4 of a mile in length, and 1,500 to 2,000 feet in width so filled with a herd or flock of sheep as to fairly cover the whole surface of the earth itself within those lines from your sight, at frequent intervals, and never let you see more than a scattered glimpse of it at any one place or time."

"Then sixteen years later to stand

worked. It was in the Russian times, a pet sealing ground with them."

July 14, 1874.

"The vast numbers of the holluschickie on this ground of Polavina, where they have not been disturbed for some five years, to mention, in the way of taking."

THE STATUS OF 1872-74.

Novastoshnah, July 2, 1872.

It was a view of such multitudes of amphibians, when I first stood upon the summit of Hutchinson's Hill, and looked at the immense spread around me that suggested to my mind a doubt whether the accurate investigation which I was making would give me courage to maintain the truth in regard to the subject."

"Hutchinson's Hill is the foundation of this point, which is itself a solid basaltic floor upon a mass of breccia has been poured at its northwest corner; it is rough, very rough in spots, and smoother in other places, but everywhere indicated on my chart it has been polished clean and clear of every spear of grass or trace of moss; the hill is about 120 feet high, and has a rounded summit, over which, and swarming up and down over its flanks to the west and the east is an astonishing aggregate of young male seals or holluschickie; these herds taken together with the three and a half miles of unbroken rookery belt of solid massed life in reproduction make a truly amazing sight this afternoon, amazing in its aggregate, and infinite in its vast detail."

July 16, 1872.

"Webster gets all the holluschickie again there as I stood to-day here, and look again upon that same place and the assembled life, and then to see nothing of them but a few lonely pods of sheep, and they all timidly huddled down at one margin of this pasture, and so few in number that it required really no effort for you to count them one by one, that is precisely the way this rookery and this hauling-ground looks to me to-day."

June 25, 1890.

The poverty of these celebrated hauling grounds of Polavina is well illustrated by the catch from the drive to-day 263 skins: At this time in 1872, I could have driven from the great parade plateau behind these breeding grounds, under precisely the same circumstances surrounding the drive to-day 10,000 killable seals, not one over 4 years old, and very few under 3 years old. Comment is needless."

July 2, 1890.

"Now to-day, every good 2-year old, every 3- and 4-year old was knocked down here out of this 1930 animals to get 240 skins, — where at this rate is the new blood for the rookeries to come in, now so desperately needed?"

THE STATUS OF 1890.

Novastoshnah, June 15, 1890.

"Arrived at Webster's House at 12.30 P. M.

The two natives stationed here on watch, declared that yesterday, which was a fine day, was employed by them in making a circuit of the hoint; that they carefully inspected the rookery margin and found only about 300 holluschickie hauled immediately up on the north side of the sea-lions on the 'Neck'. Peter Peshenkove declared that nowhere

that he wants from one spot on the north shore of the sand neck beach, west of the foot of Cross Hill: a short drive, and only what he wants for each day's work is driven: he says that he could kill every day three and four times as many as he does, if he had the men here to handle the skins: he takes nothing but large skins, nothing under 7 lbs."

else was there any holluschickie; that there were a few polsea-catchie on the beach just below the 'south shoulder', and nothing in the line of killable seals, except under the north slope of Hutchinson Hill, about 200 'good ones.'

July 13, 1890.

Fowler had over 5,000 seals driven up this morning, and when he had finished the killing, he had only 473 skins, — all the rest too small, — chiefly last year's pups; then in the afternoon, rain coming up, he made a rapid drive of those holluschickie which he had been saving for to-morrow, fearing that the rain would send them into the sea, and secured 168 more, making a total of 641, being the extreme limit reached in any one day's killing up here this year, and a total of 4,135 only; on this day here last year Webster had killed 17,168 seals: Fowler will have no holluschickie to-morrow. Webster killed on the 15th, 1,838 more."

"The driving up here has radically altered for the worse since 1872-74. It is a mere raking and scraping now of the rookery margins, no killable seals anywhere else."

"The parade fields of this once magnificent breeding ground are positively vacant to-day, — grass and flowers growing and springing up everywhere all over them. The holluschickie as they hauled to-day did not occupy a space 500 feet by 50 feet in depth: over the entire extent of this immense habitat of 1872, and the drive of 5,000 seals which we saw on the killing grounds *had been scraped from seven different points* back of the rookery between the base of Hutchinson Hill, and the S. E. terminus of the breeding grounds on the point."

SECTION III

THE METHOD OF DRIVING AND TAKING FUR-SEALS
ON THE PRIBYLOV ISLANDS OF ALASKA,
IN 1872-74, 1890

SECTION III

THE METHOD OF DRIVING AND TAKING FUR-SEALS ON THE PRIBYLOV ISLANDS OF ALASKA, IN 1872-74, 1890

The increasing difficulty of getting that regular quota of 100,000 young male fur-seal skins annually ever since 1882 due to the steady diminution of supply on the Pribylov Islands, has made it necessary to drive right from the breeding grounds incessantly with an annual increased severity during the last six or seven years; the hauling grounds of 1872-'74 which were far distant from these rookeries, and upon which large surplus herds of seal rested from the beginning to the end of each season, undisturbed, were all abandoned as the seals fell away in numbers until by 1889-'90 grass grew and grows right to the waters edge over them.

The remnants of these herds began as early as 1884 to seek quiet and protection by hauling under the lee of the breeding animals, and in doing so hauled out and laid down upon the immediate flanks of the breeding cows and bulls, close to them, and often intermingled at the outer edge; therefore, in order to get the young male seals thus hauled, it became necessary as early as 1884-'85, to scrape the edges of the rookeries in driving out, and up, the killable seals; and, in 1889 it was done with great vigor, which was increased, if anything, during the past season.

This extraordinary driving was never dreamed of in 1872-'74, much less done. Then the young male seals, being in great numbers landed in the following manner which I have spoken of in 1874, thus :

"By reference to the habit of the fur-seal, which I have discussed at length, it is now plain and beyond doubt, that two-thirds of all the males which are born, and they are equal in numbers to the females born, are never permitted by the remaining third, strongest by natural selection, to land upon the same breeding-ground with the females which always herd thereupon *en masse*. Hence this great band of 'bachelor' seals, or 'holluschickie', so fitly termed, when it visits the island is obliged to live apart entirely sometimes, and some places, miles away from the rookeries; and, in this admirably perfect method of nature are those seals which can be properly killed without injury to the rookeries, selected and held aside by their own volition, so that the natives can visit and take them without disturbing, in the least degree, the entire quiet of the breeding-grounds, where the stock is perpetuated".

Such was the number and method of the young male seals in 1872-'74 : it is very different to day : from the hour of the first driving of 1890, May 21st up to the close of the season, July 20th, all the driving was regularly made from rookery grounds from the immediate margins of the breeding animals with the solitary exception of that one place, Middle Hill, English Bay, St. Pauls Island. Not a drive made elsewhere in the course of which cows and pups and bulls were not disturbed and hustled as the young males were secured. As long as the breeding season was unbroken, very few cows were swept into these drives, though the disturbance was incessant and great : but, when after the 18th, 20th, July, the rutting season subsided, and the pups began to pod out-i. e. scatter back over thrice and five times as much ground as they had previously laid upon, then the cows followed them, and then the young males mixed up right and left and mingled with the herd, since they were no longer attacked or driven here and there by the old bulls; hence the day or two preceding July 20th was marked by a large increased number of cows and old bulls in the drives, and had the driving been permitted later the cows and old bulls would have been swept into the droves of small male seals by the hundreds where tens had previously been taken in this manner.

The driving of a cow with her udder distended, and dragged for miles over rough sharp rocks bumping heavily in and out of holes and over tussocks, cannot result in aught else than her physical ruin, and the death of her young pup which is left behind. Therefore any driving on these islands which, in order to get the holluschickie, necessitates the sweeping into it of cows, pups and bulls, should terminate instantly on that day it begins; and since the breaking up and spreading of the breeding animals begins as a rule on the 20th of July (a few days earlier, if it should rain hard), that date is the very latest day of permission to drive that can be safely given, whenever killing is resumed again for tax and shipment of skins from these islands.

Of course, when seals were in abundance, as in 1872-'79, inclusive and the sealing gangs never were obliged to go near a rookery to get their quota daily, it did not signify one way or the other as to when and how they went about their work; then they never disturbed the breeding animals no matter when they drove in June, July or August.

But to-day the whole order of hauling is changed, the scanty residuum of that surplus thousands and tens of thousands of killable seals of 1872-'74, haul now in close contact with the rapidly diminishing breeding animals in the rookeries, everywhere in fact but on those broad hauling grounds of 1872-'74 as they were wont to do then. They do so naturally and intelligently enough since it is the last resort for protection and rest that the islands afford.

From the beginning of this season of 1890, and it was so last year also, the moment a small pod of a few hundred holluschickie hauled up into the rear of a rookery or appeared on the sand beach just above the surf wash in English Bay under Middle Hill that very moment these seals were marked and ordered driven, they were never allowed to rest long enough to become even acquainted with *terra firma* ere they were hustled up by the drivers and urged over to the killing grounds.

Last season, during that desperate effort made then to get the catch of 100,000, parties were regularly sent over to drive the holluschickie off from Seevitchie Kammen, from Otter Island, from all points under the high bluffs at Zapadine and S. W. Point — St. Paul and the north shore of St. George : — this year however there were too few hauled out on these spots to warrant this effort — there was no sign of seals hauling at all on Otter Island.

When I expressed my surprise at this ferocious driving begun early in June, I was met by apparent equal surprise on the part of the drivers, who wondering at my ignorance, assured me that they had been driving seals in this method ever since 1885. — " had been obliged to, or go without the seals "!

The driving itself, in so far as the conduct of the natives conducting the labor was concerned, was as carefully and well done as it could be ; they avoided to the very best of their ability any undue urging or hastening of the drive overland from the rookeries; they avoided, as nearly as they could, under the circumstances sweeping up pods of cows and pups — did all that they could to make as little disturbance among the breeding animals as possible : but even with all their care and sincere reluctance to disturb the rookeries, cows were repeatedly taken up in their scraping drives on the margins of all the rookeries and their pups left floundering behind to starve and perish ultimately.

The manner to-day of driving overland to the killing grounds is unchanged from the methods of 1872, but the regular driving from every spot resorted to by the holluschickie on both islands has caused the establishment of killing grounds and a salt house

1. The subjoined extract is from my field notes under date of " Sunday, July 13th, 1890 " : " Walked up to North East Point this morning for the purpose of plotting the area and position of the breeding seals on Novastoshnah and the Polavinas. Also to see the natives drive at Polavina. I was on the ground at 5 A.M. and saw the whole *modus operandi*, at this place; the holluschickie haul close up against the sand beach drop to the rookery at Polavina, and the drivers in getting the young males, swept four cows into the drove, and their pups were left behind them on the sand, bruised, mauled and paralyzed by the stampeding flippers of the herd. To get the holluschickie they are obliged to drive in this violent manner.

" Another squad of say 1,000, mostly 2-year olds and yearlings was swept up by these drivers on the parade plateau, and another squad was driven from Little Polavina rookery the first drive that the natives have been able to find there thus far this season.

" Along the entire spread of Lukannon, Polavina, and N. E. Point sand beach — eight miles nearly of it — I did not see a single young seal — only a dozen or two worthless bulls scattered here and there at wide intervals : — over this extent and at this time in 1872 such a walk as mine this morning would have brought me in contact with, and in sight of 50,000 to 100,000 holluschickie; and the weather now simply superb hauling weather all day yesterday, last night, and this morning ".

as early as 1879 at Stony Point (Tonkie Mees), and a slaughter field at Zapadnie on St. Paul the skins being taken from the latter point by a bidarrah to the village; (which was sent over from there every time a killing was made) and are now hauled down in wagons, (mule teams) from the former locality, to the salt houses of St. Paul.

In 1872-'74 the work of getting the seals on the killing grounds was conducted in the following manner:

" The manner in which the natives captured and drove the ' holluschickie ' up from the hauling-grounds to the slaughter fields near the two villages of St. Pauul and St. George, and elsewhere on the islands cannot be improved upon. It was in this way; at the beginning of every sealing season, that is, during May and June, large bodies of young ' bachelor ' seals do not haul up on land very far from the water a few rods at the most, and when these first arrivals are sought after, the natives, in capturing them, are obliged to approach slyly and run quickly between the dozing seals and the surf, before they can take alarm and bolt into the sea; in this manner a dozen Aleuts, running down the sand beach of English Bay, in the early morning of some June day, will turn back from the water thousands of seals, just as the mouldboard of a plough lays over and back a furrow of earth. When the sleeping seals are first startled, they arise, and, seeing men between them and the water, immediately turn, lope, and scramble rapidly back up and over the land; the natives then leisurely walk on the flanks and in the rear of the drove thus secured, directing and driving it over to the killing-grounds, close by the village ".

1. The task of getting up early in the morning, and going out to the several hauling-grounds, closely adjacent, is really all there is of the labor involved in securing the number of seals required for the day's work on the killing-grounds. The two, three, or four natives upon whom, in rotation, this duty is devolved by the order of their chief, rise at first glimpse of dawn, between 1 and 2 o'clock, and hasten over to Lukannon, Tolstoi, or Zoltoi, as the case may be, " walk out " their " holluschickie ", and have them duly on the slaughtering-field before 6 or 7 o'clock, as a rule, in the morning. In favorable weather the " drive " from Tolstoi comsumes two and a half to three hourstime; from Lukannon, about two hours, and is often done in an hour and a half; while Zoltoi is so near by, that the time is merely nominal.

I heard a great deal of talk among the white residents of St. Paul, when I first landed and the sealing-season opened, about the necessity of " resting " the haulinggrounds; in other words, they said that if the seals were driven in repeated daily rotation from any one of the hauling-grounds, that this would so disturb these animals as to prevent their coming to any extent again thereon, during the rest of the season.

"**Progression of a seal-drive.** — A drove of seals on hard or firm grassy ground, in cool and moist weather, may be driven with safety at the rate of half a mile an hour; they can be urged along, with the expenditure of a great many lives, however, at the speed of a mile or a mile and a quarter per hour; but this is seldom done. An old bull seal, fat and unwieldy, cannot travel with the younger ones, though it can lope or gallop as it starts across the ground as fast as an ordinary man can run, over 100 yards; but then it fails utterly, falls to the earth supine, entirely exhausted, hot, and gasping for breath. "

" The ' holluschickie ' are urged along the path leading to the killing-grounds with very little trouble, and require only three or four men to guide and secure as many thousand at a time. They are permitted frequently to halt and cool off, as heating them injures their fur. These seal-halts on the road always impressed me with a species of sentimentalism and regard for the creatures themselves. The men dropping back for a few moments, the awkward shambling and scuffling of the march at once ceases, and the seals stop in their tracks to fan themselves with their hind-flippers, while their heaving flanks give rise to subdued panting sounds. As soon as they apparently cease to gasp for want of breath, and are cooled off comparatively, the natives step up once

This theory seemed rational enough to me at the beginning of my investigations, and I was not disposed to question its accuracy; but, subsequent observation directed to this point particularly, satisfied me and the sealers themselves with whom I was associated, that the driving of the seals had no effect whatever upon the hauling which took place soon or immediately after the field for the hour, had been swept clean of seals by the drivers. If the weather was favorable for landing, i. e., cool, moist, and foggy, the fresh hauling of the " holluschickie " would cover the bare grounds again in a very short space of time sometimes in a few hours after the driving of every seal from Zoltoi sands over to the killing fields adjacent, those dunes and the beach in question would be swarming anew with fresh arrivals. If, however, the weather is abnormally warm and sunny, during its prevalence, even if for several consecutive days, no seals to speak of will haul out on the emptied space; indeed, if these " holluschickie " had not been taken away by man from Zoltoi or any other hauling-ground on the island when " tayopli " weather prevailed, most of those seals would have vacated their terrestrial loafing places for the cooler embraces of the sea.

The importance of understanding this fact as to the readiness of the " holluschickie " to haul promptly out on steadily " swept " ground, provided the weather is inviting, is very great; because when not understood, it was deemed necessary, even as late as the season of 1872, to " rest " the hauling grounds near the village (from which all the driving has been made since), and make trips to far away Polavina and distant Zapadnie — an unnecessary expenditure of human time, and a causeless infliction of physical misery upon phocine backs and flippers.

more, clatter a few bones with a shout along the line, and the seal-shamble begins again — their march to death and the markets of the world is taken up anew."

"**Docility of fur-seals when driven.** — I was also impressed by the singular docility and amiability of these animals when driven along the road; they never show fight any more than a flock of sheep would do; if, however, a few old seals get mixed in, they usually get so weary that they prefer to come to a stand-still and fight rather than move; otherwise no sign whatever of resistance is made by the drove from the moment it is intercepted, and turned up from the hauling-grounds to the time of its destruction at the hands of the sealing-gang."

"This disposition of the old seals to fight rather than endure the panting torture of travel, is of great advantage to all parties concerned; for they are worthless commercially, and the natives are only too glad to let them drop behind, where they remain unmolested, eventually returning to the sea. The fur on them is of little or no value; their under wool being very much shorter, coarser, and more scant than in the younger seals; especially so on the posterior parts along the median line of the back."

"It is quite impossible, however, to get them all of one age without an extraordinary amount of stir and bustle, which the Aleuts do not like to precipitate; hence the drive will be found to consist usually of a bare majority of three and four-year olds, the rest being two-year olds principally, and a very few, at wide intervals, five-year olds, the yearlings seldom ever getting mixed up."

"**Method of land travel.** — As the drove progresses along the path to the slaughtering grounds, the seals all move in about the same way; they go ahead with a kind of walking step and a sliding, shambling gallop. The progression of the whole caravan is a succession of starts spasmodic and irregular, made every few minutes, the seals pausing to catch their breath, and make, as it were, a plaintive survey and mute protest. Every now and then a seal will get weak in the lumbar region, then drag its posteriors along for a short distance, finally drop breathless and exhausted, quivering and panting, not to revive for hours — days, perhaps — and often never. During the driest driving-days, or those days when the temperature does not combine with wet fog to keep the path moist and cool, quite a large number of the weakest animals in the drove will be thus laid out and left on the track. If one of these prostrate seals is not too much heated at the time, the native driver usually taps the beast over the head and removes its skin [1]."

"**Prostration of fur-seals by heat.** — This prostration from exertion will always happen, no matter how carefully they are driven; and in the longer drives, such as two and a half, and five miles from Zapadnie on the west, or Polavina on the north, to the village at St. Paul as much as three or four per cent of the whole drive will be thus dropped on the road; hence I feel satisfied, from my observation and close attention to this feature, that a considerable number of those that are thus rejected from the drove and are able to rally and return to the water, die subsequently from internal injuries sustained on the trip, superinduced by this over-exertion. I, therefore think it highly improper and impolitic to extend the drives of the ' holluschickie ' over any distance on St. Paul Island exceeding a mile, or a mile and a half; it is better for all parties concerned, and the business too, that salt-houses be erected, and killing-grounds established contiguous to all of the great hauling-grounds, two miles distant from the village on St. Paul Island, should the business ever be developed above the present limit; or should the exigencies of the future require a quota from all these places, in order to make up the 100 000 which may be lawfully taken."

"**Abundant supply of ' holluschickie '.** — As matters are to day 100 000 seals alone on St. Paul can be taken and skinned in less than forty working days, within a radius of one mile and a half from the village, and from the salt-house at North East Point; hence the driving, with the exception of two experimental droves

---

1. The fur-seal like all of the pinnipeds, has no sweat glands; hence, when it is heated, it cools off by the same process of panting which is so characteristic of the dog, accompanied by the fanning that I have hitherto fully described; the heavy breathing and low grunting of a tired drove seals, on a warmer day than usual, can be heard several hundred yards away. It is surprising how quickly the hair and fur will come out of the skin of a blood heated seal — literally rubs off bodily at a touch of the finger. A fine specimen of a three-year old " holluschak " fell in its tracks at the end of the lagoon while being driven to the village killing-grounds. I asked that it be skinned with special reference to mounting; accordingly a native was sent for, who was on the spot, knife in hand, within less than 30 minutes from the moment that this seal fell in the road; yet, soon after he had got fairly to work, patches of the fur and hair came off here and there wherever he chanced to clutch the skin.

which I witnessed in 1872, has never been made from longer distances than Tolstoi to the eastward, Lukannon to the northward, and Zoltoi to the southward of the killing grounds at St. Paul village. Should, however, and abnormal season recur, in which the larger proportion of days during the right period for taking the skins be warmish and dry, it might be necessary, in order to get even 75 000 seals within the twenty-eight or thirty days of their prime condition, for drives to be made from the other great hauling grounds to the westward and northward, which are now, and have been for the last ten years, entirely unnoticed by the sealers."

"**Killing the seals.** — The seals, when finally driven upon those flats between the east landing and the village, and almost under the windows of the dwellings, are herded there until cool and rested. The drives are usually made very early in the morning, at the first breaking of day, which is half-past one to two o'clock of June and July in these latitudes."

"They arrive and cool off on the slaughtering grounds, so that by six or seven o'clock, after breakfast, the able bodied male population turn out from the village and go down to engage in the work of slaughter. The men are dressed in their ordinary working garb of thick flannel shirts, stout cassimere or canvas pants, over which the 'tarbossa' boots are drawn; if it rains they wear their 'kamlaikas', made of the intestines and throats of the sea-lion and fur-seal. Thus dressed, they are each armed with a club, a stout oaken or hickory bludgeon, which have been made particularly for the purpose at New London, Connecticut, and imported here for this especial service. These sealing clubs are about five or six feet in length, three inches in diameter at their heads, and the thickness of a man's fore arm where the are grasped by the hands. Each native also has his stabbing-knife, his skinning-knife, and his whetstone; these are laid upon the grass convenient, when the work of braining or knocking the seals down is in progress. This is all the apparatus which they have for killing and skinning."

"**The killing gang at work.** — When the men gather for work they are under the control of their chosen foremen or chiefs; usually on St. Paul, divided into two working parties at the village, and a sub-party at Northeast Point, where another salt-house and slaughtering field is established. At the signal of the chief the work of the day begins by the men stepping into the drove, corraled on the flats; and, driving out from it 100 or 150 seals at a time, make what they call a pod, which they surround in a circle, huddling the seals one on another as they narrow it down, until they are directly within reach and under their clubs. Then the chief, after he has cast his experienced eye over the struggling, writhing ' kautickie ' in the centre, passes the word that such and such a seal is bitten, that such and such a seal is too young, that such and such a seal is too old; the attention of his men being called to these points, he gives the word ' strike ', instantly the heavy clubs come down all around, and every one that is eligible is stretched out stunned and motionless, in less time, really, than I take to tell it. Those seals spared by the order of the chief, now struggle from under and over the bodies of their insensible companions and pass, hustled off by the natives, back to the sea [1]. "

" The clubs are dropped, the men seize the prostrate seals by the hind-flippers, and drag them out, so they are spread on the ground without touching each other; then every sealer takes his knife and drives it into the heart at a point between the fore-flippers of each stunned form; the blood gushes forth, and the quivering of the animal presently ceases. A single stroke of a heavy oak bludgeon, well and fairly delivered, will crush in at once the slight, thin bones of a fur-seal's skull, and lay the creature out almost lifeless. These blows are, however, usually repeated two or three times with each animal, but they are very quickly done. The bleeding which is immediately effected is so speedily undertaken in order

1. The aim and force with which the native directs his blow, determines the death of the seal; if struck direct and violently, a single stroke is enough; the seals' heads are stricken so hard sometimes that those crystaline lenses to their eyes fly out from the orbital sockets like hail stones, or little pebbles, and frequently struck me sharply in the face, or elsewhere, while I sood near by watching the killing gang at work.

 A singular lucid green light suddenly suffuses the eye of the fur-seal at intervals when it is very much excited, as the " podding " for the clubbers is in progress; and, at the moment when last raising its head it sees the uplifted bludgeons on every hand above, fear seems then for the first time to posses it and to instantly gild its eye in this strange manner. When the seal is brained in this state of optical coloration, I have noticed that the opalescent tinting remained well defined for many hours or a whole day after death; these remarkable flashes are very characteristic to the eyes of the old males during their hurly-burly on the rookeries, but never appear in the younger classes unless as just described, as far as I could observe.

that the strange reaction, which the sealers call ' heating ', shall be delayed for half an hour or so, or until the seals can all be drawn out, and laid in some disposition for skinning. "

" I have noticed that within less than thirty minutes from the time a perfectly sound seal was knocked down, it had so ' heated ', owing to the day being warmer and drier than usual, that, when touching it with my foot, great patches of hair and fur peeled off. This is a rather exceptionally rapid metamorphosis — it will, however, take place in every instance, within an hour, or an hour and a half on these warm days, after the first blow is struck, and the seal is quiet in death; hence no time is lost by the prudent chief in directing the removal of the skins as rapidly as the seals are knocked down and dragged out. If it is a cool day, after bleeding the first ' pod ' which has been prostrated in the manner described, and after carefully drawing the slain from the heap in which they have fallen, so that the bodies will spread over the ground just free from touching one another, they turn to and strike down another ' pod '; and so on, until a whole thousand or two are laid out, or the drove, as corraled, is finished. The day, however must be raw and cold for this wholesale method. Then after killing, they turn to work, and skin; but, if it is a warm day, every pod is skinned as soon as it is knocked down. "

" The labor of skinning is exceedingly severe ; and is trying even to an expert, demanding long practice ere the muscles of the back and thighs are so developed as to permit a man to bend down to, and finish well, a fair day's work. The knives used by the natives for skinning are ordinary kitchen or case handle butcher-knives. They are sharpened to cutting edges as keen as razors; but, something about the skins of the seal, perhaps fine comminuted sand along the abdomen, so dulls these knives, as the natives work, that they are constantly obliged to whet them. "

" The body of the seal, preparatory to skinning, is rolled over and balanced squarely on its back ; then the native makes a single swift cut through the skin down along the neck, chest, and belly, from the lower jaw to the root of the tail, using, for this purpose, his long stabbing knife [1]. The fore and hind flippers are then suc-

---

[1]. When turning the stunned and senseless carcasses, the only physical danger of which the sealers run the slightest risk, during the whole circuit of their work, occurs

cessively lifted as the man straddles the seal and stoops down to
his work over it, and a sweeping circular incision is made through
the skin on them just at the point where the body-fur ends; then,
seizing a flap of the hide on either one side or the other of the
abdomen, the man proceeds with his smaller, shorter butcher-
knife, rapidly to cut the skin, clean and free from the body and
blubber, which he rolls over and out from the hide by hauling up
on it as he advances with his work, standing all this time stooped
over the carcass so that his hands are but slightly above it, or the
ground. This operation of skinning a fair sized ' holluschak '
takes the best men only one minute and a half; but the average
time made by the gang on the ground is about four minutes to
the seal. Nothing is left of the skin upon the carcass, save a small
patch of each upper lip on which the coarse mustache grows, the
skin on the tip of the lower jaw, the significant tail[1], together with
the bare hide of the flippers."

thus: at this moment the prone and quivering body of the "holluschak" is not
wholly inert, perhaps, though it is in nine times out of ten; and, as the native takes
hold of the fore-flipper to jerk the carcass over on to its back, the half-brained seal
rouses, snaps suddenly and viciously, often biting the hands or legs of the unwary
skinners, who then come leisurely and unconcernedly up into the surgeon's office at
the village, for bandages, etc.; a few men are bitten every day or two during the season on the islands, in this manner, but I have never learned of any serious result following any case.

The white sealers of the Antarctic always used the orthodox butchers' "steel" in
sharpening their knives, but these natives never have; and, probably never will abandon those little whet stones above referred to.

During the Russian management, and throughout the strife in killing by our own
people in 1868, a very large number of the skins were cut through, here and there, by
the slipping of the natives' knives, when they were taking them from the carcasses,
"flensing" them from the superabundance, in spots, of blubber. These knife-cuts
through the skin, no matter how slight, give great annoyance to the dresser; hence
they are always marked down in price. The prompt scrutiny of each skin on the
islands, by the agent of the Alaska Commercial Company, who rejects every one of
them thus injured, has caused the natives to exercise greater care, and the number
now so damaged, every season, is absolutely trifling.

Another source of small loss is due to a habit which the "holluschickie" have of
occasionally biting one another when they are being urged along in the drives, and
thus crowded once in a while one upon the other; usually these examples of "zooba-
den" are detected by the natives prior to the "knocking down", and spared; yet
those which have been nipped on the chest or abdomen cannot be thus noticed; and,
until the skin is lifted, the damage is not apprehended.

1. This tail of the fur-seal is just a suggestion of the article and that is all. Unlike
the abbreviated caudal extremities of the bear or the rabbit, it does not seem to be
under the slightest control of its owner — at least I never could see it move to any
appreciable degree, when the seal is in action on land. Certainly there is no service
required of it, but it does appear to me rather singular that none of the changeful

But during the last five or seven years, a somewhat different method has been in vogue, by which change the work has been expedited very much. Two or three white men, servants of the company leasing the islands, together with two or three of the natives alone constitute the killing or clubbing force; they make the selection, and knock down the killable seals as the pods are driven up by them in swift rotation then; four or five of the younger sealers constitute a force known as the " flippering " and stabbing or " sticking " men : these workmen seize each seal immediately after it is knocked down and plunge a long knife into its heart at a point directly in the centre of its chest between its fore flippers — then with a single swift sweep of this knife, the skin of the prostrate seal is cut through to the blubber in a straight line from the rims of the lower jaws to the fundament, another circular sweep cuts the skin right around the head so as to just leave all that forward of the eyes and the tip of the lower jaws; then another sweep of the keen blade cuts the furred skin clear from its junction into each naked fore flipper, and a final sweep separates it from the same junction with its hind flippers, and the abortive tail; this done the work of the flippering man ceases; and he is succeeded by the regular skinner who steps in soon after and completes the skinning out of the carcass, as was done in 1872, and described above.

The wooden clubs and steel knives are not essentially different to day from those used in 1872, and the treatment of the skins not materially changed in the salt houses; only they are cured more rapidly, salted over and changed five days after first salting into a fresh kench where they lay ready for final bundling in ten or

moods of *Callorhinus* are capable of giving rise to even a tremor in its short stump of a tail. It is never raised or depressed, and, in fact, amounts to a mere excrescence, which many casual observers would not notice. The shrinking, twitching movements of the seal's skin, here and there at irregular intervals, are especially noticed when that animal is asleep, so that even when awake, I believe that dermatological motion is an involuntary one. The tail of the sea-lion is equally inconsequential; that of the walrus, even more so, while *Phoca vitulina* has one a trifle longer, relatively, and much stouter, fleshier than that of the seal.

I found that the natives here were pronounced evolutionists, as are all the many Indian tribes with which I have been thrown in contact during my travels from Mexico to the head of the Stickeen river. They declare that their remote ancestry undoubtedly were fur-seals; indeed, there is a better showing for the brain cases of the fur-seal over that of the monkey's skull as to weight with reference to physical bulk; while their tails are as short or even shorter than most of the anthropoid apes.

twelve days time from date of first salting. I say five days after first salting, because it is done as soon as that if possible, though it is not essential — ten days often elapses; this re-salting is necessary to insure a complete curing of the edges of the pelts; if it is not done, then a great many " soft " spots will be found on the outer edges of the skins, from which the fur pulls out and thus destroys the par value of those skins.

Touching this subject, in 1874 I said in relation to the work :
" The skins are taken from the field[1] to the salt-house, where they are laid out, after being again carefully examined, one upon another, ' hair to fat ', like so many sheets of paper, with salt profusely spread upon the fleshy sides as they are piled up in the ' kenches ', or bins[2]. The salt-house is a large barn-like frame

1. Under the old order of affairs, prior to the present management, the skins were packed up and carried on the backs of the boys and girls, women and old men, to the salt-houses, or drying-frames. When I first arrived, season of 1872, a slight variation was made in this respect, by breaking a small Siberian bull into harness and hitching it to a cart, in which the pelts were hauled. Before the cart was adjusted however, and the " buik " taught to pull, it was led out to the killing-grounds, by a ring in its nose, and literally covered with the green seal hides, which were thus packed to the kenches. The natives were delighted with even this partial assistance ; but now they have no further concern about it at all, for several mules and carts render prompt and ample service. They were introduced here, first, in 1874. The Russian American Company and also the Alaska Commercial Company have brought up three or four horses to St. Paul, but they have been unfortunate in loosing them all soon after landing, the voyage and the climate combined being inimical to equine health; but the mules of the present order of affairs have been successful in their transportation to, and residence on, the Pribilov Islands. One of the first of these horses just referred to, perhaps did not have a fair chance for its life. It was saddled one morning, and several camp kettles, coffee pots, etc., slung on the crupper for the use of the Russian agent, who was going up to Northeast Point for a week or ten days' visit. He got into the saddle, and while *en route*, near Polavina, a kettle or pot broke loose behind, the alarmed horse kicked its rider promptly off, and disappeared on a full run, in the fog, going towards the bogs of Kamminista, where its lifeless and fox-gnawed body was found several days afterward.

2. The practice of curing in early times was quite differen from this rapid and effective process of salting. The skins were then all air dried; pegged out, when " green ", upon the ground, or else stretched upon a wooden trellis or frame, which stood like a rude fence adjacent to the killing-grounds; it was the accumulation of such air-dried skins from the Pribilov islands, at Sitka, which rotted so in 1803, that " 750,000 of them were cut up, or thrown into the sea ", completely destroyed. Had they been treated as they now are, such a calamity and hideous waste could not have occurred.

The method of air drying which the old settlers employed, is well portrayed by the practice of the natives now, who treat a few hundred sea-lions skins to the process every fall ; preparing them thus for shipment to Oonalshka, where they are used by brother Aleuts in covering their bidarkies or kyacks.

The natives in speaking to me of this matter, said that whenever the weather was

structure, so built as to afford one-third of its width in the center, from end to end, clear and open as a passage way; while on each side are rows of stanchions, with sliding planks, which are taken down and put up in the form of deep bins, or boxes — 'kenches ', the sealers call them. As the pile of skins is laid at the bottom of an empty 'kench', and salt thrown in on the outer edges, these planks are also put in place, so that the salt may be kept intact until the bin is filled as high up as a man can toss the skins. After lying two or three weeks in this style they become ' pickled ', and they are suited then at any time to be taken up and rolled into bundles, of two skins to the package, with the hairy side out, tightly corded, ready for shipment from the islands. "

" The bundled skins are carried from the salt houses to the baidar, when the order for shipment is given, and pitched into that lighter one by one, to be rapidly stowed; 700 to 1,800 bundles make the average single load; then, when alongside the steamer, they are again tossed up, on her deck, from whence they are stowed in the hold. "

" **Description of killing ground at St. Paul village.** — The killing ground of St. Paul is a bottomless sand flat, only a few feet above high water, and which unites the village hill and the reef with the island itself; it is not a stone's throw from the heart of the settlement — in fact, it is right in town — not even surburban, and a most singular and striking characteristic of the island of St. Paul, is the fact that this immense slaughtering field, upon which 55,000 to 70,000 fresh carcasses have laid every season sloughing away into the sand beneath, has not, and does not cause any sickness among the people who live right over them, so to speak. The cool, raw temperature, and strong winds, peculiar to the place, seem to prevent any unhealthy effect from the fermentation of decay. The *Elymus* and other grasses once more take heart and grow with magical vigor over the unsightly spot, to which the sealing gang again return, repeating their bateau, which we have marked before, upon this place, three years ago. In that way this strip of ground, seen on my map between the village, the

rough and the wind blowing hard, these air-dried seal skins, as they were tossed from the bidarrah to the ship's deck, numbers of them would frequently turn in the wind and fly clean over the vessel into the water beyond, where they were lost.

east landing, and the lagoon, contains the bones and the oil drippings and other fragments thereof, of more than 4,000,000 seals slain since 1786, thereon, while the slaughter fields at Novastoshnah record the end of a million more."

"I remember well the unmitigated sensations of disgust that posessed me when I first landed, April 26, 1872, on the Pribylov islands, and passed up from the beach, at Lukannon, to the village, over the killing grounds; though there was a heavy coat of snow on the fields, yet each and every one of the 55,000 decaying carcasses was there, and bare, having burned, as it were, their way out to the open air, poluting the same to a sad degree. I was laughed at by the residents who noticed my facial contortions, and assured me that this state of smell was nothing to what I should soon experience when the frost and snow had fairly melted. They were correct; the odor along by the end of May was terrific punishment to my olfactories, and continued so for several weeks until my sense of smell became blunted and callous to this stench by long familiarity. Like the other old residents I then became quite unconscious of the prevalence of this rich "funk", and ceased to notice it."

"Those who land here, as I did, for the first time, nervously and invariably declare that such an atmosphere must breed a plague or a fever of some kind in the village, and hardly credit the assurance of those who have resided in it for the whole period of their lives, that such a thing was never known to St. Paul, and that the island is remarkably healthy. It is entirely true, however, and, after a few week's contact, or a couple of month's experience, at the longest, the most sensitive nose becomes used to that aroma, wafted as it is hourly, day in and day out, from decaying seal-flesh, vicera, and blubber; and, also, it ceases to be an object of attention. The cool, sunless climate during the warmer months has undoubtedly much to do with checking too rapid decomposition, and consequent trouble therefrom, which would otherwise arise from the killing grounds."

"The freshly skinned carcasses of this season do not seem to rot substantially until the following year; then they rapidly slough away into the sand upon which they rest; the envelope of blubber left upon each body seems to act as an air-tight receiver, holding most of the putrid gas that is evolved from the decaying viscera until their volatile tension causes it to give way; fortunately the line of least resistance to that merciful retort is usually right where it is adjacent to the soil, so both putrescent fluids and much of the stench within is de-odorized and absorbed before it can contaminate the atmosphere to any great extent. The truth of my observation will be promptly verified, if the skeptic chooses to tear open any one of the thousands of gas-distended carcasses in the fall, that were skinned in the killing season; if he does so, he will be smitten by the worst smell that human sense can endure; and should he chance to be accompanied by a native, that callous individual, even will pinch his grimy nose and exclaim, it is a ' keeshla pahnoot ".

" At the close of the third season after the skinning of the seal's body, it will have so rotted and sloughed down, as to be marked only by the bones and a few of the tendinous ligaments; in other words, it requires from thirty to thirty-six month's time for a seal carcass to rot entirely away, so that nothing but whitened bones remain above ground. The natives govern their driving of the seals and laying out of the fresh bodies according to this fact; for they can, and do, spread this year a whole season's killing out over the same spot of the field previously covered with such fresh carcasses three summers ago; by alternating with the seasons thus, the natives are enabled to annually slaughter all of the ' hollus chickie ' on a relatively small area, close by the salt houses, and the village, as I have indicated on the map of St. Paul. "

" **Description of the killing-ground at St. George village.** — On St. George the ' holluschickie ' are regularly driven to that northeast slope of the village hill which drops down gently to the sea, where they are slaughtered, close by and under the houses, as at St. Paul; those droves which are brought in from the north rookery to the west, and also Starry Ateel, are frequently driven right through the village itself. This slaughtering field of St. George is hard tufa and rock, but it slopes down to the ocean rapidly enough to drain itself well; hence the constant rain and humid fogs of summer carry off that which would soon clog and deprive the natives from using the ground year after year in rotation, as they do. Several seasons have occurred, however, when this natural cleansing of the ground above mentioned has not been as thorough as it must be to be used again immediately; then the seals were skinned back of the village hill, and in the ravine to the west on the same slope from the summit."

" This village site of St. George to-day, and the killing-grounds adjoining, used to be, during early Russian occupation, in Pribilov's time a large sea-lion rookery, the finest one known to either island, St. Paul or St. George. Natives are living there who told me that their fathers had been employed in shooting and driving these sea-lions so as to deliberately break up the breeding ground, and thus rid the island of what they considered a superabundant supply of the *Eumetopias*, and thereby to aid and encourage the fresh and increased accession of fur-seals from the vast majority peculiar to St. Paul, which could not take place while the sea-lions held the land."

" These killing grounds at the villages of St. George and St. Paul islands, are the chief slaughtering fields: but another killing ground at " Zapadnie " is established on St. George with a small salt-house, in which the skins as taken are temporarily cured, and then transported over the trail on the backs of donkeys, to the village salt-house for final salting and bundling. On St. Paul at North-east Point, a regular salt-house and killing ground has been ordered and maintained ever since 1868, and some 25,000 to 30,000 skins have been regularly taken there every year since 1870, until last season (1890), when only a trifle over 8,000 were scraped up. Also, on St. Paul, a small killing ground has been established at Stony Point, or Tonkie Mees, ever since 1879 : a salt-house was built there then, but during the last four or five years, so few seals have been secured in its vicinity, that teams have gone, and now go up from the village, on the killing days, and haul the fresh pelts directly down to the village salt-houses; another killing ground at Zapadnie close by ' Antone's House ' has been used ever since 1879; but no salt-house erected here, since the natives now row one of their big skin lighters or ' bidarrahs ', right over from the village to this spot, and sail back with the catch for each days work. No where else on either island, have seals been killed by the lessees since 1870.

SECTION IV

THE SELECTION OF SKINS, GRADE AND SUPPLY IN 1872-74, 1890

SECTION IV

THE SELECTION OF SKINS, GRADE AND SUPPLY IN 1872-74, 1890

As the law of 1870 permits the lessees of the seal islands to kill male seals of any age that they may select from the herds of holluschickie there assembled above one year old, this selection has been very rigorously made from the beginning of the leasing, in 1870; it is entirely natural and in accord with business sense that the aim should have been every year to get only that grade of skins which will bring the most money in the best market : London, England.

In that regular effort made since 1870 to get annually 100,000 seal skins, all to be of the best possible grade, it has been customary during each season to drive up to the killing grounds every herd as it was found hauled out; then when ready to kill. pods of from 50 to 100 animals at a time would be taken from this herd, as drivers, and only those of the best grade in that pod were clubbed, the rest permitted to shamble off and back to the sea. The grade for each summer's work was proclaimed by the general superintendent of the lessees on the islands before the work of the killing season opened, and the clubbing of the pods was then executed in accordance with this order; therefore, no seals were killed above that standard set, or below it, no matter how many or how few were driven up.

This growth and grading of the fur seal on the Pribylov Islands, I found last summer to be the same as it was in 1872-74; the following table expresses it :

SECTION IV.

Table showing the weight, size, and growth of the fur-seal (*Callorhinus ursinus*), from the pup to the adult, male and female.

AGE.	LENGTH.	GIRTH.	GROSS WEIGHT OF body.	WEIGHT of skin.	REMARKS.
	Inches.	Inches.	Pounds.	Pounds.	
One week........	12 to 14	10 to 10-1/2	6 to 7-1/2	1-1/4	A male and female, being the only ones of the class handled, June 20, 1873.
Six Months.......	24	25	39	3	A mean of ten examples, males and females, alike in size, November 28, 1873.
One year.........	38	25	39	4-1/2	A mean of six examples, males and females, alike in size, July 14, 1873.
Two years........	45	30	58	5-1/2	A mean of thirty examples, all males, July 21, 1873.
Three years......	52	36	87	7	A mean of thirty-two examples, all males, July 24, 1873.
Four years.......	58	42	135	12	A mean of ten examples, all males, July 24, 1873.
Five years.......	65	52	200	16	A mean of five examples, all males, July 24, 1873.
Six years........	72	64	280	25	A mean of three examples, all males, July 24, 1873.
Eight to twenty years..	75 to 80	70 to 75	400 to 500	45 to 50	An estimate only, calculating on their weight when fat, and early in the season.

I did not permit myself to fall into error by estimating this matter of weight, because I early found that the apparent huge bulk of a sea-lion bull or fur-seal male, when placed upon the scales, shrank far below my notions; I took a great deal of pains, on several occasions, during the killing season, of 1872-'73, to have a platform scale carted out into the field, and as the seals were knocked down, and before they were bled, I had them carefully weighed, constructing the table above from these records thus obtained; also, I made the following classification then (1872), which is still entirely applicable to these seals, as they exist now (1890).

Classing the "holluschickie" by age. — When the " holluschickie " are up on land, they can be readily separated into their several classes as to age, by the colour of their coats and size, when noted, namely, the yearlings, the two, three, four, and five year old males. When the yearlings, or the first-class, haul out, they are dressed just as they were after they shed their pup-coats and took on the second covering, during the previous year in September and October; and now, as they come out in the spring and summer, one year old, the males and females cannot be distinguished apart, either by color or size, shape or action; the yearlings of both sexes have the same steel-gray backs and white stomachs, and are alike in behavior and weight.

Next year these yearling females, which are now trooping out with the youthful males on the hauling-grounds, will repair to the rookeries, while their male companions will be obliged to come again to this same spot.

Shedding the hair : stagey seals. — About the 15th and 20th of every August, they have become perceptibly " stagey ", or, in other words, their hair is well under way in shedding. All classes, with the exception of the pups, go through this process at this time every year. The process requires about six weeks between the first dropping or falling out of the old over-hair, and its full substitution by the new. This takes place, as a rule, between August 1 and September 28.

The fur is shed, but it is so shed that the ability of the seal to take to the water and stay there, and not to be physically chilled or disturbed during the process of moulting, is never impaired. The whole surface of these extensive breeding grounds, traversed over by us after the seals had gone, was literally matted with the shed hair and fur. This under-fur or pelage is, however, so fine and delicate, and so much concealed and shaded by the coarser over-hair, that a careless eye or a superficial observer might be pardoned in failing to notice the fact of its dropping and renewal.

The yearling cows retain the colours of the old coat in the new, when they shed it for the first time, and from that time on, year after year, as they live and grow old. The young three-year-olds and the older cows look exactly alike, as far as colour goes, when they haul up at first and dry on the rookeries, every June and July.

The yearling males, however, make a radical change when they shed for the first time, for they come out from their "staginess" in a nearly uniform dark gray, and gray and black mixed, and lighter, with dark ochre to whitish on the upper and under parts, respectively. This coat, next year, when they appear as two-year-olds, shedding for the three-year-old coat, is of a very much darker gray, and so on to the third, fourth, and fifth season; then after this, with age, they begin to grow more gray and brown, with rufous-ochre and whitish-tipped over-hair on the shoulders. Some of the very old bulls change in their declining years to a uniform shade all over of dull-grayish ochre. The full glory and beauty of the seal's moustache is denied to him until he has attained his seventh or eighth year.

Change in pelage. — This change for the worse or deterioration of the pelage of the male fur-seals takes place, as a rule, in the fifth year of their age; it is thickest and finest in texture during the third and fourth year of life; hence, in driving the seals on St. Paul and St. George up from the hauling grounds the natives make, as far as practicable, a selection from males of that age.

Comparative size of females and males. — The female does not get her full growth and weight until the end of her fourth year, so far as I have observed, but she does most of her growing longitudinally in the first two; after she has passed her fourth and fifth years, she weighs from 30 to 50 pounds more than she did in the days of her youthful maternity.

The male does not get his full growth and weight until the close of his seventh year, but realizes most of it, osteologically speaking, by the end of the fifth; and from this it may be perhaps truly inferred, that the male seals live to an average age of eighteen or twenty years, if undisturbed in a normal condition, and that the females attain ten or twelve seasons under the same favorable circumstances. Their respective weights, when fully mature and fat in the spring, will, in regard to the male, strike an average of from four to five hundred pounds, while the females will show a mean of from 70 to 80 pounds.

Gradation of the fur of *Callorhinus ursinus*. — The gradation of the fur of *Callorhinus ursinus* may, perhaps, be best presented in the following manner :

One-year old ♂ : well grown : at July 1 of every season :

Fur fully developed as to uniform length and thickness and evenness of distribution; it is lighter in color, and softer in texture, than hereafter, during the life of the animal; average weight of skin as removed by the sealers from the carcass, 4-1/2 pounds.

Two-year old ♂ : well grown : at June 1 of every season :

Fur fully developed as to even length and thickness and uniformity of distribution; it has now attained the darker buff and fawn color, sometimes almost brown, which it retains throughout the life of the animal; it is slightly and perceptibly firmer and stiffer than it was last year, not being at all " fluffy " as in the yearling dress now; average weight of skin, as taken from the body, 5-1/2 pounds.

Three-year old ♂ : well grown : at June 1 of every season :

Fur fully developed, as to even length, but a shade longer over the shoulders, where the incipient " wig " is forming; otherwise perfectly uniform in thickness and even distribution; this is the very best grade of pelt which the seal affords during its life; average weight of skin, as taken from the body, 7 pounds.

Four-year old ♂ : well grown : at June 1 of every season :

Fur fully developed as to even length, except a decided advance in length and perceptible stiffness over the shoulders, in the " wig "; otherwise perfectly uniform in thickness and even distribution; this grade is almost as safe to take, and as good as is the three-year-old; average weight of skin, as removed, 12 pounds.

SECTION IV.

Five-year old ♂ : well grown : from May to June 1 of every season :

Fur fully developed but much longer and decidedly coarser in the "wig" region; otherwise uniform in tkickness and distribution; the coarseness of the fur over the shoulders and disproportionate length thereon destroys that uniformity necessary for rating A 1 in the market; in fact it does not pay to take this skin; average weight, 16 pounds.

Six-year old ♂ : well grown : from May to June 1 of every season :

Fur fully developed, still longer and stiffer in the "wig" region, with a slightly thinner distribution over the post-dorsal region, and shorter; this skin is never taken — it is profitless; average weight, 25 pounds.

Seven-year old and upward ♂ : from May to June 1 of every season :

Fur fully developed but very unevenly distributed, being relatively scant and short over the posterior dorsal region, while it is twice as long and very coarse in the covering to the shoulders especially, and the neck and chest. Skins are valueless to the fur trade; weights, 45 to 60 pounds.

The analysis, as above, is a brief epitome of the entire subject; only, it should be added that the female skins are as finely furred as are the best grades of the males; and also, that age does not cause the quality of their pelage to deteriorate, which it does to so marked an extent in the males. But, taking them into consideration is entirely out of the question, and ought to be so forever.

The fœtal coat of the pup is composed of coarse black hair alone, the underwool not at all developed; when this is shed and the new coat put on in September and October, it is furred and haired as a yearling, which I diagnose above; this pelage has, however, no commercial value.

All the skins taken by the company have been prime skins, in the fair sense of the term.

To this diagnosis of 1872-'74, I may add the 4-year olds are divided by the sealers into "smooth" 4-year olds and "wigged" 4-year olds: the "smooth" skin is the finest one in the field: the "wigged" skin is way below par and never taken unless fear of not getting the quota for the season impels the clubbing of them. These young bulls vary remarkably in this matter of being "wigged", or not, at the culmination of their fourth year — just as young men at 18 vary as to having moustaches and beard, or not.

THE SELECTION OF SKINS.

Therefore, since the finest skins are the 3-year and " smooth " 4-year olds, the standard set for killing has been kept steadily at that mark, and unless a 2-year old was unusually well grown, it and the yearling male has not been clubbed at all to speak of until 1887-'88 : then it became absolutely necessary to kill a large proportion of these smaller seals or fail to get the quota of 100,000 annually, since the larger seals were missing — (had been killed by the driving and clubbing of the preceding seasons) : in 1889, in order to get the quota of 100,000, more than half of the entire catch were "long" and " short " 2-year olds, more than 25,000 "long" yearlings were taken for the first time in the whole period dating from 1870, the balance, some 20,000 only, being the prime 3-year and "smooth" 4-year old skins, which have hitherto, prior to 1887, been the only ones taken as a rule.

Among the many bits of evidence of the rapid elimination of the " holluschickie " which I gathered last season (1890), one of the most self-asserting is the following statement of the percentage of rejection which took place on these killing-grounds of St. Paul in 1872-1874, contrasted with that which I recorded last summer: — the standard for 1872-1874 was three-and " smooth " 4-year old skins (7 lb. and 12 lb. pelts); and it was not lowered; the standard for 1890, at the outset, was the same *until the 4th of July*, then, the supply of those skins having pratically failed, the standard was dropped on that day to " long " 2-year olds (5 1/2 to 6 1/2 lb. skins), and finally on the 18th-20th July, the days of the last killing permitted, the standard was again dropped so as to take in " short " 2-year olds and a few " long " yearlings! Yet with all this effort (and the attempt this year to get 60,000 skins was most vigorously made), only 21,000 skins in round numbers were thus secured, with all possible exertion.

1. A " long " 2-year old is one that is well grown, or above the average size for that age : i. e., 6 lb. skins; a " short " 2-year old is one that is under-grown for its age : i. e. a 5 lb. skin; the same classification is applicable and given to the yearlings.

2. In the report of the Treasury Agent in charge, Mr Charles J. Goff, for the current year, will be found a detailed daily statement of this work last summer, together with a full and exhaustive tabulation of the work as it has been done during the last 20 years upon these islands. I take much pleasure in reprinting this work of Mr Goff; it will be be found in the Appendix, *postea*.

SECTION IV.

Detailed exhibit of percentages of rejection : on the killing grounds under the village at Zapadnie and at Stony Point, St. Paul Island.

DATE 1890.	WHOLE NUMBER of seals in the driven herd.	WHOLE NUMBER of seals killed.	PERCENTAGE of rejection.	SKIN STANDARD of acceptance.	WHERE DRIVEN FROM.	REMARKS.
June 11	about 1,200	539	p. 100. 60	Nothing under 7 lb. skin	"Reef Crest".............	4 yr. & 3 yr. olds only taken; 12 & 7 lb. skins.
— 18	1,750	470	70	—	"Tolstoi", "Middle Hill"...	—
— 23	2,400	518	75	—	—	—
— 24	1,300	426	71	6 1/2 lb. skin	"Reef ,, & " Zol. Bluffs"..	Standard lowered so as to take the long 2 yr. olds; 6 1/2 lb. skins.
— 25	800	263	70	—	"Polavina " & " Stony Pt." .	—
— 26	344	97	72	—	"Zapadnie "............	—
— 27	1,628	392	79	—	"Tolstoi" & " Middle Hill.	—
— 29	1,317	203	83 1/2	—	"Reef Crest "...........	—
— 30	1,262	203	84 1/2	—	"Middle Hill ", "Tolstoi" & " English Bay"........	—
July 1	1,103	120	90	—	"North East Point ".....	—

THE SELECTION OF SKINS.

			Standard again lowered so as to take the average 2 yr. olds; 5 1/2 lb. skins.										
"Reef Crest"	"Polavina"	"Zapadnie"	"Tolstoi", "Middle Hill", "English Bay", "Lukannon" & "Ketavie"		"Polavina"	"Zapadnie"	"Reef Crest"	"Tolstoi", "Middle Hill", "English Bay", "Lukannon" & "Ketavie"	"Reef Crest"	"Tolstoi", "Middle Hill", "English Bay", "Lukannon" & "Ketavie"	"Polavina"	"Lukannon" & "Ketavie"	"Zapadnie"
			5 1/2 lb. skin										
89	88 1/2	81	90 1/2	92	87	83 1/2	89	88 1/2	93	93	87	85 1/4	79
115	210	180	432	350	255	462	377	633	101	309	172	197	211
2,000	1,920	925	4,323	4,001	1,863	867	3,246	5,150	1,592	4,644	1,514	1,320	1,192
1	2	3	4	7	8	9	10	12	14	15	17	17	18

143

10

SECTION IV.

Comments. — The detailed figures upon which the foregoing tabulation is based appear in Section VIII of this report.

In the drive from July 17th from " Polavina ", above cited, in order to swell the shrinking catch, all the 4-year old " wigs " in the drive were knocked down — they have been regularly rejected thus far as they came up daily in the drives; out of the total of 172 killed in this " Polavina " drive, 82 were 4-year old " wigs "; had the standard not been lowered so as to take them, the percentage of rejection would have been 95 °/°. In the drive of July 18th from " Zapadnie ", also cited above, all the 4-year old " wigs " were again taken to swell the diminishing catch ; 94 out of the total here of 241 were " wigs "; had they not been taken, 88 % of rejection would have been the record of that killing.

On the two last days of killing permitted by the Secretary, viz. July 19th and 20th, the standard was again lowered so as to take all the " short " 2-year olds : and the catch of those last killings was increased more than 70 °/° by the acceptance of 5 lb.skins, which had been rejected emphatically up to that hour.

Had the lessees been permitted to kill longer, the result would have been another quick " run to emptyings " by the lapse of three or four more killings; the supply of " short " 2-year olds would then have been exhausted in turn, as the higher grades had hitherto; the seals are simply not in existence sufficient to fill the quota; and, the above statements of fact prove it.

Summary of the percentage of seals rejected from the herds (as driven from the hauling-grounds) when upon the killing-grounds of St. Paul Island, Pribylov group, Bering Sea.

AVERAGE PERCENTAGE OF SEALS " TURNED OUT " FROM THE DRIVEN " PODS ", SEASONS OF 1872-1874, INCLUDING NOTHING BUT 7 TO 12 LB., SKINS TAKEN FROM THE START TO THE FINISH.

From June 5th to 15th, incl.
                                  5 % to 8 % of each driven herd.
— June 15th to 30th, incl.
                                  10 % to 12 % —
— July 1st to 15th, incl.
                                  35 % to 40 % —
— July 15th to 20th, incl.
                                  60 % to 75 % —

THE SELECTION OF SKINS.

AVERAGE PERCENTAGE OF SEALS "TURNED OUT" FROM THE DRIVEN "PODS". SEASON OF 1890. NOTHING BUT 7 TO 12 LB. SKINS TAKEN UP TO 4TH JULY; THEN ALL 5-1/2 LB. SKINS INCLUDED; LAST TWO DAYS, ALL 5 LB. SKINS WERE TAKEN.

From June 5th to 15th, incl.
                                60 % to 70 % of each driven herd.
— June 15th to 30th, incl.
                                70 % to 85 %   —
— July 1st to 15th, incl.
                                85 % to 90 %   —
(Standard lowered to 5-1/2 lb. skins.)
— July 15th to 20th, incl.
                                90 % to 93 %   —
(Standard again lowered to 5 lb. skins.)

The foregoing statement declares that in 1872-74 to get the quota, then secured, of 100,000, 7 lb. and 12 lb. skins (3- and 4-yr. olds chiefly then taken) *required the driving of only* 126,000 *seals from the hauling grounds* to the slaughter fields.

But in 1890, if a quota of 100,000 such skins could have been secured, it would have *required the driving of at least* 1,000,000 *seals!*

It is today an extremely liberal estimate of mine when I admit the existence *of* 80,000 " *holluschickie* ", or male seals from 1 yr. old to 4-yr. olds, *as left upon these islands of Pribylov, July* 31, 1890; and 90 % of this 80,000 are yearlings.

The strange absence of a due proportion of 2-yr. olds in the assembled " holluschickie " of this year, 1890, I believe is largely due to the killing of some 25,000 yearlings, last summer, in that desperate effort made then to fill out the quota allowed of 100,000; coupled with the subsequent deadly effect of last summer's driving upon the spared yearlings.

The following field notes and data are now given in this connection :

" June 23rd, Monday, 1890. Those two pods of holluschickie which I have observed under Middle Hill and Tolstoi, during the last two days, were driven up this morning. I made an itemized count of percentages — the number driven up in each pod' and the number turned out to the sea from it. "

SECTION IV.

Pod No.						
— —	1	(Not in time to count it).				
— —	2	79	animals driven up;	9	of them killed.
— —	3	27	—	— —	7	— — —
— —	4	37	—	— —	8	— — —
— —	5	61	—	— —	13	— — —
— —	6	46	—	— —	10	— — —
— —	7	61	—	— —	15	— — —
— —	8	50	—	— —	13	— — —
— —	9	47	—	— —	7	— — —
— —	10	39	—	— —	9	— — —
— —	11	45	—	— —	6	— — —
— —	12	69	—	— —	9	— — —
11 Pods;	of	561	animals and only	110	of them taken,

or 80 % of the whole number driven, rejected. "

" This gives a fair average of the whole drive today, some 2,800 animals, since 518 skins were taken. "

" At this time in 1872, only 10 to 12 % of such a drive were turned away, the standard being the same to-day as it was then. To-day all the seals taken, with the rare example of a few 4-yr. olds, were 3-yr. olds, not one 4-yr. old in twenty taken, and a remarkable absence of 2-yr. olds — a few only. "

" Those turned away were, 95 % of them at least, " long " and ' short ' yearlings ! a few 5-yr. olds, and a very few 6-yr. old bulls, and a very few ' short ' 2-yr. olds, also. "

" A small pod of holluschickie have just made their appearance, close up under the bluffs at Zoltoi, 100 to 150 of them at about 11 A. M. Now, that calls up to my mind this question — where have those tired seals, driven this morning, and released from the pods into the Lagoon Slough and from there, direct into the sea, — where do they go? Do they haul up again? Yes, everybody says so, and I do not know anything to the contrary, and much in affirmation. Then, that being so, these seals spared today, may be driven tomorrow from Zoltoi Bluffs; to be spared again, and driven next week, and so on, all over through the season. What indication, truthful one, have we of what number of fresh holluschickie really arrive from this time forth if these released seals are to continually present themselves? as they do ! So, as matters go, the steady increase daily of discarded seals, together with the fresh or new arrivals, are driven day after day over and over again throughout the killing season."

"Now, in 1872-'74, this proportion of rejected or turned away' seals from all the drives up to the 1st of July was not over 10 % or 12 % of the whole drove driven — *now, it is* 80 % and 90 %! of this number, yearlings that will require 6 years of rest ere they are fit for rookery service. This is the status at the present moment on the killing grounds right in the very height of the best hour for sealing in the whole season; and this, too, must be considered in the light of the positive declaration of the natives that this repeated driving renders the spared males wholly unfit for rookery service".

"How many of these released seals this morning have been driven over that road before this season? On the 17th, the last drive prior to this one to-day from Middle Hill and Tolstoi was made, 70 % of that drove was turned away; and now, to-day, the same drive is made over again, after an interval of 6 days rest of the ground and 80 % is turned away. I shall observe the next drive very closely as it comes in from Middle Hill and Tolstoi. At this rate of increase of rejection, where will the driving be in July? when the yearlings begin to haul in bodies."

"On June 24th, 1890. 5,50 A. M. A drive this morning from the Zoltoi Bluffs of about 500 all told, and another " pod " from the ' Reef ', some 750 coming. Yesterday morning at 7 o'clock there was not a single holluschakhie under Zoltoi Bluffs. But in less than three hours after the killing began on the Lagoon flats and the turning out there of 80 % of all that Middle Hill drive, I observed holluschickie hauling under these bluffs at Zoltoi, and a few on the sands, the first that have hauled there this year. Now the query enters my mind of — were any of these spared seals of yesterday, hauling up at Zoltoi yesterday? Look at the map and observe the significance of the surroundings. Everybody in 1872, and everybody to-day, admits that these seals which are released from the drives haul up again, are driven over again, released once more and still driven again and again throughout the season."

"In 1872, on this St. Paul village ground, a five-year old bull was pointed out to me by Chief Booterin, which was marked by some curious pink-white mottles on its dark fore flippers.

Booterin said to me that 'polseacatch¹' had been driven up in this way already twice from the hauling grounds, and this made its third trip since the season opened. It was not noticed in any of the subsequent drives, — it may have gone over to St. George in disgust, or have hauled at Zapadnie, at South-west Point, Polavina, Tonkie Mees, where at any one of these resorts at that date, it would have remained in peace, for no seals were then driven from any of these points. Or it may have gone to N. E. Point and exhibited itself to Webster and his men, and again this last drive above noted may have so enfeebled it as to cause its subsequent death at sea."

That these "1/2 bulls" or "polseecatch" thus driven in 1872 should not attempt then to land on the rookeries, was not surprising they simply could not for the crowds of old and virile bulls stationed there, never let them. But to-day where there are wide gaps in the water lines and above these breeding "bulls", why is it that these "1/2 bulls" in these drives to-day (5- and 6-yr. olds) do not ever attempt to go there now, where there is no sign of opposition? It is remarkable; — the statement made by the natives in 1834-'35 and today, that this driving renders them unfit for breeding, is the only solution.

At 7 A. M. I went down to the killing grounds and followed the podding and clubbing of the entire drive as brought up from the "Reef" crest and Zoltoi bluffs early this morning; the "Zoltoi" pod arrived on the ground long before the "Reef" pod, 2 hours sooner; it was made up largely of "polseecatchie" and yearlings the oldest bulls thus far of the season, 6- and 7-yr. olds, and in this drive were many bulls which the natives said, as they pointed them out, had come over from the Lagoon killing yesterday they knew the individuals by certain clubbing marks, etc.

"The seals turned aside this morning were exclusively yearlings and 'short' 2-yr, olds, and a large number of '1/2 bulls'. No 'long' 2-yr. old escaped, so, therefore, many 5-1/2 and 6 lb. skins will appear in this catch; there was, however, a notable absence of 2-yr. olds in proportion to the number driven, and the bulk of the catch was 3-yr. olds as was yesterday's killing, with

---

1. "*Polseacatch* or half-bull"; name given by natives to all fur-seal males over 4 and under 7 years of age.

a very large number of 4-yr. olds in proportion for the small number of skins secured A few cows appeared in the drive, two of them were rookery cows, and two or three were what I called ' barren females ' in 1872-'74. It is impossible, as the driving is now conducted, to avoid getting a few cows in the herd, since nearly two-thirds of that drive this morning came from the breeding lines on the ' Reef Crest '. Driving, thus from the close proximity of breeding lines was not done in 1872-'74; and then, too, I never saw such an extraordinary number of 6-yr. old bulls driven up here before. True it was that in 1872 great numbers of these ' vagrants ' or ' driven bulls ' were to be seen on the hauling grounds then, yet the natives could and did ' walk them out ' on the start, and very few of them came along in the drive. I have often watched them ' cut out ' these large young bulls and any older ones from the drives as they started from English Bay or Lukannon : they don't do it now they are afraid to lose a single eligible seal ! "

" June 27th, 1890. In 1872-'74, very little attention was paid to driving seals until the 12th or 14th of June; true it was that bands of thousands of holluschickie were then already long before that date hauled out on the several resorts, yet, then, because these animals were not in greater numbers, and were nearly all of them down by the surf margin, it was deemed best to wait until the 12th or 14th before beginning in earnest to drive; but after the 14th of June usually, there was such an abundant supply of holluschickie an hand within a mile and a half of this village, and from the salt-house at North-east Point, that no concern was ever given as to the number that they *could* get — it was the number that they *should* get — (just the other way from the present condition and desire) — for, if it was a warmish, dry day in 1872, then only a small drive, so as to get some 1,200 or 1,500 skins, was made; if it was a cool, favorable day, then the driving would be so ordered as to bring in some 2,500 or 3,000 skins, which was about the utmost number that they could handle at the village, in those times, *per diem*, under the most favorable circumstances. "

" How different now, eighteen years since the above cited order of affairs on this ground ! By the 6th of June the most eager, energetic driving began simultaneously with the arrival of each and every squad of holluschickie and has been kept up ever since; but up to the 11th June, these drives were nothing-better than 'food drives', so scant was the supply of killable seals."

"June 28, 1890. 5 A. M. The superb sealing weather still continues; the natives are bringing up a small squad from the "Reef" (some 1,300), as I write. Not a single seal on the sands of Zoltoi this morning, nor has there been one since the last drive, 24th instant, or any prior to that this season. This is remarkable — most remarkable : — this squad of holluschickie driven up from the 'Crest', when released from the several pods on the killing grounds adjacent to Zoltoi, went directly to the sea over by ' Gull Hill' then headed back for the Reef Point — a few for Ketavie, and many of the '1/2 bulls' actually hauled out under ' Gull Hill' and ' Grassy Summit' in less than an hour after their release from the driven herd in which they formed quite a large element this morning."

As these field notes of my daily investigation last summer appear *seriatim* and *in extenso*, in Section VIII following, I will make but one more quotation in this connection illustrative of the utter failure of the supply of killable seals over 1yr. old on these islands today; under date of "June 30th, 1890. The signifiance of this day's work can be seen by the most casual observer. I counted over twenty-four 'moon-eyed' or blind, or semi-blind holluschickie as they escaped in the several ' zapooskas' all of which have been crippled in this manner this season by the effects of prior driving! How many of these yearlings and ' short' 2-yr. olds that were released this morning will again be driven before the season is over? Nearly all of them : — they pass from the pods into the sea over the Lagoon Bar; they meet squadrons of cows playing and lolling in the water around the rookeries — they pause, — listen, — and join in the general comfort which the water certainly affords them; and as the females and fresh arrivals of their own sex haul out on land, these unfortunate seals are beguiled again very soon or a few days later into that deadly procession to that ground from which they were driven early this morning. How the significance — the death of this driving — now keeps rising to my mind! I had little occasion in 1872-'74 to give it thought, and what I did was only in a suggestive mood."

THE SELECTION OF SKINS.

"I passed up from the killing grounds over to Tolstoi Rookery and gave the seal-path or road a careful review. A few holluschickie were again hauled out under Middle Hill and a dozen perhaps on the Tolstoi Rookery sand intersection; but the great hauling grounds of English Bay are utterly destitute of seal life at the hour of this writing, and have been so ever since the season opened with the marked exception of those small squads under Middle Hill, in the rear of Nearhpahskie Kammen, and the sand beach at the immediate ending of the Tolstoi breding lines; these microscopic areas are the only points now in all that vast extent of ground over which, in 1872-'74, the holluschickie of English Bay spread their heavy squadrons.

"Not a holluschik on Zoltoi Sands today, and only a handful on the rocks beyond and above, from which the ' Zoltoi ' drives, so called, have all been thus far. Mr Goff assures me that there was no driving from the ' Sands ' here last year — it was all from those rocks above the Zoltoi Bluffs. When this famous hauling ground began to fail, was the time for a note of warning to have been heard, when did it fail?"

From the Journals of the Treasury Agent's office on St. Paul and St. George islands I have extracted the following data which declares plainly enough that until the season of 1885 closed the annual quota of 100 000 prime skins was easily taken on these islands between the 1st-14th June and the 20th of July; that in 1885 the work suddenly dropped behind and continued to lag until the total failure of 1890 closes this record.

Table showing dates of the first and last killings of each official sealing season on the Pribylov Islands; the season of 1890 closed on the 20th July by order of the Secretary of the Treasury.

ISLAND OF ST. PAUL.

First, 1870. No record	1883.	June 4
Last, 1870. No record	1883.	July 19
First, 1871. May 16	1884.	June 2
Last, 1871. July 31	1884.	July 21
First, 1872. June 1	1885.	June 3
Last, 1872. July 30 The catch of 75,000 was substantially taken on 17th July. A few thousand skins left for food driving until 30th.	1885.	July 27

First, 1873. June 1. 1886. June 2
Last, 1873. July 24   The catch of 75,000 was substantially   1886. July 26
taken by the 20th. A few thou-
sand skins left for food driving
until the 24th.
First, 1874. June 3. 1887. June 6
Last, 1874. July 28   The catch of 90,000 was substantially   1887. July 23
taken on the 16th July; but a few
thousand skins for food driving
were left over to 28th.
First, 1875. June 1. 1888. June 2
Last, 1875. July 23. 1888. July 27
First, 1876. June 6. 1889. June 5
Last, 1876. July 10. 1889. July 31
First, 1877. June 4. 1890. June 6
Last, 1877. July 18. 1890. July 20
First, 1878. June 8
Last, 1878. July 18
First, 1879. June 2
Last, 1879. July 16
First, 1880. June 3
Last, 1880. July 17
First, 1881. June 6
Last, 1881. July 20
First, 1882. June 2
Last, 1882. July 20

ISLAND OF ST. GEORGE.

First, 1870. No record. . . . . 1883. June 11
Last, 1870. No record. . . . . 1883. July 31
First, 1871. June 4. 1884. June 4
Last, 1871. July 31 (Delayed for "food drives" after 22nd). 1884. Aug. 4
First, 1872. June 3. 1885. June 1
Last, 1872. July 27. 1885. July 27
First, 1873. June 4. 1886. June 10
Last, 1873. July 28. 1886. July 23
First, 1874. June 1. 1887. June 9
Last, 1874. July 27. 1887. July 22
First, 1875. June 1. 1888. June 6
Last, 1875. July 17. 1888. July 27
First, 1876. June 1. 1889. June 4
Last, 1876. July 7. . . . . 1889. July 29
First, 1877. June 9. 1890. June 2
Last, 1877. July 10. 1890. July 20
First, 1878. June 10.
Last, 1878. July 21
First, 1879. June 3   This season's work covers
the first draft made upon
the reserves.

THE SELECTION OF SKINS.

Last, 1879. July 16
First, 1880. June 3
Last, 1880. July 9
First, 1881. June 9
Last, 1881. July 16
First, 1882. June 12   Heavy draft begun this year
                          upon the reserves.
Last, 1882. July 19

Official entries in the Journal of the Chief Special Agent of the Treasury Department, in St. Paul Island relative to the close of the sealing season on that island since 1879, the year of first hint of diminution :

July 14, 1879. Drive from Zoltoi, 2,632 skins taken.
July 16, 1879. Last day of the sealing season. Drive from Middle Hill making up the full quota for this island. The natives wound up the sealing with a yell.
                                  (H. G. OTIS, p. 99.)

July 17, 1880. Drive from Zoltoi, the last drive of the regular season, making up the full quota, 80,000.
                                  (H. G. OTIS, p. 181.)

July 20, 1881. Drives from Tolstoi, Zoltoi, Ketavie and Lukannon, the last of the regular sealing season, 2,530 skins taken, filling the island's quota of 80,000.
                                  (H. G. OTIS, p. 231.)

July 20, 1882. The seals killed to-day fill the quota of 1882; total killed 81,510.
                                (H. A. GLIDDEN, p. 268.)

July 19 1883. This entry closes the sealing season.
                                (H. A. GLIDDEN, p. 305.)

July 21, 1884. To-day's killing closes the sealing season of 1884; total killed 88,051.
                                (H. A. GLIDDEN, p. 347.)

July 27, 1885. The A. C. Co. made a final drive from Zoltoi Reef and Middle Hill, and killed 983, which closes the season's quota, making in all 99,996.
                                (G. R. TINGLE, p. 379.)

July 26, 1886. The A. C. Co. completed the season's killing today securing the full quota for this island, viz. 85,000.
                                (G. R. TINGLE, p. 449.)

July 12, 1887. A. C. Co. killed and salted 4,812 skins.

SECTION IV.

July 13, 1887. A. C. Co. killed and salted 4,958 skins; the last two killings are the largest for years in a single day.
July 23, 1887. A. C. Co. made a drive at S. W. Bay to close the season.

(G. R. TINGLE, p. 13.)

July 27, 1888. The sealing season closed to-day, completing the full quota of 100,000, being 85,000 for this, and 15,000 for St. George island. "

(G. R. TINGLE, p. 76.)

July 31, 1889. The season closed today, the full quota being secured for this island (85,000).

(C. J. GOFF.)

The foregoing statements of fact declare that the first breakdown from the regular time, July 20th, of getting the whole catch since 1870, took place in 1885, when it fell suddenly to the 27th of July, rallied a little in 1887, but fell back again in 1888, and down to the bottom in 1889. This season of 1890 never had a real beginning if a comparison of the seals killed daily since it opened is made with the daily record of any of the preceding 20 years.

The custom on both islands in driving of combining the herds from several localities into one drive as it is brought upon the killing grounds makes a direct comparison between years of the catch taken from any one hauling ground very difficult, indeed incorrect if attempted.

But there are two localities, North-east Point on St. Paul, and Zapadnie on St. George island, where there is no opportunity to merge any other seals driven, except those found there alone; this makes the following contrast between the work of 1889 and 1890 very direct and honest :

Daily record of seals taken at Novastoshnah, seasons of 1889-1890.

Date.	1889. No. of skins.	1890. No. of skins.	Skin grade; Nothing under 1889.	1890.
June 17	1,034	16	6-lb.	7-lb.
— 18	1,270	78	—	—
— 19	494	»	—	—
— 20	»	438	—	—
— 21	1,205	96	—	—
Carry foward.	4,023	628		

THE SELECTION OF SKINS.

Date.	1889. No. of skins.	1890. No. of skins.	Skin grade: Nothing under. 1889.	1890.
Brought forward :	4,023	628		
— 22	»	»	—	—
— 23	»	176	—	—
— 24	754	202	—	—
— 25	1,407	164	—	—
— 26	441	»	—	—
— 27	844	225	—	—
— 28	479	79	—	—
— 29	355	»	—	—
— 30	»	97	—	—
Total. . .	8,403	1,601		
July 1	1,200	130	—	—
— 2	968	96	—	—
— 3	»	380	—	—
— 4	1,559	118	—	5-1/2 lb.
— 5	1,524	74	6·lb.	5-1/2 lb.
— 6	376	»	—	—
— 7	»	336	—	—
— 8	914	378	—	—
— 9	641	271	—	—
— 10	800	112	—	—
— 11	»	»	—	—
— 12	»	»	—	—
— 13	793	641	—	—
— 14	»	»	—	—
— 15	1,838	243	—	5-lb.
— 16	1,156	311	—	—
— 17	948	485	—	—
— 18	1,282	405	—	—
— 19	834	446	—	—
— 20	243	464	—	—
— 22	350	»	—	—
— 23	740	»	—	—
— 24	610	»	—	—
— 26	1,433	»	—	—
— 29	1,625	»	—	—
— 31	938	»	—	—

Season closed for 1890 by order of Secretary of Treasury.

The contrast thus clearly drawn between the work at Northeast Point last year, and this season of 1890, tells its own story; down on the killing grounds at the village of St. Paul, the general manager became alarmed at the prospect of failure to get the season's quota of 100,000 for both islands; he accordingly lowered, on the 13th of July, the standard from a 6 lb. skin to a 4-1/2 lb. skin; thus taking in all the " long " yearlings, and everything above to the 5 yr. olds. But Webster, then at N. E. Point, stubbornly refused-to kill anything under a "short"2 yr. old or 5 lb.skin.

At the Village, however, over 20,000 of these "long" yearlings were knocked down and taken after the 13th July, 1889; that enabled the shipment of that season's quota of 85,000 skins from St. Paul after the 31st July.

Daily record of seals taken at Zapadnie, St. George Island; Seasons of 1889-1890; between the 10th June and 20th July.

Date.	1889 No. of skins.	1890 No. of skins.	Skin grade Nothing under	
			1889	1890
June 10	207	»	6-lb.	7-lb.
— 17	244	»	—	—
— 20	»	394	—	—
— 24	505	»	—	—
— 27	223	189	—	—
Total..	1,269	583		
July 1	167	»	—	—
— 7	»	58	—	—
— 8	229	»	—	—
July 12	192	»	6-lb.	7-lb.
— 14	»	53	—	—
— 15	371	»	—	—
— 18	439	»	—	—
— 20	»	527	—	5-lb.
Total..	1,498	635		
July 22	500		—	
— 25	279		—	
— 28	568		—	

Extracts from the Journal of the Treasury Agent, St. Paul Island, showing the dates of the first regular drafts made upon the reserved male life at Zapadnie ("S. W. Bay"), and Polavina. These dates also declare the time of that exhaustion in part of the regular sources of hitherto abundant supply at Tolstoi, Middle Hill, Lukannon and Zoltoi :

Page 92. June 9, 1879. Antone Meloviedov started with a gang to make a drive at Half-way Point Polavina.

THE SELECTION OF SKINS. 159

Page 93. June 10, 1879. The drive to day (at Polavina) resulted in the taking of 1,118 skins. (H. G. Otis.)

Page 93. June 11, 1879. Drive made from S. W. Bay (Zapadnie) today. and 1,462 skins taken. (H. G. Otis.)

From this day on to the close of that sealing season's work, July 20th, Zapadnie was driven often, and Polavina also; but in 1880 *only one drive was made* from this reservoir at Zapadnie, that on the 7th of June, in which 1,496 skins were taken; and, again, in 1881, *it was not driven from at all*, and *only one drive that year made from the Polavina reserve*, on the 10th June, in which 474 skins were taken :

But in 1882, the draft began in earnest and has never ceased up to the end of the present season of 1890.

The work of rapid depletion of the seal life on the hauling grounds of the Pribilov islands takes its origin at the beginning of this season of 1881; the following citations from the Treasury Agent's Journal on St. Paul's Island, show the suddenness, the regularity, and the frequency of these heavy drafts of 1882 upon that surplus male life which was wholly undisturbed by man in 1872-'74.

1882 : June	2nd.	"Drive made from S. W. Bay", etc.		
—	7th	—	—	— —
—	12th	—	—	— —
—	13th	—	—	Polavina", etc.
—	17th	—	—	S. W. Bay", etc.
—	20th	—	—	— —
—	23rd	—	—	Polavina", etc.
—	26th	—	—	S. W. Bay", etc.
—	27th	—	—	— —
—	30th	—	—	Polavina", etc.
July	3rd	—	—	S. W. Bay", etc.
—	8th	—	—	Polavina", etc.
—	13th	—	—	S. W. Bay", etc.
—	20th	—	—	— —

Season closed on the 20th, the full quota then taken of 85,000 for St. Paul.

And another feature of this draft is that the skins taken from these reserves were all large skins nothing under 3-and 4-yr. olds, or 7-1/2 to 12 lb. skins, until the end was reached in 1889, after the 13th of July, of that season.

SECTION V

CHARACTER, CONDITION AND NUMBER OF NATIVES
OF THE PRIBYLOV ISLANDS IN 1872-74,
AND 1890

SECTION V

CHARACTER, CONDITION AND NUMBER OF NATIVES OF THE PRIBYLOV ISLANDS IN 1872-74, AND 1890

What constitutes a native. — There has been some divergence of opinion on the islands as to who are the real " natives " thereof, because these natives enjoy certain privileges that are very valuable to them and coveted by all outside Alaskan brethren.

In this connection the people living here are divided into three classes; that is, the males :

First. — The natives, properly speaking, or those who have been born and raised upon the Pribylov Islands; not over one-tenth of the present adult population can lay claim to this title.

Second. — The people who were living thereon, but not born natives at the time of the transfer of all Alaska, July, 1867; this class constitutes a majority of the citizens of the two islands as they exist to-day.

Third. — The people who were living and working as sealers on the Pribylov Islands at the date of the granting by the government of the present lease to the Alaska Commercial Company, August 3rd, 1870.

Of the above three divisions, strict justice and true equity unite in recognizing the third class as the " natives " of the Pribylov Islands. This settles the question also to the best satisfaction of these people themselves, and removes every quibble of dispute in the premises. Accurate records of the men, women, and children living on each island at the date of the lease in 1870 can be found in the church registers on both St. Paul and St. George.

According to Bishop Veniaminov, the inhabitants of the Pribylov Islands belonged to the parish of Unalashka, the priest of which was obliged to visit them once every two years ("to marry, baptize", etc.) "These islands were not known before the year 1786; mate G. Pribylov, then in the service of a swan-hunting company, first, in the Russian name, found them, but at the same time he was not the first discoverer, because, as before said (Part I, chap. 1,) on one of them (southwest side of St. Paul) signs such as a pipe, brass knife-handle, and traces of fire, were found, indicating that people had been there before, but not long, as places were observed where the grass had been burned and scorched. But if we can believe the Aleuts in what they relate, the islands were known to them long before they were visited by the Russians. They knew and called them "Ateek", after having heard about them."

When Pribylov, in taking possession, landed on St. George a part of his little ship's crew, July, 1786, he knew that, as it was uninhabited, it would be necessary to create a colony there from which to draft labourers to do the killing, skinning, and curing of the peltries; therefore he and his associates, and his rivals after him, imported natives of Unalashka and Atkha, passive, docile Aleuts. They founded their first village a quarter of a mile to the eastward of one of the principal rookeries on St. George, now called "Starry Ateel", or "Old settlement"; a village was also located at Zapadnie, and a succession of barrabaras planted at Garden Cove. Then, during the following season, more men were brought up from Atkha and taken over to St Paul, where five or six rival traders posted themselves on the north shore, near and at "Maroonitch", and at the head of the Big Lake, among the sand dunes there. They were then, as they are now, somewhat given to riotous living, if they only had the chance, and the ruins of the Big Lake settlement are pleasantly remembered by the descendants of those pioneers to-day, on St. Paul, who take off their hats as they pass by, to affectionately salute, and call the place "Vesolia Mista", or "Jolly Spot"; the elder men told me, with great unction, that "in those good old days they had plenty of rum." .But when the pressure of competition became great, another village was located at Polavina, and still another at Zapadnie, until the activity and unscrupulous energy of all these rival settlements well-nigh drove out and eliminated the seals in 1796. Three years later the whole territory of Alaska passed into the hands of the absolute power vested in the Russian-American Company. These islands were in the bill of sale, and early in 1799 the competing traders were turned off neck and heels from them, and the Pribylov group passed under the control of a single man, the iron-willed Baranov. The people on St. Paul were then all drawn together, for economy and warmth, into a single settlement at Polavina. Their life in those days must have been miserable. They were mere slaves, without the slightest redress from any insolence or injury which their masters might see fit, in petulance or brutal orgies, to inflict upon them. Here they lived and died, unnoticed and uncared for, in large barracoons half under ground and dirt-roofed, cold and filthy. Along toward the beginning or end of 1825, in order that they might reap the advantages of being located best to load and unload ships, the Polavina settlement was removed to the present village site, as indicated on the map, and the natives have lived there ever since.

On St. George the several scattered villages were abandoned, and consolidated at the existing location some years later, but for a different reason. The labour of bringing the seal-skins over to Garden Cove, which is the best and surest landing, was so great and that of carrying them from the north shore to Zapadnie still greater, that it was decided to place the consolidated settlement at such a point between them, on the north shore, that the least trouble and exertion of conveyance would be necessary. A better place, geographically, for the business of gathering the skins and salting them down at St. George cannot be found on the island, but a poorer place for a landing it is difficult to pick out, though in this respect there is not much choice outside of Garden Cove.

The Aleutian stock on the islands, as it appears to-day, has been so mixed up with Russian, American, and Kamtschadale blood, that it presents characteristics, in one way or another, of all the various races of men, from the negro up to the Caucasian. The predominant features among them are small, wide-set eyes, broad and high cheek-bones, causing the jaw, which is full and square, to often appear peaked; coarse, straight, black hair, small, neatly shaped feet and hands, together with brownish-yellow complexion. The men will average in stature five feet, four or five inches; the women less in proportion, although there are exceptions to this rule among them, some being over six feet in height, and others are decided dwarfs. The manners and customs of these people to-day possess nothing in themselves of a barbarous or remarkable character, aside from that which belongs to an advanced state of semi-civilization. They are exceedingly polite and civil, not only in their business with the agents of the Government and the company on the seal-islands, but among themselves; and they visit, the one with the other, freely and pleasantly, the women being great gossips. But, on the whole, their intercourse is subdued, for the simple reason that the topics of conversation are few, and, judging from their silent but unconstrained meetings, they seem to have a mutual knowledge as if by sympathy as to what may be occupying each other's minds, rendering speech superfluous. It is only when under the influence of beer or strong liquor, that they lose their naturally quiet and amiable disposition; they then relapse into low, drunken orgies and loud brawling noises. Having been so long under the control and influence of the Russians, they have adopted many Slavic customs, such as giving birthday-dinners, naming their children, etc.; they are remarkably attached to their church, and no other form of religion could be better adapted to or have a firmer hold upon the sensibilities of the people. Their inherent chastity and sobriety cannot be commended. They have long since thrown away the uncouth garments of the Russian rule the shaggy dog-skin caps, with coats half seal and half sea-lion for a complete outfit, *cap-à-pié*, such as our own people buy in any furnishing house; the same boots, socks, underclothing and clothing, with ulsters and ulsterettes; but the violence of the wind prevents their selecting the hats of our *haut ton* and sporting fraternity. As for the women, they too have kept pace and even advanced to the level of the men, for in these lower races there is much more vanity displayed by the masculine element than the feminine, according to my observation; in other words, I have noticed a greater desire among the young men than among the young women of savage and semi-civilized people to be gaily dressed and to look fine. But the visits of the wives of our treasury officials and the company's agents to these islands, during the last twenty years, bringing with them a full outfit, as ladies always do, of everything under the sun that women want to wear, has given the native female mind an undue expansion up there, and stimulated it to unwonted activity. They watch the cut of the garments, and borrow the patterns; and some of them are very expert dress-makers to-day. When the Russians controlled affairs, the women were the hewers of the drift-wood and the drawers of the water. At St. Paul there was no well of drinking-fluid about, nor within half a mile of, the village; there was no drinking-water unless it was caught in cisterns, and the cistern-water, owing to the particles of seal-fat soot which fall upon the roofs of the houses, is rendered undrinkable; so that the supply for the town, until quite recently, used to be carried by the women from two little lakes at the head of the lagoon, a mile and a half, as the crow flies, from the village, and right under Telegraph hill. This is quite a journey, and when it is remembered that they drink so much tea, and that water has to go with it, some idea of the labour of the old and young females can be derived from an inspection of the map. Latterly, within the last fourteen years, the company opened a spring less than half a mile from the "gorode", which they have plumbed and regulated, so that it supplies them with water now, and renders the labor next to nothing, compared with the former difficulty. But to-day, when water is wanted in the Aleutian houses at St. Paul, the man often has to get it; he trudges out with a little wooden firkin or tub on his back, and brings it to the house.

The fact that among all the savage races found on the northwest coast by Christian pioneers and teachers, the Aleutians are the only practical converts to Christianity, goes far, in my opinion, to set them apart as very differently constituted in mind and disposition from our Indians and our Eskimos of Alaska. To the latter, however, they seem to be intimately allied, though they do not mingle in the slightest degree. They adopted the Christian faith with very little opposition, readily exchanging their barbarous customs and wild superstitions for the rites of the

Greek-Catholic church, and its more refined myths and legends.

At the time of their first discovery, they were living as savages in every sense of the word, bold and hardy, throughout the Aleutian chain, but now they respond, on these islands, to all outward signs of Christianity, as sincerely as our own church-going people.

Up to the time of the transfer of the territory and leasing of the islands to the Alaska Commercial Company, in August, 1870, these native inhabitants all lived in huts or sod-walled and dirt-roofed houses, called " barrabkies, " partly under ground. Most of these huts were damp, dark and exceedingly filthy; it seemed to be the policy of the short-sighted Russian management to keep them so, and to treat the natives not near so well as they treated the few hogs and dogs which they brought up there for food and for company. The use of seal-fat for fuel caused the deposit upon everything within doors of a thick coat of greasy, black soot, strongly impregnated with a damp, mouldy, and indescribably offensive odour. They found along the north shore of St. Paul and at Northe-ast point, occasional scattered pieces of drift-wood, which they used, carefully soaked anew in water if it had dried out, split into little fragments, and, trussing the blubber with it when making their fires, the combination gave rise to a roaring, spluttering blaze. If this drift-wood failed them at any time when winter came round, they were obliged to huddle together beneath skins in their cold huts, and live or die, as the case might be. But the situation to-day has changed marvelously.

When Congress granted to the Alaska Commercial Company of San Francisco the exclusive right of taking a certain number of fur-seals every year, for a period of twenty years on these islands it did so with several reservations and conditions, which were confided in their detail to the Secretary of the Treasury. This officer and the president of the Alaska Commercial Company agreed upon a code of regulations which should govern their joint action in regard to the natives. It was a simple agreement that these people should have a certain amount of dried salmon furnished them for food every year, a certain amount of fuel, a school-house, and the right to go to and come from the islands as they chose; and also the right to work or not, understanding that in case they did not work, their places would and could be supplied by other people who whould work.

The company, however, went far beyond this exaction of the government; it added an inexpressible boon of comfort, in the formation of those dwellings now occupied by the natives, which was not expressed nor thought of at the time of the granting of the lease. An enlightened business policy suggested to the company that it would be much better for the natives, and much better for the company too, if these people were taken out of their filthy, unwholesome hovels, put into habitable dwellings, and taught to live cleanly, for the simple reason that by so doing the natives, living in this improved condition, would be able physically and mentally, every season when the sealing work began, to come out from their long inanition, and go to work at once with vigor and energetic persistency. The sequel proved the wisdom of the company[1].

Many experiments, however, were made, and a dozen houses built, ere the result was as good as the style of primitive housing when it had been well done. and kept in best possible repair. In such a damp climate, naturally, a strong mouldy smell pervades all inclosed rooms which are not thoroughly heated and daily dried by fires; and in the spring and fall frost works through and drips and trickles like rain adown the walls. The present frame houses occupied by the natives owe their dryness, their warmth and protection from the piercing "boorgas", to the liberal use of stout tarred paper in the lining. The overpowering mustiness of the hall-ways, outhouses, and, in fact, every roofed-in spot, where a

1. Before this action on their part, it was physically impossible for the inhabitants of St. Paul or St. George islands to take the lawful quota of 100,000 seal-skins annually in less than three or four workings months. They can take them in less than thirty working days now with the same number of men. What is the gain? Simply this, and it is everything. The fur-seal skin, from the 14th of June, when it first arrives, as a rule, up to the 20th of July, is in prime condition; from that latter date until the middle of October it deteriorates, to slowly appreciate again in value as it sheds and renews its coat; so much so that it is practically worthless in the markets of the world. Hence the catch taken by the Alaska Commercial Company every year was a prime one, first to last there were no low-grade or " stagey " skins in it; but under the old regime, three-fourths of the skins were taken in August, in September, and even in October, and were not worth their transportation to London. Comment on this is unnecessary; it is the contrast made between a prescient business policy, and one that was as shiftless and improvident as language can well devise.

stove is not regularly used, even in the best-built residences, is one of the first disagreable sensations which the new arrivals always experience when they take up their quarters here. Perhaps, if it were not for the nasal misery that floats in from the killing-grounds to the novice, this musty, mouldy state of things up here would be far more acute, as an annoyance, than it is now. The greater grief seems to soon fully absorb the lesser one; at least in my own case, I can affirm the result.

We see here now at St. Paul and on St. George, in the place of the squalid, filthy habitations of the inmediate past, two villages neat, warm and contented. Each family lives in a snug, frame-dwelling; every house is lined with tarred paper, painted, furnished with out-houses, etc., with a stove complete; streets laid out, and the foundations of these habitations regularly plotted thereon. There is a large church at St. Paul, and a less pretentious but very creditable structure of the same character on St. George; a pharmacy on St. Paul, with a full and complete stock for the people, free of cost. There is a school-house on each island, in which teachers have been paid by the company eight months of every year, to instruct the youth; while the Russian church is sustained entirely by the pious contributions of the natives themselves on these two islands, and sustained well by each other. There are 63 family-houses, on St. Paul, in the village, with 20 or 24 such houses to as many families at St. George, and 8 other structures. The large warehouses and salt-sheds built by the Alaska Commercial Company's skillful mechanics, as have been the dwellings just referred to, are also neatly painted; and, taken in combination with the other features, constitute a picture fully equal to the average presentation of any one of our small, eastern towns. There is no misery, no downcast, dejected, suffering humanity here to-day. These Aleuts, who have enjoyed as the price of their good behaviour, the sole right to take and skin seals for the company, to the exclusion of all other people, are known to and by their less fortunate neighbors else-where in Alaska as the "Bogatskie Aloutov", or the "rich Aleuts". The example of many of the agents of the Alaska Commercial Company on both islands, from the beginning of its lease, and the course of some of the treasury agents during the last twenty years, have been silent but powerful promoters of the welfare of these people. They have maintained perfect order; they have directed neatness, and cleanliness, and stimulated industry, such as those natives had never before dreamed of; and have enforced sobriety.

The agents of the Government and the company found so much difficulty at first, in getting the youth of the villages to attend their schools, taught by our own people, especially brought up there and hired by the company, that they adopted the plan of bringing one or two of the brightest boys down every year and putting them into our schools, so that they might grow up here, and be educated, in order to return and serve as teachers there. This policy is warranted by the success attending the experiment made at the time when I was up there first, whereby a son of the chief was carried down and over to Rutland, Vermont, for his education, remained there four years, then returned and took charge of the school on St. Paul, which he served until his death, with the happiest results in increased attendance and attention from the children. But, of course, so long as the Russian church service is conducted in the Russian language, we will find on the islands more Russian-speaking people than our own. The non-attendance at school was not and is not to be ascribed to indisposition on the part of the children to our English school; but if their boys and young men neglected their Russian lessons, they knew not who were going to take their places, when they died, in their church, at the christenings, and at their burial? To any one familiar with the teachings of the Greek-Catholic faith, the objection of old Philip Volkow seems reasonable. I hope, therefore, that in the course of time, the Russian church service may be voiced in English; not that I want to substitute any other religion for it — far from it; in my opinion it is the best one we could have for these people, but until this subtitution of our language for the Russian is done, no very satisfactory work in my opinion, will be accomplished in the way of an English education on the seal-islands.

As they are living to-day up there, there is no restraint such as the presence of policemen, courts of justice, fines, etc., wich we employ for the suppression of disorder, and maintenance of the law in our own land. They understand that if it is necessary to make them law-abiding, and to punish crime, that such officers will be among them; and hence, perhaps, is due the fact, that, from the time that the Alaska Commercial Company's lease was made, in 1870, there has not been one single occasion where the simplest functions of a justice of the peace would or need have been called in to settle any difficulty. This speaks eloquently for their docile nature und their amiable disposition. Surprise has often been genuine among those who inquire, over the fact that there is no law officer here at either village, and wonder is expressed why such provision is not made by the government. But, when the following facts relative to this subject are understood, it is at once clear that a justice of the peace and his constabulary, would be entirely useless, if established on the seal-islands. As these natives live here, they live as a single family in each settlement, having one common purpose in life and only one; what one native does, eats, wears, or says, is known at once to all the others, just as whatsoever any member of our household may do will soon be known to us all who belong to its organization; hence if they steal or quarrel among themselves, they keep the matter wholly to themselves, and settle it to their own satisfaction. Were there rival villages on the islands and diverse people and employment, then the case would be reversed, and need of legal machinery apparent.

As it is, the agent of the Treasury Department is clothed with all the power necessary to maintain order up there : he is recognized and respected as the trusted representative of the Secretary of the Treasury, who is the supreme temporal ruler of their little commonwealth; and, as such, he is never disobeyed.

Seal-meat is their staple food, and in the village of St. Paul they consume on an average fully 500 pounds a day the year round; and they are, by the permission of the Secretary of the Treasury, allowed every fall to kill 5000 or 6000 seal-pups, or an average of 22 to 30 young "kotickie" for each man, woman and child in the settlements. The pups will dress 10 pounds each. This shows an average consumption of nearly 600 pounds of seal-meat by each person, large and small during the year. To this diet the natives add a great deal of butter and many sweet crackers. They are passionately fond of butter, no epicure at home, or butter-taster in Goshen, knows or appreciates that article better than these people do. If they could get all that they desire, they would consume 1,000 pounds of butter and 500 pounds of sweet crackers every week, and indefinite quantities of sugar the sweetest of all sweet teeth are found in the jaw of the average Aleut. But it is of course unwise to allow them full swing in this matter, for they would turn their stomachs into fermenting tanks if they had full access to an unlimited supply of saccharine food. If unable to get sweet crackers they will eat about 300 pounds of hard or pilot bread every week, and in addition to this nearly 700 pounds of flour at the same time. Of tobacco they are allowed 50 pounds per week; candles, 75 pounds; rice, 50 pounds. They burn, strange as it may seem, kerosene oil here to the exclusion of the seal-fat, which literally overruns the island. They ignite and consume over 600 gallons of kerosene oil a year in the village of St Paul alone. They do not fancy vinegar very much, perhaps 50 gallons a year is used up there. Mustard and pepper are sparingly used, one to one and a half pounds a week for the whole village; beans they peremptorily reject, for some reason or other they cannot be induced to use them. Those who go about the vessels contract a taste for split-pea soup, and a few of them are sold in the village store. Salt meat, beef or pork, they will take reluctantly, if it is given to and pressed upon them, but they will never buy it. I remember, in this connection, seeing two barrels of prime salt pork and a barrel of prime mess salt beef opened in the company's store, shortly after my arrival in 1872, and, though the people of the village were invited to help themselves, I think I am right in saying that the barrels were not emptied when I left the island in 1873. They use a very little coffee during the year, not more than 100 pounds, but of tea a great deal, — about 100 chests every year, but I can say that they do not drink less than a gallon of tea apiece per diem. The amount of this beverage which they sip, from the time they rise in the morning until they go to bed late at night, is astounding. Their "samovars", and latterly, the regular tea-kettles of our American make, are bubbling and boiling from the moment the housewife stirs herself at daybreak until the fire goes out when they sleep. It should be stated in this connection, that they are supplied with a regular allowance of coal every year by the company, gratis, each family being entitled to a certain amount which alone, if economically used, keeps them warm all winter in their new houses; but, for those who are extravagant and are itching to spend their extra wages, an extra supply is always kept in the store-houses of the company for sale. Their appreciation of and desire to possess all the canned fruit that is landed from the steamer is marked to a great degree. If they had the opportunity, I doubt whether a single family on that island to-day would hesitate to bankrupt itself in purchasing this commodity. Potatoes they sometimes demand as well as onions, and perhaps if these vegetables could be brought here and kept to advantage, the people would soon become very fond of them. Six or seven years ago, and after the supply of sugar had been cut off from their purchase at the store, on account of their abuse of it in making quass and getting frequently drunk, they developed a great fondness for canned milk, — ordered it at all times, and never got enough of it; soon the reason appeared, — there was and is a good body in two cans of Borden's condensed milk for the making of several gallons of beer.

Most of these articles of food just mentioned are purchased by the natives in the company's store[1] at either island; this food and the wearing apparel, crockery, etc., which the company bring up here for the use of the people, is sold to them at the exact cost price of the same, plus the expenses of transportation; and, many times within my knowledge, they have bought goods here, at these stores, at less rates than they would have been subjected to in San Francisco; the object of the company is not, under any circumstances, to make a single cent of profit out of the sale of these goods to the natives; they aim only to clear the cost and no more. Instructions to this effect were given to its agents, while those of the Government were called upon to take notice of the fact.

Another important factor to the physical well-being of these people, is the presence on the Pribylov Islands of an abundant

[1]. The store at St. Paul, as well as that at St. George, has its regular annual "opening" after the arrival of the steamer in the spring, to which the natives seem to pay absorbed attention; they crowd the buildings day and night, eagerly looking for all the novelties in food and apparel; these slouchy men and shawl-hooded women, who pack the area before the counters here, seem to feel as deep an interest in the process of shopping as the most enthusiastic votaries of that business do in our own streets; it certainly seems to give them the greatest satisfaction of their lives on the Pribylov Islands.

number of big sea-lions (*Eumetopias Stelleri*); this animal supplies them with its hide, moustaches, flesh, fat, sinews and intestines, which they make up into as many necessary garments, dishes, etc. They have abundant reason to treasure its skin highly, for it is the covering to their neat bidarkies and bidarrahs, the former being the small kyak of Behring Sea, while the latter is a boat of all work exploration and transportation. These skins are unhaired by sweating in a pile; then they are deftly sewed and carefully stretched over a light keel and frame of wood, making a perfectly water-tight boat that will stand, uninjured, the softening influence of water for a day or two at a time, if properly air-dried and oiled. After being used during the day, these skin boats are always drawn out on the beach, turned bottom-side up and air-dried during the night; in this way made ready for employment again on the morrow.

A peculiar value is attached to the intestines of the sea-lion, which, after cleansing, are distended with air and allowed to dry in that shape; then they are cut into ribbons and sewed strongly together into that most characteristic water-proof garment of the world, known as the "kamlaika[1]"; which, while being fully as water-proof as India rubber, has far greater strength, and is never affected by grease and oil. It is also transparent in fitting over dark clothes. The sea-lion's throats are served in a similar manner, and, when cured, are made into boot-tops, which are in turn soled by the tough skin that composes the palms of this animal's fore-flippers. Around the natives' houses, on St. Paul and St. George, constantly appear curious objects, which to the unaccustomed eye, resemble overgrown gourds or enormous calabashes with attenuanted necks; an examination proves them to be the dried, distended stomach-walls of the sea-lion, filled with its oil (and

---

1. The Aleutian name for this garment is unpronounceable in our language, and equally so in the more flexible Russian; hence the Alaskan "kamlaika", derived from the Siberian "kamlaia". That is made of tanned reindeer skin, unhaired, and smoked by larch bark until it is colored a saffron yellow; and is worn over the reindeer skin undershirt, which has the hair next to the owner's skin, and the obverse side stained red by a decoction of alder bark. The kamlaia is closed behind and before, and a hood, fastened to the back of the neck, is drawn over the head, when leaving shelter; so is the Aleutian kamlaika; only the one of Kolyma is used to keep out piercing dry cold, while the garment of the Behring Sea is a perfect water repellant.

sometimes with dried meat) which, unlike the offensive blubber of the fur-seal, boils out clear and inodorous from its fat.

The flesh of an old sea-lion, while not very palatable, is tasteless and dry; but the meat of a yearling is very much like veal, and when properly cooked I think it is just as good; but the superiority of the sea-lion meat over that of the fur-seal is decidedly marked. It requires some skill, in the cuisine, ere sausage and steaks of the *Callorhinus* are accepted on the table; while it does not, however, require much art, experience, or patience for the cook to serve up the juicy ribs of a young sea-lion so that the most fastidious palate will not fail to relish it.

The carcass of the sea-lion, after it is stripped of its hide, and disembowelled, is hung up in cool weather by its hind-flippers, over a rude wooden frame or " labaas ", as the natives call it, where, together with many more bodies of fur-seals treated in the same manner, it serves from November until the following season of May, as the meat-house, of the Aleut on St. Paul and St. George. Exposed in this manner to the open weather, the natives keep their seal-meat almost any length of time, in winter, for use; and, like our old duck and bird hunters, they say they prefer to have the meat tainted rather than fresh, declaring that it is most tender and toothsome when decidedly " loud ".

In 1872, when slowly sketching by measurements, the outlines of a fine adult bull sea-lion which the ball from Booterin's rifle had just destroyed, an old " starooka " came up abruptly; not seeming to see me, she deliberately threw down a large, greasy, skin meat-bag, and whipping out a knife, went to work on my specimen. Curiosity prompted me to keep still in spite of the first sensation of annoyance, so that I might watch her choice and use of the animal's carcass. She first removed the skin, being actively aided in this operation by an uncouth boy; she then cut off the palms of both fore-flippers; the boy at the same time pulled out the moustache bristles; she then cut out its gullet, from the glottis to to its junction with the stomach, carefully divested it of all fleshy attachments, and fat; she then cut out the stomach itself, and turned it inside out, carelessly scraping the gastric walls free of copious biliary secretions, the inevitable bunch of *ascaris;* she then told the boy to take hold of the duodenum end of the small intestine, and as he walked away with it she rapidly cleared it of its attachments, so that it was thus uncoiled to its full length of at least 60 feet; then she severed it, and then it was recoiled by the " melchiska ", and laid up with the other members just removed, except the skin, which she had nothing more to do with. She then cut out the liver and ate several large pieces of that workhouse of the blood before dropping it into the meat-pouch. She then raked up several handfulls of the " leaf-lard ", or hard, white fat that is found in moderate quantity around the viscera of all these pinnipeds, which she also dumped into the flesh-bag; she then drew her knife through the large heart, but did not touch it otherwise, looking at it intently, however, as it still quivered in unison with the warm flesh of the whole carcass. She and the boy then poked their fingers into the tumid lobes of the immense lungs, cutting out portions of them only, which were also put into the grimy pouch aforesaid; then she secured the gall-bladder, and slipped it into a small yeast-powder tin, which was produced by the urchin; then she finished her economical dissection by cutting the sinews out of the back in unbroken bulk from the cervical vertebra to the sacrum; all these were stuffed into that skin bag, which she threw on her back and supported it by a band over her head; she then trudged back to the barrabkie from whence she sallied a short hour ago, like an old vulture to the slaughter. She made the following disposition of its contents. The palms were used to sole a pair of tarbosars, or native boots; of which, the uppers and knee tops were made of the gullets, one sea-lion gullet to each boot-top; the stomach was carefully blown up, and left to dry on the barrabkie roof, eventually to be filled with oil rendered from sea-lion or fur-seal blubber. The small intestine was carefully injected with water and cleansed, then distended with air, and pegged out between two stakes, 60 feet apart, with little cross-slats here and there between to keep it clear of the ground. When it is thoroughly dry, it is ripped up in a straight line with its length and pressed out into a broad band of parchment gut, which she cuts up and uses in making a water-proof " kamlaikie " sewing it with those sinews taken from the back. The liver, leaf-lard, and lobes of the lungs were eaten without further cooking, and the little gall-bag was for some use in poulticing a scrofulous sore.

The moustache-bristles were a venture of the boy, who gathers all that he can, then sends them to San Francisco, where they find a ready sale to the Chinese, who pay about one cent apiece for them. When the natives cut up a sea-lion carcass, or one of a fur-seal, on the killing grounds for meat, they take only the hams and the loins. Later in the season they eat the entire carcass, which they hang up by hind-flippers on a " labaas " by their houses.

The St. George natives manage to secure a good many cod and halibut; but the St. Paul people have very poor luck fishing; so what they get in this line is really unimportant : in the early years, 1870-'78 they all used their own boats. i. e., bidarkas, but during the last ten or twelve years they have purchased yawls and whitehall boats of our make, for fishing, egging trips, etc., they are not active fishermen in any sense of the word ; they are very fond, however, of sea-eggs, and frequently the natives have brought a dish of sea-urchins' ovaries for our table, offering it as a great delicacy. I do not think any of us did more than to taste it. The native women are the chief hunters for *Echinidæ*, and, during the whole spring and summer seasons they may be seen at both islands, wading in the pools at low water, with their scanty skirts high up, eagerly laying possessive hands upon every " bristling " egg that shows itself. They vary this search by poking, with a short-handled hook, into holes and rocky crevices for a small cottoid fish, which is also found here at low water in this manner. Specimens of this " kalog ", which I brought down, declared themselves as representatives of a new departure from all other recognized forms in which the sculpin is known to sport ; hence the name generic and specific, *Melletes papilio*.

By the 28th of May to the middle of June, a fine table crab, large, fat, and sweet, with a light, brittle shell is taken while it is skurryng in and out of the lagoon as the tide ebbs and flows. It is the best-flavored crustacean known to Alaskan waters. The natives affirm the existence of mussels here in abundance when the Pribylov group was first discovered, but now only a small supply of inferior size and quality is to be found.

The native cooking is now all done in their houses, on small cast-iron stoves of American pattern and make. In olden times the unavoidable use of fur-seal blubber in culinary operations caused the erection, outside of most " barrabaras ", of a small sod-walled and low, dirt-roofed kitchen, in which the strong-smelling blubber fires were kindled. Indifferent as the native became to smells and smoke in the filthy life of early days upon these islands, yet the acrid, stifling, asthmatic effect of the blubber clouds never failed to punish him whenever he attempted to make use of such a fire in his living-room. Most of these " cookhnets ", or " povaèniks ", were in full blast when I first landed at St. Paul, and coming frequently into range of their smoky effluvium, I was infinitely annoyed; now, however, the complete substitution of new frame houses for the " barrabkies " has, I believe, caused a perfect abatement of the nuisance.

On account of the severe climatic conditions it is of course impracticable to have any sort of a vegetable garden or keep stock here with any profit or pleasure. The experiment has been tried faithfully. It is found best to bring beef-cattle up in the spring on the steamer, turn them out to pasture until the close of the season, in October, and November, and then, if the snow comes, to kill them and keep them refrigerated the rest of the year. Stock cannot be profitably raised here, the proportion of severe weather annually is too great, from three to perhaps six months of every year they require feeding and watering, with good shelter. To furnish an animal with hay and grain up there is a costly matter, and the dampness of the growing summer season on both islands renders hay-making impracticable. The natives keep a few chickens, — some years they do very well, then epidemic will break out and, for several seasons thereafter, poultry raising is a complete failure on the islands; in short, chickens are kept with much difficulty; in fact, it is only possible to save their lives when the natives take them into their own rooms, or keep them above their heads, in the little attics to their dwellings during severe winters.

But for some reason or other, these people have a strange passion for seal-fed pork, and in 1872-74, there were quite a large number of hogs on the islands of St. Paul and a few on St. George. The pigs soon become entirely carnivorous, living, to the practical exclusion of all other diet, on the carcasses of seals; it appears, however, that these hogs became so numerous by 1879-80 that the agents of the Government and company in 1881-84 made up an indictment against the Seal Island hog and proceeded to shoot them right and left, until the extermination of the species soon followed. The natives offered no resistance, but they still plead for permission to keep hogs[1]. Last but not least in this statement of native food-resources, is the annual unlimited supply of waterfowl from May until November, auks, arries, gulls, many ducks and a few geese; the flesh and eggs of which are extensively consumed. After the dead silence of a long ice-bound winter, the arrival of large flocks of those sparrows of the north, the " chootch kies ", *Phaleris microceros*, is most cheerful and interesting. Those plump little auks are bright, fearless, vivacious birds, with bodies round and fat. They come usually in chattering flocks on or immediately after the 1st of May, and are caught by the people with hand-scoops or dip-nets to any number that may be required for the day's consumption; their tiny, rotund forms making pies of rare savory virtue, and being also baked and roasted and stewed in every conceivable shape by the Russian cooks — indeed they are equal to the reed-birds of the South. These welcome visitors are succeeded rapidly by thousands and countless tens of thousands of guillemots or " arries ", *Lomvia arra;* this bird is the great egg producer of that region.

These people are singularly affectionate and indulgent towards their children. There are no " bald-headed tyrants " in our homes, as arbitrary and ruthless in their rule as are those snuffly babies and young children on the seal-islands. While it is very young the Aleut gives up everything to the caprice of his child, and never crosses its path or thwarts its desire; the " deetiah " literally take charge of the house ; but as soon as these callow members of the family become strong enough to bear burdens and to labour, generally between 12 and 15 yers of age, they are then pressed into hard service relentlessly by their hitherto indulgent parents; the extremes literally meet in this application. The urchins play marbles, spin tops, and fly kites, intermittently, with all the feverish energy displayed by the youth of our own surroundings ; they frolic at base-ball, and use " shinny " sticks with much volubility and activity. The girls are, however, much more

---

1. I think that they should be permitted to keep a few, if they will pen them up and care for them properly.

repressed, and thought they have a few games, and play quietly with quaintly dressed dolls, yet they do not appear to be possessed of that usual feminine animation so conspicuously marked in our home life.

One of the peculiarities of these people is that they seldom undress when they go to bed — neither the men, women, nor children; and also that at any and all hours of the night during the summer season, when I have passed in and out of the village to and from the rookeries, I always found several of the natives squatting before their house doors or leaning against the walls, stupidly staring out into the misty darkness of the fog, or chatting one with the other over their pipes. A number of the inhabitants, by this disposition, are always up and around throughout the settlement during the entire night and day. In olden times, and even recently, these involuntary sentinels of the night have often startled the whole village by shouting at the top of their voices the pleasent and electric announcement of the " ship's light " : or have frozen it with superstitious horror in the recital, at daybreak, of ghostly visions.

The inherent propensity of man to gamble is developed here to a very appreciable degree, but it in no way suggests the strange gaming love and infatuation with which the Indians and Eskimo of Alaska are elsewhere possessed. The chief delight of the men and boys of the two villages is to stand on the street-corners, " pitching " half dollars; so devoted, indeed, have I found the native mind to this hap-hazard sport, that frequently I would detect groups of them standing out in pelting gales of wind and of rain, " shying " the silver coin at the little dirt-driven pegs. A few of them, men and women, play cards with much skill and intelligence.

The attachment which the natives have for their respective islands was well shown to me in 1874. Then, a number of St. George people were taken over to St. Paul, temporarilly, to do the killing incidental to a reduction of the quota of 25,000 for their island and a corresponding increase at St. Paul; they became homesick immediatly, and were never tired of informing the St. Paul natives that St. George was a far handsomer and more enjoyable island to live upon: that walking over the long sand reaches of " Pavel " made their legs grievously weary, and that the whole effect of this change of residence was " ochen scootchnie ". Naturally, the ire of the St. Paul people rose at once, and they retorted in kind, indicating the rocky surface of St. George, and its great inferiority as a seal-island. I was surprised at the genuine feeling on both sides, because, as far as I could judge from a residence on each island, it was a clear case of tweedle-dee and tweedle-dum between them, as to opportunities and climate necessary for a pleasurable existence. The natives, themselves, are of one and common stock, though the number of creoles on St. George is relatively much larger than on St. Paul; consequently the tone of the St. George is rather more sprightly and vivacious.

This question is often asked: " How do these people employ themselves during the long nine months of every year after the close of the sealing season and until it begins again, when they they have little or absolutely nothing to do? It may be answered that they simply vegetate; or, in other words, are entirely idle, mentally and physically, during most of this period. But, to their credit, let it be said, that mischief does not employ their idle hands; they are passive killers of time, drinking tea and sleeping, with a few disagreeable exceptions, such as the gamblers. There are a half-dozen of these characters at St. Paul, and perhaps as many at St. George, who pass whole nights at their sittings, even during the sealing season, playing games of cards, taught by Russians and persons who have been on the island since the transfer of the territory; but the majority of the men, women and children not being compelled to exert themselves to obtain any of the chief, or even the least, of the necessaries of life, such as tea and hard bread, sleep the greater portion of the time, when not busy in eating, and in the daily observances of the routine belonging to the Greek Catholic church. The teachings, pomp, and circumstance of the religious observances of this faith alone preserve these people from absolute stagnation. In obedience to its teachings they gladly attend church very regularly. They also make and receive calls on their saints' days, and these days are very numerous. I think some 160 of the whole year's calendar must be given up to the ceremonies attendant upon the celebration of some holy birth or death.

In early times the same disgraceful beer-drinking orgies, which prevailed to so great an extent, and still cause so much misery and confusion seen elsewhere in the territory, prevailed here, and I remember very well the difficulty which I had in initiating the first steps taken by the Treasury Department to suppress this abominable nuisance. During the last fourteen or fifteen years, it gives me pleasure to say, since the new order of things was inaugurated, the several agents of the department have faithfully executed the law.

The natives add to these entertainments of their saints'days and birth festivals, or " Emannimiks ", the music of accordeons and violins; upon the former and its variation, the concertina, they play a number of airs, and are very fond of the noise. A great many of the women, in particular, can render indifferently a limited selection of tunes, many of which are the old battle-songs, so popular during the rebellion, woven into weird Russian waltzes and love ditties, which they have jointly gathered from their former masters and our soldiers, who were quartered here in 1869. From the Russians and the troops, also, they have learned to dance various figures, and have been taught to waltz. These dances, however, the old folks do not enjoy very much. They will come in, and sit around and look at the young performers with stolid indifference; but, if they manage to get a strong current of tea setting in their direction, nicely sugared and toned up, they revive and join in the mirth. In old times they never danced here unless they were drunk, and it was the principal occupation of the amiable and mischievous treasury agents, and others, in the early days to open up this beery fun. Happily, that nuisance is abated. During the last six or eight years they have organized a very good string and brass band on St. Paul Island, and play well.

Number of the Islanders. — The population[1] of St. Paul Island in 1872, was 235 souls : to-day, in 1890, it is 171 souls : of St. George Island in 1872 it was 127 souls : to-day it is 98. This declares a decrease since then of 93. Prior to 1873, they had neither much increased nor diminished for 50 years, but would have

1. In the report of Mr Goff, which I reprint in Section VIII, will be found all the details of this Census for 1890 : to it, I add there a note giving the details for 1872.

fallen off rapidly (for the births were never equal to the deaths) had not recruits been regularly drawn from the mainland and other islands every season when the ships came up. As they lived then, it was a physical impossibility for them to increase and multiply; but since their elevation and their sanitary advancement became so marked, it was reasonably expected that those people for all time to come would at least hold their own, even though they do not increase to any remarkable degree. Perhaps it is better that they should not. They are, of all men, especially fitted for the work connected with the seal-business; no comment is needed; nothing better in the way of manual labor, skilled and rapid, could be rendered by any body of men, equal in numbers, living under the same circumstances, all the year round. They appear to shake off the periodic lethargy of winter and its forced inanition, to rush with the coming of summer into the severe exercise and duty of capturing killing and skinning the seals, with vigour and with persistent and commendable energy.

To-day only a very small proportion of the population are descendants of the pioneers who were brought here by the several Russian companies, in 1787 and 1788: a colony of 137 souls, it is claimed, principally recruited at Oonalashka and Atkha.

The principal cause of death among the people, by natural infirmity, on the seal-islands, is the varying forms of consumption and bronchitis, always greatly aggravated by that inherited scrofulous taint or stain of blood which was, in one way or another, flowing through the veins of their recent progenitors, both here and throughout the Aleutian Islands. There is nothing worth noticing in the line of nervous diseases, unless it be now and then the record of a case of alcoholism superinduced by excessive quass drinking. This "makoolah" intemperance among these people, which was not suppressed until 1876, was a chief factor in the immediate death of infants, for, when they were at the breast, the mothers would drink quass to intoxication, and the stomachs of the newly born Aleuts or Creoles could not stand the infliction which they received, even second-hand. Had it not been for this wretched spectacle so often presented to my eyes in 1872-'73, I should hardly have taken the active steps which I did to put the nuisance down; for it involved me, at first, in a bitter personal

CHARACTER, CONDITION AND NUMBER OF NATIVES. 185

controversy, which, although I knew at the outset it was inevitable, still weighed nothing in the scales against the evil itself[1].

A few febrile disorders are occurring, yet they yield readily to good treatment, but they have this peculiarity : when they are ill, slightly or seriously, no matter which, they maintain or affect a stolid resignation, and are patient to positive apathy. This is not due to deficiency of nervous organization, because those among them who exhibit examples of intense liveliness and nervous activity, behave just as stolidly when ill as their more lymphatic townsmen do. Boys and girls, men and women, all alike are patient and resigned when ailing and under treatment; but it is a bad feature after all, inasmuch as it is well-nigh impossible to rally a very sick man who himself has no hope, and who seems to mutely deprecate every effort to save his life.

1. This evil of habitual and gross intoxication, under Russian rule was not characteristic of these islands alone, it was universal throughout Alaska. Sir George Simpson, speaking of the subject, when in Sitka, April, 1842, says : " Some reformation certainly was wanted in this repect; for of all the drunken, as well as of all the dirty places that I had visited, New Archangel (Sitka) was the worst. On the holidays in particular, of which, Sundays included, there are one hundred and sixty-five in the year, men, women, and even children were to be seen staggering about in all directions. " (Simpson : Journey Around the World; 1841-42, p. 83.)

SECTION VI

CONDUCT OF NATIVE LABOUR, AND PAY, IN 1872-74, 1890

SECTION VI

CONDUCT OF NATIVE LABOUR, AND PAY, IN 1872-74, 1890

Living as the seal-islanders do, and doing what they do, the seal's life is naturally their great study and objective point. It nourishes and sustains them. Without it they say they could not live, and they tell the truth. Hence, their attention to the few simple requirements of the law, so wise in its provisions, is not forced or constrained, but is continuous. Self-interest in this respect appeals to them keenly and eloquently. They know everything that is done and everything that is said by anybody and by everybody in their little community. Every seal-drive that is made, and every skin that is taken, is recorded and accounted for by them, by their chiefs and their church, when they make up their tithing-roll at the close of each season's labour. Nothing can come to the islands, by day or by night, without being seen by them and spoken of. I regard the presence of these people on the islands at the transfer, and their subsequent retention and entailment in connection with the seal-business, as an exceedingly good piece of fortune, alike advantageous to the government, to the company, and to themselves.

When we go back to the beginning of the sealing industry on these islands, the time of Pribylov and his rivals in 1786 to 1799-1801, and attempt to find any record of the conduct of the labour or compensation paid to labourers here, we discover nothing that throws the least light upon the subject; when the old Russian-American Company was put into supreme control of all Alaska in 1799, and Baranov had time in 1803 to visit these islands and close them to everybody save his own agents, we may safely assume to know pretty well what was done in this respect; we know it because we have the following statement from the best authority.

"The Aleuts serving the company sustain the following relations between themselves and it, to wit. Each of them worked without solicitation, were ordered to do whatever was found, and to which they were directed, or at that which they understood best. Payment for their toil was not established by the day, or by the year, but in general for each thing taken by them, or standing or put to their credit by the company, for instance, especially, the skins of animals, the teeth of walrus, barrels of oil, etc. These sums, whatever they might be, were placed by the company to their credit, for all general working and hunting was established or fixed for the whole year fairly. These Aleuts, in general, receive no specific wages and they are all not alike or equal, there being usually three or four classes.

In these classes, to the last or least the sick and old workmen are counted in, although they are only burdens, and therefore they receive the smaller shares, about 150 rubles (i. e., $40) a year, and the other and better classes receive from 220 to 250 rubles per year ($55 to $60). Those who are zealous are rewarded by the company with 50 to 100 rubles ($10 to $25). The wives of the Aleuts who worked at the seal hunting received from 25 to 35 rubles ($6 to $9) per annum".

(Veniaminov : " Zapieska ", etc. St. Petersburg, 1840).

This definition of the subject by Bishop Veniaminov shows us the precise relation and nature of pay that we are looking for; it covers the whole of that extended period from 1801 to 1868, 67 years; the " rubles " that all payment in Alaska during that time was made in, were paper or parchment tags, stamped with the private mark of the old Company, and rated at about 20 cents per ruble, in the Aleutian district, according to Veniaminov; inasmuch as he states that in 1835 " 4 paper rubles here are worth 1 of silver ".

At the time of the transfer of Alaska, July, 1867, and from that time until December, 1867, nothing was known by the people on these islands of the change, and they had no realization of the significance of that change until April, 1868, when three rival American sealing parties all landed on St. Paul Island within a few days of each other, and promptly began to make preparations for the coming of the seals, and taking their skins; and four different parties under the American flag established themselves a little later if at all behind, on St. George; these several parties, all bent on sealing, and many of them having old Antarctic fur-sealers in control, were anxious and desirous of securing all the native labour each one to itself, as against its rivals. The foremen then began to offer to pay the natives more and more, as they bid over one another, per skin, when delivered during the sealing season; they finally found that they would bid so high for the native labour in this manner, as to leave no profit; this brought them to an amicable agreement among themselves by which they would, none of them, pay more or less than 40 cents per skin delivered by the natives; then the natives worked for all hands during the season of 1868 without any particular advantage in serving one party better than the other.

This season's work of 1868 fixed the price of labour for skinning a young male fur-seal at 40 cents for the first time on these islands, — a tariff at least four times greater than ever before received by the native sealer here : and this rate of 40 cents was at once assumed and paid by the Alaska Commercial Co at the inception of its lease in 1870, and continued in the new lease of 1890 to the North American Commercial Co, by order of the Secretary of the Treausury for the present season of 1890.

During the last 20 years, and throughout the present season, the natives themselves worked under the direction of their own chosen foremen, or " toyone ". This chief calls out the men at the break of every working-day, divides them into detachments according to the nature of the service, and orders their doing. All communication with the labourers on the sealing-ground and the company passes through his hands ; these chiefs having every day an understanding with the agent of the company as to his wishes, and they govern themselves thereby.

The company directs its own labour, in accordance with the law, as it sees fit; selects its time of working, etc., in accordance with, and obedience to the regulations of the Secretary of the Treasury from year to year.

The treasury officials on the seal-islands are charged with the careful observance of every act of the company; a copy of the lease and its covenant is conspicuously posted in their office is translated into Russian, and is familiar to all the natives. The care and supervision of the welfare of the rookeries, and of natives was and is their chief charge.

The old company paid, and the new company pays 40 cents for the labour of taking each skin. The natives take the skins on the killing-ground. Then the skins are brought up and counted into the salt-houses, where the agent of the company receives them from the hands of his own employés. When the quota of skins is taken, at the close of two, three, or four weeks of labour, as the case may be, the total sum for the entire catch is paid over in a lump to the chiefs, and these men divide it among the labourers according to their standing as workmen, which they themselves have exhibited on their special tally-sticks. For instance, at the annual divisions, or " catch " settlement, made by the natives on St. Paul Island among themselves, in 1872, when I was present, the proceeds of their work for that season in taking and skinning 75,000 seals, at 40 cents per skin, with extra work connected with it, making the sum of $30,637.37, was divided among them in this way: There were 74 shares made up, representing 74 men, though in fact only 56 men worked, but they wished to give a certain proportion to their church, a certain proportion to their priest, and certain proportion to their widows; so they watered their stock, commercially speaking. The 74 shares were proportioned as follows :

37 first-class shares, at.	$431.22 each
23 second-class shares, at.	406.08 each
4 third-class shares, at.	360.97 each
10 fourth-class shares, at.	315.85 each

And since 1870, up to 1890, they have never received less than this, except in one season (*sic*) when only 80,000 instead of 100,000 was taken. But last summer, the catch on St. Paul was little more than 16,500 skins, so that the division was but slightly over one-fifth of the cash equivalent of the annual settlement hitherto during the last nineteen years.

In August, 1873, while on St. George Island, I was present at a similar division, under similar circumstances, which caused them to divide among themselves the proceeds of their work in taking and skinning 25,000 seals, at 40 cents a skin, $ 810,000. They made the following subdivision :

	Per share
17 shares each, 961 skins	$ 384.40
2 shares each, 935 skins	374.00
3 shares each, 821 skins	328.40
1 share each, 820 skins	328.00
3 shares each, 770 skins	308.00
3 shares each, 400 skins	160.00

These 29 shares referred to represent only 25 able-bodied sealers; two of them were women. This method of division as above given, is the result of their own choice. Four shares went to the church.

In August, 1890, I was again present on St. George, when the list was made up, but instead of the division being based upon the proceeds of taking 25,000 skins, it was the mere form of dividing $ 50 or $ 60 apiece among the sealers who have been able to take only 4,132 skins on St. George this year.

There has always been much difference of opinion as to how this annual settlement should be made among the natives. I said in 1874.

" It is an impossible thing for the company to decide their relative merits as workmen on the ground, so they have wisely turned its entire discussion over to them. Whatever they do they must agree to, whatever the company might do they possibly and probably would never clearly understand, and hence dissatisfaction and suspicion would inevitably arise; as it is, the whole subject is most satisfactorily settled ", and I am still of that opinion; but since then a gradual removal of the whole control from the natives has been made in the following manner : At the close of the season's work, *i. e.* when the quota had been secured, by the 16th to 20th of July as a rule, the chiefs and their people would make up their division, in the method above described;

this when submitted to the company's agent and the Treasury officer was usually altered by changing the names of the notorious loafers in the sealing gang into those lower grades of the division, and putting better men up : the loafers were usually men of "influence" with the church and strange as it may seem, with their own industrious townsmen, and so they were able to have their names generally placed at the top of this list. Strictly speaking, this action of the agents of the company and Government in revising the list was entirely in the right; but still the natives were better satisfied with their old way of 1872-1874, for the reason which I gave in the citation above.

This payment of 40 cents per skin taken by the natives covers nothing except the labor of driving the seals, skinning them, and helping the outside employés of the lessees to salt these skins in the salt-houses. The extra work of bundling these skins for shipment was paid for by the bundle, 1 cent per bundle, so that a smart native could make $2 per day, while at this work; then, when the ships arrived and sailed, the great and necessary labour of lightering their cargoes off and on from the roadsteads where they anchor, was principally performed by these people, and they were paid so much a day for their labor, from 50 cents to $1, according to the character of the service they rendered; this operation, however, is much dreaded by the ship-captains and sea-going men, whose habits of discipline and automatic regularity and effect of working render them severe critics and impatient coadjutors of the natives, who, to tell the truth, hated to do anything after they had pocketed their reward for sealing; and when they did labor after this, they regarded it as an act of very great condescension on their part.

Until 1882, all the labour outside of sealing incident to the business on these islands was executed by the natives of the two settlements of St. Paul and St. George, with the aid of a half-dozen of white men on shore, employés of the lessees, and the crews of their vessels. But in 1882 an epidemic of typhoid pneumonia scourged the village of St. Paul, and fully one-half of the able-bodied men were dead when it subsided in 1883; this made it necessary for the lessees to bring up thirty or forty natives from Unalashka every sealing season thereafter to do this work of salt-

CONDUCT OF NATIVE LABOUR. 193

ing and bundling skins, and unloading and loading the vessels. These outside laborers came upon the lessees' steamer every May or by the 1st of June were quartered ashore and worked here until the close of the season in July; then returned by the 3rd to 10th of August to Unalashka, receiving pay at the rate of $ 40 per month, all found; they never have been permitted to drive or skin seals; that work has been done entirely by the Pribylov men ever since 1870 up to the present hour.

In 1872-1874 and up to 1885, these seal-islanders elected their chiefs after their own choice : but they finally got into so much internal liking and disliking over this selection, that the chiefs so elected began to be disobeyed and slighted by many of their men. Thereupon the Treasury Agent and the company's representative, in charge, took the matter up, selected a new man, and ordered him chief; that settled the difficulty, and ended it; he was promptly obeyed.

Some of the natives save their money; but there are very few among them, perhaps not more than a dozen, who have the slightest economical tendency. What they cannot spend for luxuries, groceries, and tobacco, they manage to get away with at the gaming-table. They have their misers and their spendthrifts, and they have the usual small proportion, who know how to make money and then how to spend it. A few among them who are in the habit of saving opened a regular bank-account with the Company; some of them have to-day two or three thousand dollars saved, drawing an interest of 4 per cent.

1. Full details of this topic appear in Mr. Goff's report; *post*. This report is not in fact included in the appendix to Mr. Eliotts report but it is doubtless the report appearing in the British Case Appendix. vol. III., U. S., n° 2, p. 14. (Ed.)

SECTION VII

THE PROTECTION AND PRESERVATION OF THE FUR-
BEARING INTERESTS OF OUR GOVERNMENT IN THE
PRIBYLOV ISLANDS: THE IMMEDIATE ACTION
NECESSARY VIEWED IN THE FULL LIGHT
OF EXISTING DANGER

SECTION VII

**THE PROTECTION AND PRESERVATION
OF THE FUR-BEARING INTERESTS OF OUR GOVERNMENT
IN THE PRIBYLOV ISLANDS
THE IMMEDIATE ACTION NECESSARY VIEWED IN THE FULL
LIGHT OF EXISTING DANGER.**

The statements and exhibitions of fact contained in the foregoing Sections I — IV inclusive warrant me in declaring that the close of the present season's work of 1890 brings this question and its alternative promptly forward " Shall our Government make no further effort to prevent the extermination of its sealing preserves on the Pribylov Islands? " or " Will it step forward again and try anew to prevent that ruin? "

There is a universal — a unanimous wish not only at home but abroad that these Alaskan fur-seal rookeries be preserved, and a hope that these anomalous and valuable interests can be saved, and every reputable commercial, scientific, and political organization throughout the whole civilized world will applaud any action that will draw the Powers of Great Britain, Russia and the United States together in harmonious effort to that end.

Telling the truth, as I have been compelled to tell it in detail, will have however, this compensation — it will arouse and enlist the sympathy and support of a very large element that has hitherto declared its utter indifference as to whether the hunting of fur-seals in the open waters of Bering Sea was prohibited, or not, since it believed that the last official reports published up to 1889 as filed in the Treasury Department were correct in declaring that the Pribylov fur-seals were vastly increased and increasing still over their fine form and number of 1872-'74. And it also said, " What real harm are these poachers doing — why only look at the figures, after all their work, yet in spite of it, there are more seals than ever on those islands, " " their work may annoy and injure somewhat the leased monopoly up there, but what of that? if the seals can stand it, we do not feel concerned. "

These erroneous statements made in 1886-'87-'88 by official reports to the Treasury, declaring a steady increase of seals on the Pribylov Islands have given the seal poachers during the last three or four years, great aid and comfort, which has been advanced to them from official circles not only at home, but in Great Britain and Canada; and which would not have been proffered from any quarter for a moment had the fact been known that ever since 1882, the Pribylov seals have been declining in number, — rapidly dwindling ever since 1886.

Those who did not, and do not believe that we are right in claiming Bering Sea as a *mare clausum* will at once heartily unite with those who do believe in that doctrine, in so far as making it a closed sea to all pelagic sealing, the moment it becomes necessary to do so to prevent an extermination of those world renowned rookeries of Behring Sea; and in the face of the present danger the most pronounced opponents of the leasing system, monopolies, etc., will be equally prompt in joining hands with those who do believe in this plan, to forward any plan that promises preservation and conservation.

But this plan of restoration must be an unselfish one — must be free from any taint of private gain or profit, or it will fail to receive this universal sympathy and endorsement — it will fail, and it ought to fail, if it is not so planned.

Before sketching an outline of the action which I deem necessary for the Secretary of the Treasury to take for the coming season of 1891, and that legislation by Congress to strengthen his hands, the following account[1] of a similar decline of the seal life

---

1. Translated by the writer, from Veniaminov's *Zapieski*, etc.; St. Petersburg, 1840; vol. ii, pp. 568. The italics are mine, and my translation is nearly literal, as might be inferred by the idiom here and there.

in these Pribylov Islands, and its restoration way back in 1817-1834 in pertinent in this connection.

" **Indiscriminate slaughter by the first discoverers.** — From the time of the discovery of the Pribylov Islands up to 1805 (or, that is until the time of the arrival in America of General Resanov[1]), the taking of fur-seals on both islands progressed without count or lists, and without responsible heads or chiefs, because then (1787 to 1805, inclusive) there were a number of companies, represented by as many agents or leaders, and all of them vied with each other in taking as many as they could before the killing was stopped. After this, in 1806 and 1807, there were no seals taken, and nearly all the people were removed to Unalashka. "

" **Partial check ordered** ". — In 1808 the killing was again commenced; but the people in this year were allowed to kill only on St. George. On St. Paul hunters were not permitted this year or the next. It was not until the fourth year after this that as many as half the number previously taken were annually killed. From this time (St. George 1808, and St. Paul 1810) up to 1822, taking fur-seals progressed on both islands without economy and with slight circumspection, as if there were a race in killing for the most skins. Cows were taken in drives and killed, and were also driven from the rookeries to places where they were slaughtered. "

" It was only in 1822 that G. Moorayvev (governor) ordered that young seals should be spared every year for breeding, and

---

1. Resanov in his official letter to the Emperor of Russia dated Unalashka Island, July 28, 1805, says. " The multitude of seals in which St. Paul abounds, is incredible; the shores are covered with them. They are easily caught, and as we were short of provisions, eighteen were killed for us in half an hour. But, at the same time we were informed that they had decreased in number ninety per cent since earlier times. These islands would be an inexhaustible source of wealth were it not for the Bostonians who undermine our trade with China in furs, of which they obtain large numbers on our American coast. As over a million had already been killed, I gave orders to stop the slaughter at once, in order to prevent their total extermination, and to employ the men in collecting walrus tusks as there is a small island near St. Paul covered with walrus ": he adds that he met with sufficient evidences of carelessness and wast : " The skins of the fur seal were scattered about over the beach and the bluff in various stages of decomposition ". " The store-houses were full, but only a smale part of their contents was in a marketable state ". As many as " thirty thousand had been killed for their flesh alone ", the skins having been " left on the spot or thrown into the sea ". After questioning the Aleutian laborers and Russian overseers Resanov came to the conclusion that unless an end were put to this wanton destruction a few years more would witness the extirpation of the fur seal.

from that time there were taken from the Pribylov islands, instead of 40,000 to 50,000, which Moorayvev ordered to be spared in four successive years, no more than 8,000 to 10,000. Since this, G. Chestyahkov, chief ruler after Moorayvev, estimated that from the increase resulting from the legislation of Moorayvev, which was so honestly carried out on the Pribylov islands, that in these four years the seals on St. Paul had increased to double their previous number, (*that*) he could give an order which increased the number to be annually slain to 40,000; and this last order of course directed for these islands, demanded as many seals as could be got; but with all possible exertion hardly 28,000 were obtained."

"**Poor results.** — After this, when it was most plainly seen that the seals were, on account of this wicked killing, steadily growing less and less in number, the directions were observed for greater caution in killing the grown seals and young females, which came in with the droves of killing-seals, and to endeavor to separate, if possible, these from those which should be slain."

"**Partial checks again ordered.** — But all this hardly served to do more than keep the seals at one figure or number, and hence did not cause an increase. Finally, in 1834, the Governor of the company, upon the clear (*or* " *handsome* ") argument of Baron Wrangel, which was placed before him, resolved to make new regulations respecting them, to take effect in the same year (1834), and, following this, on the island of St. Paul only 4,000 were killed, instead of 12,000 ".

" On the island of St. George the seals were allowed to rest in 1825 and 1827, and since that time greater caution and care have been observed, and headmen or foremen have kept a careful count of the killing ".

" From this it will be seen that no anxiety or care as to the preservation of the seal-life began until 1805 (*i.e.* with the united companies) ".

" It is further evident, that all half measures, seen or not seen, were useful no longer, as they only served to preserve a small portion of the seal life and only the last step (1834) with the present people or inhabitants has proved of benefit. And if such regulations of the company continue for fifteen years (*i.e.* until 1849), it may be truly said that then the seal-life will be attracted quite rapidly, under the careful direction of headsmen, so that in quite a short time a handsome yield may be taken every year. In connection with this subject, if the company are moderate and these regulations are carried out, the seal-life will serve them and be depended upon, as shown in this volume, Table No. 2. "

"Ideas of the old natives. — Nearly all the old men think and assert that the seals which are spared every year (" *zapooskat kotov* ") — *i.e.* those which have not been killed for several years, are truly of little use for breeding, lying about as if they were outcasts or disfranchised. About the seals, they show that after the seals were spared, they were always less than they should be, as, for instance, on the island of St. George, after two years of saving or sparing of 5,500 seals, in the first year they got, instead of 10,000, or 8,000 as they expected, only 4,778. "

"Why the seals diminished. — But this diminution, which is shown in the most convincing manner, is due to wrong and injustice, because it would not have been otherwise with any kind of animals — even cattle would have been exterminated — because a great many here think and count that the seals mother brings forth her young in her third year, *i.e.* the next two years after her own birth [1]. As it is well shown here the spared seals ('*zapooskie*') were not more than three years old, and therefore it was not possible to discern the correct and true numbers as they really were. Taking the females killed by the people, together with all the seals which were purposely spared, it was seen that the seal-mothers did not begin to bear earlier than the fifth year of their lives. Illustrative of this is the following."

"*a* On the island of St. George, after the first 'zapooka', in 1828, the killing of five-year-old seals was continued gradually up to five times as many as at first. With those of five years old the killing stopped. Then next year twelve times as many six year-olds were observed on the islands, as compared with their number of the last year, and with or in the seventh year came seven times as many. This shows that females born in 1828 did not begin to bear young until their fifth year, and become with

1. And these natives were right; the females do bear their first young in the third year of their lives. Veniaminov falls into an error when he concludes that they do not, he has read a little too much of Buffon, better not have read at all. H. W. E.

young accordingly; that the large ones did not appear or come in six years (from 1828), as is evident, for in the fifth year all the females did not bring forth."

"*b* It is known that the male seals cannot become 'seccatchies' (*adult bulls*) earlier than their fifth or sixth year; following this, it may be said that the female bears earlier than the fourth year.

"*c* If the male seal cannot become a bull ('seccatchie') earlier than the fifth year, then, as Buffon remarks, ' animals can live seven times the length of the period required for their maturity '; therefore, a ' seccatch ' cannot live less than thirty years, and a female not less than twenty-eight '."

Veniaminov's belief that females cannot bear young until four years old. — "Taking the opinion of Buffon for ground in saying, that animals do not come to their full maturity until one-seventh of their lives has passed, it goes also to prove that the female seal cannot bear young before her fourth year."

"It is, without doubt, a fact that female seals do not begin to bear young before their fifth year, *i.e.* the next four years after the one of their birth, and not in the third or fourth year. That, however, is not the rule, but the exception. To make it more apparent that females cannot bear young in their third year, consider two year old females, and compare them with ' seccatchie ' (*adult bulls*) and cows (*adult females*), and it will be evident to all that this is impossible."

"Do the females bear young every year; and how often in their lives do they bring forth?"

His doubts on the subject. — "To settle this question is very difficult, for it is impossible to make any observations upon their movements; but I think that the females, in their younger years (of price) bring forth every year, and as they get older, every other year; thus, according to people accustomed to them, they may each bring forth in their whole lives from ten to fifteen young, and even more. This opinion is founded on the fact that never (except in one year, 1832) have an excessive number of females been seen without young; that cows not pregnant hardly ever come to the Pribilof islands; that such females cannot be seen every year. As to how large a number of females do not bear, according to the opinions and personal observations of the old people, the following may be depended upon whith confidence; not more than one fifth of the mature or 'effective' females are without young; but to avoid erroneous impressions or conflicting statements between others and myself, I have had but one season (*trayt*) in which to personally observe and consider the multiplication of seals."

His thoughts on Birth of Pups. — "There is one more very important question in the consideration of the breeding or the increase of seals, and that is, of the number of young seals born in one year, how many are males; and is the number of males always the same in proportion to the females?"

"Judging from the 'holluschickie' accumulated from the 'zapooska' in 1822-'24 on the island of St. Paul, and in 1826-'27 on the island of St. George, the number of young males was widely variable; for example on the island of St. Paul, in three years, 11,000 seals were spared and in the following three years there were killed 7,000 *i. e.*, about two-thirds of the number opposed to this, on the island of St. George from 8,500 seals spared in two years, less than 3,000 were taken hardly one-third."

"Why this irregularity? Why should more young males be born at one time, and at another less? Or why should there be years in which many cows do not bear young?"

"According to the belief of the people here, I think that of the number of seals born every year, half are males and as many females (*i. e.*, *the other half*)."

Table No. I : *Its use.* — "To demonstrate the above mentioned conditions of seal-life, the table No. 1 has been formed of the number of seals annually killed on the Pribilov islands, from 1817 to 1838 (when this work was ended)."

"From this it will be seen that :

"1. No single successive year presents a good number of seals killed, as compared with the previous year; the number is always less."

"2. The annual number of seals killed was not in a constant ratio."

"3. And, therefore, in the regular hunting season there is less need or occasion, during the next fifteen years, to demand the whole seal kind."

"4. Fewer seals were killed in those years, generally, following a previous year in which there were larger numbers of the 'holluschickie', that is, when the young males were not completely destroyed, and more were killed when the number of 'holluschickie' was less."

"5. The number of 'holluschickie' is a true register or showing of the number of seals; i. e., if the 'holluschickie' increase and exist like the young females, and conversely."

"6. 'Holluschickie' break from the (common) herd and gather by themselves no earlier than the third year, as seen in the case of the spared seals on the islands of St. George and St. Paul, the latter from 1822-'24 to 1835-'37, inclusive; the former from 1826-27."

"7. The number of seals killed on the island of St. George, after two years ("zapooska") was resumed, and gradually increased to five times as many."

"8. In the fifth year from the first 'zapooska' (*or saving*) it became impossible to count or reckon on the number remaining, and six-year olds began to appear twelve times as numerous, and seven-year olds came in numbers sevenfold greater than their previous small number; and, therefore, the number of three-year-old seals was quite constant."

"9. If on the island of St. George, in 1826-'27, the seals had not had this rest ('Zapooska') and the killing had been continued, even at the diminished ratio of one-eighth, in 1840 or 1842 there would not have been a single seal left, as appears by the following table:

	Seals.		Seals.
1825.	5,500	1833.	1,360
1826.	4,400	1834.	1,190
1827.	3,520	1835.	1,040
1828.	2,816	1836.	850
1829.	2,468	1837.	700
1830.	2,160	1838.	580
1831.	1,890	1839.	500
1832.	1,554	1840.	400

10. **Results of the " Zapooska ".** — " Following two years of ' zapooska ' (saving), the seals life is enhanced for more than ten years, and the loss sustained by the company in the time of

'zapooska' (about 8,500) is made good in the long run. The case may be thus stated: if the company had not spared the seals in to 1826-27 they would have received, from 1826 to 1838 (twelve years), no more than 24,000, but by making this 'zapooska' regulation for two years, they got in ten years 31,576, and, beyond this, they can yet take 15,000 without another, or any 'zapooska.'

"11. And in this case, where such an insignificant number of seals was spared on St. George (about 8,500), and in such a short (two years), the result was at once significant every year; that is, three times more appeared than the number spared. The result therefore, must be large annually on the island of St. Paul, where in consequence of the last orders or directions of the governor, already four years of saving have been in force, in which time over 30,000 seals have been left for breeding."

"On this account, and in conformity with the above, I here present a table, a prophecy of the seals that are to come in the next fifteen years from 7,060 seals saved on the island of St. Paul in 1835."

"On the island of St. Paul, at the direction of the governor, a 'Zapooska' or saving was made of 12,700 seals; that is, before the year 1834 there were killed 12,700 seals, and on the following year, if this saving had not been made, according to the testimony of the inhabitants no more than 12,200 seals would or could have been taken from the islands, it being thought that this number (12,200) was only one-twenty-fifth of the whole; but instead of killing 12,000, only 4,052 were taken, leaving in 1835, for breeding, 8,118 fresh yong seals, males and females, together."

"In making this hypothetical table of seals that are to come, I take the average killing, that is one-eighth part, and proceed on the supposition that the number of saved seals will not be less than 7,060."

"In the number of 7,060 seals we can calculate upon 3,600 females; that is, a slight majority of females. With the new females born under this 'zapooska' I place half of those born the first year, and so on."

"Females, in the twelve or eighteen years next after their birth, must become less in number from natural causes, and by the twenty-second year of their lives they must be quite useless for breeding."

"Of the number of seals which may be born during the next four years of ' zapooska ', or longer, we may take half for females. This number is included in the table, and the males, or ' holluschickie ', make up the total.

Table No. II: its showing. — " From the table II observe that :

" 1. Old females, that is, those which in 1835 were capable of bearing young, in 1850 must be cancelled (minus). They probably die in proportion of one-eighth of the whole number every year. "

" 2. For the first four years of ' zapooska ', until the new females begin to bear, their number will generally be less. "

" 3. A constant number of seals will continue during the first six years of their ' zapooska '; in twelve, these seals will double; in fourteen years they will have increased threefold; and after fifteen years of this ' zapooska ' or saving of, 7,060, in the first year, 24,000 may be taken from them; in the second, 28,000; in the third, 32,000; in the fourth 36,000; in the fifth, 41,000; thus in five years more than 160,000 can be taken. Then, under the supervision of persons who will see that one-fifth of the seals be steadily spared, 32,000 may be taken every year for a long time. "

" 4. Moreover, from the production of fifteen years' ' zapooska ', there can be taken from 60,000 to 70,000 " holluschickie ", which, together with 160,800 seals, makes 230,000. "

" 5. If this ' zapooska ' for the next fifteen years is not made for the seals life, diminution will certainly ensue, and all this time, with all possible effort, no more than 50,000 seals will be taken."

"Here it should be said that this hypothetical table of the probable increase of seals is made on the supposition of the decrease of females, and an average is taken accordingly. Furthermore, on the island of St. Paul, in 1836-'37, instead of 7,900 seals being killed, but 4,860 were taken. Hence, it follows that these 1,500 females thus saved in two years, and which are omitted from the table, will also make a very significant addition to the incoming seals[1]."

---

[1]. The reader, in following the calculations of the Bishop, as exhibited by this table, must not forget to bear in mind, as he runs it over, that it is arranged with a sliding scale of increase, that counts steadily down from 1840 to 1849; and also, a sliding down scale of decrease by reason of natural death-rates, that works steadily accross these figures of increase just specified.

TABLE II. — Showing the number of seals that will visit the island in the next twenty-two years

(A prophecy made by Veniaminov in 1834.)

N=	YEARS.	1 1835	2 1836	3 1837	4 1838	5 1839	6 1840	7 1841	8 1842	9 1843	10 1844	11 1845	12 1846	13 1847	14 1848	15 1849	16 1850	17 1851	18 1852	19 1853	20 1854	21 1855	22 1856
1	1835	3,600	0	0	0	0	900	1,200	1,200	1,200	1,200	1,200	1,200	1,200	1,200	1,200	1,000	800	400	200	"	"	"
2	1836	"	3,150	0	0	"	"	785	1,050	1,050	1,050	1,050	1,050	1,050	1,050	1,050	1,050	1,000	700	300	100	"	"
3	1837	"	"	2,755	"	"	"	"	680	918	918	918	918	918	918	918	918	918	900	600	300	10	"
4	1838	"	"	"	2,410	"	"	"	"	600	805	805	805	805	805	805	805	805	805	805	750	500	300
5	1839	"	"	"	"	2,410	"	"	"	"	450	700	700	700	700	700	700	700	700	700	700	600	400
6	1840	"	"	"	"	New.	1,815	"	"	"	"	"	450	615	615	615	615	615	615	615	615	600	500
		"	"	"	"	"	900	"	"	From old arrivals.	"	"	"	200	315	200	200	200	200	200	200	150	100
7	1841	"	"	"	"	Total new.	"	1,580	"	From new comers.	"	152	"	525	525	525	525	525	525	525	525	525	500
		"	"	"	"	"	Total new.	1,983	"	"	From new ones	"	"	"	572	572	572	572	572	572	572	572	500
8	1842	"	"	"	"	"	"	"	1,355	1,130	"	"	"	420	325	451	451	451	451	451	451	572	451
		"	"	"	"	"	"	"	2,930	3,768	"	From new ones	"	"	650	903	909	909	909	909	909	909	909
9	1843	"	"	"	"	"	"	"	"	4,898	900	"	"	"	"	376	376	376	376	376	376	376	376
		"	"	"	"	"	"	"	Total new.	4,102	4,423	725	From new ones	"	"	"	"	"	"	"	"	"	"
10	1844	"	"	"	"	"	"	"	"	Total new.	"	5,275	"	"	"	1,188	1,188	1,188	1,188	1,188	1,188	1,188	1,188
		"	"	"	"	"	"	"	"	"	Total new.	"	580	From new ones	"	"	300	300	300	300	300	300	200
11	1845	"	"	"	"	"	"	"	"	"	"	Total new.	6,225	430	"	"	"	241	241	241	241	241	241
		"	"	"	"	"	"	"	"	"	"	"	"	7,560	"	From new ones.	180	1,687	1,687	1,687	1,687	1,687	1,687	1,440
12	1846	"	"	"	"	"	"	"	"	"	"	"	Total new.	"	258	225	1,240	125	190	190	190	190	190
		"	"	"	"	"	"	"	"	"	"	"	"	"	880	1,020	"	1,500	1,994	1,094	1,994	1,994	1,994
13	1847	"	"	"	"	"	"	"	"	"	"	"	"	Total new.	"	"	From new ones.	"	100	143	143	143	143
		"	"	"	"	"	"	"	"	"	"	"	"	"	"	"	"	"	1,810	"	83	83	83
14	1848	"	"	"	"	"	"	"	"	"	"	"	"	"	Total new.	"	From new ones.	"	"	61	2,420	2,420	2,420
		"	"	"	"	"	"	"	"	"	"	"	"	"	"	"	"	"	"	2,254	25	2,908	2,908
15	1849	"	"	"	"	"	"	"	"	"	"	"	"	"	"	10,651	From new ones.	"	"	"	2,500	3,187	40
		"	"	"	"	"	"	"	"	"	"	"	"	"	"	"	"	"	"	"	"	"	3,187
TOTAL ♀		3,600	3,150	2,755	2,410	2,410	2,745	3,565	4,285	4,898	5,323	6,000	6,805	7,990	9,333	10,735	12,369	14,153	16,148	18,216	20,820	20,105	19,358
TOTAL ♂		3,460	3,150	2,755	2,410	2,410	2,745	3,435	4,215	4,102	5,378	6,000	6,795	8,010	9,367	10,746	12,331	14,147	16,102	18,184	20,820	20,093	19,342
ALL. . .		7,060	6,300	5,510	4,820	4,820	5,490	7,000	8,500	9,700	10,700	12,000	13,600	16,000	18,600	21,500	24,700	28,300	32,250	36,400	41,640	40,200	38,700

SECTION VII.

"From this table behold that:

"*a.* Every fifteen years, from 3,600 females, there can be received in sixteen years 24,700 seals; in sixteen years still more; and in twenty years 41,640."

"*b.* In the twenty-first year, the incomes begin to diminish, provided that if in the meantime, or the following sixteen years, a certain number of young seals are not left to breed; and if every year a known number are left to breed, then in all following years the yield will never be less than 20,000 every year."

The foregoing chapter of Bishop Veniaminov was written in 1837; and closes his knowledge of the topic with that year; the "zapooska" of 1834 which stopped all killing except a few food seals for the natives in the seasons of 1835-'40 ran on in the following manner for St. Paul Island until the restoration of the rookeries in 1846-'50: this is the only record extent, and I was fortunate in getting it.

**Proeezvodaytva Pooshnik Promissloo vie e droogich.
sah, 1835, zoda Zapooska.**

(List of the killing for furs and other purposes since the Zapooska of 1835).

1st 1835	100 skins.	Bachelor Fur Seals.	
	3,052 —	Pups —	Gray.
2nd 1836	1,200 —	Bachelor Fur Seals.	
	2,840 —	Pups —	Gray.
3rd 1837	2,000 —	Bachelor Fur Seals.	
	2,020 —	Pups —	Gray.
4th 1838	2,560 —	Bachelor Fur Seals.	
	1,380 —	Pups —	Gray.
5th 1839	5,000 —	Bachelor Fur Seals.	
	230 —	Pups —	Gray.
6th 1840	5,350 —	Bachelor Fur Seals.	
	650 —	Pups —	Gray.
7th 1841	7,100 —	Bachelor Fur Seals.	
	900 —	Pups —	Gray.
8th 1842	8,800 —	Bachelor Fur Seals.	
	1,260 —	Pups —	Gray.

1. This list above quoted is a record kept by the Rev. Kazean Shaisnikov who lived on St. Paul Island throughout the period covered by it; the autographic original was given to me to copy by his son Father Paul Shaishnikov and Kenick Artamanov, who had it in their possession, on the 2nd of July, 1890. No similar writing exists for the same period on the island of St. George.

9th 1843	{	10,030 skins	Bachelor Fur Seals.	
		1,294 —	Pups	— Gray.
10th 1844	{	10,150 —	Bachelor Fur Seals.	
		2,632 —	Pups	— Gray.
11th 1845	{	9,550 —	Bachelor Fur Seals.	
		3,428 —	Pups	— Gray.
12th 1846	{	12,000 —	Bachelor Fur Seals.	
		3,503 —	Pups	— Gray.
13th 1847	{	13,300 —	Bachelor Fur Seals.	
		450 —	Pups	— Gray.
		3,258 —	—	— —
14th 1848	{	13,600 —	Bachelor Fur Seals.	
		3,370 —	Pups	— Gray.
15th 1849	{	10,000 —	Bachelor Fur Seals.	
		3,350 —	Pups	— Gray.
16th 1850	{	2,450 —	Bachelor Fur Seals.	
		3,080 —	—	— —
		538 —	Pups	— Gray.
17th 1851	{	1,200 —	Bachelor Fur Seals.	
		9,095 —	—	— —
		935 —	Pups	— Gray.
18th 1852	{	5,300 —	Bachelor Fur Seals.	
		4,080 —	—	— —
		1,250 —	Pups	— Gray.
19th 1853	{	8,950 —	Bachelor Fur Seals	
		5,046 —	—	— —
		1,700 —	Pups	— Gray.
20th 1854	{	29,850 —	Bachelor Fur Seals.	
		4,011 —	—	— —
		1,400 —	Pups	— Gray.

Now with this list in hand, the following " table 1 " of Bishop Veniaminov becomes inintelligible; without it, I have hitherto been unable to reconcile his statement that all killing was stopped in 1835, on the one hand and on the other, with the figures which he gives below for 1835, and up to the end of his record in 1837; but, on turning to Shaishnikov's item for that year, we see that the Bishops total of " 4,052 " as taken that year on St. Paul really *was only* " 100 *skins of Bachelor fur-seals*", and " 3,952 *skins of pups*" " *gray* " *pups or five months old*, having by that time shed their black natal coats, and donned their gray overhair sea-going jackets; thus we observe that the killing was literally stopped : The pups were taken for natives food and clothing.

TABLE I, PART. II. — **Bishop Veniamonov's zapooska, etc., showing the seal catch during the period of gradual diminution of life on the islands, from 1817 down to 1837.**

TAKEN FROM.	1817.	1818.	1819.	1820.	1821.	1822.
St. Paul Island	47,860	45,932	40,300	39,700	35,750	28,15
St. George Island	12.328	13,924	11,925	10,520	9,245	8,319
Total	60,188	59,856	52,225	50,220	44,995	36,469

TAKEN FROM.	1823.	1824.	1825.	1826.	1827.
St. Paul Island	24,100	19,850	24,600	23,250	17,750
St. George Island	5,773	5,550	5,500		1,950
Total	29,873	25,400	30,100	23,250	19,700

TAKEN FROM.	1828.	1829.	1830.	1831.	1832.
St. Paul Island	18,450	17,150	15,200	12,950	13,150
St. George Island	4,778	3,661	2,834	3,084	3,296
Total	23,228	20,811	18,034	16,034	16,446

TAKEN FROM.	1833.	1834.	1835.	1836.	1837.
St. Paul Island	13,200	12,700	4,052	4,040	4,220
St. George Island	3,212	3,051	2,528	2,550	2,582
Total	16,412	15,751	6,580	6,590	6,802

Grand total for St. Paul Island 464.259
Grand total for St. George Island 114,665

Total catch during nineteen years of diminution . . 578,924

It should be borne in mind as this table I is scanned, that during all this time from 1817 up to 1834, all sorts of " half way measures " were being tried, without success, by the Russian American Co. so as to try and save the seal life and yet at the same time, continue a modified annual killing for shipment; they finally concluded that in 1834, as a result of a half measure of saving, they ought to get at least 20,000 to 25,000 skins of, one and two year olds, (taking them just as they came for that matter); but after " all possible exertion " only 12,700 skins were secured, and the natives declared the ruin of these rookeries at hand if another such a season of driving and killing was inaugurated; then the Company reluctantly, but wisely ordered that cessation of sealing which Shaishnikov's list testifies to.

A study of this killing throughout the " zapooska " of 1834 on St. Paul Island shows that for a period of seven years, from

1835 down to the close of the season of 1841, no seals practically were killed save those that were needed for food and clothing by the natives; and that in 1835 for the first time in the history of this industry on these islands was the vital principle of not killing female seals, recognized ; it will be noticed that the entry for each and every year distinctly specifies so many " bachelor seals " or "holluschickovkotovie " (*Korocmekobkomobrozrs*). The sealing in those early days was carried on all through the summer until the seals left in October or November, on account of the tedious method then in vogue of air drying the skins. This caused them in driving after the breaking up of the breeding season by the end of July, to take up at first, hundreds and thousands, later on, of the females in the same manner that they have been driven up during the last two seasons of 1889 and 1890 : but, they never spared those cows then when they arrived in the droves on the killing grounds, prior to this date above quoted, of 1835.

In 1842-'43, it will be observed, the killing is advanced to a otal of 9,000 and 10,000 skins for these years respectively; and until 1854, this killing was not greatly increased, per annum ; then it was suddenly put up to 33,000 " bachelor seals " and in 1857 the old natives assured me last summer, that there was as many seals on the islands then as there was when I recorded their area and position during 1872-'74; and that from the year 1854, the Russian Company never had any more concern as to the supply of killable seals on the Pribilof Islands; they got annually thereafter " all that was ordered taken ", each season.

While the supply of killable seals in 1890 was not quite so low as that of 1834, yet it was nearly as bad — worse perhaps when the calculations of the old and new companies for the seasons catch are taken into account, and with reference to next year, far worse, because the additional danger and source of injury from pelagic sealing is added to the cause for present declination of these rookeries : it did not enter into Russian calculations — the seals of Bering Sea were never seriously disturbed by these hunters until 1886.

The condition of the Pribylov rookeries to-day is such as to make the following imperative demands upon our Government, if they are to be saved as they should be from speedy ruin.

FIRST. *That no young male seals whatsoever shall be killed on these islands as a source of revenue either to the public treasury or to private corporations for the next seven years : i. e. during the seasons of* 1891-98 *inclusive.*

This step is imperative since there was scarcely a drop of young male blood in service on the breeding grounds of either St. Paul or St. George throughout the reproductive season of 1890. There are no young bulls left to speak of on these hauling grounds above the one and two year old grades, very few of the latter, and not many of the former; it will take at least five years of perfect rest for the scanty stock now left of this character in which to mature so as to |serve on these breeding grounds; and it will be two years after this new service is first rendered before the appreciable gain can be well seen and in this necessary period of five years growth, not more than one-half of these young bulls thus maturing can be estimated as certain to survive the attacks of their natural enemies at sea (sharks, killer whales, etc.)

SECOND. *That all pelagic sealing in the waters of Bering Sea be prohibited and suppressed throughout the breeding season, no matter how, so that it is done, and done quickly.*

This step is equally imperative: the immorality of that demand made by the open water sealer to ruin within a few short years and destroy forever these fur bearing interests on the Pribylov Islandss the immorality of this demand cannot be glossed over by any sophistry; the idea of permitting such a chase to continue where five thousand female seals heavy with their unborn young are killed in order to secure every one thousand skins taken is repugnant to the sense of decency and the simplest instincts of true manhood. I cannot refrain from expressing my firm belief that if the truth is known, made plain to responsible heads of the civilized powers of the world that not one of these governments will hesitate to unite with ours in closing Bering Sea and its passes of the Aleutian chain, to any and all pelagic fur sealing, during the breeding season of that animal.

If these two steps are taken next year, and a perfect rest established throughout the breeding seasons on the islands, and in the waters of Behring Sea for the next seven years inclusive then

PROTECTION AND PRESERVATION. 215

the restoration of these sadly diminished interests to their good form of 1872-'74, will have been well advanced, if not wholly realized by the expiration of the season of 1898.

Then with revised and proper regulations for driving and killing, the 20th century may open with another era of commercial prosperity for these islands and pleasure and profit for those not only at home but all over the world where furs are worn and valued.

In taking these two steps, the Government cannot divide the responsibility; it must assume the entire order and conduct of affairs on these seal islands of Alaska for the next seven years : the new lessees of 1890 should have a fair rebate — they are not to blame in any sense whatsoever for the present condition of the rookeries and hauling grounds — not at all : they cannot be asked to nurse these shrivelling rookeries into shape, to feed and clothe the natives and maintain an establishment on these islands for that purpose during this necessary period of rest; and if they offered to do it, this offer, for obvious reasons, should be refused.

The skins of a few thousand yearlings and pups which the natives may safely kill under order of the Secretary of the Treasury every year, for food and clothing just as they killed them in 1834-'43 inclusive, will, when sold by the Secretary of the Treasury, fully meet all the cost of caring for these dependent people properly, and enable them to live just as comfortably as they have been living; these food skins can be annually brought down to market on the revenue cutters and these vessels can bring up the supplies of food, fuel and clothing necessary for the natives after their purchase in due form by the Treasury Department.

The new lessees of 1890 in full belief, and warranted by official reports in believing that they would get at least 60,000 prime skins in the first season of their contract and annually more thereafter during the period of their contract, purchased the entire land plant of the old lessees *i.e.* the salt-houses, dwelling and school houses, barns, stores and goods, and divers chattels, and paid for it together with the eighty-one small dwelling houses which the old company built for the natives occupation, about $61.000; those people have lived in these cottages, rent free, during the last eighteen years, and do live in them now under the same privilege; repairs and paint being also furnished gratis.

Under the present changed order of affairs, the Government needs at once, part of this plant above cited, at least, and for that matter should not hesitate to take it entirely off the hands of the new lessees, as the condition of the business now stands; also the money paid on account of the native houses should be promptly refunded by the Government to the new lessees; for as I have said there cannot be any division of responsibility in the coming change of nursing these exhausted rookeries back to good order; the work has got to be entirely free from any and all suspicion, of private intrigue and gain during the next seven years, or it had better not be undertaken; this will require the removal of everybody from these islands except the natives, and the Government officers and employes : these men resident should consist of the existing staff of four Treasury agents, a physician for each island, and a school-teacher and store-keeper also in each village, including a mess cook and laundryman.

On account of the remoteness of their situation, those officers and employes of the Government should be housed on these islands, and supplied with rations and fuel free of cost to themselves : otherwise the enforced abnormal expense of living there would render their salaries absurdly inadequate; these supplies can be regularly purchased in San Francisco every spring by the Collector of Customs of that port, and sent up to the Seal Islands on the revenue cutters which annually have cruised, and will cruise around about them throughout each coming season[1].

While the Secretary of the Treasury is fully empowered by existing law I believe to take any or all steps necessary to preserve and protect these interests of the Government on the Seal Islands of Alaska, yet the passage of a bill substantially like the following draft will save him from some misunderstanding and doubt in the minds of our people, as to the precise limit of his authority; also he needs the authority of law for the establishment of the school teachers, physicians, etc.

1. It is wholly unnecessary to enter into the details of this programme they will all suggest themselves in due form to the officers of the Treasury Department and be promptly attended to; when the work is undertaken.

A BILL

For the protection and preservation of the interests of the Government on the Fur-seal Islands of Alaska (Pribylov group) Bering Sea.

ALASKA

Sec. 1. *Be it enacted, etc.* — That for the period of seven years from and after the passage of this Act, no fur-seals shall be killed for their skins, on or around the Fur Seals Islands (Pribylov Group), of Alaska, by any person or persons whatsoever, Provided : That the natives of said islands shall have the privilege of killing such young male seals, only, as may be required for their food and clothing and the construction of their small boats for their own use, which killing shall be limited and controlled by the Secretary of the Treasury, as he may prescribe, and he is hereby authorized to incur any and all proper and necessary expenses incident to the establishment, and maintenance and employment of one physician, one school-teacher, one storekeeper, and one cook on each island, also for the proper housing of the natives, the government officers in charge, and property, with rations for the same and fuel, throughout the time specified in the foregoing section.

Provided also : That such food-skins taken as above cited shall be sold annually for the defrayment in part or in whole of these expenses, at public auction by the Secretary of the Treasury; said food-skins to be classified for such sale by the Treasury Agent in charge, and accompanied by him from the islands until sold as prescribed by the Secretary of the Treasury.

Sec. 2. *And be it enacted, etc.* — That no persons, other than the natives, and the authorized Agents of the Government shall be permitted to occupy said islands, or either of them, from and after the passage of this Act, and any person or persons who may attempt or attempts to violate this order of this section or that of the first section of this Act, shall be punished on conviction thereof for each offence by a fine of not less than one thousand dollars, or more than ten thousand dollars, or by imprisonment not exceeding one year, or by both such fine and imprisonment at the discretion of the Court having jurisdiction and taking cognizance of the offences : and all vessels, their tackle, apparel and furniture, whose crew shall be found engaged in the violation of any of the provisions of this Act, shall be forfeited to the United States.

Sec. 3. *And be it further enacted*, *etc.* — That the provisions of the seventh and eighth sections of an act entitled " An Act to extend the laws of the United States relating to customs, commerce and navigation over the territory ceded to the United States by Russia, to establish a collection district therein, and for other purposes ", approved July 27th, 1868, shall be deemed to apply to this Act : and all prosecution for offences committed against the provisions of this Act, and all other proceedings had, because of the violation of the provisions of this Act, and which are authorized by the said Act above specified, shall be in accordance with the provisions thereof, and all Acts and parts of Acts inconsistent with the provisions of this Act are hereby repealed.

THE EXISTING LAW, READS AS BELOW AN ACT TO PREVENT THE EXTERMINATION OF FUR-BEARING ANIMALS IN ALASKA

Be it enacted by the Senate and House of Representatives of the United States of America in Congress assembled. — That it shall be unlawful to kill any fur-seal upon the islands of St. Paul and St. George, or in the waters adjacent thereto, except during the months of June, July, September, and October, in each year; and it shall be unlawful to kill such seals at any time by the use of fire-arms, or the use of other means tending to drive the seals away from said islands : *Provided*, that the natives of said islands shall have the privilege of killing such young seals as may be necessary for their own food and clothing during other months, and also such old seals as may be required for their own clothing and for the manufacture of boats for their own use, which killing shall be limited and controlled by such regulations as shall be prescribed by the Secretary of the Treasury.

Sec. 2. *And be it further enacted, etc.* — That it shall be unlawful to kill any female seals, or any seal less than one year old, at any season of the year, except as above provided : and it shall also be unlawful to kill any seal in the waters adjacent to said islands, or on the beaches, cliffs, or rocks where they haul up from the sea to remain; and any person who shall violate either of the provisions of this or the first section of this act, shall be punished on conviction thereof, for each offence, by a fine of not less than two hundred dollars nor more than one thousand dollars, or by imprisonment not exceeding six months, or by both such fine and imprisonment, at the discretion of the court having jurisdiction and taking cognizance of the offenses; and all vessels, their tackle, apparel, and furniture, whose crew shall be found engaged in the violation of any of the provisions of this act, shall be forfeited to the United States.

Sec. 3. *And be it further enacted, etc.*—That for the period of twenty years from and after the passage of this act, the number of fur-seals which may be killed for their skins upon the island of St. Paul is hereby limited and restricted to seventy-five thousand per annum; and the number of fur-seals which may be killed for their skins upon the island of St. George, is hereby limited and restricted to twenty-five thousand per annum : *Provided*, that the Secretary of the Treasury may restrict and limit the right of killing, if it shall become necessary for the preservation of such seals, with such proportionate reduction of rents reserved to the government as shall be right and proper; and if any person shall knowingly violate either of the provisions of this section, he shall, upon due conviction thereof, be punished in the same way as provided herein for a violation of the provisions of the first and second seétions of this act.

Sec. 4. *And be it further enacted, etc.*—That immediately after the passage of this act, the Secretary of the Treasury shall lease, for the rental mentioned in section 6 of this act, to proper and responsible parties, to the best advantage of the United States, having due regard to the interests of the government, the native inhabitants, the parties heretofore engaged in the trade, and the protection of the seal-fisheries, for a term of twenty years from the last day of May, 1870, the right to engage in the business of taking fur-seals on the islands of St. Paul and St. George, and to send a vessel or vessels to said islands for the skins of such seals, giving to the lessee or lessees of said islands a lease duly executed, in duplicate, not transferable, and taking from the lessee or lessees of said islands a bond, with sufficient sureties, in a sum not less than $500,000, conditioned for the faithful observance of all the laws and requirements of Congress, and of the regulations of the Secretary of the Treasury touching the subject-matter of taking fur-seals and disposing of the same, and for the payment of all taxes and dues accruing to the United States connected therewith. And in making said lease the Secretary of the Treasury shall have due regard to the preservation of the seal-fur trade of the islands, and the comfort, maintenance, and education of the natives thereof. The said lessees shall furnish to the several masters of vessels employed by them certified copies of the lease held by them, respectively, which shall be presented to the government revenue-officer for the time being, who may be in charge at the said islands, as the authority of the party for landing and taking skins.

Sec. 5. *And be it further enacted, etc.*—That at the expiration of said term of twenty years, or on surrender or forfeiture of any lease, other leases may be made in manner as aforesaid for other terms of twenty years; but no persons other than American citizens shall be permitted, by lease or otherwise, to occupy said islands, or either of them, for the purpose of taking the skins of fur-seals therefrom, nor shall any foreign vessel be engaged in taking such skins; and the Secretary of the Treasury shall vacate and declare any lease forfeited, if the same be held or operated for the use, benefit, or advantage, directly or indirectly, of any person or persons other than American citizens. Every lease shall contain a covenant on the part of the lessee that he will not keep, sell, furnish, give, or dispose of any distilled spirits or spirituous liquors on either of said islands to any of the natives thereof, such person not being a physician and furnishing the same for use as medicine; and any person who shall kill any fur-seal on either of said islands, or in the waters adjacent thereto (excepting natives as provided by this act), without authority of the lessees thereof, and any person who shall molest, disturb, or interfere with said lessees, or either of them, or their agents or employés, in the lawful prosecution of their business, under the provisions of this act, shall be deemed guilty of a misdemeanor, and shall for each offence, on conviction thereof, be punished in the same way and by like penalties as prescribed in the second section of this act; and all vessels, their tackle, apparel, appurtenances, and cargo, whose crews shall be found engaged in any violation of either of the provisions of this section, shall be forfeited to the United States; and if any person or company, under any lease, therein authorized, shall knowingly kill, or permit to be killed, any number of seals exceeding the number for each island in this act prescribed, such person or company shall, in addition to the penalties and forfeitures aforesaid, also forfeit the whole number of the skins of seals killed in that year, or, in case the same have been disposed of, then said person or company shall forfeit the value of the same. And it shall be the duty of any revenue officer, officially acting as such on either of said islands, to seize and destroy any distilled spirits or spirituous liquors found thereon; *Provided*, that such officer shall make detailed report of his doings to the collector of the port.

 Sec. 6. *And be it further enacted, etc.* — That the annual rental to be reserved by said lease, shall be not less than fifty thousand dollars per annum, to be secured by deposit of United States bonds to that amount, and in addition thereto a revenue tax or duty of two dollars is hereby laid upon each fur-seal skin taken and shipped from said islands during the continuance of such lease, to be paid into the Treasury of the United States; and the Secretary of the Treasury is hereby empowered and authorized to make all needful rules and regulations for the collection and payment of the same; and to secure the comfort, maintenance, education, and protection of the natives of said islands, and also for carrying into full effect all the provisions of this act; *Provided*. That the Secretary of the Treasury may terminate any lease given to any person, company, or corporation, on full and satisfactory proof of the violation of any of the provisions of this act, or rules and regulations established by him.

 Sect. 7. *And be it further enacted, etc.* — That the provisions of the seventh and eight sections of an act entiled " And act to extend the law of the United States relating to customs, commerce, and navigation over the territory ceded to the United States by Russia, to establish a collection district therein, and for other purposes ", approved July 27th, 1868, shall be deemed to apply to this act; and all prosecution for offences committed against the provisions of this act, and all other proceedings had because of the violations of the provisions of this act and which are authorized by said act above mentioned, shall be in accordance with the provisions thereof, and all acts and parts of acts inconsistent with the provisions of this act are hereby repealed.

Sect. 8. *And be it further enacted*, *etc*. — That the Congress may at any time hereafter alter, amend, repeal this act.

Approved July 1st. 1870.

Amended, March 24th, 1874. — *Be it enacted*, *etc*. — That an act entitled " An act to prevent the extermination of fur-bearing animals in Alaska ", approved July first, eighteen hundred and seventy, is hereby amended so as to authorize the Secretary of the Treasury, and he is hereby authorized, to designate the months in which the fur-seals may be taken for their skins on the islands of St. Paul and St. George, in Alaska, and in the waters adjacent thereto, and the number to be taken on or about each island respectively.

In pursuance of this Act of July 1st, 1870, on the 3rd of August 1870, the Secretary of the Treasury executed the following lease :

Terms of the Seal Island lease from the Government. — This indenture in duplicate, made this 3rd day of August, A. D. 1870, by and between William A. Richardson, Acting Secretary of the Treasury, in pursuance of an act of Congress approved July 1, 1870, entitled " An Act to prevent the extermination of fur-bearing animals in Alaska, " and the Alaska Commercial Company, a corporation duly established under the law of the state of California, acting by John F. Miller, its president and agent, in accordance with a resolution at a meeting of its Board of Trustees, held January 31, 1870. Witnesseth :

That said Secretary hereby leases to the said Alaska Commercial Company, without power of transfer, for the term of twenty years from the 1st day of May, 1870, the right to engage in the business of taking fur-seals on the islands of St. George and St. Paul within the territory of Alaska, and to send a vessel or vessels to said island for the skins of such seals.

And the said Alaska Commercial Company, in consideration of their right under this lease, hereby covenant and agree to pay for each year during said term and in proportion during any part thereof, the sum of $55,000 into the Treasury of the United States in accordance with the regulations of the Secretary to be made for this purpose under said act, which payment shall be secured by deposit of United States bonds to that amount, and covenant and agree to pay annually into the Treasury of the United States, under said rules and regulations, an internal-revenue tax or duty of $2 for each seal-skin taken and shipped by them in accordance with the provisions of the act aforesaid, and also the sum of 60 1/2 cents for each fur-seal skin taken and shipped, and 55 cents per gallon for each gallon of oil obtained from said seals, for sale in said islands or elsewhere, and sold by said company; and also covenant and agree, in accordance with said rules and regulations, to furnish, free of charge, the inhabitants of the islands of St. Paul and St. George annually during said term 25,000 dried salmon, 60 cords firewood, and a sufficient quantity of salt and a sufficient quantity of barrels for preserving the necessary supply of meat.

And the said lessees also hereby covenant and agree during the term aforesaid to maintain a school on each island, in accordance with said rules and regulations and suitable for the education of the natives of said islands, for a period of not less than eight months in each year.

And the said lessees further covenant and agree not to kill upon said island of St. Paul more than seventy-five thousand fur-seals, and upon the island of St. George not more than twenty-five thousand fur-seals per annum; not to kill any fur-seal upon the islands aforesaid in any other month except the months of June, July, September and October of each year; not to kill said seals at any time by the use of firearms or means tending to drive said seals from said islands; not to kill any female seals or seals under one year old; not to kill any seal in waters adjacent to said islands, or on the beach, cliffs, or rocks, where they haul up from the sea to remain.

And the said lessees further covenant and agree to abide by any restriction or limitation upon the right to kill seals under this lease that the act prescribes, or that the Secretary of the Treasury shall judge necessary for the preservation of such seals.

And the said lessees hereby agree that they will not in any way sell, transfer, or assign this lease, and that any transfer, sale, or assignment of the same shall be void and of no effect.

And the said lessees further agree to furnish to the several masters of the vessels employed by them certified copies of this lease, to be presented to the government revenue officers for the time being in charge of said islands, as the authority of said lessees for the landing and taking of said skins.

And the said lessees further covenant and agree that they or their agents shall not keep, sell, furnish, give, or dispose of any distilled spirituous liqours on either of said islands to any of the natives thereof, such person not being a physician and furnishing the same for use as medicine.

And the said lessees further covenant and agree that this lease is accepted, subject to all needful rules and regulations which shall at any time or times hereafter be made by the Secretary of the Treasury for the collection and payment of the rental herein agreed to be paid by said lessees for the comfort, maintenance, education, and protection of the natives of said islands, and for carrying into effect all the provisions of the act aforesaid, and will abide by and conform to said rules and regulations.

And the said lessees, accepting this lease with a full knowledge of the provisions of the aforesaid act of Congress, further covenant and agree that they will fulfil all the provisions, requirements, and limitations of said act, whether herein specifically set out or not.

In witness whereof the parties aforesaid have hereunto set their hands and seals the day and year above written.

WILLIAM A. RICHARDSON (Seal.)
Acting Secretary of the Treasury.

Executed in presence of
J. H. SAVILLE.

Alaska Commercial Company :
By JOHN F. MILLER, *President.* (Seal.)

This lease having terminated on the 1st day of last May (1890), the following new lease was executed in accordance with the law.

This indenture, made in duplicate this twelfth day of March 1890, by and between William Windom, Secretary of the Treasury of the United States, in pursuance of Chapter 3 of Title 23, Revised Statutes, and the North American Commercial Company, a Corporation duly established under the laws of the State of California, and acting by I. Liebes, its President, in accordance with a resolution of said corporation adopted at a meeting of its Board of Directors held January 4th, 1890. Witnesseth :

That said Secretary of the Treasury, in consideration of the agreements hereinafter stated, hereby leases to the said North American Commercial Company, for a term of twenty years, from the 1st day of May, 1890, the exclusive right to engage in the business of taking fur-seals on the islands of St. George and St. Paul in the territory of Alaska and to send a vessel or vessels to said islands for the skins of such seals.

The said North American Commercial Company, in consideration of the rights secured to it under this lease above stated, on its part covenants and agrees to do the things following that is to say;

To pay to the Treasurer of the United States each year during the said term of twenty years, as annual rental, the sum of sixty thousand dollars; and in addition thereto agrees to pay the revenue tax, or duty, of two dollars laid upon each fur-seal skin taken and shipped by it from said islands of St. George and St. Paul; and also to pay to said Treasurer the further sum of seven dollars sixty-two and one half cents apiece for each and every fur-seal skin taken and shipped from said islands; and also to pay the sum of fifty cents per gallon for each gallon of oil sold by it made from seals, that may be taken on said islands during the said period of twenty years; and to secure the prompt payment of the sixty thousand dollars rental above referred to, the said company agrees to deposit with the Secretary of the Treasury bonds of the United States to the amount of fifty thousand dollars, face value, to be held as a guarantee for the annual payment of said sixty thousand dollars rental, the interest thereon when due to be collected and paid to the North American Commercial Company, provided the said company is not in default of payment of any part of the said sixty thousand dollars rental.

That it will furnish to the native inhabitants of said islands of St. George and St. Paul, annually, such quantity or number, of dried salmon, and such quantity of salt and such number of salt barrels for preserving their necessary supply of meat, as the Secretary of the Treasury shall from time to time determine.

That it will also furnish to the said inhabitants eighty tons of coal annually, and a sufficient number of comfortable dwellings in which said native inhabitants may reside; and will keep said dwellings in proper repair, and will also provide and keep in repair such suitable schoolhouses as may be necessary, and will establish and maintain during eight months of each year proper schools for the education of the children on said islands; the same to be taught by competent teachers who shall be paid by the company a fair compensation; all to the satisfaction of the Secretary of the Treasury; and will also provide and maintain a suitable house for religious worship; and will also provide a competent physician or physicians, and necessary and proper medicines and medical supplies; and will also provide the necessaries of life for the widows and orphans and aged and infirm inhabitants of said islands who are unable to provide for themselves; all of which foregoing agreements will be done and performed by the said company free of all costs and charges to said native inhabitants of said islands or to the United States.

The annual rental, together with all other payments to the United States, provided for in this lease, shall be made and paid on or before the first day of April of each and every year during the existence of this lease, beginning with the first day of April 1891.

SECTION VII.

The said company further agrees to employ the native inhabitants of said islands to perform such labour, upon the islands, as they are fitted to perform and to pay therefor a fair and just compensation, such as may be fixed by the Secretary of the Treasury, and also to contribute, as far as in its power, all reasonable efforts to secure the comfort, health education, and promote the morals and civilization of said native inhabitants.

The said company also agrees faithfully to obey and abide by all rules and regulations that the Secretary of the Treasury has heretofore or may hereafter establish or make in pursuance of law concerning the taking of seals of said islands, and concerning the comfort, morals and other interests of said inhabitants, and all matters pertaining to said islands and the taking of seals within the possession of the United States: It also agrees to obey and abide by any restrictions or limitations upon the right to kill seals, that the Secretary of the Treasury shall judge necessary, under the law, for the preservation of the seal fisheries of the United States; and it agrees that it will not kill or permit to be killed, so far as it can prevent, in any year a greater number of seals than is authorized by the Secretary of the Treasury.

The said company further agrees that it will not permit any of its agents to keep, sell, give, or dispose of any distilled spirits or spirituous liquors or opium, on either of said islands, or the waters adjacent thereto, to any of the native inhabitants of said islands, such person not being a physician and furnishing the same for use as a medicine.

It is understood and agreed that the number of fur-seals to be taken and killed for their skins upon said islands by the North American Commercial Company during the year ending May 1st 1891, shall not exceed sixty thousand.

The Secretary of the Treasury reserves the right to terminate this lease and all rights of the North American Company under the same at any time, on full and satisfactory proof that the said company has violated any of the provisions and agreements of this lease, or of any of the laws of the United States, or any Treasury regulation respecting the taking of fur-seals, or concerning the islands of St. George and St. Paul or the inhabitants thereof.

In witness whereof, the parties have set their hands and seals the day and year above written.

WILLIAM WINDOM,
Secretary of the Treasury.

North American Commercial Company by : I. LIEBES,
President of the North American Commercial Company.

Attest : H. B. PARSONS,
Asst. Secretary.

In both of these instruments it will be observed that the old and the new lessees emphatically and unreservedly " agree to abide by any restriction or limitation upon the *right to* kill seals under the lease that the act prescribes or that the Secretary of the Treasury shall judge necessary for the preservation of such seals ".

Had there been any refusal on the part of the lessees to thus covenant and agree in this important regard, no seal-island lease ever could have been sustained by its friends. The powerful and jealous opponents of this system would have carried the day in 1870, and again in 1890.

The wisdom and propriety of this express reservation in behalf of the Government is now apparent : there is no legal or moral obstacle in the way of taking the action which I suggest for the restoration of these interests on the seal islands themselves, and I firmly believe that a visit by some representative Commission of Great Britain to these Pribylov rookeries next season will result in securing the prompt, hearty co-operation of that power with our Government in protecting these seals from slaughter in the open waters of Behring sea and certain portions of the North Pacific Ocean during the breeding season of those animals.

SECTION VIII

APPENDIX CONTAINING THE AUTHOR'S DAILY FIELD
NOTES TOGETHER WITH OTHER MEMORANDA
ILLUSTRATIVE OF THE PRECEDING
SECTIONS I TO VII, INCLUSIVE

SECTION VIII

APPENDIX CONTAINING THE AUTHOR'S DAILY FIELD NOTES TOGETHER WITH OTHER MEMORANDA ILLUSTRATIVE OF THE PRECEDING SECTIONS I TO VII, INCLUSIVE

I give *in extenso* the following field notes, because each one belongs to a particular place, day and date for every sealing season that is to follow this one just ended of 1890. These notes on hand on the islands during the coming years will aid the officers of the Government up there to observe and contrast the condition of the rookeries and hauling-grounds as it shall change for better or worse hereafter.

For convenience and easy reference, I divide my notes into three subdivisions. *.i.e.* " *Rookery Notes* ", " *Hauling Ground Notes* ", and " *Notes on the Driving and Killing* ", together with a following of *general memoranda*.

ROOKERY NOTES. — ST. PAUL ISLAND, 1890.

The Reef and Garbotch.

" Thursday, May 22, 1890. The " Reef and Garbotch ".

Spent the day in taking a fresh set of angles over this fine area of breeding ground; the sand has drifted very slightly from its boundaries on Zoltoi during the last 18 years, but a large field of basaltic rocks has been uncovered by the holluschickie just wearing away the grassy covering; that opens the sand to the full play of the wind and away it goes, down to the rocky foundations; the Reef Point from Gull Hill down to the extreme S. W. "drop" of Garbotch is a solid lava table with " bubbles " of hot eruption at later intervals — all pushed up from the sea; then from old John's Rock down to the slopes of Parade Pinnacle, is a thick superstratum of volcanic cinders — all reddish and fine, polished and smoothed in 1872 into that remarkable " parade ground " which I have plotted carefully as it lies; below Fox Cliff, strewn from the beginning of the Reef Rookery, is a surface profusion of basaltic boulders, all knee and waist high as a rule, though many of them are nearly sunken; this covering is characteristic of the entire Reef Rookery and of Garbotch as far down as the intersection of the " 1st Point " of rocks, on that ridge S. W. But, that N. slope of Garbotch is as smooth as a floor — a hard cinder pavement that slopes down gently, yet rapidly, with its broad expanse to the sea. It looks as though it might have been graded by the hand of man. In the bight of this rookery and in the rocks awash at its point, 25 or 50 hair seals, *Phoca vitulina*, were basking, lulled into a sense of security by the hauling fur-seal bulls.

The whole of the Reef Point south of Grassy Summit and Fox Cliff, was entirely bare of grass, or any vegetation except lichens on rocks inaccessible to fur-seals, and tufts of grass only grew on the points and cliff edges of the west shore; tufts of grass and a few flowers appeared also over the " 2nd Drop ". It looks to-day as though much vegetation had crept in and over this field since then, but it is too early now to fairly observe it.

I gathered and gave to Palmer (for the S. I.) a lovely sample of that characteristic green confervoid growth that appears so strange to me growing only upon these hauling grounds and the rookeries; it seems to grow on the pulverized shedded hair and fur comminuted; this makes a beautiful green carpet and it seems to be in its best form at this time of the year; in other words, I take it to be in blossom; by the 10th — 12th June, it shrinks and crocks up but is as bright as it is now.

I do not observe one bull here today where I saw at least 20 at this time 18 years ago; then these slopes of Garbotch were covered with angry, lusty bulls, in solid mass from the shore line to the ridge summit — so far over, even, that it required a club vigorously used before we could get up on Old John's Rock, so as to look over and below; then they were fighting in every direction under our eyes; now, not a fight in progress anywhere, not bulls enough to quarrel — they are scattered so widely over this same ground where in 1872 an interval of ten feet between them did not exist — today there are intervals of hundreds of feet !

June 7, 1890. The kelp on the submerged reef extends at least 1000 feet to S. S. W. from the rocks awash as indicated on my chart of the peninsula; this kelp marks a shoal everywhere rough and rocky

APPENDIX. 233

within its borders, of a fathom to 6 fathoms depth, making it a very dangerous point for vessels especially when picking up the land in a fog.

In this kelp and over these rocks awash, the first bands of holluschickie that reach these islands every spring, sport and haul. A few of them may be seen here at or about the arrival of the first bulls, and it is from this point that the first " drives " of the year are regularly made by the natives for food — as early as the 10th — 14th May, some seasons, and the 20th — 24th May in late or cold springs.

June 8, 1890.

This pencil sketch of the sweep of Garbotch, I have made this afternoon with extreme care, since it shows to the best advantage the real character of a first class breeding ground in the eyes of a fur-seal.

The entire underpinning to the Reef and Garbotch is lava, — basalt in which at some points, notably on the Reef Point, much iron is embodied; this basalt is either dark purplish or reddish black, or else of light gray tint; sometimes it is solid and compact, then again thickly peppered with air holes and bubbles; on the point of Garbotch in this picture, the breeding ground is a smooth slope down to the sea from the summit of polished breccia of soft grayish black and dull red scoriae; worn entirely with a gravelly surface by the attrition of the flippers of hauling seals. But under Old John's Rock large boulders are heaped promiscuously from the crest of the ridge to the surf; and this rough surface continues to the limit of the rookery under my seat by the edge of these bluffs by the " Cap ". When I first came down to this rookery in May (21) 1872, I had great difficulty in getting in from behind to Old John's Rock; clubs had to be used to drive the bulls away first; now, there is nothing in the road there, or anywhere else on the crest of the entire rookery. It does not seem to me, as I write, that there are 5 bulls here to-day where there were 100, eighteen years ago! lichens and mosses now growing on rocks here where restless breeders annually polished them brightly then.

June 11, 1890.

Natives made their first drive of the year for the Company this morning, early, from the " Crest "; about 1,000 holluschickie (See Note Book II, hauling grounds). This picture opposite shows the ground as it is really occupied by the bulls today; it is a fair sample of the occupation of every other one of the great breeding grounds of St. Paul. In 1872, there were right on the field of this drawing, just as many bulls to be seen as there were rocks uncovered — look at the scene now! This is a pre-Raphaelitic sketch. Visited " Reef " and Garbotch this morning, no change in bulls substantially from what is above noted; 2 cows on Garbotch, and Antone reports a pup on the " Reef ".

June 17, 1890.

The cows are hauling in small squads; this is about as in 1872; but not a single " polseecatch " along the water margin of this rookery to-day: not a single one, and none upon the ground with the old males, where there is plenty of vacant space and nothing to oppose them. Where are the " half-bulls " which played so prominent a part in the rookeries, 1872-74? I asked T. this evening and his assistant, Mr. R.; they replied that they observed that this class of seals were not on the rookeries to-day. Mr. T. said that five years ago he saw the last of them in so far as his observation went at Tolstoi. On calling Mr. Goff's attention to it, he declared that he never observed a young bull attempting to land on the rookeries last year, and that he believed that the natives told the truth, when they said to me in his presence at N. E. Point that these animals were " quite all killed ".

June 18, 1890.

How singularly regular the fog and drizzle is around and on these islands! Here, during the last two weeks, with only one or two brief intervals, the wind has blown from every point of the compass, from a stiff breeze to a gentle air, yet the fog and the drizzle have been and are constant, just as it was in 1872. Not so much rain, but a steady drizzle daily beaten into your eyes and clothes by fresh to violent winds. A thick fog and " booze " or drizzle does not prevent seals from landing, indeed it seems to encourage them; but a heavy rain with hail or sleet will drive them into the water from the hauling grounds. They will, however, soon reappear after the cessation of this particular kind of meteorological disturbance.

June 19, 1890.

I myself have not seen a " killer " (*Orca*), yet thus far, but I am credibly informed that these enemies do appear here every summer, later on and in the fall (when the pups are just beginning to go to sea) in greater and greater numbers every year.

Also, that within the last three years, two exceedingly severe October gales have prevailed, causing those deadly " surf-nips " by which an immense number of pups were destroyed.

If it be true what I hear now, then between the " killer whales ", the " surf-nips ", the killing of the " half-bulls ", the killing of yearlings, driving from rookery margins, and pelagic poaching, the seals of these islands have little chance short of extermination unless the remedy is applied at once.

June 21, 1890.

Again I look over the sea margin, and not a single " polseecatchie " at the water's edge. In this connection arises the strong assurance which the natives here gave Bishop Veniaminov, in 1832, that these "half-bulls" which are driven up in the daily drives become thereby utterly useless as breeders thereafter, that they are demoralized and broken up physically so that they lay around simply as outcasts or vagrants.

I took notice in 1872 of the fact that there was a large number of these apparently big able-bodied bulls always hauled up out and hauling with the holluschickie, and laying in squads along on the sand beaches whenever and wherever I went out in June and July during the inception and height of the breeding season. I then gave them only a thought of their being "soured" and beaten bulls, since the rookeries then simply rung with the noise of fighting "seecatchie"; and there were then so many bulls on these grounds that the absence of these was not of the least account.

But, now this feature comes up again to me; and is not this plaint of the natives to Veniaminov, in 1832, wholly correct? and does this not account in a very large measure for the vacancies of and the astonishing somnolence of the scattered old bulls which I see to-day on the breeding grounds?

June 22, 1890.

The cows are just faintly showing themselves on this Garbotch side, and a little better, but not much on the Reef line; they are falling far behind the record of 1872 at this hour.

June 27, 1890.

As the Garbotch side of this Rookery is in full view from the Village Hill, I have come down here since the above note; I can see the sweep of Garbotch, and that tells the story just as I have recorded it under Tolstoi and Lukannon; as this, however, was the first rookery I took the land angles of, so it will be the first one to be mapped with the cows on the 10th prox.

June 28, 1890.

Made a tour of Garbotch and the Reef this morning and find a feeble suggestion of the hauling of the cows in 1872-74. Although there yet remains ten days, ere the full limit to the coming of the females is reached, yet enough is suggested by the exhibition of the hour to make one very thoughtful — as much, nearly, as the extraordinary scant hauling of the bulls did early in the month; the wide empty areas between the podding females in which nothing now is seen, and upon which bulls were thickly clustered in 1872, all roaring and fighting incessantly — these empty areas strike me most unpleasantly, and fore-tell what the result of my survey must be, in a measure.

The females are hauling very slowly, and that point below the "crest" where the holluschickie were driven from this morning, is swept bare — not a bull on it — showing the result of the present method of driving from the outskirts, or immediate line of the breeding seals, is to break up and dissolve that organization at that place.

The Reef rocks which lay awash S. S. W. from the Reef Point seem to have a bond of submerged union with the S. end of Seevitchie Kammen, for the sea breaks in a continuous roll across; and again from its N. end to the coast of the Reef rookery, S. S. E. from Reef Pinnacle this reef continues; the water is bold enough all around outside of this.

July 1, 1890.

A circuit of the Reef and Garbotch this morning shows that the bulls are certainly inadequate for the service which their scant number, and wide hauling entails upon them. Scattered harems of 65 and 70 cows are stretched along Garbotch, with but a single bull to each, while at the same moment there are vacant intervals of a hundred and hundreds of feet between them, in which old bulls, all without cows, are placidly sleeping! No fighting, no young bulls landing, and the ragged rookery belt does not mend. The cows are slowly arriving, and will until the 10th instant; then I shall map them down. But, as I view them today, it is impossible to avoid the plain evidence of imperfect, dilatory and feeble service, as contrasted with the vim and vigor here of 1872. What with grass rapidly covering the grand Reef " parade " of 1872-74, and that algoid growth which always appears immediately the next season after the one the seals cease to haul on an old hauling ground, I cannot walk over this place without positive feelings of regret and astonishment; the alteration is simply immense, and all for the worse ".

July 10, 1890.

In company with Mr. Goff and Dr. Lutz, I made my plotting of the breeding seals as they lay on the Reef and Garbotch today;

Here at the very height of the breeding season, when the masses were most compact and uniform in their distribution in 1862-74, I find the animals as they lay today scattered over twice and thrice as much ground as a rule as the same number would occupy in 1872- scattered because the virile bulls are so few in number and the service which they render so delayed or impotent. In other words, the cows are restless, not being served when in heat, they seek other bulls by hauling out in green great jagged points of massing, (as is shown by the chart), up from their landing belts.

This unnatural action of the cows, or rather unwonted movement, has caused the pups already to form small pods everywhere, even where the cows are most abundant, which shadows to me the truth of the fact that in five days or a week from date, the scattering completely of the rookery organization will be thoroughly done; it did not take place until the 20th-25th July, 1872.

In 1872, these cows were promptly met with the service which they craved the rookery ground. The scattering of these old bulls today over so large an area, is due to extreme feebleness and combined in many cases to a recollection of no distant day when they had previously hauled thus far out on this very ground surrounded by bareness, though all is vacant and semi-grass grown under and around them now.

It is impossible not to consider the question which this scene every moment prompts — " what proportion of these old males which we see here now, over-done and scant in number — what ratio of their number will live to return next year? — and if they do all live to return, what manner of good will they be? — in many cases will they be potent at all? " And again, not a single young bull to be seen on the breeding grounds or at the breeding margins! Where are they coming from? They, so conspicuous by their numbers and aggressiveness in 1870-'74! Where is the new blood which must take the place of the old and enfeebled sires before us? already failing to meet the demands of the hour on every side and ahead of us! Where is it?

The only answer which my study of this season gives me is *there is no new blood, mature enough, left.* The club and effects of driving has destroyed it, slowly at first, but surely through-out the last eight years! and rapidly during the last three of this period—especially rapid last year and at the present hour.

The poacher at sea has lent his aid since 1885 to this destruction; he has destroyed the cows in especial but the " half-bulls " have been chiefly eliminated by driving, and the club, which has smitten every one of them as " smooth " 4-year-olds, whenever they appeared in the drives during the last 20 years, throughout the killing seasons.

In 1872-'74, when no driving was made from S. W. Point, from the Zapadnies, and all English Bay to the westward of Neahrpahskie Kammen, from Polavina, or any where between it and the hauling grounds of Lukannon, then there were reservoirs of young male life which were not drawn upon or disturbed, from which a steady stream of new male blood for the breeding grounds could and did flow. That year here when they first began to systematically drive from these places marks the beginning of the decay and present deplorable condition of these rookeries of the Pribylov Islands. This systematic driving began in 1882, and was firmly established in 1884; the poaching began in 1886 and from that year these two agencies have gone hand in hand forward with this work of ruin and depletion.

The Lagoon.

June 13, 1890.

" I think that there has been little or no change in the topographical character of this Lagoon sea-wall since my surveys of 1872-74, except that in its height I think the boulders are shoved up higher by ice floes, some 6 or 10 feet, perhaps; the lower segments of the rookery wall are unchanged, being just above surf wash at high water.

The shoving up of these boulders which compose the Lagoon seawall, on which this rookery is established, has also resulted in perceptibly shoaling the cove; although the sand therein has shifted some, yet it all appears very natural to me.

The rookery itself does not show up any better than a ragged remnant of what it was in 1872.

My sketch shows the Lagoon Rookery, the slough and the killing gang at work on the village killing grounds, Lagoon salt-house, all, as they appeared this afternoon at 4 P. M.

Lukannon.

June 2, 1890.

A strong W. N. W. wind blew all day yesterday with snow and covered everything white and wet last night — the wind still blew this morning, but the sky cleared at noon, and the snow quit. I made a visit to Ketavie, taking angles from the base of Black Bluff up to Lukannon Hill. I do not observe any great increase of bulls today, a few more, but still, large areas unoccupied by these animals right down to the water line. They have hauled at odd intervals as far back as they did in 1872, but no crowding into the same area at all.

Some bulls have ascended high up on the flanks of Lukannon Hill, but large intervals of vacant ground lie between them of from 50 to 100 feet! and this day is not more than two or three days in advance of the first arrival of the females. I cannot avoid taking significant note of this point. These old bulls that do appear are all in good physical trim outwardly — they look well.

The snow seems to surprise some of these bulls; they smell at it, then roar angrily. These small holluschickie were in the centre of the rookery area on Keetavie this A. M.

June 12, 1890.

Very slight change in bulls during the last ten days; they have hauled here very widely far back from the water, with large areas of 30 and 40 feet between them; 2 cows in sight here; one " rusty ", so must have been hauled out several days — she has a pup. Mr. Goff reported the arrival of a cow here two days ago — perhaps this is the one, so that this pup has not been born long, a few hours or a day at the most.

June 22, 1890.

A survey of Lukannon Rookery this afternoon shows an astonishing apathy among the bulls, and not a single " half-bull " on the shore, or in the water — a few clusters of cows just along the water margin are

APPENDIX. 239

all I see. They have been out at least 4 or 5 days because they all look rusty; the newly arrived cows are very conspicuous for a day or two after arrival by reason of their shining white abdomens, and silvery gray backs and necks. There is not a bright cluster of cows anywhere in sight today on Keetavie, Tolstoi, Lagoon Reef or Garbotch; this shows how gradually and slowly these small clusters have grown in size since the first arrivals on the 4th-5th inst.

June 24, 1890.

Scarcely any change for the cows today; those holluschickie on the sand have hauled up on the hill, about 100 feet, and are now sleeping in among the breeding bulls.

June 27, 1890.

Scarcely any change.

July 1st, 1890.

I have passed three hours this afternoon marking and watching the service of the bulls in their harems; it is simply lifeless, languid and fairly impotent — wholly so in many cases at this early date — what will it be ten days from now? if it is so feeble now at the outset. Saw 2 "polseecatchie " at the water's edge, and one at the rear; where, indeed, are these animals? What, indeed, is on hand, or will be for the next 6 years to come, to supply the places of these scattered and already enfeebled sires of the rookery?

July 10, 1890,

" I made a careful survey of the area and position of the breeding seals on Lukannon and Keetavie this afternoon in company with and aided by Mr Charles J. Goff. On Lukannon, while there appears to be 2/3 as many cows as in 1872, yet the bulls do not average more than 1/15 of the number they showed in 1872. No better on Keetavie; if any thing, a shade or two worse. No young bulls any where offering service or attempting to land on the rookery.

Keetavie.

June 13, 1890.

A comical picture was made today when in the afternoon the entire herd of mules, 10 in number, filed over from the village and pastured on the seal grass that grows on the deserted outskirts of the rookery at Ketavie; the old bulls in waiting paid not the least attention to them that I could see, while the mules were equally indifferent.

I presume that such a pastoral scene as this has never been witnessed outside of these islands.

June 22, 1890.

As this is the time the cows begin to haul in appreciable numbers, I took a careful view at this (Ketavie) Rookery today from that point of sight in the sketch opposite. I saw but three clusters of cows in all the sweep of this picture, and they in the fore-ground right between the 1st and 2nd rollers as they come in; these pods were bevies of from 30 to 50 cows each, all thickly clustered around a single bull with all the other bulls stretched in somnolence around them, just as I recorded the state of affairs on Tolstoi yesterday; and as I go over the field on Lukannon right after this I find it precisely that way there, too; this apathy of the bulls coupled with the total absence of the " polseecatchie " (or " half-bulls ") on these breeding grounds at this hour is a striking contrast with that vim and fury that was so marked among the swarming bulls of 1872 on this and every other one of the breeding grounds of the Pribylov Islands. It is in order to record the fact that the cows are not hauling in anything like the numbers of 1872-74. On Lukannon and the Lagoon, the dearth of cows to-day is noteworthy, while at Tolstoi nearly every cow there this afternoon is as I described it yesterday — three small pods right down at the junction of rocks and sand under the cliffs — 250 cows perhaps on that whole ground this P. M.!

Tolstoi.

June 12, 1890.

A tour to-day on Tolstoi shows little or no change in " seecatchie " from last date I saw no cows; quite a troop of holluschickie on the sand just above surf wash and beyond the drop of the rookery to the sand beach.

The old bulls are hauling here very wildly — way back 500 feet with 50 to 100 feet between them in many instances. No fighting anywhere, and no young bulls at the water's edge; the polseecatchie; perhaps I shall see some of them when the cows begin to haul next week, but they were in swarms by this time in 1872-74.

June 21, 1890.

An inspection to-day shows the odd scattering of cows as they haul, and which Mr. Goff early called my attention to as a great deviation from the habit which they exhibited in my work of 1872. As this is the date in which this class begins to haul in appreciable numbers, I now begin my daily examination of the manner and number in which the cows arrive.

They commenced just as they did in 1872 a few cows here and there by the-4th 6th June; then by the 15th, little clusters appeared of 10 to 50 along the water's edge, and to-day here instead of that exhibi-

APPENDIX.

tion of solid " wave-like " streaks spread up from the water's margin, to the rear limits of the breeding grounds, which they gave me in 1872, I can see nothing of the kind—not even an approximation of that stage. Still these animals have yet 20 days in which to fill up the rookeries as they did in 1872, and it is not the time to finally speculate on their coming or number, merely idle now to do so.

But the behavior of the old bulls is extraordinary this morning at this time of the inflowing cows; they are listless; three-fourths of their scanty number, stretched out sound asleep, while right alongside of these sleepers, a pod of 15 or 30 cows will be closely clustered around a single alert bull, or one that at least is not inert and stupid. There are three such pods as that right under my eyes as I make this note, lying at the junction of the sand beach and rocks of Tolstoi rookery; no such scattering of bulls and indifference was ever witnessed on any of these breeding grounds in 1872-'74; then every bull was alert and furious in his struggles to get possession of at least one, if not all the females within reach; — now, look at them! Why, it seems to me that these bulls are enfeebled and sick. At least it is a most remarkable deviation from the method and order of first arrival of the females in 1872; such a picture of perfect listlessness and indifference as this is, from the beginning to the end of the season, never met anybody's eye on these breeding grounds then.

No young bulls anywhere along the water's edge, or back among the old bulls — widely scattered as they are — way upon the hill slopes of Tolstoi this morning at least 550 to 600 feet away from these first cows widely and thinly scattered old bulls, all of them now stretched out in sound sleep.

June 23, 1890.

" This is the day in 1872 when the cows had hauled in sufficient numbers to impress me deeply for the first time as the season then advanced; at this time in 1872 the most casual observer would note the arrival of the cows as " coming up in families, or streaks as it were from the waters line upon the ridge " (as per MS. note of June 23, 1872, made as I looked then at Garbotch slope). The peculiar " fanning " of the cows then as they used their hind flippers, made their resting places conspicuous at any moment to the eye glancing then over the rookeries.

To-day it takes a sharp trained eye to find the scant scattered pods of cows, as they rest just above the surf margin, and as for ' hauling back ' up on the ridge, — not the first symptom of such a movement is in progress.

As you stand and look across the cove at the Lagoon Rookery not over 900 feet away you cannot see the least visible evidence of the landing of females this morning. I can make out a few scattered heads, but no concerted arrival of these animals, so very obvious in 1872-'74, at this time of the season ".

June 24, 1890.

That peculiar podding of the cows which I note on the 22nd still continues here : — the cows still cluster in groups at the water's edge, with no attempt yet made to haul up in long " wavelike streaks " to the high ground in the rear.

Strange, in this connection is the hauling of these somnolent scant bulls, why, several of them, yes, a dozen are now up 600 feet back from these cows at the surf margin on the sand, and vacancies of hundreds of feet between them : Not a fight in progress, and not a single young bull in sight at the landing of the cows.

June 27, 1890.

I observed on Tolstoi the arrival of a few more cows, the first I have yet seen that wore the fresh attractive toilet of these creatures; they are still crowding in on the sand in that strange manner above alluded to, and still but a very faint advance made in any single spot towards filling in the ground back from the surf margin. The bulls are still hauled in that wild manner which I have so frequently noted, and are sleeping stupidly everywhere, with the cows landing just around them and below them!

June 30, 1899.

A survey of Tolstoi this morning shows the most striking want of bulls — that there are pods or harems of 60 females with only one bull ; that the sand beach end is the chosen resort of the solid hauling of cows, while the rocks up in their rear are positively deserted. I do not see that the cows are arriving so as to make any considerable number of them show white and silvery. But the few that are here are under full swing. The strange wild hauling of old bulls, and the remarkable absence of the " polseacatchie " is still prominent. I see two " half-bulls " at the lower end of the rookery ground right under Fox Castle; these are the only examples of their kind on the field. I have been constantly saying to myself, "now I can easily count every bull on this rookery that is here to-day ! " They certainly do look lost among the rocks in the rear, and in the large pods of cows at the water's edge.

The cows are pupping, are caring for themselves precisely as I have hitherto recorded the act, in 1872, at this time.

July 1, 1890.

A survey of Tolstoi this afternoon shows little change during the last three days, if any, it has been an increased solidity to the belt of the females on the sand. I think their hauling here as they do one of the anomalies of this all around extraordinary state of affairs.

APPENDIX. 243

As I again look at these old bulls hauled out here above those cows, 500 and 600 feet away from them and not a half dozen bulls between them, I begin to think that perhaps they do so because a few years ago when they were here cows then hauled out to them, in solid masses from the water—they did so in 1872, I find by my maps; and so perhaps that is the reason why they, the bulls are out here again without any visible reason for their so being. It is the same way on the Reef and Garbotch, at Lukannon, and especially so at Zapadnie.

I took notice of a large proportion of small or 2-year old females, and the unusual slowness of hauling, compared with 1872, which was not at its greatest activity up to July 7th.

The usual parade of foxes in and out among the breeding seals now presents itself. I saw one to-day running off with a fresh placenta, or " after-birth ", in its mouth; there is a marked diminution of the number of foxes as contrasted with my notes of 1872. They have been mercilessly hunted during the last ten years, and last winter Mr. Goff ordered a " zapooska " for their benefit and preservation. This season is one of unalloyed physical and mental comfort for Reynard; he has all the fresh meat, waterfowl, eggs and beetles that he can eat, and the delightful assurance that he is never shot at or trapped at this time of the year. At the present hour they are shedding, and they look scrubby enough; generally, the old hair on the tail hangs the longest, even after all is renewed everywhere else on their bodies; thus you constantly see around you now a bluish gray fox running off with a fluffy, dried grass colored tail, a very odd looking contrast.

July 7, 1890.

From a station on the bluffs overlooking the entire stretch of the cliff belt the breeding seals at Tolstoi, I passed two hours this afternoon intently observing the service which the bulls below were rendering; there were 67 bulls directly within distinct sweep of my vision; distinctly and widely separated; and these bulls had some 2,000 to 2,500 cows! It is fairly idle to attempt to express the perfect impotency of these overdone and feeble old males; sleeping or dozing nearly all of the time, and on waking, teased by the females without arousing them in the least. I saw in these two full hours of attentive watching, only three attemps to serve the cows by these 67 bulls; and each attempt was a languid failure. Not a single " half-bull " or polseecatch attempting to land here or anywhere else for that matter on the rookeries to-day. How many of these cows are going off without impregnation if not served when in heat? Do they ever return for it? And if they do, where is that service to come from? Certainly not from those already useless bulls which are hourly growing weaker as the season culminates. I saw to-day a mobile virgin cow, and an older one, engaged at the same moment in teasing a languid old bull, which made an ineffectual attempt to satisfy one of them and failed. I never witnessed such a scene in all of my observations of 1872-'74. Then there were 20 bulls where there is 1 now, and three times or four times as many cows. Late in the rutting season, about 20th-24th July, an occasional exhibition of languid impotence was seen, but it made no impression on my mind other than to note the fact that here and there have and there was a bull which was physically exhausted, chiefly from the effects of fighting; but there were then so many virile bulls right around it ready and eager, that it did not signify.

One of the odd orders at Tolstoi is the fact that the best massing of the cows now is seen down on the sand at the extreme extension of the rookery out towards Middle Hill; it gives one the only suggestion of what the compact, solid massing of the rookery was in 1872, and which massing is now utterly lacking on these breeding grounds of St. Paul and St. George.

There are so few cows, pups and bulls today on that cliff belt of Tolstoi that instead of an area there of 36 feet in width, densely covered as in 1872, actually today there is great difficulty in reconciling the mind to allow a depth so covered of 10 feet: as I look down upon this same ground — that gives us 1750 feet by 10 = 17,500, or ground for 8,750 seals ♂., ♀. and ○. instead 36,750 in 1872.

That parade ground up and over this breeding belt under the cliffs at Tolstoi is wholly deserted by the holluschickie — not a single animal has hauled out there upon its grassy patched surface thus far this season. Out near the point is that queer climbing path up the cliffs from the sea to this ground; here, in 1872, I have sat for hours at a time watching the seals come up and go down in ceaseless files of hundreds and thousands, actually climbing up places so steep that it was all an agile man could do to follow them safely!

I saw about 50 or 60 holluschickie on the cliff steps to this path to-day; but none of them seem inclined to go up on to the old parade ground above; the natives call this particular locality "Bobrovia yama", or the " sea otter cave ".

July 10, 1890.

Made a careful survey of the area and position of the breeding seals on Tolstoi this day in company with Mr. Charles J. Goff. In July (14th), 1872, this Tolstoi Rookery held 225,000 ♂., ♀. and ○., a startling decrease here of nearly 3/4 or 72/00, or loss here, since 1872, of 162,600 seals!"

Zapadnie.

June 13, 1890.

I think the bulls on Lower Zapadnie show the thinnest in distribution: — certainly this great rookery which swarmed with rousing fighting bulls, closely massed over all the breeding space mapped out on this ground at this time in 1872, is in a great decline. The few bulls that here are hauled out so widely and so far from the water in places they are a 1,000 feet! I think they act as though they were anticipating nothing. A few cows, perhaps 4 or 5, are all that I saw this day here, and 3 on Upper Zapadnie.

I have fairly got this rough surfaced rookery charted to-day it is a queer place to view the seals — they lay in curious little valley and canons which have been created by hot lava bubbles in pre-biological days. But that scant distribution of the bulls in these places to-day puts me continually in mind of that song of the — " banquet hall deserted, — whose garlands dead and guests have fled ", etc. Upper Zapadnie is equally thin and distribution its hill slopes, and what is more, the water's edge line, is vacant on frequent intervals; there is an occasional roar and some characteristic " spitting ", but none of that desperate, incessant fighting that prevailed among the closely thronged bulls on all these places in 1872; the rookeries to-day, on this occasion of the first arrival of the females, are positively quiet! The unbroken uproar that boomed night and day from them then in 1872 is not more than even suggested by what I hear now ".

June 26, 1890.

I have not seen much of Lower Zapadnie to-day, only a running survey from the sand beach, while I had a fine view of Upper Zapadnie and its beach extension. Upper Zapadnie shows the same decadence, but not so painfully marked as in Lower Zapadnie; the beach extension, however, is remarkably vacant in so far as cows are concerned.

July 3, 1890.

The hauling of the cows on Zapadnie to-day is extraordinary in contrast with its appearance here in 1872 at this time, and only a week from the hour of its utmost limit of expansion. Really, I cannot see much increase since my notes last week, but such rusty cows, such somnolent stupid bulls! such an abnormal average as 60 to 75 cows in the harems! while lots of sleeping bulls all around, though only some 40 or 50 feet away from these harems, where the bulls in charge are so feeble that they have refused the advances of eager cows repeatedly under my eyes within less than 20 minutes after I had set a fixed watch on half a dozen right within my view and near by.

Driving as they are obliged to do has the deplorable effect of widening and scattering the already too wide and scattered distribution of these breeding animals. I saw this result on the Reef after it had been swept on the 1st inst. the same extending vacancies on the water line of this once great compact breeding ground is plainly visible to-day. Every little pod of holluschickie that creeps in now behind a harem, laying close up to it instinctively for shelter, is at once marked and swept out, up and into the drives, this huddles the cows into larger and larger masses, sweeps off and away the few surplus old males, and leaves the ground in worse and worse shape for a bad season at the least. This driving from the immediate vicinity of a breeding ground was never done after June 5th in my time; then rarely and only to get a few hundred seals early as they first arrived, for the natives food; this always took place before any noteworthy arrival of the cows.

July 9, 1890.

I made a close recognoissance of the breeding seals as they lay upon the ground at Zapadnie, both Upper and Lower wings, this morning immediately after the natives had driven the small squads of holluschickie which they alone find here now, and only in spots, laying up in close proximity to the cows. I went over at 4 A. M. purposely to see the *modus operandi* of the driving here, and then to get a fair idea now at this proper time of the full expansion of Zapadnie as it stands to-day.

July 11, 1890.

In company with Mr Charles J. Goff I visited and surveyed the entire sweep of Upper and Lower Zapadnie rookery to-day...

It is impossible to convey the queer sense of utter desolation which the vacant seal area of 1872 on this fine rookery carries to my mind this morning. Grass and flowers springing up over those broad areas back of the breeding grounds where in 1872 thousands upon thousands of young male seals hauled out and over during the entire season, without being visited by any man then except myself! Nobody in 1872 ever thought of such a thing as coming over from the village to make a killing at Zapadnie; and then too, those splendid areas of hauling-ground in English Bay, all grass grown, mosses, lichens, and flowers, which in 1872-'74 so astonished Maynard and myself at this date that year by their teeming squadrons of young male seals.

Judging from the appearance of the grass, I should say that the seals must have ceased to haul here to any great extent as late as 1883, and by 1884-'85 to have suddenly dropped out of the field in large numbers. No seals have hauled in the rear of these breeding lines of 1872-'74 since 1878-'79; that is certain because this area is now well sodded and sprinkled with a full crop of *Archangelica* which never comes in sooner than 8 or 10 years after the seals have once destroyed it. This time of the re-growth of "*pochkie*" was well demonstrated to me at Zapadnie in 1876; there, in 1868, Morgan's sealing party built a salt house right in the center of a well polished hauling ground of holluschickie. The seals at once, of course, abandoned a large space directly and indirectly dominated by this salthouse and the killing gangs; the grass upon this abandoned haulingground of 1868 was pretty well tufted and established when I first saw it in 1872, and in 1876 small heads of the *Archangelica* began to sprout everywhere anew over it; this shows that 8 years after the seals ceased to haul upon a hitherto well polished area by them, plenty of rank grass was growing upon it with many flowering plants, and a beginning of a new garden of that rank, umbelliferous *Archangelica*, above specified.

Polavina.

June 3, 1890.

As there is not the slightest appearance of change to the sea margin of this bluff-banded rookery during the last 16 years, nor is there ever likely to be, I simply re-draw my original land angles of 1872-'73, establishing, however, two additional stations. One on the Point, at the "Grotto", "B", and the other on the beach below at "C"; this will cover the showing of any change that the breeding seals may present on that portion of the rookery ground which can be altered by surf and ice-floe pressure during storms in the fall and the winter and early spring. The land angles of "Little Polavina" are precisely as they were in 1872.

June 4, 1890.

An odd seal bridge and grotto is on the extreme point of Polavina, and makes one of the queerest sort of subjects for the pencil; when I shall visit it in July, I presume I shall find it tenanted with a harem, although it may be a thoroughfare, since the seals can haul up through it.

I take this sketch of Polavina Point from my Sta. "C", just 300 feet below those bulls in the foreground and which map out as they lay today the southern limit of the present extent of this breeding grounds. On this flat of sand, just above surf wash, basaltic boulders, mostly small ones, are strewn thickly over, and many pieces of driftwood. That remarkable reef table which projects out under Polavina Point is well bared to-day by the low water and gives me a full view. It is a solid, flat table of basalt covered with innumerable pools of water and forests of sea-weed, which fairly glisten as they are now bared damp and dripping by the tide".

June 25, 1890.

I revisit this morning the spot from which this sketch is taken; a few small clusters of females have arrived as shown in the sketch on the other side of this page. The number of vagrant bulls dozing on this sand beach in the fore-ground has increased vastly, but the cows are very scant in number for the day; they are feebly suggestive of that wonderful massing which they were making on this ground in 1872 at this time.

I thought at the time which I established this Sta. " C " (on 4th inst.) that it was way below where the rookery would go this year, judging from the lay of the bulls then; I now see it plainly.

July 3, 1890.

Visited this rookery ground and surveyed the area and position of the breeding animals in company with Mr. Goff.

My final survey of this rookery shows it to be one of the two rookeries only which seem to have suffered only half in loss of form and numbers. I cannot avoid the conclusion, however, that this rookery like Zapadnie, has been cruelly driven during the last four or five seasons, perhaps the last eight years, since the chief hauling-grounds always laid up behind the breeding lines of Polavina; therefore, when the shrinking of holluschickie began, the scraping of the large semi-circular edge of Polavina Rookery commenced in earnest, since the young males naturally do here as they do everywhere else on this island to-day — they lie up closer and closer to the lines of the breeding seals.

Novastoshnah.

June 2, 1890.

Came into the great rookery ground this morning from the "Arago"; made my headquarters in Webster's new house, and prepared for the day's work; a clear day with light N. wind; I find the bulls here in as good or better number than on any other rookery of this island; still, large vacancies and several wholly deserted sections.

A greater number of sea-lions than I expected to see; several thousand of them clustered principally on Sea Lion Neck and N. E. Point, although they haul all along the East, North and West shores of this Point; the bulls were in full rutting ardor, and several cubs or pups newly born; their stifled wheezing roaring, deep gutterals and grunting groans, come out into sharp contrast with the clear cut voices of the fur-seal bulls which haul out here side by side with their huge cousins.

I saw very few holluschickie to-day, although I inspected every foot of the great rookery.

That slope of Hutchinson's Hill which drops to the westward is certainly the most imposing single sweep of seal ground on the islands — it is impressive and extensive; the seacatchie here today appear in as good numbers as anywhere else on St. Paul Island; still, I must truthfully add that they are in woeful contrast with what I have recorded here in 1874.

APPENDIX.

June 4, 1890.

These sand dune tracts at and around the "Neck" of N. E. Point have changed character somewhat since 1872. Then, everything on this high, bare sand knoll of to-day, which rises from the Big Lake and separates it from the surf sand flat level of the "Neck" — then this knoll was grassed firmly over; but now, from some cause or other, sand has been blown up and over, completely covering the lower grassy hummocks or knolls and has blown out and away entirely from the highest points. It leaves now a desolate, deep sand ridge to cross and recross, as you go to and from the point; and also, the surf now beats upon a wider spread of sand on both sides of the "Neck", washing completely across in storms with much driftwood and many small basaltic "donicks" or boulders interspersed in lines with the wash of the surf.

This sand is simply powdered volcanic rock with a liberal admixture of comminuted sea-shells, and other marine conchological forms.

The Big Lake seems wholly as it was; likewise, the trail down among the sand dunes on its eastern shore. The genesis of a finely fixed sand dune here, is as follows: first a heap of wind-drifted sand from its the drying out above surf wash, into this the seeds of the *Elymus arenaria*, are carried and sprouting, throw the strong deep roots of that coarse grass down deep, binding the heap as it were; this grass alone seems to possess the power of taking hold at first and successfully growing — the other plants and grasses can and do germinate but the first strong wind thereafter raises the sand about them or from under them, or destroy their roots; but this "wild wheat", the *Elymus*, has such deep-reaching roots — as pronounced in this respect as those of the alfalfa are, that it cannot be blown out, or blown under very often.

But when the *Elymus* has firmly anchored a sand dune, then a grass closely resembling our timothy or orchard grass takes hold in its company, and with several species of mosses and the creeping willows (*Salix*), and wild pea-vines, finally crowds the hardy *Elymus* fairly out within a few years, or at least leaves but a scanty remnant of its former exclusive holding; however, there are extensive tracts on St. Paul where the sand is unusually light, deep and restless; upon these areas, and on the killing grounds where the bodies of millions of seals have decayed, making a rich, hot compost out of the dry, sterile sand, there the *Elymus* grows strong and luxuriant, without a rival, — nothing else can get in.

July 13, 1890.

I made my land survey of this point on the 2nd and 4th of June; and from that time until this day I have not been on the breeding-grounds here; but now the hour having arrived in which to see the breeders at their finest limit of expansion on the ground occupied by them, I made this morning, in company with Mr. Goff, a careful, rod by rod, inspection and survey of the field; every section from point to point as we advanced from station to station was carefully plotted on the chart with a distinct memorandum of its massed depth, the land angles giving the exact number of feet of sea margin which each section possessed. In this way, foot by foot we progressed around the entire circuit, jotting down every expansion and contraction of the breeding lines and every vacancy. This is the only method by which a uniform fair statement of fact and estimation of the numbers, area and position of these rookeries can be made. To attempt to carry in your mind an estimate over this irregular ground and distribution of life upon its surface, is simply a physical impossibility; and an attempt to measure this area with the life as massed upon it with a tape line, is equally abortive and ludicrous.

But, my angles taken with a fine prismatic compass from my several stations established with initial base lines, locate these herds just as they rest upon the ground to-day. By having the topography all finished June 2nd-4th, now I rapidly and accurately plot upon it as I traverse the field, these herds, just as they lie under my eyes.

Thus all guess work is wholly eliminated, as it should be, from the exact location of the position and area of these rookeries; then upon this known ground of occupation, a sensible rule for estimation can be based.

July 26, 1890.

Daniel Webster is the veteran white sealer on these islands; he came to St. Paul in 1868, and, save the season of 1876 (then on a trip to the Russian Seal Islands), he has been sealing here ever since, being in charge of the work at North East Point, annually, until this summer of 1890, when he has conducted the killing on St. George. He spoke very freely to me this afternoon while calling on me and said there is no use trying to build these rookeries up again so as to seal here as has been done since 1868, unless these animals are protected in the North Pacific Ocean as well as in Behring Sea; on this point the old man was very emphatic.

Webster came ashore on St. Paul Island in the spring (April) of 1868, an employé of Williams and Haven, of New London, Ct. He took charge of the sealing then begun in behalf of this firm at Novastoshnah or North East Point. Hutchinson, Kohl and Co. had the only other party up there at that time. This was the first irregular sealing ever done upon this island since 1804.

Webster said that H. K. and Co. and he took over 75,000 young male seals at N. E. Point alone, that summer of 1868, and only stopped work from sheer exhaustion of their men, who were not only physically "used up", but also they had used up all their salt and had no suitable means left of saving any more skins.

When, then both parties stopped work he said that no apparent diminution of the number of holluschickie was evident to any of them; and that this fact created much comment; he declares that there has never been so many seals on that ground since; that " although there was a fine showing of seal, Mr. Elliott, when you were there in 1872, yet there never has been so many there as in 1868. "

He says that ever since 1876-'77 he has observed a steady shrinking of the hauling grounds at North East Point a very rapid contraction during the last six years, especially rapid since 1887-'88.

That he never agreed with the statement recently made of the great increase of seals over my record of 1872-'74; but on the contrary has always said that no increase ever followed it, and that he always said so to both Treasury and company agents whenever questioned he declared a steady diminution; he says that when down in San Francisco last (about 5 years ago, winter of 1885-86) he was not asked any questions by anybody as to the increase of seals, and he volunteered no information; if he had been asked, he would have spoken his mind freely.

Webster says that in 1872-'74 he was then able to get all the holluschickie he wanted from that sand beach on the North shore of the "Neck" at N. E. Point " never went anywhere else for them, or near a rookery.

He says that the holluschickie never again came down upon the southern slope of Hutchinson's Hill, after the season's work of 1868 closed.

On the rookeries : St. George Island. " North. "

July 19, 1890.

I came upon this breeding-ground to-day after an absence of just sixteen years. I find the topography unchanged — the hauling-grounds all grass grown, and the usual flowering plants that seem to follow the abandonment of hitherto polished ground laid upon by holluschickie.

The seals upon its breeding area are in the usual form and number characteristic of this season over on St. Paul — a scanty supply of old bulls — no young bulls in the rookery or outside — large scattered harems, and every evidence of imperfect service — in all these forms, precisely as they are over on St. Paul.

But this rookery which held 76,250 ♂, ♀, ○. in 1874, has suffere a loss of — only one-half of its cows and pups; of the bulls, however, a vastly greater proportion, five-sevenths of them, are missing; this rookery was the largest on St. George in 1874, it has been so ever since, and is to-day diminished as it is, but large as it is over here, there are only two on St. Paul smaller; one is the " Lagoon ", and the other Ketavie, though it was twice as large as this breeding ground in 1874.

SECTION VIII.

July 25, 1890.

Capt. Lavender and Dr. Noyes made a careful survey of the holluschickie that have hauled out here since they were driven up on the 19th inst.; they agreed that if driven to-day this rookery would not yield 300 holluschickie of over 5-1/2—7-lb skins.

July 26, 1890.

No increase of holluschickie on this ground.

If I may believe the apparent honest statement of Dr. Noyes and Mr. Webster (agents N. A. C. Co.), this rookery has shrunk 1/2 from its margins of 3 years ago, *and, it is greatly worse today, than it was at this time last year.*

This is the testimony also of Mr. Goff as to the status of the St. Paul rookeries as between this season and last; *it now points with my work, to the certainty of a still further marked reduction in the form and number of the breeding seals next year*, while the killable seals or holluschickie, will simply be minus.

July 27, 1890.

The cows and pups in full swing of " podding "; the holluschickie scant in numbers and mixing up with the scattered harems; a small pod, chiefly yearlings, hauled out on the extreme western extension and the two other small pods at the " Raichka ", and " Scraidnee " on this rookery — altogether, not 200 of them 9-lb. skins.

I am surprised at not seeing the due proportion of yearlings out now, that a rookery of this size should claim. At least 20,000 pups left this ground last October; half of them should be back now as yearlings; and as such, show up a thousand or two every day now until the end of the season. I am therefore inclined to think that the pups are suffering a heavier ratio of loss than in 1872-'74; they are now fewer in number and their natural enemies, such as " killer-whales " here and sharks in the North Pacific, and the " killers " there too, are just as numerous and voracious as of old; the loss therefore inflicted from this source would be more apparent now than when the pups were twice and thrice as numerous; in 1872-'74, I estimated that about one million pups left St. Paul every October and November, in fine physical trim; and of this one million, not over half of the number came back next June and July as yearlings.

To-day, judging from the scanty returns of yearlings, I know that the loss in pup returns is far greater — it looks as though not more than one-quarter are returning this season of 1890 as yearlings.

There should be at least from 3,000 to 5,000 yearlings out on the hauling grounds of this rookery daily now, estimating that only half of them, as in 1872, are or have been destroyed at sea since they left this ground of their birth last autumn. But raking and scraping the whole extent of this rookery to-day would not produce a " drive " of

600 holluschickie of all ages — 450 of them to 500 yearlings and the balance chiefly 2-year-olds.

I have been looking every day after another since the 15th inst. over the rookeries and hauling grounds for the percentage of yearling returns. By this time all those seals should show up if they are to show up at all this year. They all arrived here by the 20th July 1872-'74, and I presume now this 27th day of July, that it is fair to demand a count.

July 30, 1890.

The pups nearest the water's edge on this rookery under the bluffs are all attempting to swim this afternoon; a high S. S. W. wind has caused a heavy black swell, and that throws up a series of odd yet perfect salt water bath tubs, caused by the foundation of several basaltic basins in the beach margin of the rookery here; above and below this place, those pups which are exposed to the full and direct wash of the surf are not making any effort to play and swim in the water, but have crept higher up and are still crawling up so as to get entirely out of the spray.

Most of the pups today on this Rookery have "podded" back — some of them 150 feet from the sea margin, where with their mothers they are mixed up, and mixing all the time with the holluschickie that are hauling.

The holluschickie are chiefly one-year olds; 9/10 of the several pods hauled out here today are yearlings; a great many yearling females are halting down at landings in and among the scattered harems, aimlessly paddling about : — their slight forms and bright silvery backs, white throats and abdomens, are shining out very brightly in contrast with the dark rocks, the dull brown and rusty coats of the "Matkahs", and still rustier forms of the old "seacatchie"; these young yearling cows finally drift up into the rear, join in the medley of sex and age there, and go and come with the rest as they go and come during the remainder of the season.

I have noticed this year, because I began at the outset to look for them, the yearlings which come out in June were invariably males as far as I could see, whenever they were examined (as I had frequent opportunity to do, as they easily and often smother and fall, in the pods, into a sort of stupor which permits you to lift them by their hind flippers and drag them out of the way.) But when the cows begin to arrive in full form and number about the 1st — 10th July, then the female yearlings also appeared in the herds as a class, for the first time.

This points to the natural fact that the young yearling males instinctively flock together and follow the older males on their return trip to the islands while the cows attract the young females as a class,

— just as toddling boys will follow the older boys and men, while the little girls avoid them and flock with the young women and their elders of the same sex.

By the 20th of every July all the cows, mobile and maternal, have arrived, and that arrival brings in the last wave of yearling animals for the season; so that all of the seals that are to appear for the year are now on land, have hauled out, and now finally haul out; it is this final and finishing arrival of the yearling cows that swells the numbers of the yearlings as a class, so markedly, after the 5th — 10th July — sometimes as early as the 1st to 5th of that month, if the season happens to be a very forward one. Still, I find that the records of the arrival of the females on the rookeries during the last 20 years, as they have been annually recorded on these islands — these yearly entries show that the cows came here every season with an amazing regularity, and precisely in this respect as I observed them in 1872-'74.

The old bulls are more irregular, varying as to the character of the seasons, favorable seasons early in May; unfavorable seasons, only three or four days later; and all of them invariably on land by the 1st of every June.

Since the holluschickie here have been permitted to rest for a few days without being at once swept up, after landing, and over to the village killing grounds, they have become sensibly tamer; and like the foxes here, when trapping ceases, they seem to know that they are not going to be hustled over to the shambles again when we come in sight; today, Capt. Lavender, who is a very large man, and myself, walked to within a few yards distance from every pod of holluschickie on this rookery, and save in case where the Captain happened to vigorously flourish his cane (in emphasis of something said), these animals gave no sign of rushing into the water or of stampeding.

This simply goes to prove that the " wildness " of these holluschickie of 1890, which some of the sealers attempted to tell me was a marked natural change in their habit of 1872-'74, is naturally due to the extraordinarily changed fashion of driving which the sealers themselves have instituted during the last six or eight years of increasing scarcity of killable seals; from the time since 1881, when the first regular driving began early in June, until the catch of 100,000 was secured in July, following, these animals have never been allowed to rest anywhere on the islands as they hauled out, long enough to become wonted to the grounds. Naturally enough, we find them " wild ", especially when there is not a tenth of the number on the ground there to-day of the holluschickie which used to be here in 1872.

August 3, 1890.

The pups in that small area under the bluffs where the surf has filled certain cavities so as to form incipient bath tubs—these pups are now all swimming outside, in the gentle swell that now rolls in. They have learned to swim, but the great majority of their kind are still far back on the uplands to the rear, and wholly unused as to water yet. Also, I notice that those pups on the sea margin which are not in the immediate vicinity of these " bath tubs " are still hanging aloof from the surf; they will, however, soon begin their water exercises, by the 13th inst., at the latest, as they did so in 1872.

The numbers of yearling females that are loitering on the rookery ground, lolling over the rocks and nagging the pups, are larger than I have usually observed thus far since the season for their arrival opened on the 15th of July last.

But the mixture to-day of all classes of holluschickie, with the cows and pups, is complete; it would be a matter utterly impossible to make a " drive " of a 100 killable seals from this place today, and not sweep into that " drive " as many cows, drag pups out and demoralize things generally.

The number of holluschickie out this afternoon is not equal to half the of what I observed here day before yesterday during the prevalence of that S. W. gale, which threw up a heavy, furious surf; when the ocean is troubled, the non-breeding seals always haul out in greatest numbers; the breeding seals are, however, quite uniform in their attendance, however, without much reference to weather, unless it be a very abnormally warm, sunshiny day; then the cows nearly all take to the water, leaving their pups with the bulls behind them; they dont go far away, but lie in the rollers idly scratching in the cool embrace of the sea.

I noticed one action this afternoon which has hitherto completely escaped my eyes. A young pup near these " bath tubs " under the bluffs was eagerly endeavouring to get over the rocks and join those sporting pups which were so joyously splurging in and out of the pools there; but no sooner did the little fellow fairly get started than its mother would lunge after, and catching the pup precisely as a cat does a kitten, would pitch it rudely back, sometimes full three feet at a swing, bumping it without mercy on the boulders; the pup would then for a few moments lie perfectly quiet, then start up suddenly, get a few feet under way for the pools again, when the mother would repeat the lesson just cited. I watched her check and bump this pup of hers against the rocks for nearly half an hour; then seeing no sign of cessation of this action of the mother, or desire of the pup to have its own way, I did not wait for the ending of the controversy. It shows very plainly, however, that so far from learning their pups to swim, the mother seals try to keep their pups from the water as long as they can, seeming to have an instinctive appreciation of the fact that a heavy swell and surf could and would drown their offspring when so young, should these little creatures happen to get out and within the reach of its breaking force.

SECTION VIII.

Great Eastern.

July 23, 1890.

I passed up above this rookery in going to Tolstoi Mees and the sea-lion rookery this morning; no holluschickie, save a small pod, hauled out; and I also observe that the holluschickie have not put in an appearance in the North Rookery either — have not hauled since the 20th inst., simply because there are none left to haul. There are very few seals in the water — no " killer whales " about either — they were here in large numbers up to the 20th June, then suddenly departed. Capt. Lavender informs me that he has seen schools of " killers "; " hundreds of them " skimming along close to the shore between the Village landing and the North Rookery; that they have probably gone north into some of the bays there or river estuaries where shoal water permits them to calve and get food; and then returning this way they hang around these islands for several weeks, in October, then leave for the North Pacific; that they suddenly left this island on the 20th of June this year.

I, myself, have not been able to see one of these animals thus far this season, beginning at St. Paul, May 21st, up to date.

July 26, 1890.

I made a thorough survey of this Eastern Rookery in the morning, since now is the proper time to look for a showing of last year's pups or yearlings. I saw about 600 only of them (500 in one pod and the others, scattered); there were also about 100 2-yr. olds and a few 3-and 4-yr. olds—very few.

Some 6,000 pups must have been born on this rookery last June-July (1889), and half of them should be back this summer; perhaps they will show up better; it is, however, not reasonable to expect to see more than half of them hauled out at any one time, even now in the very height of their hauling season. I was much impressed when viewing them at this time in 1872-'74 on St. Paul by their habit of ceaseless travel out from and then back into the sea; i.e. they were constantly coming up from the surf to haul a thousand or two thousand feet back, and others were as steadily marching down to the water from the uplands where they had been laying out — returning to the water for baths and food.

What is left of the cows and pups as to numbers, on this breeding ground, as well as the other rookeries here, seem to be healthy and free from any visible, physical disorder. The most unique feature of this rookery to-day is the hauling of some 450 to 500 sea lions, ♂., ♀., and ○., on the surf-washed beach of its sea margin right under the bluffs; the breeding fur-seals lay up just above that surf-wash, while the huge yellow bodies of *Eumetopias* crowd close up to them from below, on a narrow belt which only high water and a stiff wind can dislodge them from; they, however, never haul anywhere else out higher from the water than this, since their young can take to the water and swim in a few days at the longest after birth.

Not so with the fur-seal; such a location means the death of every pup born upon it from June until Sept.15th inclusive, whenever the sudden rising of a gale might raise, in an incredibly short time, a heavy, churning surf, But after the middle of September the fur-seal pup has become pretty well used to the water and can swim well. Yet, severe gales in October have caught even these pups at that time so savagely as to destroy thousands of them and their lifeless bodies will be thrown high up by the surf to decay on the rocks and sand.

It is a queer sight to see here today those little black fur-seal pups podding hither and thither rubbing up against the big sea-lions in the most fearless and familiar manner, causing those animals no annoyance whatever, and arousing them not a particle : a very queer picture indeed, these small black clusters of fur-seal pups crowding in against the yellow bulk of the big sea-lions.

Starry Arteel.

July 20, 1890.

The green growing grasses, flowers and confervae that fairly border this breeding ground today, on this steep bluff slope — this odd rookery — makes a most startling change in its appearance contrasted as it is in my mind with what it was sixteen years ago; then, a polished hauling ground fully 1,000 to 1,500 feet deep encircled the breeding ground and restless troops of holluschickie in squads of hundreds clambered incessantly up and down the steep, abrupt slopes of Starry Arteel hill. To-day it looks as though a seal never had pattered over those hauling grounds of 1873, and even now, where the breeders themselves are lying and podding, the ground is not wholly free from scattered vegetation.

The natives assure me that this rookery actually increased in 1876-'78 considerably over my lines of 1873-'74; also, the East Rookery; but to-day it has shrivelled up to half its numbers of that time and the East Rookery to less than one-third!

Why the breeding seals should elect to haul up on this unusual spot in this queer manner is difficult to positively say, because there is more vacant space at North Rookery or Little Eastern than is necessary for the reception of ten times as many as are here assembled; perhaps, however, the drainage is so perfect that it meets exactly the wishes of the breeding seal, since it is compelled to rest from two to three months upon a single spot ere the work of reproduction is completed.

This rookery and Zapadnie are the only ones on this island thus far raided ashore by pirates; the high bluff on which the breeding seals rest, just N. N. E. about 800 feet sharp into the sea from the straight W. and E. trend of the North shore of the island. This abrupt projection of the ground makes a pretty snug shelter from human observation in the village, or from any other point East; there is no rookery and nobody living west of it; and unless somebody stands upon the extreme summit of the rookery bluffs, or west of it, nothing can be seen of anybody below.

Behind the Starry Arteel bluff on its western face, just at and only a trifle above surf-wash, is a water-worn cave — a small cavern in which a dozen men can huddle; here, in 1886, a sealing schooner's crew systematically passed their days in hiding, and their nights in raiding the rookery. They worked some three weeks ere they were detected by the natives, who, in searching along the shore for driftwood, after the sealing season had ended for them, found the freshly killed bodies of a number of cows at the mouth of this cave, the sealers having skipped.

Again, at Zapadnie, in the month of August last year, 1889, a similar raiding of that rookery was attempted; but as the pirates' boats came in at, 10,40 P. M. from their schooner, they fired into them, and the startled marauders turned about and disappeared in the fog. Zapadnie has been visited three times prior to this in this manner by pirates — but no great number of seals has been taken by them — a hundred or so perhaps; but it is a chosen spot for the marauders to anchor off from, one half to one mile at sea, where they have shot a great many seals; at no other rookery on either island have they done so to any extent.

At Starry Arteel, in 1886, those cave pirates above described took several hundred skins, some 600; this is the largest haul made by illegitimate landing on either island, also.

July 27, 1890.

I made a circuit of this unique breeding ground today; climbed up through a few scattered pups, cows and holluschickie, all commingled on its steep hill slope of breccia and cement, which these seals seem to love so well, happy as to drainage, and free from dust.

The podding of the pups here since the 28th July has made the driving of holluschickie simply impossible from this place, for the mixture of all classes is thorough today.

I notice also that the effect of that peculiar driving (which has been in vogue here ever since the shrinking of 1882 caused its establishment), of the holluschickie in creating an undue extension of sea margin for the number of animals occupying it as a breeding ground. In 1873 this rookery was a compact, oblong, oval mass of breeding seals, 500 feet by 125 feet, in which my figures declared a gathering of 30,000 cows, pups and bulls; today there is a straggling belt of 800 feet by 40 feet (a very liberal estimate) on which only 16,000 ☿., ♀., and ○. rest...

Zapadnie.

July 20, 1890.

I often wondered in 1873 why this little rookery over here was always the best hauling ground on St.George's; I now believe that it is due to its location on the south side of the island where the scent and noise of the breeding seals must appeal strongly to those bands of holluschickie that are upward bound from the Aleutian passes for St.Paul Island; the largest and best drives are always secured here, i. e. when taken from any one place on the island, the rookery was one of the two smallest on St.George then, and is a small one to-day; and it is the only one on the south side of that island...

It was here to-day that the evidence of excessive cow-driving (which can not be avoided if the holluschickie are to be secured) was plainly given by our finding in the fresh track of the "drive" (made this morning just as we came on the ground), several pups, feebly "bleating" for their mothers, who could never answer in time, even if they ever came at all.

This podding of the pups on and after the 15th and 20th July every year, makes it simply ruinous to drive a day after that date; the holluschickie now are so few in number that they do not haul out by themselves as they were in the habit of doing when they were in abundance here, but mix in at once after they land with the straggling cows and podded pups; as the season advances, and this podding progresses, the mingling becomes still more and more effected, so that by the 24th-25th July, it becomes impossible to drive from any rookery margin now without getting hundreds of cows in the drive of a thousand holluschickie.

Comment is needless: the impropriety of the act asserts itself...

July 24, 1890.

It was off this rookery, Sep. 1rst, 1874, that the first "pirate" or pelagic sealer began operations, since the Seal Islands became the property of the United States: this schooner, the *avant courier* of that destructive fleet of 1886-90, was the "Cygnet" of San Francisco, Capt. D. Kimberley, and the "San Diego", of San Francisco, Capt. E. P. Herendeen, was the next craft in order, having paid St.Paul's island a visit of that doubtful character, designated as 'piracy' in 1875.

August 1, 1890.

A careful review of the rookery to-day disclosed some 1,200 holluschickie, half of that number apart from the cows, the other half commingled with the podded females and their young: 9/10 of this squad of holluschickie were yearlings.

I observed not only here but on all the other rookeries a strange absence of the proportion of two-years-olds which should show up now.

the fact that 25,000, possibly 30,000 yearlings were killed last year after the 13th July may account for this, — it simply shows, however, what an empty shell now remains.

The condition of these breeding seals at Zapadnie barring their scant numbers, is good physically; the pups and cows have podded out in some places, nearly 1,000 feet back, up and away from the sea; these pups on the uplands so far back will not get into the water much earlier tham the 1st of next month, while a few of these pups on the beach margin are now swimming and learning to swim.

The heavy surf of yesterday and the day preceding has not injured any pups here as far as I can observe : they are all safely hauled up out of its fury. When, however, they fairly get under way in swimming at first, then such a storm catches thousands of them unawares, and destroys them.

On the hauling-grounds : St. Paul Island.

May 21, 1890.

The first " drive " for food of the season made this morning on Seevitchie Kammen by the natives : about 300 holluschickie. In 1872 on May 14th, I made the following note : " First drive of the season made to-day, some 200 holluschickie from the point on or near the reef. They drove slowly but well. Strong N. W. wind and dry". Substantially this same time in arriving now as in 1872.

June 11, 1890.

The first regular business drive of the season made this morning at 3 A. M., from the " Crest " on the Reef rookery. The natives made this drive of about 1300 holluschickie, half of it made up of mostly 3-year-olds, some " long " 2 and a few 4-year-olds, the balance, a large proportion of it, " long " yearlings and " short " 2-year-olds : the drive was made from the south slope of the " Crest " where about 150 feet back from the surf on the rocks, these animals had hauled, having slipped in between the breeding bulls, which are widely scattered there on the sea-margin; this ground when visited by myself, four or five hours later, was filling ap again with holluschickie, showing clearly that the act of visiting and driving from this point early this morning has had no effect in preventing or delaying the continued hauling of this class of seals... (539 skins taken, — 60 per cent. rejected) :

These old bulls by the way on the rookeries, behave now as they did in 1872, precisely : they are a little shy and sensitive when they first haul up in May (or late in April) and for the next ten days thereafter; but by the 15th — 20th of May, they have become so settled that they will not leave their positions, but boldly face and defy you, when you walk down to them to inspect their lines of hauling. Not a single bull on any one of these seven breeding grounds of St. Paul from the

22nd of May up to the hour of the completion of my survey of them, manifested the least fear of my presence, when I was in their immediate vicinity.

There are, however; always a number of bulls that haul on the outskirts of these well defined rookeries which I term " vagrants " because they have no location, — these bulls will scuttle away precisely as the holluschickie do.

June 13, 1890.

During the last ten days while inspecting the land angles and bulls on the several breeding grounds of this island, I have paid careful attention to every squad of holluschickie that has appeared, and except as to numbers, I do not observe any change up to date in their habit or of hauling early in the season, from my notes of 1872.

These early squads appear just above the surf-margin in English Bay, just at the back of the breeders on Lukannon, Ketavie, and the Reef; they are captured by the natives just in the manner that I describe as characteristic of the work so early in season of 1872, and they are driven overland also in the same method, except that the drivers use whistles occasionally, instead of bones, grass, etc., to start the lagging herd.

There is not much change, however, in the method of handling the skins after they are taken, which is also done exactly as I have described it, only a white man supervises the clubbing. Now a team of mules and a full sized " Studebaker " farm wagon is busy in carrying the skins from the field to the salt-houses; and two men easily do this part of the work to-day, which all hands had to keep to do in 1872; in 1874 carts and mules were first employed for this purpose, and these teams aforesaid, soon followed.

At 8 A. M. a report came down from N. E. Point which declared the presence of two marauding schooners up there nearly, with their boats down, sealing. This is the first notification of the kind for the season. Mr. Goff and I started at once for Novastoshnah with four selected men. I went with him because independent of the legitimate errand, I desired to personnally experience a ride up on a two-wheeled cart, as he rode in a gig drawn by a team of mules; the road is bad, — very bad and will require considerable work laid out on it before it is fit even for slow driving over in any vehicle; thus far the mule-back ride is best, and after all, I prefer my own legs.

We arrived at Webster's house at 12.30 P. M. Stiff N. E. gale charged with rain and hail whole way. The two natives stationed there on watch were not clear in their understanding of the vessel which they saw yesterday; because it was at one time a steamer, and at another, a schooner, etc.; we came to the conclusion that it was and is one of the several steam whalers that we know to be cruising in Bering Sea this season.

Peter Pesherkov, one of these watchmen, said that yesterday was a fine day, still and semi-clear; he went around the entire circuit of the rookery here, carefully inspecting the sea-margin; he says that he found about 200 holluschickie, only, hauled immediately up on the north side of Sea-lion Neck: he says that nowhere else was there any holluschickie, except a few polseacatchie on the beach just below the south shoulder, and everywhere else outside of the straggling old bulls, nothing. Peter and Carp Booterin came into the house in the afternoon while the storm was in progress and talked to Mr. Goff and myself freely over the condition of this rookery, as well as the others.

June 16, 1890.

Webster House, 9 A.M. Carp Booterin and Neon Mandriggan made a circuit of N.E. Point this morning; they report to Mr. Goff no sign of vessel landing or sealing anywhere on the circuit: they say that there are about 300 holluschickie on the "Staff Right"; about 200 good ones on the North slope of Hutchinson's Hill, and a few, very few at or near the South Shoulder.... I came down on foot to the Village, giving Polavina a survey along outside so as to see the old and new seal grass on that famous parade; it is somewhat too soon to arrive at a conclusion, but what I saw and noted causes surprise.

Suppose you had sixteen years ago stood on an eminence overlooking a sheep-pasture, 3/4 of a mile in length and 3/4 to 1/2 a mile in width, — this lot filled with a flock of sheep so full as to fairly whiten with their bodies the whole surface of the green earth upon which they slept, gazed and stood in groups.

Then to-day to stand again upon the same eminence, overlooking the same ground and life, and see nothing but a few lonely wide scattered bands of sheep, and these so few in number that it requires no effort to count them one by one, - that desolate impression made thus upon you is precisely the impression that these hauling grounds of St. Paul Island make upon me to-day.

Perhaps the next month may improve matters, — but Mr. Goff says that it will not, — that I will see.

June 17, 1890.

I made a review of the abandoned site of Nah Speel rookery this morning. The best bulls and cows hauled here in 1886. In 1872-'74, there were some 8,000 Bulls, Cows, and Pups here; 400 feet of sea-margin, 40 feet deep: in 1876, they had fallen off to less than half that number, having gone over across the way to Lagoon Rookery.

This abandonment gives me a good basis for estimation of the time it takes to remove striking traces of seals hauling on the rocks. Now, these rocks of Nah Speel rookery under my feet this morning were in 1872-'74 so polished by the flippers of *Callorhinus* that nothing save the shiny basalt, olivine and grey lava was to be seen : to-day they are literally covered with yellow and gray lichens, and were it not for the evidence of those seal-grass tussocks up above them, a practiced eye would not, could not detect the previous existence of a breeding rookery on them and this all effaced in less than twelve years, partially then, and wholly within the last five years. How important it is therefore to have these breeding grounds correctly surveyed at frequent intervals so that ebb or flow of this seal-life tide can be truthfully registered. Certain, it is, nothing can be definitely trusted to memory in this respect.

June 17, 1890.

On the Reef and Garbatch. — Where are the polseacatchie or "1/2 bulls"? where, indeed, are those young 5 and 6 years old bulls which were literally swarming at the water's edge of these breeding grounds in 1872? trying to land and repelled in vicious battle offered and waged by the old bulls : then thousands and thousands of these young bulls were incessantly essaying to land on the rookery sea-margins, and were as incessantly fought off by the elder, heavier seecatchie then in possession of the water's edge.

I have been carefully watching the field this morning on these two great breeding grounds : the cows are arriving, and it was at this time and occasion in 1872, that the polseacatchie appeared as I have above noted.

But, *not a single example presents itself to my eye this morning!* Where are these young bulls which must step in next year to supply the vacancies which the law of nature is to create in the ranks of the old bulls? These seals are not here to-day, will they appear later?

There has been no change in the numbers of the old bulls on the rookeries since the 10th instant, none whatever : and there are frequent intervals on these sea-margins to all these rookeries where vacancies exist from 15 to 40 feet wide between the located old bulls : thus every inducement is offered to a young bull to land without the fear even or certainty even of being obliged to fight savagely, which must have prevailed in its mind in 1872, and which then did not deter it from incessant attempt to land on the breeding ground.

Are these young "1/2 bulls" all gone? if so, then every thing else will soon follow, unless the check is applied. Then, again, in this connection, let me put it on record as I come in now from the field, that *none* of the scattered bulls now hauled out on the rookery grounds, are those known as half bulls, or "polseecatchie".

Only 73 skins taken from the drive at N. E. Point to-day : First drive of the season up there.

June 19, 1890.

I ascended the basaltic ridge between Lukannon Sands and the village Lakes, this morning, beetween 8 and 9 o'clock, — not a single seal, old or young on these hauling grounds and sands of Lukannon : then from the summit of Telegraph Hill, I had a full sweep of English Bay, only a small squad of perhaps 150 holluschickie under Middle Hill and another small pod at the intersection of the sand-beach with Tolstoi Rookery... A small drive from English Bay was made yesterday, some 300 skins taken, and the first drive from N. E. Point yesterday gave only 78 skins! Whether this trouble begins on the rookeries or on the killing grounds I have to find out, and it is important to know it.

Not a single holluschak of any age whatsoever on Zoltoi Sands this day, and there has not been a killable seal thus far there this season!

June 21, 1890.

From the high sand-dunes of Tolstoi I have a full sweep of English Bay, — a few hundred holluschickie only under Middle Hill, and right down under me at the intersection of the sand-beach with the breeding ground of Tolstoi are a few more, 200!

The weather has been good for hauling ever since the last drive (17th) from this place, yet it has not filled up any better than this?

From this time on, the killable holluschickie should appear in as good or better number up to the 4 th of July, — better form than they will thereafter. In other words the best classes of these killable seals, viz., the 2, 3, and 4 year olds were here now in their finest form and number for the season during the seasons of 1872-74.

From the Volcano Ridge I had a clear view of Lukannon beach and hauling grounds, — not a seal of any age upon it, and the weather superb for seals to haul in, cool, moist and foggy.

June 22, 1890.

Fine weather for seals to haul in continues but the seals do not haul; not a single seal on Zoltoi Sands this morning, — has not been a holluschak there yet ! and this spot was the never failing resort of the natives in 1872-74, according to my own observation. Sometimes two drives of thousands each would be taken, one right after the other, in the same morning from this place right under the village at this time in June. Every seal would be swept off from the sands of Zoltoi then in the early hours of a morning like this, — a drove of anywhere from 3,000 to 5,000, and even more holluschickie of all sizes, and thousands permitted to hustle into the water at the moment of driving; then after breakfast, at 7 o'clock I would again go up to look, and behold ! these sands of Zoltoi only a few hours earlier which were swept bare of every seal, were now fairly covered with a fresh swarm of holluschickie; and which, later in the day, might be driven up to the killing grounds not more than 1,000 feet away ! provided that the day was a very favorable one for work there, and the men on the killing grounds were not unwilling to meet the active labor for the day, etc.

Now, not a single young male seal has hauled on Zoltoi thus far this season : (June 22nd, 6 A. M.) This is the day and this is the hour of the season in which to see the holluschickie in their best form and number, — all classes, except the yearlings.

Therefore this vacancy on Zoltoi Stands, on Lukannon Beach and the uplands of Volcanic Ridge, on Ketavie uplands, on the sands of English Bay, on those of Polavina and the utter solitude of those of S. W. Point and of Novastoshnah makes a deep impression on one, who has, like myself, stood upon them all in 1872-74, and observed the swarming platoons of young male seals then existing, — now entirely vanished.

Yesterday, when the work on the killing grounds closed, only 3,010 skins have thus far been taken and every little squad of holluschickie that has showed itself above surf margin on this island has been secured to get even this pitiful number: the same ruthless driving in the same time, 13,000 odd skins; — at this rate of decrease, or less than one quarter, and the season for hauling far better than it was last year, — what indeed will be the catch next year? not more than a few hundreds ! these are facts which the status of the hour declares, and which can not be sensibly overlooked at this finest season of the catch.

Then, too, the utter shift of method in driving which characterizes the present from the past. Now, with the solitary exception of the small drives from Middle Hill, every drive has been right from the borders of the breeding rookeries; from right in and among the old bulls as they lay in waiting for the incoming females! This fact, in itself, is a most eloquent pointer to the truth, — to the utterly depleted condition to-day of these hauling grounds and their abundant reserves of 1872-'74.

At this time in 1873-'74, inclusive, I never glanced over at Zoltoi Sands, but I saw holluschickie coming and going from and to the sea in steady files and platoons. I never looked over the broad sweep of English Bay beach from the hight sand-dunes of Tolstoi, but to see the same sight only in vaster greater form and numbers : — so, too, as I viewed the beach and volcanic ridge of Lukannon Bay and at Polavina it was an impressive spectacle, and the sand reaches of North East Point were simply alive with the restless multitudes of holluschickie that were hauling out and into the sea.

I do not observe to-day, except at Middle Hill, the least, the faintest suggestion even, of that past. Will it improve? the 20th of July will tell the whole story beyond speculation or cavil.

June 22, 1890.

" From the fact that this morning opened warm, clear, and bright sunshine, I did not expect to see any hauling of the holluschickie, — it has been the first day since the 12th instant, that has not been suitable for hauling; the weather hitherto has been excellent. Lukannon Beach is as bare as it was yesterday, and the two small pods at English Bay remain at the close of the day just as they were hauled yesterday, — no more of them. I rather expected to see them all in the water since it has been so warm, — the first warm day of the year, — but they were not.

It thickens up this evening and becomes cool. Not a seal on Zoltoi Sands this morning and not one since during this day.

June 23, 1890.

Those two pods of holluschickie which I have observed under Middle Hill and Tolstoi during the last two days were driven up this morning; I began an itemized account of percentages, — the number driven up in each pod and the number turned out to the sea, or rejected from it.

No. of Pods.	Whole No. Driven.	No. Taken.	No. of. Pods.	Whole No. Driven.	No. Taken.	Remarks.
1			7	61	15	
2	79	9	8	50	15	Pod. No. 1, 1 did not get a correct count of, so it is omitted.
3	27	7	9	47	7	
4	37	8	10	39	9	
5	61	15	11	46	6	
6	46	10	12	69	9	

11 pods of 561 animals driven up; 110 of them killed or 1/5 taken or 80 per cent turned away, —all under 7 lb. skins, with the exception of a few wigged 4-year olds, and a dozen or two old bulls.

This gives a fair average of the whole drive to-day, some 2,500 animals, since 518 were taken only.

At this time in 1872, with the same standard of nothing under 7 lb. skins, only 10 per cent. to 12 per cent. were turned away.

To-day all the seals taken with the rare examples of a few 4-year-olds (11 lb. skins) were 3-year-olds, (7 1/2 lb. skins); not one 4-year-old in 20 taken; and a remarkable absence of two-year-olds.

Those turned away (nearly 2,000) were 95 per cent. at least, "long" and "short" yearlings ! a very, very few 5-year-olds and a -very few 6-year-old bulls: very few 2-year-olds also.

A small pod of holluschickie have made their appearance close up under the bluffs of Zoltoi, 100 to 150 of them at about 11 A. M. Now, this calls up to my mind, where have those tired seals gone? which were driven this morning, and let loose from the pods on the killing grounds into the Lagoon Slough from there, direct to the sea, — where do they go? do they haul up again? Yes, everybody says so, and I do not know anything to the contrary, and do know a great deal in affirmation. Then, if that be so, these seals spared to-day may be driven to-morrow, to be spared again, and driven next week, and soon all over the island through the season. What indication then really have we, of what number of fresh holluschickie really arrive from this time forth, — if these released seals are to continually present themselves anew as they do? So, as matters go we will note the steady increase daily of discarded seals in the drives together with the new arrivals, or freshly driven seals throughout the killing season.

Now in 1872-'74, this proportion of rejected or turned away seal, from all the drives up to 1st of July was not over 10 per cent or 12 per cent of the whole number driven, *now, it is between 70 per cent. and 80 per cent.*! and 95 per cent. of the rejection yearlings, that will require 6 years of rest ere they are fit for rookery service : this is the status at the present moment on these killing grounds, and, this also, must be considered in the light of the native's positive declaration in 1834 that this repeated driving renders the spared male seals wholly unfit for rookery service.

How many of these released seals this morning have been driven over this road before this season? On the 17th instant the last drive prior to this one to-day was made from Tolstoi and Middle Hill; 70 per cent. of that drove was turned away; and now, to-day, the same ground is driven over again, and 80 per cent. is turned away. I shall observe the next drive very closely. At this rate of increase, where will the driving be in July? when the yearlings then begin to haul in bodies.

June 24, 1890. 5.50 A. M.

A drive this morning from Zoltoi Bluffs of about 500 all told and also pod from the Reef, 750 coming. Yesterday morning at 7 o'clock there was not a single holluschickie on Zoltoi Bluffs. But in less than three hours after the killing began on the Lagoon Flats, and the turning out from the pods there, I observed that holluschickie were hauling under the bluffs at the intersection of Zoltoi Sands, — the first that have hauled there this year; — (they drove from there on the 14th instant last year). Now, the query cannot leave my mind of " Were any of those spared seals of yesterday, hauling up soon thereafter at Zoltoi? " " look at the map and observe the significance of the surroundings. Everybody in 1872 and everybody to-day admits that these seals which we released from the drives haul up again, are driven over, released, and still driven again and again throughout the season. In 1872 on this St. Paul Village killing ground such a 5-year-old bull was pointed out to me by Chief Booterin;

At 7 A. M., I went down to the killing grounds and followed the " podding " and " clubbing " of the entire drive brought up from the Reef Crest and Zoltoi Bluffs, this morning; the Zoltoi pod arrived on the ground long before the Reef pod, — two hours sooner; it was made up largely of polseacatchie and yearlings, — the oldest bulls of the season, 6 and 7 year-old, and in this pod were many bulls which the natives said had come over from the Lagoon killing yesterday, — they knew them as they pointed them out to me by certain clubbing marks.

Field Notes of the Podding and Clubbing of the Drive made from Zoltoi and the Reef : June 24, 1890. Killing began at 7 A. M. Ended by 9. 30 A. M.

No. of Pod.	Whole No. Driven.	No. Taken.	"Half-bulls".	No of. Pod.	Whole No. Driven.	No. Taken.	"Half-bulls"
1	53	13	6	Brought forw.	781	234	62
2	39	14	4	20	38	13	3
3	41	12	2	21	28	12	1
4	48	12	3	22	34	9	3
5	27	11	3	23	25	6	2
6	54	20	4	24	36	11	5
7	30	15	3	25	47	15	4
8	42	10	4	26	50	12	3
9	52	12	3	27	29	9	4
10	40	16	2	28	34	7	3
11	39	13	3	29	17	7	1
12	27	7	1	30	37	8	4
13	36	10	2	31	20	8	2
14	61	14	7	32	52	11	1
15	46	10	3	33	38	10	0
16	40	10	5	34	46	14	0
17	35	9	3	35	24	9	0
18	36	14	0	36	28	15	
19	35	12	4	37	30	15	
Carry forw.	781	234	62	Total.	1,386	426	96

Summary : Whole number of animals podded or driven, . . . 1,386
— — — skins taken, ... 426
— — — half-bulls in it, ... 96

or 71 per cent. of this drive rejected. Every 3 and " smooth" 4 year old taken, and every " long " 2 year old : nothing under or over that grade.

The seals released this morning were exclusively yearlings, " short " 2-year-olds, and the 5-and 6-year-old "half-bulls " or " polseecatchie ". No " long " 2-year-old escaped, and so, therefore, many 5 1/2 lb. and 6 lb. skins will appear in this catch; there was a notable absence, however, of 2-year-olds in proportion, and the bulk of the catch was 3-year-olds, as was yesterday's killing with a very large number of 4-year-olds in proportion to the whole number of skins taken...

In the afternoon I took a survey of Lukannon Bay and its hauling grounds, — not a seal on the beach, except a half dozen half-bulls, abreast of the Volcanic Ridge; thence over to Tolstoi sand-dunes, where I saw about 600 or 700 yearlings conspicuous by their white bellies, — and a few killable seals sandwiched in : another small pod under Middle Hill.

I should remark that the driving of the seals has been very carefully done, no extra rushing and smothering of the herd, as it was frequently done in 1872. Mr. Goff began with a sharp admonition and it has been scrupulously observed, thus far, by the natives. This dropping of exhausted seals along the road in 1872-'74 was a matter which then aroused both Lt. Maynard and myself in 1874 : the agent of the A. C. Co. then promised to correct the evil; but it will always require the eye of the Treasury Agent to rest upon this feature of the business since he is the executive head in this small community, unique and isolated, and he should be.

June 23, 1890.

An inspection of Zoltoi beach this morning does not show a single seal upon this famous hauling-ground; yesterday morning a small drive of considerably less than 500 was taken from the rocky eminence just to the southward of this spot, being also the first drive made from there this year. When driven from in such fine sealing weather as that now prevailing in 1872-'74, these sands in less than an hour afterwards would begin to fill up again with fresh arrivals from the sea; and often after the lapse of seven or eight hours after the first drive had been made, to fill up an additional demand another drive would be ordered from the same spot, and duly driven. Also, I did not see this morning a single seal sporting in the waters of Zoltoi Bay, and the only one in sight was right under the Village bluffs where I stood by the flagstaff.

June 25, 1890.

I went up at 6 A.M. to the killing at Tonkie Mees or Stony Point, where over since 1879, the seals that have hauled at Polavina, and on the sand beach between and towards Lukannon below, have been driven for slaughter: a small herd collected this morning, and only 263 taken, — the balance, some 500 or 600 turned back to the sea : the selection was made in the same manner as yesterday, and the same class of seals spared; — an enormous number of 5-and 6-year-old bulls in it for the whole number driven, even greater than that I recorded yesterday : I tallied these pods thus :

Pod 1 : 76 driven in it : 9 taken, — all 3 and 4 year-olds.
— 2 : 35 — 9 — — — —
— 3 : 56 — 16 — — — —

Then after the killing-gang had finished, and started to return to the village at 8.30 A.M., I proceeded up to Polavina following the seal drive path made by the natives early this morning. I observed at Stony Point, or Tonkie Mees, the spared seals as they were released from the pods, plunge back into the surf, and to my surprise all of these seals headed directly back for Polavina jumping in rapid " dolphin " leaps and swimming rapidly. As I walked along, I repeatedly stepped up on to the summit of a sand-dune, and continued to watch the progress of these liberated herds; they all headed directly for Polavina, and filed right along in swift procession, passing me continually as I walked in the same direction; when I came up to my land angle, Sta. " C. ", I saw these small seals liberated only a few hours ago at Tonkie Nees, beginning to haul anew at Polavina, from whence they had been driven overland early this morning; they were lured up as they returned, just below the rookery ground proper on a broad sand beach by the large number of somnolent apathetic bulls that are stretched out here in a confused medley, — all quiet, however, or heavily sleeping.

From this station (" C ") I could easily see distinctly that last remnant of the Zapooska at Stony Point, 2 miles below, creeping down into the surf, then heading towards me, join the others all swimming up along shore, just outside of the outer breaker margin of the rollers, up to that point of retarding, as I have stated above. Thus, in this way, for the first time, I have seen myself an unbroken circuit of released seals as it plunged back into the water, and hauled out again within the space of three hours from the time of the release until the landing was made anew.

The present poverty of these celebrated hauling grounds of Polavina is well illustrated by the catch from the drive of to-day, only 263 skins: At this day and date in 1872, I could then have driven from the great parade plateau, behind this breeding ground, under precisely the same circumstances surrounding the drive of to-day, 10,000 killable seals: not one of them over four years old, and not one, not a single one of them under a good 2-year-old, *i.e.* all 5/2 lb. to 12 lb. skins. Comment is unnecessary.

Yesterday from the summit of Volcanic Ridge, I saw three released holluschickie sporting in the Village lake, right under my feet; they seemed to be thoroughly happy; were lolling on their backs with their flippers lazily held up or turned up and over on their chests, scratching, etc. I sat down, and watched them sport for some ten minutes; this morning while on my way up to Stony Point and Polavina I saw that one of them had died, — its body laid just awash at the water's margin, — and only one of the three was remaining in the lake. Now, certainly, this particular seal died last night from, the strain or effect of that drive overland from Tolstoi or English Bay, — in getting over here from that point, for it was driven this far from there on the morning of the 23rd instant. So, again, this question keeps rising of "how many of these driven seals, that are released, finally die of internal injuries received during their overland trip to the slaughtering grounds?" and "how many of them really can live after they have been redriven in this manner, many times from these several hauling grounds of St. Paul?" More and more forcibly arises to my mind the statement of the natives in 1834 who then on this island assured Bishop Veniaminov that the young, males driven here and spared never became fit afterwards for breeding purposes, and never went after this driving upon the rookeries.

Certainly it becomes clearer and clearer to my mind that those young males which as yearlings survive the driving here of that year of their age, and then return to survive the driving of the second year of their age; — then surviving this trial, reappear to be driven over again in their third year, — to be released and again if alive to be redriven up here in their fourth year, and then finally if surviving these five consecutive seasons of unwonted violent physical effort, — unnatural efforts to be again driven as I see them to-day in their fifth year of growth, what indeed can we reasonably expect of them in their sixth year, even if they do manage to endure, (some of them, not many of them), all of this intense physical suffering, exhaustion, straining of tendons, congestions of lungs and brain, and heart suffusions: The more I think over this matter, the more I believe that the natives were right and Veniaminov says that they " truly assert " it.

I had this point in my thought during my studies of 1872-'74: but at that time, no holluschickie were driven from S. W. Point, from Zapadnie, from Tonkie Mees or Stony Point, or from Polavina, — no seals were driven from these places where everybody admitted that full half of the entire number belonging to the island, laid, and then, the percentage of rejected or turned-out seals on the killing grounds was really very small, — there was not much wasted energy, — most of the seals driven there were killed and duly skinned.

Thus, then it did not impress me, — it seemed immaterial for there was an immense reserve of undriven, undisturbed young male life; and the natives themselves said that all was well even if those spared seals of 1872 never went to the rookeries. How different at this writing! in 1879 the distant driving began here; and that marks the date of the decline of the hauling grounds : — at that rate of decrease up to the present wretched order of affairs it will require seven years of unbroken rest to bring back at the earliest moment, a condition such as I found and recorded here in 1872-'74, — perfect rest must be given here on the islands and full protection in Bering Sea.

June 26, 1890.

Not a single holluschak or " half-bull " either on Zoltoi Sands this morning, and there has not been one near it since that sweep, of 500 half bulls to yearlings made there on the morning of the 14th instant, — this time in 1872, it would have been overrunning with seals from the Bay, clear over to the summit of Gull Hill, even if driven clear every morning! The sealing weather here since the 1st June has simply been perfect: it is as fine as could be desired, and yet the astonishing poverty of these empty hauling grounds is sought to be ignored in certain quarters: a hundred gifted tongues speaking in emphatic harmonious accord could not tell the story of destruction better than those vacant sands of Zoltoi, as they appeal to your eye and understanding this morning.

I walked over to the Zapadnie killing grounds this morning, arriving there about 9 o'clock. The drivers had collected a squad of about 340 holluschickie, which were clubbed thus;

No. of Pod.	Whole No. Driven.	No. Taken.	"Half-bulls"	No. of Pod.	Whole No. Driven.	No. Taken.	"Half-bulls"
1	30	12	2	Brought forw.	186	60	19
2	37	13	1	6	407	1	
3	56	11	9	7	53	12	4
4	40	15	2	8	47	12	1
5	23	9	3	9	18	6	5
Carry forward	186	60	16	Total.	344	97	30

or about 72 per cent. unfit to take, being made up chiefly of (1) yearlings, (2) "short" 2-year-olds, and (3) "wigged" 4-year-olds, and 5-year-old bulls up to 7-year-olds, — of this latter class of " 1/2 bulls " an enormous percentage in this little drive appears.

Now this little drive was not taken from the regular hauling grounds of these holluschickie as I knew them in 1872, but from the immediate line of the rookery on Lower Zapadnie at a section about midway between the point, and the sand beach. The weather cannot be blamed for the small killing to-day here at this date, on that fine hauling-ground of 1872-'74; the weather is simply superb sealing weather, and not a word over here against it was uttered by the disappointed sealers this morning.

Nearly every one of these released or spared seals this morning, returned at once to the rear of the breeding bulls on Lower Zapadnie, and right under our eyes: they refused to return to the sea, although the path was open to them and it was as near, or nearest! They will all be driven again in the next visit, plus the new arrivals which may come along between now and then. Ah! — this driving *and redriving*, — its full significance is beginning to appeal to my understanding successfully.

That pod of holluschickie which I have seen under Middle Hill during the last two days, still lies there, and also that one next to the clustered cows on the sand at Tolstoi; they will drive it to-morrow. Thus far no holluschickie have hauled-out 50 feet above surf-wash, except where they are found in back of the rookery margins as the Reef

APPENDIX. 273

" Crest ", Zapadnie, and N. E. Point, where the breeding bulls drive them back some 150 to 250 feet. In English Bay, to-day, eighteen years ago, the holluschickie were hauled by thousands upon thousands back nearly half a mile everywhere upon the soil, sand, rocks and grass of the uplands : to-day, not a sign of a seal there except the handful down close by the surf under Middle Hill...

June 27, 1890.

" The drive to-day from Middle Hill, Tolstoi, and Bobrovia Yama (of Tolstoi, near the Point), panned out as follows : this is the result of saving the drive over since the 23rd instant.

Pod.	Whole No. Driven.	No. Taken.	"Half Bulls".	Pod.	Whole No. Driven.	No. Taken.	"Half Bulls".	Pod.	Whole No. Driven.	No. Taken.	"Half Bulls".
1	108	14	»	Brought forw. 703	136	10		Brought forw.	1268	263	20
2	82	13	1	12	55	8	»	22	45	15	»
3	57	12	»	13	54	12	2	23	59	15	1
4	56	11	»	14	61	20	»	24	41	14	»
5	68	12	3	15	81	16	»	25	44	15	»
6	34	3	2	16	49	10	»	26	50	18	»
7	58	12	»	17	53	13	3	27	53	17	3
8	60	15	2	18	40	4	»	28	42	15	»
9	54	16	2	19	60	15	»	29 } 30 }	50	22	»
10	53	13	»	20	49	13	2				
11	73	15	»	21	63	16	3		1652	394	24
Carry forw. 703	136	10		Carry forw. 1268	263	20					

(Deduct 24 over 24
Counted.) 1628

Summary : Whole number of animals driven. . . 1628
  » » » » » taken . . . 394,

78 per cent. rejected : — nothing taken under a 6 lb. or " long " 2-year-old skin.

Thus this drive in the very best of the season shows that 78 per cent. had to be rejected. Now, those little fellows which were turned aside here on the 23rd instant, will be out again in a few days to be redriven, plus these that are released to-day, plus all the rest to be released likewise, — they will be all up in July, — what will these drives be ? Sixteen of the three hundred and ninety-four skins taken in the killing grounds as above cited, were rejected in the salt-house by the company's manager, because they were too small, — they were normal 2-year-olds, 5 1/2 lb. skins; perhaps they will be glad to get them later.

In 1872-'74 very little attention was paid to driving seals until the 12th-14th of every June : true it was that bands of thousands of holluschickie were hauled-out on the several resorts, yet because these animals

15

then were not in comparatively great numbers, and were nearly all down at that early date by the surf margin, it was deemed best to wait until the 12th-14th before beginning in earnest to drive; but, after the 14th June, there always was such an abundant supply of holluschickie on hand within a mile and a half of this village, and N. E. Point salthouse, that no concern was ever given as to the number that they could get, — it was just the other way; if it was a warmish dry day, then a small drive only was made so as to secure some 1,200 or 1,500 skins; if it was a cool favorable day then some 2,500 or 3,000 skins would be taken, which latter figure was then the utmost number that the working force at the village could handle under the best circumstances in one day.

How different this year! on the 6th June here, the most eager energetic driving began simultaneously with the arrival of each and every squad of holluschickie big enough to warrant it; and it has been, kept up unremitingly until the present hour.

The spared seals turned away this morning were saved by their small size, — only 24 of them, of the whole 1628 in the drive, were 5-and 6-year old bulls. Every " long " or well-grown 2-year old was taken (6 lb. skin) and every 3- and " smooth " 4-year-old.

Not a holluschak or any other class of fur-seal on Zoltoi Sands this morning, or noon. I watched the progress of the released seals this morning as they came out over the Lagoon slough and rookery; they or most of them, swam directly out to sea, — not heading in any particular way except from land; a few swam under the Village Hill bluffs and thence out across in the direction of the Reef and a few headed back for English Bay. Not one of them started for Zoltoi as they did on the 23rd instant. On that occasion it was the hauling of some 50 " half-bulls " on Zoltoi that lured the younger seals out after them; they were released together.

This afternoon I took another survey of Lukannon and Tolstoi, and the vacant hauling grounds of English Bay and the Volcanic Ridge. Another small pod of holluschickie at Middle Hill, from whence they drove last night for the day's killing, and another adjoining the podding cows on the sand beach at Polavina; about 250 or 300 in both pods, and chiefly yearlings.

June 28, 1890.

The superb sealing weather still continues; the natives are bringing up a small squad from the reef as I write, (5 A. M.)...

APPENDIX.

Field Notes of the podding and clubbing of drive from Reef and Zoltoi Bluffs, June 28th, 1890.

No. of Pod.	Whole No. Driven.	No. Taken.	"Half-bulls".	No of Pod.	Whole No. Driven.	No. Taken.	"Half-bulls".
1	71	13	3	Brought forw.	772	114	16
2	75	19	»	14	73	7	»
3	80	14	3	15	85	15	»
4	46	3	1	16	49	7	»
5	80	8	»	17	54	4	3
6	62	8	1	18	66	9	2
7	50	10	1	19	63	10	»
8	40	5	2	20	46	7	6
9	55	8	»	21	74	10	»
10	45	7	4	22	43	6	»
11	56	10	»	23	40	8	1
12	52	4	»	24	52	10	4
13	60	5	1		1417	203	27
Carry forw.	772	114	16				

Summary : Whole number of animals driven. 1417
— — — — taken 203
or 85 per cent. turned out.

Last drive from this place, June 24th, and 71 per cent. turned out. Everything taken in this day's killing above a normal 2-year old, and under 5-year olds and " wigged " 4-year olds, *i.e.* all 6 lb. skins and upwards.

June 30, 1890.

Field Notes of the podding and Clubbing of Drive from Middle Hill[1], English Bay[2], Tolstoi[3], Lukannon[4], and Keetavie[5].

No. of Pod.	Whole No. Driven.	No. Taken.	"Half Bulls".	No. of Pod.	Whole No. Driven.	No. Taken.	"Half Bulls".
1	108	11	6	Brought forw.	310	42	15
2	39	5	»	6	40	10	1
3	41	6	4	7	53	10	1
4	69	12	4	8	47	14	4
5	53	8	1	9	58	6	1
Carry forw.	310	42	15	Carry forw.	508	82	22

1. Last Drive from these places, June 27th, and 79 per cent. turned out, of rejected
2. *Ibid.*
3. *Ibid.*
4. Last Drive from this place, June 20th.
5. First Drive from this place.
   The small contingent from Lukannon and Keetavie numbered less than 300 animals before merged in the single drive.
   Everything taken that was above a 5 1/2 lb. skin and under those of the 5-year-olds and " wigged " 4-year-olds.

No. of Pod.	Whole No. Driven.	No. Taken.	"Half Bulls".	No. of Pod.	Whole No. Driven.	No. Taken.	"Half Bulls".
Brought forw. 508	82	22		Brought forw. 921	151	31	
10	58	8	»	17	70	9	4
11	51	10	»	18	47	12	5
12	53	7	»	19	49	9	1
13	56	4	»	20	46	10	»
14	55	15	2	21	48	6	5
15	63	15	2	22	81	6	»
16	77	10	5		1262	203	50
Carry forw. 921	151	31					

Summary : Whole number of animals driven. 1262
— — — — taken 203

or 84 1/2 per cent. rejected.

The significance of this day's work can be seen by the most casual observer. I counted over 24 blind-eyed or "moon-eyed" holluschickie as they escaped from the several pods; " zapooskas " — all of which have been crippled in this manner by prior driving this season ! How many of these yearlings and " short " 2-year-olds that were released this morning will again be driven, and driven before this season ends? Nearly all of them will; they pass into the sea over the Lagoon Bar; they meet squadrons of cows playing in the water around the rookery margins — they pause, listen, join in the general comfort which the water certainly affords them, and as these females and the fresh animals of their own kind haul out on land, they join again and fall into this deadly procession for them, to the land from whence they were driven early this morning. How the significance of this driving now keeps rising to my mind ! I had little occasion in 1872-'74 to give in thought, and what I did was only in a suggestive mood.

I passed up from the killing grounds over to Tolstoi Rookery and gave the drivers' path or seal-road a careful review. A few holluschickie were again hauled out under Middle Hill and a dozen perhaps on the Tolstoi rookery sand intersection; but the great hauling-grounds of English Bay are utterly destitute of seal life at the hour of this writing and have been so, with the marked exception of that small spot under Middle Hill, and the juxtaposition of Tolstoi rookery, which are the only points where the seals now haul in all that vast extent of ground pattered over by them here in 1872-'74.

Not a holluschickie on Zoltoi Sands to-day; and only one or two on the rocks beyond and above, from whence they have been driven thus far as Zoltoi seals. Mr. Goff assures me that there was no driving from the sands here last year; it was all from these rocks above. When this famous hauling ground began to fail was the time for the note of warning to have been sounded — when did it fail?

July 1, 1890.

Field Notes of the podding and clubbing of Drive made from every section of the Reef; everything in back of Zoltoi Bluffs, Garbotch, and the entire circuit of the Reef.

No. of Pod.	Whole No. Driven.	No. Taken.	"Half Bulls".	No. of Pod.	Whole No. Driven.	No. Taken.	"Half Bulls".
1	109	15	2	*Brought forw.*	1025	136	26
2	51	4	1	17	66	7	3
3	77	12	1	18	49	6	3
4	53	9	»	19	78	4	4
5	54	7	»	20	58	9	5
6	69	4	»	21	60	6	4
7	58	10	»	22	78	11	4
8	61	4	»	23	67	7	4
9	48	9	»	24	56	7	»
10	73	12	1	25	60	4	1
11	100	8	3	26	91	7	4
12	58	8	2	27	57	11	3
13	48	9	4	28	71	8	4
14	52	7	3	29	69	7	1
15	46	8	3	30	38	6	»
16	68	10	6	31	75	9	»
Carry forw.	1025	136	26		1998	245	66

Summary: Whole number of animals driven. 1,998
— — — — taken . 245, or 89 per cent. rejected.
Last drive from this place June 28th and then 85 — —

Everything taken over a 5 1/2 lb. skin and under the "wigged" 4-yr. and 5-yr. old pelts.

The seals rejected to-day were over 90 % yearlings.

This is the largest number yet driven in any one drive from this place thus far this season; and the catch among the smallest; the yearlings driven before plus the new arrivals are making the ratio.

Not a seal on the hauling grounds and sands of Lukannon Bay, and none on Ketavie; about 500 yearlings at Middle Hill, and none of that pod near the sand beach at Tolstoi rookery that I saw yesterday P. M.; they have evidently made for Middle Hill.

July 2nd, 1890.

Field Notes of the podding and Clubbing of Drive made from every section of Polavina and Stony Point.

No. of Pod.	Whole No. Driven.	No. Taken.	"Half Bulls".	No. of Pod.	Whole No. Driven.	No. Taken.	"Half Bulls".
1	83	7	»	*Brought forw.*	275	24	4
2	91	11	»	4	59	4	»
3	101	6	4	*Carry forw.*	334	28	4
Carry forw.	275	24	4				

SECTION VIII.

No of Pod.	Whole No. Driven.	No. Taken.	"Half Bull".	No. of Pod.	Whole No. Driven.	No. Taken.	"Half Bull".
Brought forw. 334	28	4		*Brought forw.* 1183	122	33	
5	50	6	»	17	104	8	2
6	56	6	2	18	113	12	5
7	63	5	3	19	73	15	»
8	65	10	»	20	62	11	3
9	102	4	»	21	91	13	5
10	90	6	5	22	63	8	7
11	100	12	7	23	49	6	2
12	71	13	2	24	47	9	7
13	72	14	3	25	40	6	5
14	65	8	2	26	43	11	4
15	60	5	3	27	54	9	6
16	55	5	2		1929	230	80
Carry forw. 1183	122	33					

Summary : Whole number of animals driven 1,929
— — — taken 230, or 88-1/2 % rejected.
(and " road and " smothered " skins 10 = 240 taken).

Last drive from this place, June 25th; then 800 animals were driven and 263 taken, or 65 % then rejected.

This drive to-day here covers a whole week's interval since the last drive from Polavina, and it shows that as the season advances, the numbers driven rapidly increase while the proportionate catch diminishes; in other words, the new arrivals, plus those redriven, will continue to steadily swell the gross aggregate driven day by day from now on, and not proportionately increase the catch. Rather, I believe that the catch will markedly diminish.

Now to-day every good 2 yr. old, every 3 and every " smooth " 4 yr. old was knocked down out of this 1,929 animals; every one; where, at this rate of killing, is the new blood left for the rookeries? now so desperately needed there! Not a single young male left between the effects of driving, and the deadly club, save a few hundred of those demoralized and worthless " half bulls " which I make note of as they come up in every drive ; and these the natives truly declare will never go upon the rookeries.

Thus far this season every seal that is eligible in weight from a " long " 2-yr. old male up to 5-yr. olds, has been ruthlessly slain within a few days after its appearance in these desolate hauling grounds of St. Paul island. They were as ruthlessly knocked down last year ; and to-day the yearlings and everything above to 5-yr. olds would be knocked down did not the new $10.22 tax per skin save their lives! The new deal in this respect was lucky for the seals.

My assistant, Palmer, comes in from N. E. Point this afternnon ; he tallied a killing there yesterday as follows : — counting the seals

APPENDIX. 279

one by one as they shamble out from the pod when released and then the ones knocked down — adding the two counts gives the whole number in the pod).

July 3rd, 1890.

Field notes of the podding and clubbing of Drive made at N. E. Point (Fowler's party), July 1st, 1890; taking nothing under a 6 lb skin, or " long " 2 yr. olds. July 3rd, 1890.

No. of Pod.	Whole No. Driven.	No. Taken.	" Half bulls ".	No. of Pod.	Whole No. Driven.	No. Taken.	" Half bulls ".
1	62	8	»	Brought forw.	744	69	
2	53	1	»	15	36	10	»
3	36	4	»	16	35	6	»
4	35	1	»	17	28	1	»
5	44	6	»	18	42	4	»
6	62	4	»	19	29	6	»
7	46	6	»	20	39	5	»
8	52	7	»	21	30	2	»
9	47	8	»	22	38	5	»
10	42	3	»	23	31	3	»
11	66	3	»	24	26	5	»
12	58	9	»	25	22	4	»
13	62	5	»		1,103	120	
14	59	4	»	— " Half bulls " not tallied.			
Carry forw.	744	69					

Summary : Whole number of animals driven 1,103
— — — taken 120, or 91-1/2 °/₀ rejected.

Field notes of the podding and clubbing of Drive made from every section of Upper and Lower Zapadnie, July 3rd, 1890.

No. of Pod.	Whole No. Driven.	No. Taken.	" Half bulls ".	No. of Pod.	Whole No. Driven.	No. Taken.	" Half bulls ".
1	99	16	5	Brought forw.	331	97	33
2	70	11	2	9	63	17	9
3	71	10	3	10	70	8	8
4	63	9	»	11	62	17	5
5	50	16	5	12	46	13	»
6	78	18	4	13	71	12	5
7	61	6	8	14	62	18	4
8	59	11	6		925	180	64
Carry forw.	331	97	33				

Summary : Whole number of animals driven, 925
— — — taken 180, or 81 °/₀ rejected.

Nothing under a 6 lb. skin taken. or " long " 2-yr. olds.

Last drive from this place, June 26, 1890—when 344 animals were driven and 97 taken, or 72 °/₀ rejected.

These drives at Zapadnie are made just as they are at all the other rookeries this season—made from the immediate outskirts of the breeding animals, cows, pups and bulls. This method of driving was not even suggested, much less done, in 1872-'74. Such a proceeding would have been voted abominable then; it is still more so now — it sweeps every young male seal that is 4, 3 and 2 yrs. old into death as soon as it hauls on these shores today! Nothing escapes except that which maturing age or extreme youth saves — or rather which the high tax of 1890 ($ 10.22) saves!

The only spot on this island where seals have hauled outside of their close and immediate juxtaposition with the breeding classes is on Middle Hill sand beach, at a point on the English Bay sea margin about half way between Neahrpahskie Kammen and Tolstoi Rookery.

I cannot summon language adequate to express my condemnation of the present method of driving, careful as it is, but it is a method made necessary by the amazing scarcity of young male seals. *Under any and all circumstances*, there should be a stated and positive reservation of half the hauling grounds on these islands as a place of undisturbed rest and refuge for these young male seals and yearlings — places where material can and would grow up in full vigor to supply the imperative demands of nature on these breeding grounds; these reserves would in fact be reservoirs that would be a steady source from which this stream of particular seal life can regularly flow without diminution in its volume from year to year.

Now, this method of driving in 1890, huddles and hustles the breeding lines and sweeps the few surplus bulls that may be outside up and away to the killing grounds — stampeded into the drive.

July 4, 1890.

To-day, finding that the supply of 3-yr. olds and 4-yr. olds and "long" 2-yr. olds was practically exhausted; in other words, that more and more seals were being driven up every day, and less and less skins taken, the company's agent dropped his standard to 5-1/2 lb. skins; this takes in all the average 2-yr. olds, which have hitherto been rejected as they appeared in the pods; but even this tumble to a lower grade did not prevent a small catch, as the following tabulation of the biggest drive of the season as to numbers, testifies :

Field notes of the podding and clubbing of Drive made from English Bay, Middle Hill, and Tolstoi, July 4, 1890.

No. of Pod.	Whole No. Driven.	No. Taken.	"Half bulls".	No. of Pod.	Whole No. Driven.	No. Taken.	"Half bulls".
1	84	4	»	*Brought forw.*	349	21	3
2	81	6	1	5	65	8	»
3	90	3	2	6	75	8	1
4	94	8	»	*Carry forw.*	489	37	
Carry forw.	349	21	3				

APPENDIX. 281

No of Pod.	Whole No. Driven.	No. Taken.	" Half Bull ".	Pod.	Whole No Driven.	No. Taken.	" Half Bull ".
Brought forw.	489	37	4	Brought forw.	2529	284	45
7	52	5	3	35	61	10	»
8	61	7	3	36	61	4	»
9	76	8	3	37	52	»	1
10	70	11	4	38	36	3	»
11	126	14	1	39	40	6	2
12	82	15	1	40	49	5	6
13	71	13	1	41	52	6	»
14	81	11	»	42	67	5	1
15	92	10	3	43	64	4	4
16	63	9	»	44	58	3	1
17	76	11	3	45	59	9	»
18	69	7	»	46	68	10	1
19	68	9	1	47	58	8	»
20	58	7	1	48	56	2	»
21	74	9	2	49	70	6	»
22	56	6	3	50	45	2	»
23	53	4	2	51	58	4	»
24	92	10	4	52	64	8	»
25	72	7	3	53	38	3	»
26	46	10	1	54	36	2	»
27	70	4	»	55	66	8	»
28	85	10	1	56	62	8	»
29	77	12	»	57	53	5	»
30	69	4	»	58	53	5	»
31	97	8	»	59	56	14	»
32	111	12	1	60	40	8	»
33	45	6	»	61	41	7	»
34	47	8	»	62	42	5	»
Carry forw.	2529	284	45		4,323	432	67

Summary : Whole number of animals driven 4,323.
— — — taken 432, or 90-1/2 °/₀ rejected.

Last drive from this place, June 30th.; 1,262 animals driven, 203 animals taken, or 84-1/2 °/₀ rejected.

July 5, 1890.

Visited Otter Island ; no seals whatsoever hauled out there save a small squad of 50 right on the rocks awash above our landing; has been none thus far this season, or no sign either of them; last year some 1,500 or 2,000 were hauled-out here at this date. Grass has thickly and solidly grown all over the hauling grounds here, clear down to the surf, all over those places which were polished bare of every trace of vegetation by the hauling seals in 1872-74.

SECTION VIII.

July 7, 1890.

Field notes of the podding and clubbing of Drive made from English Bay, Middle Hill, Tolstoi, Lukannon and Keetavie.

No. of Pod.	Whole No. Driven.	No. Taken.	"Half bulls".	No. of Pod.	Whole No. Driven.	No. Taken.	"Half bulls".
1	70	7	1	Brought forw. 2121		197	32
2	52	11	»	30	65	7	3
3	41	7	1	31	74	8	»
4	79	9	6	32	59	4	»
5	77	17	1	33	73	5	»
6	66	8	1	34	62	10	»
7	60	10	1	35	79	15	»
8	48	7	2	36	74	8	»
9	70	11	3	37	56	5	1
10	38	4	»	38	70	4	1
11	89	9	2	39	77	5	2
12	101	4	»	40	43	9	»
13	64	2	»	41	59	7	»
14	42	2	»	42	59	5	»
15	121	12	»	43	41	2	»
16	102	5	3	44	56	»	»
17	76	6	»	45	84	15	»
18	70	5	»	46	50	5	»
19	78	8	»	47	60	3	»
20	86	11	»	48	38	5	»
21	70	4	2	49	53	6	2
22	82	2	»	50	45	6	»
23	72	5	»	51	43	4	»
24	75	3	»	52	45	8	»
25	62	5	3	53	40	4	»
26	100	7	3	54	47	3	»
27	61	7	3	55	70	1	»
28	59	4	»	56	42	2	»
29	110	5	»	57	66	7	»
Carry forw.	2121	197	32		4,001	350	42

Summary : Whole number of animals driven, 4,001.
— — taken, 350, or 92 %, turned out.

Last drive from this place, July 4th; 4,323 animals driven; 432 animals taken, or 90-1/2 %. turned out.

To-day, every 2-yr. old down to middle or medium, or every 5-1/2 b. skin, was taken; had the standard been kept at original mark, the rejection would have been as high as 95% to 96%!

July 8th, 1890.

Yesterday afternon I went back to Tolstoi over the seal road on which the drive above tallied was made in the night and morning of the 7th inst.; the number of road " faints " or skins was not large, which shows that the natives had taken great care in driving these seals; this they have uniformly done thus far; but when they pick up the drives at Zapadnie, at Lukannon, on the Reef and at Polavina, they are obliged, in order to get *all* of the holluschickie, to sweep the very skirts of the rookeries there: that is wrong; it should not be permitted; when matters become so desperate here as to obligate such a method, it is time to call a halt. I went up to Stony Point this morning early and made the following:

Field notes of the podding and clubbing of Drive from Polavina and all the beach below to Stony Point.

No. of Pod.	Whole No. Driven.	No. Taken.	" Half Bulls ".	No. of Pod.	Whole No. Driven.	No. Taken.	" Half Bulls ".
1	96	9	»	*Brought forw.* 1096		119	24
2	62	5	»	15	63	16	2
3	60	5	1	16	61	4	3
4	87	9	1	17	64	12	8
5	65	6	»	18	56	7	10
6	86	5	»	19	69	9	4
7	73	13	»	20	72	14	4
8	62	9	»	21	62	9	5
9	86	9	2	22	91	20	6
10	108	7	2	23	78	19	7
11	80	8	4	24	59	8	9
12	75	7	2	25	61	11	3
13	98	14	4	26	43	7	»
14	58	13	8		1,865	255	85
Carry forw.	1096	119	24				

Summary: Whole number of animals driven, 1,865
— — — — taken 255, or 87 % turned out.
Last drive from this place, July 2nd, 1,929 animals driven,
210 — taken, or 88 %.
turned, but the standard to-day being lowered to 5-1/2 lb. skins, prevents the increase of rejection percentage;—had the same standard prevailed to-day as on July 2nd, here, the rejection would have been as high as 92 %.

" This drive was principally made from the sand beach under Polavina rookery and on its outskirts to the north; and that is where these 85 " half bulls " (really, nearly all of them were 7- and 10-year-olds!) were gathered in; the two prior drives were chiefly made from the parade ground up above the breeding-ground, and there these bulls were first gathered in; to-day every 2-yr. old was taken that was well-grown, and had not these smaller seals been taken, there would not have been over 120 or 150 skins at the most; the first citation, 120, is the nearest correct; this would have given us a rejection of over 93 %:

I came down to the village on the sand beach betwen Stony Point and Lakannon; not a killable seal has hauled there yet this year! — a place where thousands upon tens of thousands of them were to be seen at this time 1872.

Also, not a holluschak has as yet hauled upon Zoltoi Sands; that was one of the finest resorts for holluschickie that the island boasted of in 1872-'74.

July 9, 1890.

I went over to Zapadnie early (4 o'clock) this morning to witness the driving there by the natives; most of the scanty drive was taken on the immediate borders of Upper Zapadnie rookery; the whole sweep of Lower Zapadnie did not yield over 150 or 200 holluschickie which had hauled out at several places just up and above the breeding seals.

All that large space above the rookery on Lower Zapadnie, which was literally alive with trooping platoons of holluschickie in 1872, is today *entirely vacant*, not seal on it! and the natives peering down over the high bluffs on the south side and the westward of the " Point " trying to find a few seals skulking down there on the rocks awash! Their eager search in such a quarter, with their backs to this silent parade ground of 1872, made me decidedly thoughtful. They said that they would go with a " bidarrah " and pick these secluded seals up — they did so last year they averred. I made the following:

Field notes of the podding and clubbing of Drive made from Upper and Lower Zapadnie, July 9, 1890.

No. of Pod.	Whole No. Driven.	No. Taken.	" Half Bulls ".	No. of Pod.	Whole No. Driven.	No. Taken.	" Half Bulls ".
1	125	11	»	*Brought forw.*	550	108	28
2	67	19	2	10	37	6	2
3	48	9	3	11	47	8	4
4	54	12	4	12	52	9	1
5	55	9	4	13	43	15	2
6	56	17	5	14	34	9	3
7	44	7	5	15	59	6	»
8	47	11	2	16	45	9	2
9	54	13	3		867	172	42
Carry forw.	550	108	28				

Summary: Whole number of animals driven, 867
— — — — taken, 172, or 83 °/₀ rejected.

Last drive from this place, July 3rd, 925 animals driven;
180 — taken, of 81 °/₀ turned out.

APPENDIX.   285

Lowering the standard on the 4th inst. prevented an immense percentage of rejection here today; had it not been for the small 5-1/2 lb. skins taken to-day, there would have been 95 °/₀ rejection !

July 10, 1890.

Field notes of the podding and clubbing of Drive made from every section of the Reef and Garbotch, July 10, 1890.

No. of Pod.	Whole No. Driven.	No. Taken.	"Half bulls".	No. of Pod.	Whole No. Driven.	No. Taken.	"Half bulls".
1	86	5	»	*Brought forw.* 1703		201	14
2	67	8	»	26	56	10	»
3	62	8	»	27	57	1	»
4	74	7	»	28	52	8	»
5	35	9	»	29	106	1	»
6	76	14	»	30	101	14	»
7	47	8	»	31	70	7	1
8	54	7	»	32	65	7	2
9	87	11	»	33	86	7	1
10	80	5	»	34	68	6	2
11	74	13	2	35	68	19	1
12	56	9	1	36	59	10	1
13	46	4	2	37	60	10	1
14	94	4	»	38	70	7	2
15	76	6	1	39	81	7	1
16	52	4	»	40	74	3	1
17	73	10	3	41	59	15	»
18	74	9	3	42	64	15	»
19	70	15	2	43	78	6	»
20	61	12	»	44	62	5	»
21	104	5	»	45	77	3	5
22	62	9	»	46	37	7	»
23	58	10	»	47	52	3	»
24	69	6	»	48	41	7	»
25	66	3	»		3,246	377	31
Carry forw.	1703	201	14				

Summary : Whole number of animals driven, 3,246
— — — — taken, 377, or 89 °/₀ rejected.

The last drive from this place and killing was made on the 5th inst. and was not tallied by myself — I was over to examine Otter Island while the killing was in progress. 526 skins were taken, however, with the standard lowered to 5-1/2 lb. skins, and as I looked up at the drove in waiting on the killing grounds that morning, I estimated that there was at least 4,000 animals in it.

On the 1st of July a drive of some 2,000 animals was made from this place; and with the higher standard, the original standard, 245 skins were then taken; that standard, applied today would have cut the catch of 377 down to less than 200 ! more likely to 150 ! As the clubbing progresses now every 2-yr. old holluschack from average size up is taken to the 5-yr. olds and "uigged" 4-yr. olds; the "short" 2-yr. olds and the yearlings escape. The standard used on the 11th of June, by which nothing under a good 3 yr. old skin was taken, if followed to-day, though the podding and clubbing of the 3,246 driven seals above itemized, would not have given the lessees more than 80 skins !

Field notes of the podding and clubbing of Drive made from English Bay, Middle Hill, Tolstoi, Lukannon, Keetavie, July 12, 1890.

No. of Pod.	Whole No. Driven.	No. Taken.	"Half bulls".	No. of Pod.	Whole No. Driven.	No. Taken.	"Half bulls".
1	98	7	»	Brought forw.	2015	242	21
2	65	»	»	35	79	5	5
3	78	8	2	36	26	51	1
4	64	5	»	37	58	6	2
5	52	8	»	38	58	11	2
6	64	2	2	39	68	9	»
7	63	6	1	40	50	11	1
8	73	10	4	41	54	6	»
9	50	9	»	42	76	4	»
10	78	10	»	43	65	6	»
11	63	2	»	44	37	6	»
12	69	9	»	45	64	13	»
13	51	6	1	46	87	14	»
14	46	7	»	47	77	18	»
15	62	9	»	48	76	16	»
16	49	6	»	49	71	8	»
17	58	6	2	50	71	11	»
18	63	6	3	51	91	11	»
19	59	9	1	52	88	13	»
20	77	10	2	53	89	13	»
21	40	7	»	54	86	5	»
22	49	10	1	55	89	9	2
23	50	13	»	56	100	10	1
24	52	8	»	57	92	13	»
25	26	2	»	58	72	8	»
26	53	10	»	59	87	10	»
27	67	9	»	60	76	7	»
28	50	16	»	61	93	10	1
29	51	5	»	62	114	16	2
30	65	8	»	63	48	6	2
31	60	4	1	64	81	6	»
32	61	4	»	65	71	15	»
33	44	3	»	66	79	10	»
34	56	8	1	67	69	10	»
Carry forw.	2015	242	21	Carry forw.	4453	559	40

No of Pod.	Whole No. Driven.	No. Taken.	"Half Bull".	No of Pod.	Whole No. Driven.	No. Taken.	"Half Bull".
Brought forw. 4453	559	40		*Brought forw.* 4730	602	43	
68	91	12	»	72	47	4	2
69	60	6	»	73	55	5	3
70	66	12	»	74	101	13	»
71	60	13	3		5150	633	48
Carry forw. 4730	602	43					

Summary: Whole number of animals driven, 5,150
— — — — Taken, 633, or 89-1/2 °/₀ turned out.
Last drive, July 7th, from this place, 4,001 animals driven,
350 — taken, or 92 °/° issued out

This is the second drive from these places, ranking largest in number, but it has rested since July 7th, or five days, a day longer than has been given yet to it this season; and then, the natives purposely left a squad of at least 300 yearlings in the lakes at the head of the lagoon, and another squad of at least 250 under the Lukannon sand-dunes.

When it is borne in mind that in the very height of the season after five days' rest or non-attention, only 633 medium fur-seals skins, mostly 5-1/2 lb. clean, skins, or 2-year-olds can be secured from the combined scraping of everything in English Bay (on Zapadnie and S. W. Point we know there is nothing), Middle Hill, Tolstoi, Lukannon and Ketavie, the extraordinary condition of these interests can be well understood in a general way. Such a driving in 1872 at this time and circumstamces of weather would have brought at least 50,000 holluschickie up here, instead of the 5,150 to-day! There were a number of cows in this drive; I counted 3 that I was sure of ".

July 13, 1890.

Walked up to N. E. Point early this morning for the purpose of plotting the area and position of the breeding seals on the Polavina and Novastoshnah. Also, to see the natives drive at Polavina. I was on the ground at 5 A. M. and saw the whole *modus operandi* at this place; the holluschickie haul up close against the sand beach " drop " of Big Polavina rookery, and the drivers, in getting the young males, swept 4 cows into the drove, and their little black pups were left behind them on the sand, bruised and marked by the stampeding flippers of the herd. To get the holluschickie, they are obliged to drive in this violent manner.

Another squad of say 1,000 mostly young or " short " 2-year-olds and yearlings, was swept upon the parade plateau, and another squad was driven from Little Polavina parade — the first drive that has been made from there thus far this season — no seals in this division but small ones; I have charted these areas of hauling.

Along the entire spread of Lukannon, Polavina and N. E. Point sand beach — 8 miles nearly, I did not see a single young seal not one hauled out — only a dozen or two old worthless bulls scattered here and there over this extent at wide intervals. At this time in 1872 such a walk as mine this morning would have brought me in contact with and in sight of from 50,000 to 100,000 holluschickie! and the weather, too, is simply superb sealing weather — all day yesterday, last night and this morning.

About 300 yards north of that basaltic shoulder which terminates the sand beach above Little Polavina rookery, and fully one mile from that rookery, I saw on the sand beach there this morning a single cow, guarded by two old bulls; this is the first example of solitary hauling of a female (an old cow, it was), that I have ever witnessed; it is a straw, however, showing the way which the wind is blowing up here this season — points to the demoralization which the present order of affairs is working, and which has been pretty steadily at work ever since 1882.

Found Fowler busy on the killing grounds just across the lake from Webster's house, where I arrived at 7 1/2 A. M. Mr. Goff joined me soon after, and we at once take up the rookery survey.

Fowler this morning had over 5,000 seals in his drive, but took only 473 of them; then in the afternoon, the rain coming up, he made a rapid drive of those holluschickie which he had been saving for to-morrow, fearing that the rain would send them to the sea, and thereby secured 168 more, making a total of 641, being the extreme limit reached in any one day's killing up here this year. On this day last year Webster killed 1883, and the next day 1,156, but Fowler will have no holluschickie to kill to-morrow.

The driving up here has radically changed since 1872; then Webster got all the killable seals he wanted from that sand beach on the "Neck", between the foot of Cross Hill on the North Shore, and the Big Lake sand-dunes. He never went out along the outskirts of the rookery; *it was not even thought of.*

The hauling now at Novastoshnah takes place at seven intervals or breaks in the breeding belt, and right in the rear and fairly among the scattered harems in many instances. We saw the scraping tracks of the drive which had been made in the early hours of this morning (10 A. M. we are here), and found over 15 or 20 pups which had been swept away and out into the rear and killed or dying by the stampede incident to such driving, and which I witnessed at Polavina only this morning on my way up here.

The parade fields of this once magnificent breeding ground are positively vacant to-day, grass and close white bunched flowers are growing and springing up everywhere all over them, while large areas of well polished ground of 1872-'74 are sodded over. The holluschickie as they hauled to-day did not occupy a space of ground 500 feet by 50 feet

APPENDIX.   289

in depth: over the entire extent of this immense habitat of theirs, and the drive of 5,000 which we saw on the killing ground had been scraped from seven different points between the base of Hutchinson's Hill and the S. E. extremity of the rookery.

On the North West shoulder a small pod of say 400 holluschickie were laying in just back of the narrow strip of rookery there, about 250 feet back from the sea; again, a little ways right over across to the south was another small pod of less than 300, near the small sand beach between the middle and the N. W. shoulders; then another small pod appeared just below the south shoulder, laying above surf wash on the sand: and another small squad laid out on that once famous reach of sand beach under Cross Hill and the Big Lake sand-dunes — all told, there could not have been over 3,500 of them; these, plus the 5,000 which Fowler had in hand, gives us all there is on this great rookery today, 8,500 holluschickie; 95°/₀ of them yearlings!

This hauling in under the cover of the breeding seals by the non-breeding young males, as we see it today, recalls forcibly that account which the natives gave to Lt. Maynard and myself about the holluschickie as they hauled in 1835, and several years thereafter. They then " laid in among the breeding seals ".

In 1872, instead of these frequent breaks that now appear in the circuit of this rookery belt here, only one place then existed from Sea-lion Neck clear around to the end of S. W. shoulder — the holluschickie were then literally obliged to haul out over that sand beach opening in Sea-lion Bight where there was an open reach of several hundred feet of sea margin, which was avoided by the breeding seals — too much sand. Today there are 25 or 30 vacant spaces in the breeding belt of the Novastoshnah all open for the holluschickie.

July 14, 1890.

Field notes of the podding and clubbing of Drive made from every section of the Reef peninsula, July, 14, 1890.

No. of Pod.	Whole no Driven.	No. Taken.	"Half Bulls".	No. of. Pod.	Whole no Driven.	No. Taken.	"Half Bulls".
1	117	4	3	Brought forw.	605	48	7
2	51	4	»	9	69	4	1
3	80	1	»	10	73	2	1
4	73	5	»	11	82	4	»
5	68	7	»	12	71	3	»
6	77	11	»	13	69	4	»
7	69	11	2	14	69	3	»
8	70	5	2	15	63	9	»
Carry forward.	605	48	7	Carry forw.	1101	77	9

No. of Pod.	Whole No. Driven.	No. Taken.	"Half Bull".	Remarks :
Report.	1101	77	9	
16	60	7	»	This drive shows the elimination
17	61	6	»	of the 2-yr. olds which were first
18	47	3	»	taken here on the 5th. inst.
19	61	2	1	
20	38	4	»	
· 21	74	2	»	
	1,592	101	10	

Summary : Whole number of animals driven, 1,592
— — — — taken 101, or 93 °/₀ rejected.

Last drive, July 10, 3,246 animals then driven,
377 — — taken, or 89 °/° rejected.

July 15, 1890.

Field notes of the podding and clubbing of Drive made from English Bay, Middle Hill, Tolstoi, Lukannon and Ketavie, July 15, 1890.

No. of Pod.	Whole No. Driven.	No. Taken.	"Half Bulls".	No. of Pod.	Whole No. Driven.	No. Taken.	"Half Bulls".
1	82	5	4	*Brought forw.* 1991		104	25
2	90	7	9	27	80	9	»
3	89	4	»	28	109	5	1
4	77	3	1	29	93	6	5
5	69	6	1	30	117	8	1
6	80	3	»	31	104	8	2
7	66	1	»	32	102	8	»
8	77	2	»	33	76	10	»
9	83	8	»	34	85	6	1
10	70	2	»	35	88	5	2
11	79	6	»	36	77	5	3
12	76	2	»	37	102	5	1
13	57	3	»	38	84	4	»
14	55	3	»	39	74	8	1
15	84	5	»	40	76	6	1
16	80	4	»	41	120	11	»
17	66	4	»	42	91	6	»
18	80	1	»	43	76	8	»
19	78	5	»	44	84	7	1
20	79	4	2	45	78	7	»
21	68	4	2	46	81	»	»
22	89	3	»	47	80	3	»
23	53	2	»	48	84	5	»
24	98	5	»	49	119	7	»
25	90	8	4	50	94	7	»
26	76	4	2	51	83	7	»
Carry forward. 1991		104	· 25	*Carry forw.* 4248		205 ·	44

APPENDIX. 291

No of Pod.	Whole No. Driven.	No. Taken.	"Half Bulls."	No. of Pod.	Whole No. Driven.	No. Taken.	"Half Bulls."
Brought forw. 4,248	265	44		*Brought forw.* 4,472	282	47	
52	65	3	»	55	90	7	»
53	68	8	3	56	85	6	»
54	91	6	»	57	89	13	»
Carry forw. 4472	282	47		4,644	309	47	

Summary : Whole number of animals driven, 4,644,
— — — — taken, 309, or 93 °/₀ rejected.
Last drive from these places, July 12, 5,150 animals driven,
633 — taken, or 89 °/₀ rejected.

In this drive I do not think there were 60 skins taken that were 3-year-olds, or 7 lb. skins! and certainly not 20 4-year-olds; of course every one of them was instantly clubbed as they have regularly been the moment they have appeared in the pods since the season opened. No 2-year-old of normal growth escaped today, only the yearlings, the "runty" or "short" 2-year-olds and few " half bulls " which I have numbered; these " half bulls " in all my tallies are those that run all the way up from 5-years-olds to advanced age — 10 or 15 years.

The evidence of redriving was stronger than ever today; the number of " moon-eyes " being so large that every pod exhibited one or more examples; fully half of the animals in this drive have been up here repeatedly before this season. In my opinion as I have been watching the course of these released seals, I believe that some go back at once on the day of their release to the hauling-grounds; not all return to the same place from whence driven that day, but haul out on the other grounds here, there and anywhere else on the island; they are then soon again picked up in the rapid rotation of driving, and put through this painful land journey again and again in this manner. The others go out to sea in quest of food, and perhaps are gone a week, to return and as above cited, and then be again driven and redriven, and so on. Thus, it becomes an exceedingly difficult matter or problem to solve, i. e., the query, of how many of these seals that appear in this drive to-day, 4,644 of them, are up here for the first time? How many of them have hitherto been driven from the seven or ten different hauling spots on this island this season? And how often have they been thus redriven?

Ever since the 10th—12th inst. the yearlings, i.e., last year's pups, have been hauling in greatly increased numbers daily, and will do so until the 20th inst. This was their habit in 1872-'74, and I notice by these tallies on the ground that it is their habit today. Of course, the $10.22 tax paid this year rules them out safely from the club; otherwise, they would have been slaughtered, This shift from the $3.17 tax of 1870 to the $10.22 tax of 1890 is an exceedingly fortunate one for the seals and the Government — it has prevented what would have been close to the finishing touch about the destruction of these rookeries; — yes, perhaps a killing which would have made it the labor of 15 years in which time to restore them and the hauling grounds dependent, to their standard of 1872. As it now appears, it will require at least 7 years of absolute rest — killing nothing here during that time save that small number of pups and yearlings required annually for the food and clothing of the Pribilov Islands. Had there been no killing at all this year, still it even then would have required a rest of at least 5 years, beginning with this season; the work of last year and this was and is literally "robbing the cradle and the grave".

July 17, 1890.

Field notes of the podding and clubbing of Drive made from Polavina, July, 17, 1890.

No. of Pod.	Whole no. Driven.	No. Taken.	"Half Bulls".	4 yr. wigs".	No. of Pod.	Whole of Driven.	No. Taken.	"Half Bulls ".	4 yr. wigs.
1	96	9	6	»	Brought forw. 988	100	85	49
2	84	15	6	9	10	158	18	20	8
3	81	11	5	»	11	76	6	14	4
4	124	9	6	»	12	73	15	26	7
5	134	9	13	10	13	64	18	17	8
6	101	7	8	7	14	70	3	»	1
7	114	16	10	6	15	44	5	7	1
8	124	14	14	12	16	67	7	9	3
9	130	10	17	5		1,514	172	168	81
Carry forw. 988	100	85	40						

Summary: Whole number of animals driven, 1,514
— — — — taken, 172, or 87 °/₀ turned out.

Of this 172 taken as above, 82 were 4 year-old "wigs"; this is the first killing of this low grade skin made thus far this season; they have been driven up steadily and redriven, and as steadily rejected had they not been taken today, the percentage of rejection would have been 95 ₀/°.

Field notes of the podding and clubbing of Drive made from Lukannon and Ketavie, July 17, 1890.

No. of Pod.	Whole no. Driven.	No. Taken.	"Half Bulls ".	No. of Pod.	Whole no. Driven.	No. Taken.	"Half Bulls ".
1	150	18	6	Brought forw. 440	70	19
2	137	26	3	5	80	18	7
3	91	14	5	6	73	12	6
4	62	12	5	7	83	14	3
Carry forw.	440	70	19	Carry forw. 676	114	35

No of Pod.	Whole No. Driven.	No. Taken.	"Half Bulls".	No. of Pod.	Whole No. Driven.	No. Taken.	"Half Bulls".
Brought forw.	676	114	35	Brought forw.	944	170	72
8	80	12	4	13	65	5	2
9	80	9	5	14	67	5	7
10	70	12	11	15	63	7	1
11	66	11	10	16	74	10	»
12	72	12	7		1,320	197	83
Carry forw.	944	170	72				

Summary : Whole number of animals driven, 1,320,
— — — — taken, 197, or 85 1/4 °/₀ rejected.

A small squad of 3-year- and 4-year-olds hitherto undriven, though marked on Ketavie during the last three days, some 80 or 90 all told, were secured in this day's drive, being brought right up through the scattered breeding animals from the Point of Ketavie; this raises the catch proportionaly in the little drive; the Lukannon seals were nearly all yearlings and only 7 " wigged " 4-year-olds were knocked down in this batch — at least 25 or 30 of them were released.

Thus, these two small drives for this day show an irregularity in their percentage, both being due to exceptional incidents. The Polavina, catch of 172 would not have touched 100 skins, had it not been for the sudden drop to " wigged " 4-year-old bulls, 81 of which were knocked down ; it is the very first systematic killing of this class made thus far this season : it is, however, a small matter, drive, catch and all.

The Ketavie drive was principally made from the extreme point, a new spot which has not been driven from before, but the rookery is now so thin and straggling that the drivers were able to get fairly down on the point and dislodge about 100 good 3- and 4-year-olds ; the balance of the 197 skins taken in the united drive with Lukannon are small 5-1/2 to 6 lb. skins.

Going up to Polavina early this morning, I did not see a single young male seal on that long reach of sand beach between Lukannon and Polavina — only weak, sickly or dying seacatchie, a dozen or two of them, and nothing else. The utter absence of the holluschickie from these sands of Lukannon Beach and those extensive hauling grounds back of them on the Volcanic Ridge and half a mile again to the Northward — this desolation is fully as startling a contrast with their life and animation in 1872 as is that of Zoltoi sands and English Bay.

July 18, 1890.

Field notes of the podding and clubbing of Drive made from Zapanie — the last drive here for 1890.

No. of Pod.	Whole No. Driven.	No. Taken	"Half Bulls	4 yr. "wigs".	No. of Pod.	Whole No. Driven.	No. Taken.	"Half Bulls	4 yr. "wigs".
1	94	13	5	6	*Brought forw.* 689	114	53	29	
2	50	11	11	3	10	72	15	2	5
3	76	17	9	5	11	80	15	4	6
4	78	15	5	4	12	51	12	9	3
5	82	12	2	3	13	61	20	9	7
6	85	15	»	3	14	63	15	6	6
7	81	12	5	»	15	72	23	7	8
8	74	11	8	4	16	46	11	16	5
9	72	8	8	1	17	69	16	9	5
Carry forw.	689	114	53	29		1,192	241	115	(74 wigged 4 yr. olds).

Summary. — Whole number animals driven, 1,192
— — — taken, 241, or 79 % rejected.

Minus the "wigged" 4-year-olds, 88 % turned out.

This tally of the final killing of the season at the "South-west Bay" killing ground of Zapadnie, shows that extraordinary scarcity of holluschickie in a most lucid manner when contrasted with the other drives of this year, which I have tallied on this once famous rendezvous. This last scrape made here today was opened by the appearance of only 1,192 animals on the grounds after a rest of nine days since the last drive; 115 of these 1,192 seals were old bulls — all over 6 years, and most of them 7- and 10-year-olds, and all the balance outside of the 241 animals knocked down, were yearlings, chiefly, a few "runty" 2-year-olds, a few bitten 4-year-old "wigs", and a few 5-year-olds. Every 4-year-old "wig" was taken, taken here, as at Polavina yesterday, for the first time this season; every "smooth" 4-year-old was taken in the first drives, and now the dregs are drawn also.

These young bulls vary remarkably in this matter of being with manes or "wigged", or not, at the culmination of their 4th year of growth — just as young men at 18 vary as to having moustaches or beard, or not; the "smooth" or unwigged 4-year-old is a fine skin, but the "wigged" 4-year-old is a poor one.

Thus far this season until yesterday morning, I observed that from the beginning, though every "smooth" 4 yr. old was clubbed, yet every "wigged" one of that age and upwards was never taken, unless-struck down by accident.

I have seen once in a while a 3-year-old so wigged as to be a really poor skin; but that is a rare example when found of this age; and for that matter, the "wigged" 4-year-olds do not number 1/10 of their class as they grow up ".

July 19, 1890.

4-1/2 A. M. As I go over to the " Rush " at the East landing. I observe that not a single young male seal is on Zoltoi Sands this morning — not one has hauled there thus far this season; (I leave for St. George Island on the " Rush " at 5 A. M., arrive there at 11 A. M.)

Field notes on St. George Island.

July 20, 1890.

I made a careful survey of the North Rookery this afternoon and its hauling grounds; — the perfect desolation — the grass growing, flowers blooming over the polished hauling grounds of 1873-'74 are as much or even more marked here if possible than on St. Paul; the natives, ever since this season of 1890 opened, have been scraping the rookeries and up to this morning had but 2,964 skins taken, ruled by the standard of nothing under a 7 lb. pelt (which was started as the rule on St. Paul but dropped day after day down to 5 lb. skins this morning). These St. George natives were unable to get out of every 1,000 animals driven up, more than 50 to 60 such 7 lb and 12 lb. skins as the rule of killing called for. The order was given to-day for Webster to take everything down to 5 lbs. in the drive then awaiting, and he did so for the first time this year, getting about 640 this evening out of the herd, some 2,500 or, 3,000 animals all told; the only seals escaping were the yearlings and old bulls; every " wigged " 4-year-old knocked down also, and several yearlings, by accident in shaving so fine down to 5 lb. skins.

July 22, 1890.

I examined this morning, one by one, the skins that were taken from the drive of yesterday; three-fourths of them will not weigh more than 5-1/2 lbs., or belonging to the small grade which was ordered not taken until yesterday; had this standard not been lowered to these small skins, not over 150 would have been secured as it was, 641 were taken.

At Zapadnie, where I went this morning, I observed another drive, which has been saved up for a week from date; 521 skins taken, as per the above standard ; had the standard not been thus lowered, not over 60 or 75 skins could have been taken from this drive. Mr Webster freely admitted to me in the presence of Captain Lavender and his son, that he had taken these small skins yesterday and to-day for the first time this year. Had he taken them in June and early in July, he would have nothing to-day on this field but yearlings and " half bulls ".

The hauling grounds at Zapadnie are simply grass grown; those at Starry Arteel, ditto; the Great Eastern parade is a mere suggestion, and Little Eastern has not had a single drive made from its faint reminder of a once good resort for holluschickie.

In the " wake " of this drive to-day, here, I saw a number of pups which had been swept along in the driven herd — their mothers gone in it — they, left to perish behind. The podding of these pups way back by 20th July on to the abandoned hauling-grounds, so that the holluschickie can and do mix with them and their mothers, makes the act of driving from this hour forth during the remainder of the season, simply ruinous to the rookeries; since, bad as it is to-day, it would become worse as it progressed every day after.

July 22, 1890.

These hauling grounds of St. George which were never by nature of the land and life thereon, as broad and extended as those of St. Paul, were in 1873 polished very brightly here by the holluschickie, but that same utter desolation which prevails over them at St. Paul, also prevails here; the driving, however, thanks to the good sense of Webster, has not been so excessive as it would have been had a less experienced sealer been in charge; for instance, driving every day from a given hauling ground, this season will not yield at the end of a week's work any more seals than it would were the drive made but once in all that time; in 1872-'74, however, then so many seals were on hand at every place that it was necessary to take no more each day than the working force of skinners at the village could handle; but when the seals are scarce as they are everywhere this year, it is folly to rake and scrape the ragged edges of these breeding rookeries every day or two for a mere handful of holluschickie which can be secured just as well if driven all up once a week. *It is the driving*, as well as the clubs, which kill, just as surely.

The method of driving as now ordered makes the selection of holluschickie, after the pups begin to pod in bulk on or before the 20th of July, every season, — makes such selection utterly impossible without sweeping cows into the " drive ", and dragging their young out to die in the track of this " drive. " Every day or two from this 20th July makes the work of such driving worse and worse for the rookeries; so much so that no driving under any and all circumstances after that date ever should have been permitted or will be permitted again if our Government means to preserve and perpetuate these fur-bearing interests on the Pribilov Islands.

Bad as driving in effect on the holluschickie is, the driving of cows is certain death to them; they are fuller in habit and less muscular — their milk glands become inflamed and swollen, and the result must ensue of " garget " or " milk sickness " so well known in cats, dogs and cattle; that means death or permanent disability, even if the cows are driven but once — death to both cow and her pup left behind, since that pup will not be permitted to suckle any other.

The scraping or sweeping of these rookeries on St. George did not fairly begin until 1884; while it was not really begun in earnest on St. Paul until 1886 or 1887; but the driving here has been lighter than it would have been had I not changed the quota from 25,000 to 10,000 in 1874; in 1887 the difficulty of getting even 15,000 holluschickie before the end of July was evident, far more difficult than that of securing 25,000 before the 20th July in 1872 was; yet, in spite of this marked deviation from the working record of the preceding seasons, the Treasury Agents of 1886-1887, in charge of these interests up here, actually sent in a report to the Treasury Department criticizing my figures of 1873-'74 and declaring that there were *eight times as many fur-seals* on the St. George rookeries then as when I made my surveys in 1873-1874: I cannot see any difference in the character of the holluschickie here on St. George from those I have studied all summer on St. Paul; indeed, I know that these animals haul on either island indifferently, as they go and come throughout the season; they will haul out here to-day and next week, just as likely as not, many of them will be over on St. Paul hauled out there for a spell in turn.

One of the queerest ideas of how to help the holluschickie to haul (when there were none to haul!) was the desperate notion of the lessees agent here last summer who, on the 9th of June, actually went down into the ragged sea margin at the Near or North Rookery and drove away a few old bulls which had hauled into the empty path of the holluschickie which leads up by the " Raichka ": this done to help the holluschickie " to land faster! "

July 25, 1890.

St. George Island: Weighed 100 skins as they came over from Zapadnie to-day, from the little salt-house there, and which were taken on the last day of killing, the 20th inst.; three-fifths of the whole number weighed were 5-1/2 — 6 lb. skins — average to " long " 2-year-olds; the balance, 7 to 7 1/2 lb. skins, four 8 lb. skins and one 9 1/4 lb. skins and one 4 lb. skin (or yearling).

July 26, 1890.

Weighed 176 skins of the Zapadnie catch of the 20th inst.; just as they came over on the burro train; as I handled the skins, they ran thus:

```
            64 skins, 5-1/2 lbs. =  352   lbs.
            26   —    5      —  =  130    —
             4   —    4      —  =   16    —
            42   —    6      —  =  252    —
Carry forward  136                 750
```

SECTION VIII.

Brought forward	136				750	
	20	—	6-1/2 lbs.	=	130	lbs.
	12	—	7	— =	84	—
	4	—	7-1/2	— =	30	—
	2	—	8	— =	16	—
	1	—	8-1/2	— =	8-1/2	—
	1	—	9	— =	9	—
	176 skins				1,027-1/2 lbs.	

making the average as low as a 5-7 8 lb. skin; this is the run of the last killing on St. George on the 19th-20th inst.; had the standard first ordered been adhered to, only 20 skins would have been taken instead of 176, in the above catch.

July 30, 1890.

A stiff S. W wind ever since yesterday has kicked up such a rough sea that to-day by noon nearly every seal by the island has hauled out on shore and it is a good afternoon to inspect the rookeries in so far as my search for pups of last year or yearlings, goes.

A careful examination of the largest rookery of this island, "North", revealed the presence of about 750 holluschickie 700 at the least, and possibly 900; all were yearlings, save a small percentage of 2-year-olds, with scattered examples, wide apart, of 3-year-olds and a dozen perhaps of 4-year-olds.

They were all hauled out (with the exception of one pod of some 150 near the Raichka), and commingled with podding pups and cows. A drive could not be made there to-day of more than 200 holluschickie without driving as many cows and pups:

Such a day as this should show up at least 4,000 yearlings here, on these spots of that rookery alone, this afternoon where are these yearlings?

The pups at the water's edge are beginning to familiarize themselves with their native element, essaying to swim in the pools and surf wash at sheltered spots. Those pups, where the surf directly breaks upon the sea margin and strikes the beach with unbroken force—those pups to-day are not in the water at all. A vast majority of the pups will not get into the water before the end of the next two and three weeks.

I observe a very large proportion of yearling cows scattered all over the breeding ground from end to end near the sea margin, while the yearlings of both sexes are completely mixed up on the outskirts of the rookery here and everywhere else commingled with the adult cows and their young pups.

August 1st, 1890.

Heavy rain has fallen and a stiff S. W. gale has raged all day yesterday; it clears up this afternoon. Desiring to see the hauling grounds at Zapadnie and the rookery there immediately after such a storm where the surf breaks in with full force and fury, I went over and made a survey of the entire field. Since my last visit the pups have podded to the uttermost length and breadth of the place, a 1,000 to 1,500 feet back from the surf margin of the rookery, and way up and into the green grass and moss in the rear. Squads of holluschickie mingled in with them everywhere, and their mothers, of course; but how many in proportion I cannot say, since the yearlings and the 2-year-olds so closely resemble the young cows when all huddled up and startled by the approach of man.

However, if you walk slowly, and occasionally sit or stoop down for a few minutes, when an unusual rush by the seals seems pending, you can traverse every one of these breeding grounds to-day without startling or stampeding many of the seals thereon into the water. As these animals first startled by your unexpected form, " cough ", " spit ", " snort " and then turn to fly, at that moment you gently squat down, then they pause, turn curiously to look, and notice that you are not following or moving, then they bolt, altogether, and regard you intently for a minute or two ; then if you do not move in a few moments more, they all resume their occupation of sleeping or playing one with another as they were doing when you first startled them by your coming.

Then, if you rise *slowly* to an erect posture, and resume your walk, very quietly and slowly along parallel with or away from them they do not seem to pay you any special attention further; they will not again start to run or " flipp-flapper " " back into the sea.

August 1, 1890.

Natives drive a pod of 97 seals up for food, this morning; *only 5 skins* out of the whole number of the 97 seals killed, for they were all killed, only 5 skins were 7 lb. pelts : the rest yearlings and 2-year-olds; (85 °/* yearlings).

St. Paul Island, August 9, 1890.

A careful survey of the Reef and Zoltoi, Garbotch and Gull Hill hauling-grounds this morning discloses no change whatever in the lonely character of these places, and I observe the same scarcity of yearlings that has recently impressed me on St. George.

Not a single young male seal on Zoltoi Sands this day, and none have hauled there at all this season; and now it is safe to say that none will until the pods of swimming pups in October come here from Garbotch. What few holluschickie are left here have become so demoralized by the driving early in June and up to the 20th July, as to now haul in among the podded cows where you can easily distinguish them right and left among the " matkahs " and pups. It would be very difficult now to say as we look out over the field, how many of them are thus hauled out there to-day — are here — but the spectacle is a quiet, sad one to see, is that silent parade ground of the Reef ahead of us. Over its whole smooth sweep a soft, velvety grass and moss is springing up bright and strong under the stimulus of an August air; that wide expanse is entirely deserted by seals where, in 1872, it was fairly alive with restless trooping thousands and tens of thousands.

That S. W. gale of the 30th-31st July, which I experienced and followed so closely on St. George, seems to have destroyed a great many pups over here on the Garbotch sea margin; there are 17 dead pups laying half buried in the sands of Zoltoi right before and under my eyes, as I stand."

In closing these copies of my field notes on the hauling grounds, the following is pertinent; during the killing season, several of the elder men, natives on St. Paul, expressed a desire to talk with me about the condition of affairs. I asked them to wait until the work of the season was over, then to come up to the Government House when I returned from St. George, where what they had to say could be heard by all of the Treasury officers, as well as myself; the notes below of this interview were made by Mr. Murray : I copy them literally :

Village of St. Paul.

In the presence of and hearing of Henry W. Elliott, Charles J. Goff, Joseph Murray and S. R. Nettleton, U. S. Treasury Agents :

August 6, 1890.

The following natives (old men) were called into the Government House of. Prof. Elliott and examined by (Simeon Meloviedoff, interpreter) Messrs. Elliott, Goff, Murray and Nettleton, Treasury Agents.

Mr Murray took the following notes of the conversation :

PRESENT : Kerick Artamonov, Kerick Booterin, Vaselie Sedoolie, Markeel Vollkov, Eupheem Korchootin, Fedosay Sedick.

Question. Do you remember Prof, Elliott being on this Island (St. Paul) in 1872?

Answer. Yes, we remember him well.

Question. Do you remember that thousands of holluschickie were then hauling at South-west Point?

Answer. Yes, we do remember.

Question. Were there thousands and thousands lying there undisturbed — that there were no drives made from that point?

Answer. There were no drives made from there for many years, notably, 1872-1873-1874 and 1875, and yet there were thousands and thousands there and at Zapadnie and Middle Hill from which we made no drives.

Question. Do you remember the small rookery and the hauling grounds on Prof. Elliott's map just west of Zapadnie, and called by him "Kursoolah?"

Answer. Yes, we remember it distinctly — there was a small rookery there and a large hauling ground.

Question. Are there any seals hauling there today, or have you seen any seals at South-west Point?

Answer. No, there is nothing there today but growing grass — where it used to be covered with seals from point to point.

Question. Do you remember the hauling-grounds West of Middle Hill in English Bay and Zapadnie in 1872-1873-1874?

Answer. Yes, it used to be covered with seals in those years; we drove them from English Bay — from half way over only and even then we would often leave half of the seals behind; and were often obliged to divide the drives into four or five divisions because the seals were so numerous.

(The above answer was given by Kerick Booterin, who at that time was chief.)

Question. Do you remember the hauling-grounds of Polavina, and is it true that in Mr Elliott's time there were thousands upon thousands of young male seals hauled upon those grounds undisturbed by any driving from beginning to end of the seasons of 1872-1873 and 1874 exclusive?

Answer. Yes, there were lots of seals there, thousands upon thousands undisturbed.

Question. Do you remember the hauling-grounds of Stony Point and the beach around it?

Answer. Yes, we know the place well, and there were seals scattered there all along it.

Question. Are there any seals there to-day?

Answer. No, they are all gone.

Question. Do you remember the hauling-grounds between Webster's House and Polavina?

Answer. Yes, and there used to be lots of seals there, especially at a point called "Dalnoi".

Question. Are there any seals there today?

Answer. No, there are none there — we drove there this year, but could not get more than 100 seals.

Question. Do you remember old man Webster in 1872 to 1874 at North-east Point, and where he got his seals in those days?

Answer. Yes, we do remember. Artamonov was then second chief and worked with Webster six weeks.

Question. (To Artamonov). Is it true that Webster got all his seals from that strip of sand beach on the north shore, west of Cross Hill?

Answer. Yes, there where always a sufficient number.
Question. Did Webster drive from or near a rookery then at North-east Point?
Answer. No, he never allowed the men to go near a rookery.
Question. Where do they drive from at N. E. Point today?
Answer. They drive from all around the point.
Question. Do they go among the cows to get out the holluschickie?
Answer. No, they go right above the cows and drive from the very edges.
Question. Was any man now present at N. E. Point this year?
Answer. Yes, three of us.
Question. At what date were you there?
Answer. At the beginning of the season and during the third week.
Question. Were any of you at North-east Point since the " podding " or " spreading " out of the cows and pups occurred?
Answer. No.
Question. (To Kerick Booterin and to Artamonov.) Were you born at North-east Point and what are your ages?
Answer. Yes, and Artamonov is now 65 and Booterin is 61.
Question. (To same two men.) Do you remember whether there were more or less seals before 1872 than then (1872-1874) or afterwards?
Answer. In 1868 the hauling-grounds and rookeries were at their very fullest — the entire ground from the lake upwards being covered with seals.
Question. When did you first notice the shrinking or scarcity of seals? and when did you first talk about it among yourselves? "
Answer. In 1877, we first began to notice that the holluschickie were getting fewer, and have continued from that year to grow less and less. "
Question. At what time did you talk among yourselves as to when the time would come when there would be an end to the seal business? "
Answer. (By Geo. Booterin.) I began to see in 1877 that this trouble was ahead, but whenever I or my people spoke about it we were told by the company men " Americans " (*sic*) that it was not of our business and we must not talk about it. Wenever we talked about the seals the company men threatened to send us away from the island.
Question. (By Mr Goff to Booterin). Was that the reason you would not talk to me last year?
Answer. I hardly remember now why I did not like to talk about the seals.
Question. What do you men think of the effect on seal life of the driving of the seals?
Answer. When the old Russian Company drove, and the drives came in here, they never killed anything over a three-year-old; all over that were either never disturbed, or else spared ; and if the same thing

had been praticed ever since, there would be no scarcity of seals to-day.

Question. How many three-year-olds do you think you can get next year?

Answer. If they were to drive all the seals on this island next year they would get nothing and would only disturb and injure the rookeries.

(By Kerick Booterin.) Whenever any killing is allowed, if they never kill any over three-year-olds, and kill only three-year-olds and under, I believe there would be no injury done.

Question. Do any of you remember the " Zapooska " of 1834?

Answer. Yes, Booterin and Artamonov remember it well.

Question. How many seals were killed after the first year of that order, and how were they killed?

Answer. The first year we killed only one hundred holluschickie, and we increased the number every year afterwards.

Question. What do you think of another " Zapooska " for today?

Answer. (By Kerick Booterin.) When the Russians ordered their Zapooska, little by little afterwards, everything grew better, and if the same thing is repeated today, everything will grow better, and if it is not done, no seals will come here. We observed that the men sent here by the Government since old Capt. Bryant, till we saw you men and talk now with you, took no interest in the seals, but whenever busy, were engaged in shooting our hogs, in fact they very seldom visited the rookeries.

Question. Did you men ever talk or attempt to talk about seal life to any of the Government officers before Mr Goff's time?

Answer. Yes, on several occasions, and they answered we did not know anything about it.

Question. Have you any questions you would like to ask the Government?

Answer. Yes, we want to know what is to be done about the seals?

Answer. (By Mr Elliott.) We propose to immediately inform the Secretary of the Treasury of the exact condition of affairs, and we know that he will take care of the seals and the people too. That he is the only man who can talk, but that he sent us here to get the facts, and he will act upon that information, That none of us in Washington knew of the true condition of affairs up here; until Mr Goff wrote down last year to the Secretary of the Treasury not a word has ever gone from here since 1870 which even hinted at any danger to the seals.

(By Kerick Booterin.)

We think had it not been for Mr Goff, the seals would all be gone. We are not now afraid of being hungry although we cannot take seals.

(By Mr Elliott). " We want you natives to understand that the Government cares more for the preservation of the seals than for any money that may be received in the form of a tax.

The interview closed at this point.

The foregoing statements are made only by those natives who in 1872-'74 were old enough then to really observe and think; these men above named are the only survivors of that age when I was on the island in 1872; also, when the above interview was in progress, Kerick Booterin during the whole time held a small note book in his hand, open, and not seeing him make any notes or refer to it at the close of the talk, he was asked by the interpreter what he wanted to do with the book that he had there; he then showed us the following written statement (in Russian) which he said he made for me, as he was not certain whether we should meet and talk, or not, before I left the island.

Translation.

August 6, 1890.

Pardon me, Mr Elliott, I never call myself a big man, but now I shall talk what I know, and will not tell what I do not know.

I think that as the hauling grounds were, they will be if the drives were made and the killing made from small ones, the large ones spared. If that is done, I think all will be well. If that is not done, more harm will come to the rookeries so that there will be no more hauling out on the rookeries. If a " Zapooska " is made, I think all will be well. If the " Zapooska " is not made, then we will lose the land if the Treasury does not look out. If the hauling-grounds could sustain the company, then the grass and everything like it would not grow there now. This loss will fall upon us and upon our children. We cannot longer sit quiet and talk about there being lots of seals.

General memoranda concerning the seal islands.

St. George Village, July 29, 1890.

In many respects a resident here enjoys a far more pleasureable life than if stationed at St. Paul. He has a finer view of the sea, which in storms boils at his feet, in surf of suprising power, or leaves the black basaltic base of the Village Cliff in low, rippling murmurs when calm days prevail; he can see from morning until night endless flocks of waterfowl, from the 26th of every April until the end of every October flying to and from the uplands and cliffs, some days beating their way stubbornly against a stiff head wind, or darting off through the fog or mist like bullets from a gun.

I notice a great increase in the floral display over that exhibited here in 1873-'74; indeed, now I think that the flowers at Garden Cove are as numerous and as beautiful as can be seen on St. Paul. They were not so in 1873.

The grass in and around the village here is the finest turf in Alaska; it is a close growing, fine speared species or variety that very closely resembles the blue grass of Kentucky; the seal " road " leading to the Eastern rookery is of this sod — sodded smoothly, and it crops out on the south side at Garden Cove, especially attractive.

Such a compact, smooth, glassy green turf, makes the little hamlet here look attractive; as it is kept clean everywhere and not littered or strewn; the water here is abominable, however; nothing but the seepage from the hilly tundra back of the village, and perhaps owes much of its " *flatness* " to that drainage which it represents of the " Choochkie " ridges, which rest here by millions from June to August 30th September 10th all over the uplands around the town.

On St. George in 1868 no regular list was made of the number of seals taken then; but it seems likely from all I can gather that at least 30 000 were killed. On St. Paul, also no regular count was made, but H. M. Hutchinson and Daniel Webster, who were on the ground then, sealing there, assure me that the number did not exceed 240,000; this was followed in 1869 by the killing of 60,000 or a few more on St. Paul and St. George for natives " food "; the skins being salted, and finally taken by the A. C. Co. next year; *i.e.* most of them, since they did not get possession until August, 1870 and then the sealing season was substantially ended for the year.

The condition and appearance of this little town of St. George is one of good order and cheerfulness. The 21 native houses here are occupied by 98 souls; there were 120 when I was here in 1873; the little streets or roadways are clean and well drained; the grass in and about the village is much better than that at St. Paul, and a small sheep paddock directly under the window of the Treasury Agent's house is one that suggests a Kentucky blue grass meadow most forcibly.

General memoranda, the food of the fur-seal and its relation to the fisheries of Alaska and the North-west Coast.

In my monograph of the Seal Islands of Alaska (p. 64.), I called attention to the amount of fish that a fur-seal probably consumed every day on an average throughout the year, showing that these animals undoubtedly required and secured some six millions of tons of fish as food annually.

I said. " Think of the enormous food consumption of these rookeries and hauling grounds; what an immense quantity of finny prey must pass down their voracious throats as every year rolls by. A creature so full of life, strung with nerves, muscles like bands of steel cannot live on air, or absorb it from the sea. Their food is fish, to the practical exclusion of all other diet. I have never seen them touch, or disturb with the intention of touching it, one solitary example in the flocks of water fowl which rest upon the surface of the water all about the islands. I was especially careful in noting this, because it seemed to me that the canine armature of their mouths must suggest flesh for food at times as well as fish; but fish we know they eat. Whole windrows of the heads of cod and wolf fishes, bitten off by these animals at the nape, were washed up on the south shore of St. George during a gale in the summer of 1873; this pelagic decapitation evidently marked the progress and the appetite of a band of fur-seals to the windward of the island, as they passed into and through a stray school of these fishes."

"How many pounds per diem is required by an adult seal, and taken by it when feeding, is not certain in my mind. Judging from the appetite, however, of kindred animals, such as sea-lions fed in confinement at Woodward's gardens, San Francisco, I can safely say that forty pounds for a full grown fur-seal is a fair allowance, with at least ten or twelve pounds per diem to every adult female, and not much less, if any, to the rapidly growing pups and young " holluschickie ". Therefore, this great body of four and five millions of hearty, active animals which we know on the seal islands, must consume an enormous amount of such food every year. They cannot average less than ten pounds of fish each per diem, which gives the consumption, as exhibited by their appetite, of over six million tons of fish every year. What wonder, then, that nature should do something to hold these active fishermen in check."

"I feel confident that I have placed this average of fish eat per diem by each seal at a starvation allowance, or in other words, it is a certain minimum of the whole consumption. If the seals can get double the quantity which I credit them with above, startling as it seems, still I firmly believe that they eat it every year. An adequate realization by ichthyologists and fishermen as to what havoc the fur-seal hosts are annually making among cod, herring, and salmon of the north-west coast and Alaska, would disconcert and astonish them. Happily for the peace of political economists who may turn their attention to the settlement and growth of the Pacific coast of America, it bids fair to never be known with anything like precision. The fishing of man, both aboriginal and civilized, in the past, present and prospective, has never been, nor will it be, more than a drop in the bucket contrasted with the piscatorial labours of these ichthyophagi in those waters adjacent to their birth. What catholic knowledge of fish and fishing banks any one of those old ' seecatchie ' must possess, which we observe hauled out on the Pribilof rookeries each summer. It has, undoubtedly, during the eighteen or twenty years of its life, explored every fish — eddy, bank, or shoal throughout the whole of that vast immensity of the North Pacific and Bering Sea. It has had more piscine sport in a single twelve month than Izaak Walton had in his whole life."

An old sea-captain, Dampier, cruising around the world just about 200 years ago, wrote diligently thereof (or, rather, one Funnel is said to have written for him), and wrote well. He had frequent reference to meeting hair-seals and sea lions, fur seals, etc., and fell into repeating this maxim, evidently of his own making : ' For wherever there be plenty of fish, there be seals'. I am sure that, unless a vast abundance of good fishing-ground was nearby, no such congregation of seal-life as is that under discussion on the seal-islands, could exist. The whole eastern half of Bering Sea, in its entirety, is a single fish-spawning bank, nowhere deeper than 50 to 75 fathoms, averaging perhaps, 40: also there are great reaches of fishing shoals up and down the northwest coast from and above the straits of Fuca, bordering the entire southern, or Pacific, coast of the Aleutian islands. The aggregate of fish food which the seals find upon these vast ichthyological areas of reproduction, must be simply enormous, and fully equal to the most extravagant demand of the voracious appetites of *Callorhini*."

Using the above as a suggestion, several writers have hastily assumed that it would be a good thing if the seals were exterminated—that by exterminating them, just so much more would be given to our salmon and cod fishermen to place upon the markets of the world. These men forget the fact that all animal life in a state of nature existing to-day as the fishes and seals do, is sustained by a natural equilibriun, one animal preying upon the other, so that year after year, only so many seals, so many cod, so many halibut, so many salmon, so many dog fish, and so on throughout the long list can and do exist.

Suppose for argument that we could and did kill all the seals we would at once give the deadly dog-fish (*Squalno ancarthias*), which family swarms in these waters an immense impetus to its present extensive work of destruction of untold millions of young food fishes such as herring, cod, and salmon.

A dog-fish can and does destroy every day of its existence hundreds and thousands of young cod, salmon, and other food fishes-destroys at least double and quadruple as much as a seal; what is the most potent factor to the destruction of the dog-fish? Why the seal himself, and unless men can, and will, destroy the dog-fish *first*, he will be doing positive injury to the very cause he pretends to champion, if he is permitted to disturb this equilibrium of nature, and destroy the seal.

LIST OF RESIDENT TREASURY AGENTS WHO HAVE SERVED ON THE SEAL-ISLANDS OF ALASKA FROM 1869 TO 1890.

Chief Special Agents.

No.	Name.	Seasons of Service.
1.	Charles Bryant	1869 to May 20th 1877 (incl.)
2.	John M. Morton	1877 to 1878 (incl.)
3.	Harrison G. Otis	1879 to 1881 (incl.)
4.	Henry A. Glidden	1882 to July 1st 1885 (incl.)
5.	Geo. R. Tingle	1885 to April 1889 (incl.)
6.	Charles J. Goff	1889 to date (November 1890.)

Assistant Special Agents.

No.	Name.	Seasons of Service.
7.	Samuel Falconer	1870 to 1876 (incl.)
8.	Henry W. Elliott	1872 to 1873 (incl.)
9.	Francis Lessen	1872 to 1874 (incl.)
10.	Geo. Marston	1875 to 1877 (incl.)
11.	Wm. J. Mc Intyre	1874 to 1876 (incl.)
12.	J. H. Moulton	1877 to 1882 (incl.)
13.	B. F. Scribner	1879 to 1880 (incl.)
14.	John W. Beaman	1879 to 1880 (incl.)
15.	W. B. Taylor	1881 to August 3rd, 1881.
16.	Geo. Wardman	1881 to May 29th, 1885.
17.	Louis Kimmel	1882 to 1883 (incl.)
18.	Herbert G. Fowler	1884 to 1885 (to July 1st only).
19.	A. P. Loud	1885 to 1889 (incl.)
20.	Thos. J. Ryan	1885 to 1886 (incl.)
21.	J. P. Manchester	1886 to 1889 (incl.)
22.	Wm. Gavitt	1887 to 1888 (incl.)
23.	Joseph Murray	1889 to date (Nov. 1890).
24.	S. R. Nettleton	1889 to date —
25.	A. W. Lavender	1890 to date —

In addition to the above list of names of regularly specified seal island Agents of Treasury Department, S. N. Buynitsky a clerk in the Customs Division, Office of the Secretary of the Treasury, was detailed as a temporary agent and served through the seasons work of 1870 on St. George, three months : then he passed another period of nine months on St. Paul from July 31st, 1871 to April 26th, 1872, in charge. But he was not regularly enrolled or appointed as a Treasury Agent for the seal-islands.

In 1874, under order of special Act of Congress, Henry W. Elliot, and Lt. Washburn Maynard, U. S. N. made a thorough survey of the seal-life as embodied on these islands.

APPENDIX. 309

The following citations are from the daily Journal of the Treasury Agent's Office on St. George Island in reference to the visits of marauders or pirates; a few of the extracts are given below to show the general impression made at the time, means of prevention, etc.

1884.

Sept. 10th. Schooner reported at Zapadnie.
Sept. 11th. About 12.45 A. M. we noticed boats coming towards the shore.... as a warning to let them know, and not to land, we fired a half dozen shots. The marauding boats immediately turned about and disappeared in the fog and darkness " (p. 376).

1885.

July 2nd. ... About five o'clock the watchman came over from Zapadnie with the news that a schooner was in sight and its crew were catching seals in the water by shooting ...
July 3rd. The men we sent to Zapadnie yesterday evening, returned early this morning reporting they could see no pirates or signs of any (p. 413).
July 20th. ... The men with the boat brought the information that they had seen marauders near Starry Arteel Rookery... We failed to catch the rascals, but found their marks in the shape of many seal skeletons some fresh shown (*i. e.*) that they had been killed but the night before.
July 22nd. (At same place.)... On the arrival of Mr. Morgan and myself on the ground, we found the marauders gone but their work left on the beach, one hundred and twenty seal skins and evidence enough to satisfy the Government Agent that between six and seven hundred seals had been killed nearly all female... We found hundreds of skinned seals hid under rocks and in caves ... (p. 419).
Sept. 7th... The marauders who are in the habit of hanging around this island at this season of the year are keeping themselves at a distance this year for which we are very much obliged (p. 427).

1886.

June 19th. " At 3 A. M. this morning, the Chief reported that the two watchmen at Starry Arteel discovered within 400 feet of shore a ship's boat, and they fired four shots in all, and the boats left : this occured about 1 A. M.... Arkently reported no vessels at Zapadnie last night, but fog was heavy, and it was dark (p. 469).
Aug. 6th. Dense fog. Went to Starry Arteel Rookery taking Chief with me to see the dead seals reported yesterday found there; they had been killed by clubbing and had evidently been dead a week...

Aug. 9th. "... Schooner sighted about 8 A. M. some six miles to the North, heading West. Soon after natives reported seeing a boat just off Bluff at West Point... Two boats close in shore at West Point, fired upon them when they at once pulled out into the fog in direction of the Schooner.

Sept. 24th. At about 1 P. M. the Revenue Steamer "Bear" came to anchor in front of the village... Capt. Healy reports that in his opinion all marauding vessels (*sic*) have left these waters (p. 487).

1888.

Nov. 17th. ...At 12 M. saw a schooner from the village at the west end of the Island heading to the N. W. Sent 2nd Chief and three men to Zapadnie, etc.

Nov. 18th. ...Nothing seen of the schooner to-day. 2nd Chief returned to village and reports that some persons had landed as there were fresh tracks, and the windows of the native house were all broken. No signs could be discovered of much damage being done to the rookery as the few seals left there at this time are all quiet.

1889.

Sept. 30th. ...Messenger from Zapadnie reported that men had landed and killed seals on the Rookery last night.

Oct. 1st. ...At 10 o'clock P. M. three boats hove in sight and came up to within a few yards of where we were concealed. Here they separated one going towards the end of the Rookery and two steaming towards the center of the Rookery... so I fired across the nearest boat and gave orders to the men to fire. Instantly the boats turned and pulled for the open sea (p. 277).

Oct. 21st-22nd. Schooner anchored off Zapadnie 21st. Captain came ashore on 22nd and spoke to watchmen at Barrobskie saying he belonged to the A. C. Co. Compasses out of order, etc., bound for Kamschatka. Natives refused to go aboard with him, and he went off and got under way—left. Nothing seen of him since, and no other vessel this year.

The following citations from the Treasury Agents Journal on St. George's island refer to the appearance of the "Killer" whales (*Orca gladiator*), and the havoc they create; there is but one brief entry of the kind in the St. Paul Journal : I am not surprised at it, however, because I did not see myself a killer whale around St. Paul during the whole of my visit there last season May 21st to August 11th inclusive. But at St. George, the letter of Capt. Lavender which follows, declares the presence of a great many.

1881.

Sept. 15th. A school of apparently ten or twelve killers ran into the shoal around the "near" Rookery to-day, and soon made havoc among the pups... It was estimated from the manner in which the seals were thrown up out of the water that 25 or 30 were eaten by their greatest enemies.

Sept. 18th. Another visitation of killers similar to that of 15th instant (p. 269).

1882.

May 9th. A school of killers were also seen this morning for the first time since the seals left last fall (p. 286).

Oct. 29th. The weather being fair and favourable to-day I made a trip to Starry Ateel Rookery noticing on my way there that a good many so called killers were chasing and destroying young pup seals in the sea off the beach (p. 304).

1885.

Sept. 3rd. ...The killers put in an appearance in force about the beginning of this month, remaining or coming near every day up to this date, to the great discomforture (*sic*) of the pups. The number of pups devoured by them must be great... (p. 429).

1886.

May 5th. Three killers passed by to-day, the monsters (p. 456).

1887.

Sept. 14th. ... A school of killers made their initial appearance. There were about eight in school. They passed the length of the Island three times and killed all the seal and sea-lion they could get.

Sept. 22nd. Killers again appeared this afternoon: there were about fifteen of them. They passed from East to West and killed many seals.

Oct. 16th. ... A school of killers, about four in all came at 8-30 A. M. from East... (p. 39).

Oct. 19th. ...Killers came again this evening passing from East to West. Their work as usual very destructive. The gulls followed picking up remnants of meat.

Oct. 19th. Killers at an early hour this A. M. and they cleared the sea of all the seal were in it at the time (p. 50).

1888.

July 1st. ...Killers have been in this vicinity for a week and were in front of village all afternoon (p. 158).

Oct. 23rd. ...There were many pup seals in the water now, and we often see killers among them. I think that they kill many of the pups. (p. 192).

In a letter addressed by Capt. A. W. Lavender on this subject to the writer, he says that he " is now stationed on St. George island as Treasury Agent and not having been long enough on the island to be a competent judge as to the number of seals destroyed annually by these monsters, he has asked the opinion of gentlemen who have spent every season for the last ten years here and the answers to all my inquiries have been that this species of whale must be destroyed or the seal rookeries will be something of the past in a short time; they also informed me, that during the month of October when the pups first take to the water they are killed by the thousand and that the water along the shore of the rookeries is red with the blood of young seals which fall easy victims to these monsters, having no fears of them... "

He closes with the following sensible recommendation :

" The next Congress should make an appropriation sufficient to furnish two whale boats and crews with all the modern improvements for the killing of whales and to station one boat and crew on each island during the ensuing year with orders to patrol the islands daily if possible, and destroy this whale wherever an opportunity is afforded. These boats should be in charge of experienced whalemen from some part of the New England states where this whale and other similar species exist in large numbers, there would be no trouble in obtaining men who were well versed in this kind of whaling, and it is my opinion at the end of the year it would be found that killers were very scarce and would not come near the shore while their appetite for seal and sea-pups would be changed so much, that cod fish and other similar varieties would be good enough for them. I shall endeavour to write more fully on this subject in the near future when I have had a little more experience on the islands as I consider it one of great importance. "

" Truly yours,

" A. W. Lavender. "

Extracts from the Journal of the Office of the Treasury Agent St. George Island, in reference to the number of seals thereon : the following citations show that several of the assistant agents over here have paid considerable attention to this important subject by making field observations in the breeding seasons, since my published work of 1874, the Journal of the St. Paul Office does not give any similar evidence of attention until the season of 1889, or until the notes of Mr. Chas. J. Goff were entered last year. All final surveys and population notes of the breeding grounds made before the seals arrive, and not when they are to be seen at the right time for measurement of area and position, viz. July 10th-20th inclusive, are valueless. Also that in 1884 a distinct note of warning was sounded from St. George by Assistant Agent Wardman; the St. Paul office gave it no attention.

The first survey made after my work of 1873-'74 was the following which seems to have been made in all sincerity: but the extraordinary allotment of space which he gives to the seals, two feet in some places and eight feet in others, is due to the fact that he must have struck those particular eight, four, and five feet areas when the pups were podding back and the cows scattered with them; the work, however bears evidence of pains and sincerity and is entitled to respect. I made that season of 1874 a total of 162,402; he makes it 198,648 breeding-seals and young; his figures of sea-margin and average depth, show that when contrasted with mine, that his tape-line and the podding which is evident that he encountered were not safe factors for a close calculation.

This calculation of Wm. J. Mc Intyre is copied from his autograph entry in the Journal of the Treasury Agent St. George island and is a

Table showing the present condition of the Breeding Rookeries on Saint George's Island from a survey made by Wm. J. McIntyre: The limits of expansion were defined in the middle of July 1874, and measured in April of the following year.

Rookeries.	Length of Shore Line.	Average Breadth.	Space allowed for each seals.	Total number of Bulls, Cows and Pups.	
Zapadnie.	875	136	5 square feet	24,600	
Starry Arteel.	650	173	3 — —	34,150	
North 1st part	900	31	2 — —	18,450	
— 2nd —	900	34 1/3	8 — —	6,112	86,562
— 3rd —	1,000	124	2 — —	62,000	
Little East.	650	72	3 — —	12,356	
East, 1st Part	260	240	4 — —	15,600	
— 2nd —	1,240	49	2 — —	25,380	
GRAND TOTAL.	6,475	111 1/8	3 5/8 — —	198,648	

With all due deference to Mr. Elliott's opinion that 2 square feet of ground for each seal on the breeding rookeries is approximately correct, I am inclined to the opinion that this is too liberal an estimate for all of the rookeries. In some cases I have allowed 2 square feet, in others 3, 4, 5, and 8 square feet according to the topography of the ground, its adaptability for breeding purposes, and the condition of the rookery at the time of it greatest expansion, *i. e.* about the middle of July. It would be utterly impossible for any series of measurements to give the accurate number of seals that haul up on the breeding rookeries or hauling grounds. The least that can be done under the circumstances is to form some basis for measurement during the middle of July, mark the limits of the breeding grounds, and measure them carefully with a tape line as was done in this case before the seals return. This will give their approximate number, and, if carefully done, will not be far out of the way; still these figures are not exact, and should be proven by the measurements of 1875.

WM. J. McIntyre.

Jun 30, 1877.

... The month has been rather dry for killing seal, but yet a large number has been killed for this month, a much larger number than has been taken in June in any previous year since the island has been in the hands of the A. C. Co. The number taken this month is 9,987, — lacking only 13 of being as many as was taken in the whole season of 1876. The highest number ever taken in June was 8,343 in 1872 : the number taken in June last year was 3,397. The first drive last year, June, was 108. The first drive this year was made June 1st., and numbered 198 : this drive of 198 has been equalled only once, — that was in 1873 when 198 were driven June 4th. It will be seen by the above comparisons that there was an increase of seals the 1st of June, which continued throughout the month. During this month there has been but one drive from "Zapadnie" on account of the prevailing dry weather. At this date there are at least 5,000 seals on that rookery large enough to kill. The last drive this month was made from East Rookery, numbering 1,589, and several hundred were left on hauling grounds.

After conferring with Mr. Morgan, Co.'s Agent, and the Chief of this islands, I am convinced that there is a large increase of all classes of seal this year over last year for the month of June. But whether this increase will continue to the end of the hauling season; remains to be seen.

J. H. MOULTON,
Ass't. in Charge.

July 10, 1877 (p. 115).

... The natives made a drive of 880 seals from East Rookery. This is the last drive for the season of 1877, making 14 drives in all, numbering 15,000 seals altogether. The number allowed by law to be taken from this island this season was 15,000. It is hoped that the A. C. Co. will decide to take 17,000 the next season in order that the natives may get out of debt.

J. H. MOULTON.

July 15, 1877.

... Mr. Morgan, Co.'s Agent, the chief and myself visited "Zapadnie" Rookery to make a careful examination of its condition; and, after a careful examination came to the conclusion that there is an increase of all classes of seals over last year of 33-1/3 per cent. The chief informs me that there are more seals on all the rookeries than in any former year.

J. H. MOULTON.

1881.

June 28, (p. 260.)

... The drive to-day numbered about 1,600, an unusual number of 1 and 2 year olds, — too small to kill. This has been the case with almost every drive thus far this season.

Drive for "East Rookery".

Total seals killed	746
— skins accepted	744
Rejected	2

W. B. TAYLOR.

July 16, 1881.

This makes a grand total of 20,000, the full quota for 1881, — skins all salted to-day.

W. B. TAYLOR.

June 14, 1882, (p. 290).

An examination of all the rookeries on the North side this afternoon demonstrates that there were not more than four or five hundred holluschickie hauled out, which was not considered enough to make a drive desirable. *Considerable numbers of holluschickie haul out under the cliffs of North and East Rookeries from which places they are driven out with a view to forcing them to other localities where they may be available for driving to the killing-grounds.*

G. H. WARDMAN.

June 21, 1882, (p. 291.)

As the holluschickie have taken to hauling in considerable numbers under the cliffs of East and North Rookeries from which they cannot be obtained for killing, small flags saturated with kerosene were to-day set among the rocks at those places with a view to frightening the seals to other grounds. On the men visiting the flagged places a short time afterward the seals were found sleeping between the flags. They do not scare.

G. H. WARDMAN.

June 30, (p. 291.)

The prevailing character of the June weather this year was light and dry. There was more or less fog on 27 days, but generally it was very light, and frequently modified by sunshine.

G. H. WARDMAN.

June 30, 1883 (p. 327.)

... The month of June has been very unfavourable for sealing, this year only 2,674 skins having been taken in that time. This number might have been increased at Zapadnie by killing the seals there, numbering some 2000 or more, being held as a reserve to draw upon in case the quota, 15,000, should not be available on the North side of the island. The number might also have been enlarged this month had the A. C. Co. not determined to take larger skins in the aggregate than heretofore of late years. An effort is now made not to kill seals, the skins of which will not weigh 8 lbs, at least.

G. H. WARDMAN.

June 23, 1883 (p. 326.)

On East Rookery and Starry Arteel, the gradual increase in the number of females and pups is easily seen day by day but the accessions to the holluschickie party are not so apparent.

G. H. WARDMAN.

July 19, 1883 (p. 293.)

The year's quota of 20,000 was filled to-day.

G. H. WARDMAN.

The first note of warning from St. George

Treasury Agent's Journal;

(Standard, nothing *less* than an 8 lb. skin.)

July 27, 1883.

... Skins from Starry Arteel, North and East Rookeries 606, — out of a drove of about 6,000 seals.

Having those 6,000 seals on hand at the village from the drive yesterday afternoon, the writer of this set out at seven o'clock this morning to view the hauling grounds from East to little East Rookeries. There were then in sight about 1,500 holluschek (*sic*) which had hauled out yesterday afternoon and last night. Allowing as many holuschek (*sic*) to be in the water along the beach as were hauled out, and supposing as many along Starry Arteel and North as East, we should have 12,000 on the North side of the island. Judging from the killing at Zapadnie this year there should be at least 6,000 over there. Call it 8,000 and we have all we can claim, 20,000 holuschek (*sic*) about the island; of which at least half are yearlings, which if all return will be too small for market next year. If all of the holuschek (*sic*) which we believe to be about the island return we may be able to fill a quota next year of 10,000. It now appears that more than 10,000 could not safely be demanded of St. George for 1884.

On July 30, the quota of 18,000 big skins still to be taken.

G. H. WARDMAN.

2nd note of warning from St. George.

Treasury Agent's Journal:

September 7, 1883.

At East Rookery while there are seals scattered all along from Little East to the Main East Rookery it does not seem that there are so many as in 1881. But there may be more in the water, as the long continued southerly wind makes small surf.

September 14, 1883.

Heavy surf on North shore sending nearly every seal to land. From a careful examination of Little East to-day am satisfied that there are not so many seals there as two years ago; would not estimate present number at above 8,000 of all kinds, including pups. Ass't. Agent Mc Intyre estimates 12,356 there in 1874. Elliott's estimate was 13,000 in 1873.

G. H. WARDMAN.

September 16, 1883.

... Most of seals being ashore in consequence of heavy surf, a careful view of North and Near Rookeries was made to-day. In 1874, Ass't. Agent Mc Intyre estimated the number of seals there at 36,562. This writer would consider that an extreme outside figure for the seals there now.

September 25, 1883.

... At East Rookery, seems not so many seals there now as a month later in 1881.

G. H. WARDMAN.

September 5, 1884 (p. 374.)

Walked along the cliffs and beaches to Little East and East Rookeries. After careful examination, estimate number of seals of all kinds at Little East, 12,000, and East, 23,000. Scattered along the beach between rookeries 100 : under the cliffs beyond East, 500. At East Rookery there were about 800 sea-lions. On account of the surf most every seal was on shore."

G. H. WARDMAN.

September 8, 1884 (p. 375).

... At North and Starry Arteel Rookeries; after careful examination estimate number of seals of all kinds at North, 75,000, and at Starry Arteel 40,000. Under the cliffs beyond North, about 500. The heavy surf of the past week has driven and kept ashore almost every seal. Many of them were hauled way back on the grass.

G. H. WARDMAN.

September 2, 1885 (p. 427.)

Walked to North Rookery to-day, was surprised at not finding the great numbers of seals on the rookery that has been recorded as seen by other agents in other years. So far from observations made I think some one has greatly over-estimated the number of seals on the rookeries at any time.

Elliott, I think, comes nearer the number than any of his successors.

T. F. RYAN.

With all due respect for the work, measurements and conclusions of Messrs Elliott and Mc Intyre, I am forced from close observation and tests made on the work of both to the following conclusions :

First, that Mr. Elliott's measurements are much nearer the mark than Mr. McIntyre's, and He (*sic*) is at least one thousand feet of shore line rookery by fifty feet in width too much.

Second, that Mr. Elliott's opinion that two square feet of ground for each seal or 4 square feet for cow and pup even, — taking into consideration the topography of the ground, — is none too liberal ; the lay of cows and pups at birth are very close."

T. F. RYAN.

July 26, 1886.

June 21, 1886 (p. 470.)

... The rookeries upon this island are looking finely and are showing many Bulls, Cows and Pups. The seals are coming unexceptionably fine and plenty for killing. The Alaska Comm'l Co. have already

APPENDIX. 319

taken 1,000 more than they took one year ago this time, being about 5,000 to date.

J. P. MANCHESTER.

June 26, 1886 (p. 472.)

... The seal for the past week have been coming in very slow, expecting them to do better soon.

J. P. MANCHESTER.

July 5 (p. 475.)

... We are now 23 skins behind last season. The seals are coming a little slow.

J. P. MANCHESTER.

July 7 (p. 477.)

... The seals come very slow; hope they will do better soon.

J. P. MANCHESTER.

July 15.

... Mr. Ryan measured Little East Rookery in company with the chief and called it 350 by 40 feet, well covered with cows and pups and appeared quiet and happy with big showing of pups; he estimates 7,000 cows and pups.

J. P. MANCHESTER.

July 22, 1886.

Counted in 527 skins killed yesterday. The Co. wants 294 more to fill their quota of 15,000.

J. P. MANCHESTER.

July 23.

To-day, the A. C. Co. took 294 seals.

J. P. MANCHESTER.

Treasury Agent's Journal, St. George Island :

June 15, 1887 (pp. 12-13).

The following was received on 13th. :
The measurement of rookeries by[1] Dr. Noyes, Acting Ass't.

---

1. With reference to this official entry in the St. George Journal, the following note from my journal should be transcribed in simple justice to Dr. Noyes.

Village of St-George, July 25th, 1890. : Dr L. A. Noyes who " made the measurements " of the rookeries of St. George Island in 1887 long before a breeding-seal had made its appearance upon them, and who sent them over to St. Paul to Geo. R. Tingle, who in turn under date of June 10th, 1887, orders them spread upon the record

SECTION VIII.

Treasury Agent, St. George Island, January 4th, March 1st, and April 22nd 1887.

Rookeries.	Sea-margin.	Width.	Square feet.	Seals.
East	2,200	300	440,000	220,000
Zapadnie	2,100	160	336,000	168,000
Little East	600	125	75,000	37,500
Starry Arteel	900	375	517,000	258,750
Near North	3,500	300	1,050,000	525,000
Totals	9,300		2,418,500	1,209,500

The measurement of the above rookeries by H. W. Elliott, July 12th-15th, 1873, gives as the totals of males, females and young seals on the breeding rookeries, 163,420, whilst the Co. killed 25,000 seals on St. George, or one-fourth of the catch.

The same officer gives the number of breeding seals on St. Paul Island, July 10th to 18th, at 3,030,250 or twenty times the number on St. George, and yet only three times the number of seal were taken on St. Paul. It is evident that Mr. Elliott's measurements of St. George rookeries were not correct, or the Company could not have taken 25,000 from so small a showing.

The very careful and correct measurements by Dr. Noyes shows the true condition of the rookeries, and is in proportion to the St. Paul Island seal population, as follows :

	Sea-Margin.	Square feet.	Seals.
St. Paul	49,850	10,297,000	5,148,500
St. George	9,300	2,418,500	1,209,250

St. Paul quota (*sic*) 85,000; St. George quota (*sic*) 15,000. To equalize the income of the natives on the two islands, the Company allows the St. George men to assist on the St. Paul island, where they earn about 3,000 each year equal to taking 7,500 additional seal on St. George as far as the St. George natives' income is concerned.

Please enter the foregoing in your journal for future reference.

I am, resp'y,

Signed : Geo. R. Tingle,
Treasury Agent.

St. Paul Island, June 10, 1887.

as " absolutely correct " (neither man had ever seen, up to that hour, the rookeries when covered with breeding-seals as specified in these measurements aforesaid), — Dr. Noyes entered a disclaimer, to me, as to any responsibility for these estimates of the numbers of seals on the St. George rookeries, which Tingle declares " absolutely correct ". He said to me that he did not know anything about surveying, that he made those measurements of space in length and depth at Mr. Tingle's request, and sent them over *without making, himself, any estimates of the number of seals that might be within the lines of his measurements*. That estimate of 1,209,000 seals on the St. George rookeries in 1887 was " made wholly outside of his knowledge or suggestion ".

APPENDIX.

Extract from Treasury Agent's Journal:

St. George Island, June 22, 1888, (p. 471).

... We think from the outlook under the next lease the Government will get a revenue of not less than $500,000 a year from the seal of St. Paul and St. George Islands. We think 150,000 can be taken each year instead of 100,000, especially if the Government will commence at once and give them good protection. The crop of seal are (*sic*) big upon these Islands, the largest and best in the world.

J. P. MANCHESTER.

St. George, September 25, 1888 (p. 187).

... Made an examination of all the rookeries on north side. Estimate about two thousand killable seals.

A. P. LOUD.

St. George, July 1889, 10. (p. 251)

... It is feared by Mr. Clark of the A. C. Co., that we cannot get our quota of skins this year. The seals are coming in very slowly.

JOSEPH MURRAY.

With that entry of Col. Murray of the 10th of July 1889, I close the St. George official extracts, and turning to the official entries on the pages of the St. Paul Journal, I find nothing there of the character cited from the St. George records, *i. e.* direct entries made from field observation like those quoted above, until I reach the record of last year: they are summed up in the following direct significant warning, which that gentleman (who uttered it) promptly embodied in this report to the Treasury Department: thus giving the first direct information on file in the Secretary's Office which warned him of the true state of affairs up there.

Sept. 1889, ... Dr. Lutz and myself took a walk to the Reef this afternoon: the old bulls are about all gone, pups are getting rather large, and could be seen by thousands playing in the water yet. I am satisfied that they are not *near so numerous* as in the past. It is impossible to continue killing 100,000 seals *per annum* and expect a continuation of seal life and a revenue to the Government. My observations this summer of the rookeries have fallen far short of my expectations after reading Elliott and others on seal life [1].

C. J. GOFF.

[1]. Treasury Agent's Journal, St. Paul's Island: p. 173.

SECTION VIII.

Field notes relative to Pelagic sealing.
In re : Seal Pirates.

Oonalaska, Augt. 13, 1890.

From what I saw yesterday as I came down on the "Arajo" from what Capt. Tanner of the "Albatross" informs me, and from what I learn through the Collector here, there is no doubt but that a number of pelagic sealers are at work in Bering Sea at the present hour, and getting everything that they can lay their hands upon in the form of fur-seal.

We ran down upon a typical sealing schooner yesterday morning, about 7 o'clock, as she was becalmed partly, about 60 miles north of Akootan Pass; she had her sails at first clewed up but as we drew near she hoisted her foresail and jib and lazily drew off so as to turn her stern away from sight in order that her name might not be taken : but we ran clear around so as to disclose the name " Ariel, St. John N. B". in white letters on her black hull, under her stern, passing so near to her that we could look right down upon her crowded deck — crowded with N. W. coast canoes and Indians, so that there was hardly moving room on her.

She was a small schooner, not over 50 tons, and extremely shabby in her equipment, rigging frayed and slack, sails patched like a crazy quilt, and the crew made up entirely of Indians, except three white men, some 30 or 35 in all. The Indians were dressed in blanket coats or shirts with their flaps overhanging — some breeched and some unbreeched : their canoes were telescoped on deck precisely as the dories of a Gloucester cod-fisherman are packed or stowed.

They all crowded up on the diminutive poop-deck of the schooner and stared at us in mingled fear and wrath, while some one of the white men ran below and re-appeared with a rifle under his arm.

The name of the schooner being disclosed, the "Arajo" bore away and when the craft was some 5 miles astern, we saw her canoes starting out for seals : she had 8 or 10 canoes. I am not certain as to the count, but not any less that is sure. These Indians use both spears and guns.

Capt. Tanner says that last week when at work 60 miles W. N. W. of St. Paul Island on the 100 fathom line, he saw two schooners there, with their boats out sealing, and anchored, the skinned carcasses of the seals that they had shot were floating everywhere.

The Collector here says that he has been informed — by these men who have been running in here frequently during the last three weeks ostensibly in distress, but really to find out where and what the cutters were doing — that the catch outside of Bering Sea up to July 1st was 47,000 skins; these skins were shipped on a special Victoria steamer by the sealers at a common rendez-vous at Sand Point and at Thin Point of Sannak Island before they ventured into Bering Sea : this is an enormous catch and must have been wholly taken from the cows since there are little or no male seals left. The Collector says that out of the 67 skins which he seized on, the sealers informed him that 60 of these seals were females, when killed all being with their unborn young.

Certainly the absence of seals in the water as we came down yesterday over a sea that was smooth and glassy — the absence of these animals was surprising — we saw but 4 young seals on the entire stretch between Oonalashka and the Isld. of St. George. The opportunity for viewing these animals never could be better and the inference is unavoidable that they are rapidly running out.

I find the opinion commonly expressed here, as.it was when I first came up that the active uninterrupted shooting and hunting of these seals on the several paths of travel up to the Seal Islands from the Pacific on one side, has deflected large bodies of them over to the Russian rookeries. It stands to reason that a fleet of 40 or 45 or more vessels all hovering about the entrances to the passes of the Aleutian chain on the Pacific side — the passes of Akootan, and Oonimak in especial — that such a reception would head off and turn aside a regular orderly migration of these animals. How many of them are thus turned over to the Russian herds which really belong to us, I have no idea — who can say? But at this present hour every seal lost to the rookeries of the Pribylov Group counts heavily against the future life and preservation of those interests.

Capt. Tanner has been cruising in Bering Sea between Oonalaska and Bristol Bay and as far to the westward as 175°. Long. N. E. the 59° Lat. and has seen but three schooners in Bering Sea up to date : two of those vessels were in the full tide of sealing as above stated 60 miles. west of St. Paul Island, and the other was a rusty little craft just above Anak Island west of Oonimak Island. But that does not signify that there are no more — on the contrary it is very likely that there are more.

A careful inquiry here to-day discloses the fact that fur-seals have never hauled on the beaches of Oonalaska Island, and have never come into the harbour here within sight of the natives except for a few days only when strong northerly gales prevail : as soon as it becomes calm they go out and down into the Pacific : from time immemorial, fur-seal pups have been shot and speared every fall, in November chiefly, as they migrated south into the Pacific from Bering Sea, anywhere from a few hundred to 2,500 annually have thus been secured since the Russians first opened up the country in 1768-'86. The best resort for such hunting is Oomnak Pass : it was in the past, and is now. It was this annual passage of these animals down in the autumn and up in the summer through these passes of the Aleutian Archipelago that aroused the search of the Russians for the Seal Islands.

The scarcity of seals this year has been commented upon by the fishermen of Alaska, who declare that they have been getting larger catches this season than ever before, and lay the change to the decrease of seal-life. Capt. Tanner says that he has seen several of these men who have charge of canneries and cod-fishing stations at Oorza et Paper Islands, they all said that inquestionably the increase of fish was due to the decrease of seals, — if not wholly due to that, it certainly was due in a measure to it. I myself am by no means inclined to regard the circumstance as noteworthy to any appreciable degree whatever.

Nor can I believe much in the deflection of any large body of fur-seals from the Aleutian passes up to our side of Bering Sea and the Pribylov Islands : there is not as yet enough ground covered by these poachers to make that abrupt turn down south of the Aleutian chain of the fur-seal herd — wherein too long. and too wide, and too frequent an opportunity exists for them to go wholly unmolested up to their places of birth in Bering Sea : they might be so headed off by a cordon of hundreds of schooners hovering steadily in the mouths of these passes, with the wind and weather always clear and calm, still water and foggy only at short intervals : but such is not the case here, the weather is treacherous, the winds rise and blow for days and days, the fog settles and hangs for weeks and weeks so thick that the oldest and most experienced seamen actually get lost in its confusion — during these periods the fur-seals can and do pass safely through into Bering Sea no matter how many schooners (filled with no matter how many hunters) may be in the waters outside waiting to intercept them.

Then, when it does clear up, becomes calm, and the horizon is visible in every direction — then these pelagic hunters can and do work rapidly and successfully during the brief intervals which such weather affords; brief I say because the clear calm bright day off the Aleutian Chain and in its passes is a rare one, and is easily remembered during each season.

Therefore I do not feel warranted in believing that as yet any deflection by hunting in the open waters of the ocean has been made to or in that path of migration regularly pursued by the fur-seal.

I think that such a deflection might be caused by the withdrawal of large schools of food fish supply from the Aleutio-Bering Sea region — by its abandonment of this region and location in the occident — such a course would be quite sufficient, since the seal is a hearty feeder and would follow its source of food supply. But fish are now more abundant, if anything, than ever thus far in the waters of the Alaskan coast, and the seals have no cause on that score to deviate from their regular route of travel.

Lost of seals by poachers.

Witnesses under oath before the Committee Merchant Marine and Fisheries 50 the Congress, 2nd Sess. Rep. No 3883. H. R.

Page 64.

T. F. MORGAN. — "*Question.* What number of seals are recovered that are killed in the water? — *Answer.* I could not state it as a positive fact, but I should say not over 50 per cent."

Page 54.

W. B. TAYLOR. — "*Question.* When they kill the seals in the waters, about what proportion of them do they recover? — *Answer.* I do not believe more than one-fourth of them."

Page 87.

C. A. WILLIAMS. — "*Question.* And the conditions are bad? — *Answer.* Yes, sir; and often worse, for this reason: if you kill a pup you destroy a single life, but in killing a cow you not only destroy the life that may be, but the source from which life comes hereafter, and when they are killed there in the water by a shot-gun or a spear, the proportion saved by the hunters is probably not one in seven. That was their own estimate; that out of eight shots they would save one seal and seven were lost. If they were killed on the land, those seven would go towards filling out their score."

Page 118.

H. H. McINTYRE. — "*Question.* What proportion of the seals shot in the water are recovered and the skins taken to market? — *Answer.* I think not more than one-fifth of those shot are recovered. Many are badly wounded and escape. We find, every year, imbedded in blubber of animals killed upon the islands, large quantities of bullets, shot, and buckshot. Last year my men brought to me as much as a double handful of lead found by them imbedded in this way."

Page 164.

GEO. R. TINGLE. — "*Question.* The waste of seal life was only 53 in 1887? — *Answer.* Yes, sir; in securing 100,000 skins, while these marauders did not kill last year less than 500,000. The logs of marauding schooners have fallen into my hands, and they have convinced me that they do not secure more than one seal out of every ten that they mortally wound and kill, for the reason that the seals sink very quickly in the water. Allowing one out of ten, there would be 300,000 that they would kill in getting 30,000 skins. Two hundred thousand of those killed would be females having 200,000 pups on shore. Those pups would die by reason of the death of their mothers, which added to the 300,000, makes half a million destroyed. I am inclined to think, because the seals show they are not increasing, or rather that they are at a standstill, that more than 300,000 are killed by marauders."

Page 220.

T. F. Ryan. — "The number of seals taken by marauders from seal islands or in the waters near by are very few in comparison to the great numbers taken in the 50 or 60 miles south of the islands. Old seal-hunters seldom bother the islands, and from the information to be had, 95 per cent. of seals taken by seal-hunters in Bering Sea are taken at a distance of from 40 to 75 miles south of St. George Island, and 90 per cent. of those taken are cows, the producers."

Page 237.

Capt. L. G. Shepard. — "*Question.* It has been stated in testimony here that not one out of five, six or seven of the seals wounded in the water are recovered. I think you put the estimate a little lower than that. Have you any knowledge on that subject? — *Answer.* I think they recover about one half."

Page 246.

Capt. C. A. Abbey. — "*Question.* What was your opinion about that? — *Answer.* In the earlier days they shot them with bullets and with rifles, and when they are shot with a bullet the seal sinks and probably out of half a dozen they would not get more than one. If the seals are not killed but simply wounded that leaves a chance to get them into a boat. They were very expert hunters who hired for that purpose, but I judge that they killed about three for every one they got. I got that from the conversation with the hunters themselves."

Page 316.

J. C. Redpath. — " *Question.* And if they wound a seal in the water, the seal is likely to sink before they can recover it? — *Answer.* There is no doubt about that.

Question. What proportion do they recover of those that are killed by firearms in the water? — *Answer.* Very few, I should suppose. I have never seen a seal shot in the water. I have known of sea-lions that if wounded in the water could be recovered, but if shot and killed they will sink.

Question. In your judgment, what proportion of seals that are shot in the water are recovered? — *Answer.* It is hardly possible to recover one-half of them."

Page 332.

H. H. Mc Intyre. "*Extracts from the log of the schooner Angel Dolly*, *kept by Capt. Alfred N. Tulles, who was accidentally killed by his own hand on the 28th of July,* 1887, *near Otter Island.*

July 4, 1887. — Hove to 30 miles southwest of St. George Island. At 1.30 out boats. Got 5 seals.

July 5, 1887. — Out boats at 6.30 a.m. Returned at 11.15 p.m. with 11 seals, one boat getting 6.

July 9, 1887. — I am now on the hunting-ground, but keep sail on the vessel as we may pick up a sleeping seal.

July 11, 1887. — Caught 7 seals.

July 13, 1887. — Caught 12 seals; they were around the vessel as thick as bees (the seal). Had it been clear we would have caught 100 easy.

July 16, 1887. — Saw 3 sleeping seals from the vessel. Got boat over and got them. I have not seen the sun for nine days, therefore I have had no observations, yet I know that I am not over 14 miles from St. George Island,

July 17, 1887. — Out boats at 10.30 a.m.. The seals were around the vessel in hundreds. The boats would not go any distance from the vessel. Had they gone away they could have caught 200 or 300 seals. They were afraid of the fog, yet I told them that it would clear up, which it did at 3.30 p.m., and continued thus all the rest of the day. They are the hardest set of hunters that were ever in Bering Sea, who caught 20 seals and used 250 rounds of amunition. They get 1 out of every 10 they fire at. Well, I will never be caught with such a crowd again. The head hunter fired a 100 shells and got 6 seals. The vessel is lying between the Islands of St. Paul and St. George. Just as soon as the fog clears off the land I will have to move, as I might have the cutter after me. I came here to get a load of seals, and by God, if I had any men with me, I would get them, too. They are all a set of curs, genuine ones, too.

July 21, 1887. — Out boats at 6.30 a.m. coming back to the vessel at 9 p.m. One boat returned at 7 p.m. This was the head hunter. He is last out and first back always; caught 30 seals; one boat got 14. This is the best day's work we have done yet. From the amount of growling among the boat-pullers, I conclude that they fired at and missed nearly 200 seals. They had 100 loaded shell each when they left the ship, and when they came back all were emptied, so they did some tall firing.

July 23, 1887. — To-day I asked Daniel Mc Cue, boat-puller for Charles Loderstrom, how it was that his boat got only 9 seals. I told him that I had seen 40 sleeping seals from the vessel, and that he must have seen more as he was pulling about. His answer was that if he had a man that knew how to shoot that the boat could not carry all the seals that were missed. Why captain, said he, it is enough to discourage a man. You pull up to a sleeping seal to within 10 feet, fire at him and see the shot go 6 feet the other side of him. I then asked J. Linquist, puller for boat two. He said, captain, don't ask me how many we have seen but ask me how many we missed, and I will tell you. I asked him the above question; he said 100.

I now asked Joe Spooner the same questions as above; his answer was, we only want hunters, and we would be going home now with 1,500 skins at the very least.

July 24, 1887. — As fine a day as was ever seen in San Francisco. A flat calm with the sea as smooth as glass. Got out the boats at 6.30 p.m.; coming back at 7.30 with 14 seals. Why! One boat with an ordinary hunter could get that many without going 100 yards from the ship. I killed two inside of ten minutes, and it was than nearly dark.

July 25, 1887. — Nice weather. Out boats at 7 p.m. Came back with 4 seals big catch.

July 26, 1887. — There were thousands of seals around the vessel. I shot and killed 7 from the vessel, but only got 1, through the tardiness of the hunters. At 4.30 I put the boats out; came back at 7.30 with 1 seal. The water was fairly covered with seals, yet they only caught 1.

The log closes on the 28th of July, 1887, on which day the captain was killed and his vessel seized for violation of the revenue laws.

His signals were : (1) *Come back to the vessel;* (2) *Want a boat for dead seal;* (3) *Keep near the vessel. Bad weather or fog* ; (4) *Cutter in sight.*

This paper is a transcript of the log-book of the schooner Angel Dolly, captured by Mr. Tingle in July, 1887.

Number of seals.

Witnesses under oath before the Committee Merchant Marine and Fisheries. 50nd Sess. (Rep. No. 3883. H. R.).

Page 211, 1885-1887.

T. F. RYAN. — " *Question.* Will you state about the location of these islands and the condition of the seal rookeries while you were there. — *Answer.* St. George island is in Bering Sea, 180 miles to the northwest of Oonalaska, one of the Aleutian chain of islands. It is an island about 6 miles wide and 10 miles long, to which 175,000 to 200,000 seals come annually — male, female, and pup. "

Page 162 *et seq.*, 1885-1888.

G. R. TINGLE.— "*Question.* What is your observation as to the number of seals resorting to the islands annually; are they diminishing or increasing? — *Answer.* Upon that subject, if it is in order, I would like to answer the question by reading from my report to the Treasury. May I inquire if it is in Mr. Elliott's evidence that he made his statements as to the seal life upon the island from personal observation?"

"The Chairman. Yes; and estimates."

"The Witness. Was it shown that Mr. Elliott had not been on the fur-seal islands for fourteen years?"

"The Chairman. His evidence was that he was last there in 1876, twelve years ago."

"The Witness. He made a statement that there was no greater number of seals upon the islands now than at the time he measured the rookeries. Since I have been on the islands I have observed very closely the breeding rookeries. I have visited them daily, remaining around and observing them for hours at a time. I gave them very close attention. The reason I did so was that I desired to be able to place the Department in possession of the very best information I could in regard to this seal property; whether it was increasing or diminishing. I found on the islands this book of Mr. Elliott's, giving his measurements of the seal rookeries, and I conceived the idea of making some measurements myself on the Elliott basis to find out if the seals were increasing. Mr. Elliott's measurements of the fur-seal islands showed an area of 6,021,900 square feet, and he says that upon that basis there are 3,010,950 seals. Taking Mr. Elliott's basis, I made measurements fourteen years after his, and they showed an increase of 8234 feet in sea-margin of the rookeries and an increase of 4,275,100 feet of superficial area occupied by breeding seals, showing upon St. Paul Island, at the time I made my measurement, 5,148,500 seals, or an increase of 2,137,500."

The number of seals at present shown to be on the breeding rookeries of the two islands is as follows :

St. Paul Island.	5,148,500
St. George Island.	1,209,250
Total.	6,357,750

Page 59, 1883.

W. B. Taylor. — "*Question.* Is it your opinion that a larger number of seals may be taken annually without detriment to the rookeries? — *Answer.* No, sir; I would not recommend that. The time may come, but I think that one year with another they are taking all they ought to take, for this reason : "

"I believe that the capacity of the bull seal is limited, the same as any other animal, and I have very frequently counted from thirty to thirty-five, and even, at one time, forty-two cows with one bull. I think if there were more bulls there would be less cows to one bull, and in that way the increase would be greater than now. While the number of seal in the aggregate is not apparently diminished, and in fact there is undoubtedly an increase, yet if you take any greater number of seal than is taken now, this ratio of cows to one bull would be greater, and for that reason there would be a less number of young seals, undoubtedly. I look upon the breeding of the seal as something like the breeding of any other animal, and that the same care and restriction and judgment should be exercised in this breeding.

Page 39, 1876-1880.

GEO. WARDMAN. — *"Question.* What is your impression of the number of seals that visit these rookeries annually? — *Answer.* I never could make it so much as Professor Elliott has done. I made many estimates. I have been to all the rookeries on these islands many times, and compared them with the space occupied by the carcasses on the killing-ground, and I feel pretty confident that the total number has been overestimated."

"*Question.* He estimated it at something less than 4,000,000 on the two islands? — *Answer.* I think he estimates 250,000 to 275,000 on St. George. I have figured it out in several ways, and I think 20,000 that we killed would be 10 per cent. of the killable seals."

"*Question.* Is that your estimate 10 per cent. of all that come? — *Answer.* I take that for one thing. I take our killing ground, where we kill 20,000 and where we lay these seals along as close as we could, so as to give us greater area. We want to make room to take the next year another piece so that by the third year we could get back again. I measured off that space two or three different times where 20 000 carcasses lay, and where I considered they lay as close as on the rookeries. I came to the conclusion we had about 40,000 at Zapadnie, 30,000 at Starry Arteel, and about 50,000 at North Rookery, 10,000 to 15,000 on Little East Rookery, and about 25,000 or 30,000 on East Rookery. That is all the rookeries. I could never make it any more than that during that time. I measured the places carefully."

"*Question.* Do you put it at the same numbers annually? — *Answer. About.* I think the breeding seals on the rookeries come in about the same numbers; but the first year I was up there we killed 20,000 with great ease and in a short time, and I considered that we could kill more easily; and I recommenced Colonel Otis to make a bigger allowance for St. George, because we wanted to bring up our men's dividends a little. The next year he gave permission to take 25,000 on St. George, and they would take 75,000 on St. St. Paul. We got 21,000 or 22,000 that year. We had exceeded in our estimate the number that we could take at that time; and they had to finish our quota on the other island. Later in the season, perhaps two weeks after that, we could have got perhaps 10,000 more seals, but we certainly could not get them when we wanted them. "

L. A. Noyes (pr. G. R. Tingle), p. 177, 1887.

Measurements of breeding rookeries by Dr. L. A. Noyes, Acting Assistant Treasury Agent, of St. George Island, January 4, March 12, and April 22, 1887.

Name of Rookery.	Sea Margin.	Depth.	Square feet.	Seals.
East	2,200	200	440,000	220,000
Zapadnie	2,100	160	336,000	168,000
Little East	600	125	75,000	37,500
Starry Arteel	900	575	517,500	258,750
Near and North	3,500	300	1,050,000	525,000
Total	9,300		2,418,500	1,209,250

The breeding grounds on St. George Island, surveyed July 12 and 15, 1873, gave the following figures (H. W. Elliott's "Condition of Affairs in Alaska, 1874", p. 78)[1]:

Name of Rookery.	Sea Margin.	Depth.	Square feet.	Seals.
Eastern	900	60	54,000	27,000
Little Eastern	750	40	30,000	15,000
North	2,000	25	50,000	25,000
Near	750	150	112,500	56,250
Starry Arteel	500	125	62,500	31,250
Zapadnie	600	60	36,000	18,000
Total	5,500		345,000	172,500

Page 69, 1868-1888.

T. F. MORGAN. "*Question.* Have you ever formed an estimate of the probable number of seals that visit the rookeries annually?—*Answer.* I have attempted to do but it is hard to do."

"*Question.* You are aware that Professor Elliott, in his book, estimates in the neighborhood of 4,000,000 : what do you think about that estimate?—*Answer.* I think that Professor Elliott has overestimated it. When he was there, the way he figured out the estimate was that the laid down the carcasses of seals and measured around them and then measured the rookeries."

Question. He estimated the average size of a harem?—*Answer.* Not only a harem, but every size of seal, each old bull. He measured the four-year old, the three-year old, the two-year old, and the one-year old grown male, and then he takes the extent of territory where the seal had laid and measured that, and computes his figures from the

---

1. The figures here given do not exactly agree with those in the work cited, nor with those in Elliott's " Census Report ", p. 61. The computation appears to have been revised (Ed.).

territory; but they do not lie all over the territory which he marked out."

"*Question.* He measured all around, taking a given area?—*Answer.* The seals did not cover the whole area as thoroughly as he measured it. The only time he could make his measurement was after the seals had left. These were made then. You cannot measure a rookery while the seal are lying there. But he observed the ground covered by the animals during the season and sketched out the details and where they were lying and measured that after they had left there."

"*Question.* Do you think under careful treatment and the present policy a large number might be readily taken off after a year with safety? — *Answer.* Possibly, but I would not suggest that they should increase the catch very fast. I should go carefully and observe the effect, increasing at the rate of 5,000, 10,000 or 15,000."

Page 29, 1880-1885.

H. A. GLIDDEN. "*Question.* What was your estimate of the value of those rookeries?—*Answer.* I could not estimate them. The seals are there by the millions; you cannot count them."

Page 12. 1869-1872.

S. N. BUYNITSKY. "*Question.* Have you any means of making an estimate of the probable number of fur-seals that visit these islands and rookeries?"

"*Answer.* I saw an approximate estimate made by Mr. Elliott. I do not know that I ever indulged in any figures as to that."

"I simply expressed my impression here (examining report); no, I see I did not indulge in any guessing."

"*Question.* You say that Professor Elliott has made some estimate of that? *Answer.* Yes, sir, I say I did not make any estimate. I do not think any estimate would be within a million or two. I think he puts them at five millions, but it may be three or seven millions, as they are countless. It is a sight never to be forgotten by one who saw it, and it recurs sometimes in my dreams — that vast extent of beach covered by these animals."

APPENDIX.

Table showing the number of fur seal skins taken from the Pribylov Islands since their transfer in 1867 from Russian to American ownership : tax and rental paid.

Year.	No. of Skins.	Tax and Royalty Paid	Remarks.
1868	250,000		The skins of 1869 were called "food-skins", and carried over to 1870 are added to the catch of that year of the beginning of the lease, making a seeming return for this year of 95,477 skins taken in first year of Alaska Commercial Co's lease; Tax $2.62 ¹/₂ per skin taken and Rental of $55,000 per annum. As this lease did not go into operation until August 1870, the Secretary made a rebate of some $22.000 Rental.
1869	85,901	$	
1870	9,577	101,080.001/2	
1871	99,741	317,082.621/2	
1872	99,975	317,444.371/2	
1873	99,744	316,927,00	
1874	99,998	317,494.75	
1875	99,976	317,446.971/2	
1876	89,964	291,155.50	
1877	75,526	253,255.75	
1878	99,980	317,461.39	
1879	99,962	317,410.221/2	
1880	100,036	317,594.50	
1881	99,766	316,984.75	
1882	99,925	317,295.24	
1883	75,000	251,875.00	
1884	99,962	317,410.221/2	
1885	99,996	317,488.20	
1886	99,982	317,467.94	
1887	99,950	317,378.721/2	
1888	100,000	317,500.00	
1889	100,000	317,500.00	
1890	21,000	210,000.00	Lease of Alaska Com'l Co. expires May 1st 1890. Lease renewed to North American Commercial Co. Allowed to kill 60,000 but secured only 21,000; tax $9.62, for each skin taken and $60,000 rental per annum.
TOTAL.	2,206,057	$6,208,916.17	

1. The foregoing figures only account for those skins taken and shipped from the Islands between 1870 and 1890; of those taken in 1868, no time list has been kept. Nearly 140,000 " food-skins " have been taken between 1870 and 1890 which have never gone from the islands — were wasted and destroyed. — This should never occur again. The 1869 skins paid a tax of only $1.00 per skin and the rental for that year was only $5,480.75.

SECTION VIII.

Table showing the number of Fur-seal skins taken from the Russian Rookeries on the Commander Islands, Bering Sea, since 1871, and shipped to the markets.

Year.	Robben Island.	Bering and Copper Islands.	Total.	Remarks.
1871	—	3,614	3,614	Bering and Copper Islands constitute what is known as the Commander Group. Robben Reef or Island is a small islet, or rock rather, about 30 miles off-shore from the East shore of Saghalien Island in the Okotsk Sea; it belongs to Russia, also. These skins were all taken under the Lease to Hutchinson, Kohl Philippaeus et Co. and paid a tax of $1.50 to the Imperial Treasury for each skin taken. This lease expired in November 1890, and at the date of this report, it is not known definitely as to its renewal.
1872	—	20,356	20,356	
1873	2,694	27,710	30,404	
1874	2,414	28,886	31,300	
1875	3,127	33,152	36,279	
1876	1,528	25,432	26,960	
1877	2,949	18,584	21,533	
1878	3,142	28,198	31,340	
1879	4,002	38,748	42,750	
1880	3,330	45,174	48,504	
1881	4,207	39,314	43,521	
1882	4,106	40,514	44,620	
1883	2,049	26,650	28,699	
1884	3,819	50,034	53,853	
1885	1,838	41,737	43,575	
1886	—	54,591	54,591	
1887	—	46,347	46,347	
1888	—	47,362	47,362	
1889	—	52,755	52,755	
1890	—	52,502	52,502	
			769,863	

Under Russian management the yield from these Islands I have the record of, as follows.

1862	—	4,000	4,000	No account of the proportion that Robben Reef gives to this total for each year between 1862 and 1870 has been found by the writer.
1863	—	—	4,500	
1864	—	—	5,000	
1865	—	—	4,000	
1866	—	—	4,000	
1867	—	—	4,000	
1868	—	—	12,000	
1869	—	—	24,000	
1870	—	—	24,000	

Table showing the number of Fur-seals skins taken by the pelagic sealers and poachers in the North Pacific and Bering Sea.

Pelagic and Poaching catch of 1886.	Skins.
Landed at Victoria, B. C. by British Sealers	25,538
" " " American "	5,000
" " San Francisco, Cal. " "	2,944
Seized in Behring Sea by U. S. R. M. Cutter "Rush"	2,177
TOTAL	35,659

Pelagic and Poaching catch of 1887.	Skins.
Landed at Victoria, B. C. by British Sealers	17,078
" " " by American "	2,536
" " San Francisco Cal., by " "	6,502
Seized in Behring Sea by Cutters "Rush" and "Bear"	12,345
TOTAL	38,461

Pelagic and Poaching catch of 1888.	Skins.
Landed at Victoria by British Sealers	19,011
" " " San Francisco by American Sealers	5,348
TOTAL	24,359

Pelagic and Poaching catch of 1889.	Skins.
Landed at Victoria by British and American Sealers	39,538
" San Francisco by American Sealers	1,800
Seized in Behring Sea by Cutters "Bear" and "Rush"	2,531
TOTAL	43,869

Pelagic and Poaching catch of 1890.	Skins.
Landed at Victoria, B. C. by British and American Sealers	38,404
" San Francisco by American Sealers	7,228
TOTAL	45,632

Comments : Only in a general way can the relative number of skins taken in Bering Sea, be declared, as distinct from the North Pacific catch. In 1885, the Bering Sea catch can be said to be very near 20,000 in 1887, 29,000 in 1888, 19,000 (no seizures were made that year); in 1889, 25,500; in 1890, 16,000 (no seizures).

The short supply and threatened extermination of the fur-seal together made the London sale a very lively one last October; the following citation from the " Fur Trade Review, " for December, 1890, is interesting.

October sales.

Report by Messrs. Blatspiel Stamp and Heacock.

" The sales covered six days, and comprised a larger variety of furs than previously offered in the autumn. Of course the chief item has been salted fur-seals, sold on the 27th inst., and the various catalogues have contained 20,994 Alaska, 42,721 Copper Island, 20,117 North West Coast, 9,649 Lobos, and 1,873 Cape of Good Hope., etc., making a total of only 95,354 (as against 126,217 last year), and this total was only brought together now by including the larger part of the catch from Copper Island, which were heretofore always sold in the following spring. The attendance for the seal sale was large, but for the other furs there was a smaller number of buyers from Germany present than last year, and buyers generally were not eager."

"As soon as the small catch of Alaska by the new Company became known, early in September, the fur-seal market became excited and values speedily advanced; it was mentioned that the herds on the Seal Islands had been greatly diminished by the indiscriminate slaughter of fmales on the open seas, and therefore the catch for next year on the Pribylov Islands could not now be forecast, it might again have to be very small."

"The quality of the 20,994 Alaska was excellent and chiefly large sizes, the great number of small skins which we have had the past few years being conspicuously absent. Of course, for the Alaska the demand was far greater than the supply, and consequently prices advanced rapidly and greatly, averaging about 90 per cent. all round. Separated, the ratio of advance was : On 659 middlings and smalls, 75 per cent.; on 2,939 smalls 65 per cent.; 5,144 large pups, 85 per cent.; 7,684 middling pups, 100 per cent.; 3,752 small pups, 130 per cent., and 71 extra small pups, 100 per cent. There were exceptionally few (745) low and cut skins, which were also in good demand. Nearly all were secured for America."

"The 42,721 Copper Island skins were also of somewhat superior quality, but having already somewhat improved last March, they now sold at an average advance of fully 50 per cent., being nearly level in advance in all the sizes; these were also largely secured for America, but part were taken by European dealers and furriers."

"The North West Coast skins were of average fair quality, and ranging lower in prices, were more appreciated by the English trade; the advance, however, proved about 60 per cent. on rates current last spring."

"The Lobos, although the quality was on the whole nothing choice of the sort, ranged nearly 50 per cent. dearer than last year. The small low skins hardly advanced in the same ratio; many were taken for France."

"The Cape of Good Hope, also participated in the genered advance."

(Fur Trade Review, Decr.; p. 1890 ; 462.)

INDEX

	Pages.
LETTER TO THE SECRETARY OF THE TREASURY...............	1

INTRODUCTION

GEOGRAPHICAL DISTRIBUTION OF THE FUR-SEAL AND ITS EXTERMINATION IN THE ANTARCTIC......................... 1

SECTION I

THE "ROOKERIES" OR BREEDING GROUNDS OF THE FUR-SEAL ON THE PRIBYLOV ISLANDS OF ALASKA: THEIR AREA AND CONDITION IN 1872-'74, 1890............................. 7

SECTION II

THE "HAULING-GROUNDS" OF THE FUR-SEAL ON THE PRIBYLOV ISLANDS OF ALASKA; THEIR AREA, POSITION AND CONDITION IN 1872-'74, 1890............................. 93

SECTION III

THE METHOD OF DRIVING AND TAKING FUR-SEALS ON THE PRIBYLOV ISLANDS OF ALASKA, IN 1872-'74, 1890............. 115

SECTION IV

THE SELECTION OF SKINS, GRADE AND SUPPLY IN 1872-'74, 1890... 135

SECTION V

CHARACTER, CONDITION AND NUMBER OF NATIVES OF THE PRIBYLOV ISLANDS IN 1872-'74, AND 1890................. 161

SECTION VI

CONDUCT OF NATIVE LABOUR, AND PAY, IN 1872-'74, 1890 . . .   187

SECTION VII

THE PROTECTION AND PRESERVATION OF THE FUR-BEARING INTERESTS OF OUR GOVERNMENT IN THE PRIBYLOV ISLANDS: THE IMMEDIATE ACTION NECESSARY VIEWED IN THE FULL LIGHT OF EXISTING DANGER 197

SECTION VIII

APPENDIX CONTAINING THE AUTHOR'S DAILY FIELD NOTES TOGETHER WITH OTHER MEMORANDA ILLUSTRATIVE OF THE PRECEDING SECTION TO VII, INCLUSIVE. 229

www.ingramcontent.com/pod-product-compliance
Lightning Source LLC
Chambersburg PA
CBHW020241240426
43672CB00006B/605